allenge of

an Politics

han / **Louis S. Loeb**

The Cr
Americ

Daniel M. Bern

LAWS & MEN

THE MACMILLAN COMPANY
COLLIER-MACMILLAN LIMITED, LONDON

© Copyright, The Macmillan Company, 1970

All rights reserved. No part of this book may be reproduced or transmitted in any form or by any means, electronic or mechanical, including photocopying, recording or by any information storage and retrieval system, without permission in writing from the Publisher.

First Printing

Library of Congress catalog card number: 79-96738

The Macmillan Company

Collier-Macmillan Canada, Ltd., Toronto, Ontario

Printed in the United States of America

To My Mother and Father
and
To the Memory of Dan

Preface

UNDER normal circumstances the publication of a book is an occasion for joy. But when a close friend and a respected colleague is suddenly taken from you, joy is sadly tempered. Dan Berman died while on sabbatical leave in India in the fall of 1967, at a time when we were revising the initial draft of this joint venture.

We were convinced that a book on American government could be readable and relevant as well as scholarly. Students—who, after all, are the ones who read such books—are entitled to no less. For many students, a course in American government is their only exposure to an important facet of their own culture. It seemed to us that such an exposure should not overly stress the professional aspects of political science as a discipline, but that it should be geared to the political problems and issues to which students would be most sensitive. And for majors in political science, or those contemplating such a choice, a

PREFACE

course in American government should strive to develop an already aroused interest.

Over the last fifteen years, the literature of political science has freed itself from the traditional historical and legalistic approaches to American government. Instead, the focus has been on the study of political behavior and the systematic analysis of the governmental process. In writing this book, we have tried to reflect the most pertinent aspects of this recent scholarship. We have, moreover, attempted to organize the material in a way consistent with the contemporary study of political behavior and processes.

The book begins where politics begins—with people. It develops an understanding of how individuals relate to politics and of those factors which condition their political participation. The actors and institutions of American government are then analyzed in terms of their roles in the policymaking process. In order to achieve this focus on process, the authors eschewed more conventional approaches. Although there is a chapter focusing on Congress, congressional activity is discussed wherever it has a bearing on the making of public policy. Congressional initiatives in setting the policy agenda, for example, are included in a chapter which analyzes the inputs of other political institutions in this aspect of policymaking.

Furthermore, we have chosen to deal with constitutional principles wherever they are pertinent to the discussion. But the major consideration of the Constitution and its bearing on the contemporary political system comes toward the end of the book, *after* the empirical and descriptive foundation has been laid. We thought that in this way the relation between theory and practice would be more meaningful to the student. Beyond stressing relevancy, we have sought to make the book readable. There is a minimum of detail. Consequently it is a relatively short book. This permits instructors considerable freedom to supplement their course with a variety of paperbacks consonant with their inclinations.

Consistent with the integrity of our views, we observed the professional canons of disinterest and objectivity. We thought it best, however, to provide a point of view against which students could judge their own as well as that of their instructor's. Blandness need not be a concomitant of scholarship. Our bias is apparent throughout: a technocratic, manipulative age is not inherently inconsistent with maximizing many of the norms of democratic theory that are observed in

PREFACE

rhetoric but ignored in practice. The temper of the late sixties indicated that many students and an increasing number of political scientists were beginning to share the same conviction.

Our debts are extensive. Our association with the Washington Semester program of American University influenced us in choosing the approach we did. Many of the people who participated in the program—congressional staff assistants, journalists, bureaucrats, and lobbyists—helped to shape our thinking about the contemporary realities of the policymaking process. To them an acknowledgment is in order. The contributions and insights of professional colleagues are noted in the many books and articles on which we have relied. If every idea and bit of data are not cited, it is not because we were unmindful of their sources but because we were more concerned in keeping footnotes to a minimum.

More immediate appreciation is due those who read drafts and offered comments and criticisms. It is customary to thank them, and we do so, even though they immeasurably increased our task by exposing errors of fact, poor word usage, and grammatical *faux pas*, not to mention their questioning our judgments.

Of all those who helped in one way or another, Professor A. Lee Fritschler of American University performed well beyond the conventional expectations of professional courtesy. He not only read the manuscript with an astounding thoroughness, but he also spent many hours offering suggestions for improving it. Other American University colleagues who read all or parts of the manuscript were Professors Richard G. Smolka, Jeff Fishel, his wife Lynn, Jerome J. Hanus, and Bruce F. Norton. Their time and effort are acknowledged with appreciation.

Thanks are due to several students, all of whom contributed time and ideas: Harold Relyea, a Ph.D. candidate at American, Walker J. "Musa" Foster III, Donna Jones, David Carey, and Brian Adams. Many other students, too numerous to mention here, have also contributed by the kinds of questions they have raised about the American political system.

The major typing effort was loyally and impeccably accomplished by Mrs. Marylee Buchly, whose services are gratefully acknowledged. Others who helped in typing were Lisa Pickett, Marie McNertney, Beauty Whitelow, and my wife.

PREFACE

Mr. Robert J. Patterson, formerly of Macmillan, assisted in launching the project. Mr. James J. Carroll, Jr., of Macmillan helped to counter fits of pessimism and despair, and Mr. Joe Falzone, also of Macmillan, eased some of the pains of the production process.

My wife Ruth has been patient and understanding. Her meager reward is that she can now say to Derek, Clifford, and Brian that "Daddy is finally finished with the book."

Aline Berman has been helpful and encouraging throughout. She shares with me the conviction that Dan would hope that this book will serve to arouse greater awareness of the shortcomings of the American political system and to stimulate students to do something about them.

L. S. L.

American University

Contents

Part One   Political Participation

1   The Creed Under Fire   3

Beliefs and Paradoxes / The Functions of Government / Political Behavior / Political Participation / How Decisions Are Made

2   The Voter   14

The Right to Vote / Woman Suffrage / Making the Vote Equal / The Courts Enter the Thicket / One Man, One Vote / The Nonvoter / Reasons for Nonvoting / Voter Apathy

3   Political Behavior and Public Opinion   34

Why People Vote / Factors Affecting Voting Behavior / Sense of Involvement / Partisan Preferences / Socioeconomic Factors / Individual and Group Voting Behavior / Candidate Personality / Perception of the Issues / The Uncommitted Voter / Political Attitudes / Public Opinion / Characteristics of Public Opinion / Opinion Formation / Communication and Opinions / Public Opinion and Public Policy / Other Forms of Political Activity / Political Demonstrations

CONTENTS

4 The Pressure of Interests 58

Economic Interests / The Big Three—Business, Agriculture, and Labor / The Professionals / Noneconomic Interests / A Nation of Joiners? / The Leaders and the Led / Mobilizing Grass-roots Support / The Public Relations Campaign / Campaign Contributions: Legalized Bribery? / Other Forms of Campaign Help / Lobbying Administrators / Military-Industrial Complex / Former Congressmen as Lobbyists / Lobbyists and Congressmen / Are Lobbies Effective? / Supplementary Representation / Regulation of Lobbying / Executive Lobbying / The White House Lobby / The Pressure System and Democratic Government

5 Political Parties 94

The Two-party System / Decentralization of the Parties / Party Membership / Party Differences / Choosing Presidential Candidates / Undisciplined Parties / The Nominating Conventions / The National Committees / Permanent Party Organizations / The Parties and Participation

Part Two The Political Process: Conditioning Factors

6 The Media, Public Relations, and the Political Process 123

The Magic Tube / The Press and Vietnam / Critic or Handmaiden? / The Modern Newspaper / The Rise of Public Relations / Engineering Consent / Political Public Relations / Television and Political Campaigning / Television Debates

7 Money and Politics 143

The Big Contributor / Campaign Contributions: Ineffective Regulations / Spending Patterns / The Need for Reform / Increasing Costs at All Levels / Other Costs of Political Office / Interest Group Spending / Taxes and Politics

8 Freedom of Political Expression   166
   The Alien and Sedition Acts / World War I / Clear and
   Present Danger / The Red Scare / The War Against the
   Communist Party / A Climate of Fear / Vietnam:
   The Antiwar Movement / Business and the First
   Amendment / Public Employees: Rights of Expression

Part Three   The Policymaking Process

   An Introductory Note   192

9 Formulating the Policy Agenda   195
   The President as Prime Mover / The Message Barrage / A
   National Perspective / The Budget: Instrument of Policy / The
   President Needs Help / Bureau of the Budget / White
   House Office / Commissions and Task Forces / Congressional
   Policy Initiatives / Taking Credit / Agency Initiatives / Court
   Decisions as Policy Initiatives

10 Policymaking: Focus on Congress   227
   President vs. Congress / Localism / Constituency Service / Case
   Work / There Are Two Houses / Committees / Committee
   Chairmen / Seniority System / Power Dispersed / On the
   Road: Hearings / Marking Up / White House Lobbying / To
   the Floor / Scheduling / House Rules Committee / On the
   Floor / Amendments, Debate, and Voting / The
   Filibuster / Log-Rolling / Presidential Pressure / Conference
   Committees / To the White House / Appropriations / The
   Pork Barrel

11 Policymaking: Presidency and Bureaucracy   270
   Administration and Policy / Policy Subsystems / Controlling
   the Subsystems / Presidential Appointments / Legislative
   Oversight / Control by Appropriations / The Power to
   Investigate / General Accounting Office / The Foreign
   Policy Dilemma / Crisis Policy / Treaties and Executive
   Agreements / The War Power / Suppressing Domestic
   Violence

CONTENTS

12 Policymaking by Courts   299

Judicial Policymaking / Judicial Review / Political Law / Myth and Reality / What Kinds of Cases? / Interpreting Statutes / Interpretation as Policy / The Federal Court System / Appellate Court Policymaking / Policy at the Top / Contemporary Role: Civil Rights and Liberties / Power Within Limits / Congress and the Supreme Court / Dispute Settlement: By Commissions

Part Four   Constitutional Theory and Political Reality

13 Dispersing the Powers of Government   335

Fear of the Majority / Toward Government / Federalism—The Republican Remedy / Who Has the Power? / The Commerce Power Undone / The Commerce Power Restored / Conflict and Cooperation / The Marble Cake / Separating Powers / A State of Repose / Mutual Relations

14 The Burden of the Future   369

The Drag of Tradition / A Troubled Agenda / Process and Policy

Appendix

American Politics: Reading and Research   387

Political Participation / The Political Process: Conditioning Factors / The Policymaking Process / Constitutional Theory and Political Reality / American Politics: Research

The Constitution of the United States of America   402

Index   421

Part One

Political Participation

Chapter 1 The Creed Under Fire

In studying American government, the student comes face to face with a major segment of his own culture. American government is thus a study of the familiar. Although this reduces the problem of getting to know the subject, it introduces at the same time a complicating factor. The study of chemistry, physics, mathematics, English, or even history does not have a uniquely American setting. The student can approach such matters relatively free of the cultural bias that surrounds the study of American government and politics.

The student's encounter with American government in college is usually not his first one. Under names such as civics and social studies much of the same ground has been covered, perhaps two or three times. Teaching about American government and the political values associated with it is, in fact, one of the more important functions carried on by public and private educational systems. It is little wonder, therefore, that students have well-developed and usually strong feelings about such a pervasive part of their own culture.

Beliefs and Paradoxes   Yet, with all the exposure to such training, students, like the general population, harbor some curiously mixed feelings and attitudes about American government and politics. A predominant strain in the American political character is a deep distrust—even fear—of government. Historical encounters with tyrannical and arbitrary governments were not only part of the background of the colonists, but also the very real confrontation with George III etched in the American mind the feeling that out of government only evil could come. If government must inevitably exist as a necessary evil, it should at least be as close to the people and as small in size as possible.

But if Americans have been hostile to the notion of government, they have also demanded much from it; this is not a recent phenomenon. Through the almost two centuries of native government in America, people have wanted government to undertake a bewildering variety of tasks: to carry their mail; to fight Indians; to help build highways, canals, railroads, and supersonic transports; to protect them from competition from foreign manufacturers; to open up foreign markets to American businessmen; to build schools, parks, and libraries; to forestall economic depression and to foster a healthy economy; to fight wars to further or protect the nation's interests; to provide assistance for the ill and the needy; to make charts and maps and to give weather reports.

Americans generally find little conflict between the general mistrust of government and their continually increasing demands that government do more for them. Whatever ideological inclinations are held, they are easily pushed aside by a persistently pragmatic vision that is nearsighted in result. If there is sight outward to the fine points of philosophical speculation, it is only a blurred vision.

A quarter of a century ago the Swedish social scientist, Gunnar Myrdal, wrote of the American creed "as principles which *ought* to rule" and which have "been made conscious to everyone in American Society."[1] The creed embodies economic and social ideals (for exam-

---

[1] *An American Dilemma* (New York: Harper and Row, 1962), p. 3. First published in 1944, *An American Dilemma* was an exhaustive analysis of the racial problem in the United States.

THE CREED UNDER FIRE

ple, the ideas of the land of opportunity and equality of all men) as well as political ones. In specific political terms, the creed consists of notions such as the following:

1. Democracy is the best form of government.
2. Public officials should be chosen by majority vote.
3. Every citizen should have an equal chance to influence government policy.
4. The minority should be free to criticize majority decisions.
5. People in the minority should be free to try to win majority support for their opinions.[2]

The fact that Americans have found it difficult to live up to the noble precepts of the creed has often, in the past, been a source of tension and anxiety. The basic problem stems from the inability of people to see the implications of general ideals in concrete situations. Nearly 100 percent agreement was found to exist on the series of five general propositions. Yet, when translated into specific questions, consensus on some of them melts away. When asked, for example, whether a Communist should be allowed to speak, only 44 percent of a sample in one survey gave a genuinely democratic response. And less than two thirds of the group gave a similar response when asked whether an antireligious speech should be allowed.[3]

It is, however, the abstract agreement that gives the political ideals of the American creed their force. Even though what people think may have little relation to what they do, the set of attitudes embodied in the creed places limits on what can be done and on how it will be done. The mere fact that the generalities of the creed are believed in so uncritically thus becomes one of the most important starting points in understanding the American political system.

Nor are the political values of the creed merely ends in themselves. Frequently, they are thought of in terms of what they permit the individual to do in his economic activity. The themes of the "pursuit of life, liberty, and property" and the "land of opportunity" are indicative of the feeling that the political climate of America is and should be conducive to economic gain. Although America has excelled in many things, its economic growth and widespread prosperity is perhaps the

[2] James W. Prothro and Charles M. Grigg, "Fundamental Principles of Democracy: Bases of Agreement and Disagreement," *Journal of Politics* 22 (May 1960), 282.
[3] Ibid., p. 285.

virtue most often thought of in the minds of its own people. As one observer of American culture has expressed it, most of our history has been characterized by a "lopsided preoccupation with amassing wealth and raising the standard of living."[4]

It is in the economic realm, in fact, that many prized American words—such as independence, individualism, initiative, or enterprise—take on their most widely understood meanings. Rugged individualism has been transplanted from use as a description of the rigors of life on the frontier to one that approves of the man who gets ahead by dint of his own hard work and sacrifice in the business world. Thus, although individual nonconformity is approved of in technological and economic terms, the culture is one in which there is a tendency to legislate conformity in the area of personal morals.[5] Radical ideas and their expression, unorthodox modes of dress, or the wearing of long hair or beards are just some of the expressions of individualism generally met with hostility.

In economics, as in politics, there are gaps between the set of held ideals and practice. Considerable sympathy remains for the lore of the small independent businessman in a nation in which colossal corporate enterprises dominate so heavily. A survey of teen-agers revealed a distinct hostility and fear toward big business that in the "future will see all free enterprise swallowed up in one or two gigantic trusts."[6] At the same time, the majority of boys expressed little desire to go into business for themselves, preferring instead "to find security and success in positions with important national companies."[7]

Whatever specific feelings toward business may be harbored by certain groups, there is a general belief that the political system is in large part responsible for the economic success of America. Most Americans would readily identify free enterprise as the *sine qua non* of democracy. Americans may favor government stepping in when particularly abusive practices result from the economic system, but few would favor more than a mild tinkering here and there. So pervasive does the business culture reign in America that economic attitudes and beliefs impose severe constraints on the political system.

The American tendency to embrace pragmatic solutions helps to reinforce the view that the political system should be instrumental in

---

[4] Jules Henry, *Culture Against Man* (New York: Random House, 1963), p. 5.
[5] Robin M. Williams, Jr., *American Society, A Sociological Interpretation* (New York: Alfred A. Knopf, 1960), p. 451.
[6] Henry, *Culture Against Man*, p. 38.
[7] Ibid., p. 39.

facilitating economic well-being. An additional supporting crutch is provided by the polyglot nature of the American population. Throughout the nineteenth century and for the first two decades of this century, people came to this country to seek what the "land of opportunity" offered. For these immigrants, and also seemingly for the Negro, no system of political ideals could have more closely corresponded with their interests.[8]

Yet, if this has been so in the recent past, there are signs that the cement supplied by the creed is cracking. Most immigrant groups, having achieved a modicum of economic success and a measure of social assimilation, now interpret the creed as a defensive mechanism to preserve what they have gained. But for growing numbers of young Americans and Black Americans the gaps between professed ideals and the realities of American practice had become too acute to ignore. Discontent has existed in many previous periods of American history, during the Progressive era and the Great Depression, for example. But the challenge to American institutions today seems more pervasive, and at a time when the nation is more affluent and powerful than ever before.

A variety of reasons may account for this. Affluence itself may well provide the atmosphere in which many can afford the time and luxury to think more deeply about their own society; thus, at least one consequence is that more people (in number as well as a proportion of their age group) go to college and are provided opportunities for more critical analysis of their society. Messages of political and economic discontent are more easily and more widely transmitted through modern media so that political awareness and consciousness seem at a higher level among more people (especially students) than in the past. And there seem to be more things to think about as domestic and international problems have become inordinately perplexing and difficult to solve.

Whatever the causes, the undeniable fact appears to be that in greater numbers than in the past people are asking fundamental questions about the nature of American political institutions.

Early in the sixties there was the promise of a New Frontier. But, as the decade unfolded, the New Frontier, and then the Great Society, revealed a deep and pervasive racism and militarism which have shaken the faith of many Americans in the viability of their system. And pervasive to both of these issues a belief developed that hypocrisy—in

[8] Myrdal, *An American Dilemma*, p. 13.

terms of the promises of the creed—was inherent in the country's political and economic life style.

Involvement in Vietnam and the inability of the system to respond adequately to racism and the decay of urban life have contributed to a lessening of confidence in American institutions and the creed on which they supposedly rest. As the decade drew to a close disaffection occasioned by these issues manifested itself more and more in the form of unrest on college and university campuses. The war in Vietnam and the race problem almost always lurked in the background but there were other issues too: the involvement of universities in secret government research; maintenance of ROTC programs; failure in some cases of universities adequately to take into account the needs and aspirations of the urban communities of which they were a part. And perhaps more widely supported than any of these specific issues was the quest on the part of students to exercise greater participation in the decision-making processes which deeply affected their education and their lives. Not surprisingly, a similar movement soon spread to the high schools.

America thus came face to face with demands for power: Black power and student power. At the same time, there were insistent voices raised against the power wielded in society by the military-industrial complex. Clearly a test of old values, traditions, and institutions was underway. In many facets of American life, authority was being challenged. As the seventies began, there was little sign of abatement.

Implicit in such a challenge is the whole question of legitimacy: the legitimacy of existing political institutions and the legitimacy of existing decision-making processes. Most Americans simply take for granted the legitimacy of their political institutions and processes. The symbolic focal point that sustains the belief in legitimacy is the Constitution. No other single symbol has as much significance as this chief ornament of American political culture. To many Americans the Constitution serves as a blueprint as to how government *should* work. Although it may serve as a basic guide, it is hardly an accurate description of how the political system works in the last third of the twentieth century.

Reading the Constitution might lead one to believe that there are three separate, independent branches of government—that is, the president, Congress, and Supreme Court—each exercising different kinds of power. In this triad, supposedly only Congress makes laws, the president does little more than enforce them, and the Supreme Court interprets them. Such an impression, however, would be vastly misleading.

The Functions of Government

Part of the difficulty encountered in trying to understand the complexities of any political system arises from the tendency to confuse governmental institutions or branches and governmental functions. No matter what form a government may take, it must necessarily perform certain basic functions. Rules for the members of society subject to the government must be made. This function, perhaps the most basic of all, is what government is all about—at least in the stages of growth beyond primitive social organization. Once rules are made, it becomes necessary to apply or enforce them. In primitive societies, where rules of behavior are normally unwritten and simply adhered to as a matter of received traditions, another basic function of government is to protect "members of the political community against lawlessness within and enemies without."[9]

In most cases, the concern of government in such primitive situations was the redress of wrongs. When an individual injured his neighbor, some mechanism, approved by the community, provided the means for the settlement of such disputes. Out of the community's concern for the maintenance of law and order, therefore, develops the necessity of applying or enforcing the rules in the course of settling disputes among the members of the society. Regardless of the complexity of modern societies and their governments, these three basic functions can therefore be identified: rule-making, rule-application, and rule-adjudication.[10]

All of these three basic functions can be in the hands of one man—such as a king—or in a single political institution—such as a legislature. A government, therefore, may have one, two, three, four, or any number of organized institutions or branches engaged in these three functions. There is nothing inherent in the performance of these functions which requires them to be exercised by three branches, nor is there anything which requires one branch of government to engage in one of them exclusively. The problem is not one of what a government should look like, but rather, of what a government does.[11]

Once the focus is shifted from the appearance of governmental institutions to the functions government performs, to what government does, it becomes easier to conceive of government as a system of ac-

---

[9] Lucy Mair, *Primitive Government* (Baltimore: Penguin Books, 1962), p. 16.
[10] Gabriel A. Almond and James S. Coleman, *The Politics of the Developing Areas* (Princeton: Princeton University Press, 1960), p. 17.
[11] Mair, *Primitive Government*, p. 16.

tions. The actions of the citizens or members of a political community, on the one hand, and the actions of governmental institutions or officials, on the other hand, constitute the stuff of politics. In a political community

> there are always and everywhere persons with conflicting and competing interests seeking to have disputes settled in their favour and to influence community decisions ("policy") in accordance with their interests. This is politics.[12]

A system of political action implies a reciprocal relation between what the members of the community do and what governmental institutions and officials do. This relation may be very close or only a distant one, depending on the traditions, culture, or operating rules of a particular organized political community. There are obvious differences in this respect, for example, between Sweden and Portugal, or between the United States and South Africa. The same is true even of states within the United States, as, for instance, between Mississippi and Massachusetts.

Political Behavior

Regardless of such differences, it is useful to conceive of a political system in respect to what its members do and what its rulers do, "to view political life as a system of behavior."[13] With the focus on behavior, what citizens do, what interest group leaders, political party leaders, reporters and columnists, congressmen, presidents, secretaries of departments, chiefs of bureaus and offices, members of regulatory commissions, and judges do becomes politically meaningful. All of these people—all of us, in short—pursue other than political goals and lives. But, where the emphasis of behavior is directed toward the decisions to be made by the political community, our activity is political.

The making of decisions—the making of rules which guide behavior—is the major function of government. This is what government primarily does. It matters little what form the rules take. They may be laws of Congress, or merely directives in a committee report aimed at an agency; they may take the form of executive orders of the president,

[12] Ibid., p. 10.
[13] David Easton, *A Framework for Political Analysis* (Englewood Cliffs, N.J.: Prentice-Hall, 1965), p. 23.

or administrative rules which hundreds of lesser executive officials are authorized to issue. The rules may be embodied in decisions of a regulatory commission or in the opinions or mandates of the courts. In the end, all have a similar effect—they induce people to do certain things or to refrain from doing other things.

The kinds of rules and the policies they embody are the major products of the activity of government officials. The products of governmental activity, however, must be in response to something. Something must first actuate the processes whereby the rules are made; they are not produced in a vacuum. Here is where the reciprocal relation between the rulers and the ruled comes into play. It is the rulers responding to the ruled and vice versa which produces the activity of the political system.[14]

Political Participation The study of American government, therefore, involves both what the people do in relation to government, and what government does to or for people. How the ideas, feelings, beliefs, and attitudes of the American people shape the demands they make on government, as well as determine the support they give to government, is one aspect of what people do. The way in which such demands and support express themselves may take the quite simple form of voting or may take more complex forms such as organized participation in interest groups and political parties. How the citizen relates himself to government, the forms such participation takes, and the effectiveness of that participation are thus important considerations in assessing the relation between the ruled and their rulers.

The effectiveness of participation in the political process cannot be fully measured unless account is taken of the conditions under which it is exercised. Under idealized and, to many, unrealistic conceptions of democracy, the voice of each citizen presumably is as effective as his neighbor's. But what are the factors in real-life America which condition or qualify political participation so that some citizens are substantially more equal in their political weight?

The impact that modern techniques of mass communications in mass

---

[14] A useful way of thinking about the political system is to regard the activities of the vast number of members of the political community as "inputs" and the decisions and policies of governmental institutions and officials as "outputs." Ibid., p. 112.

POLITICAL PARTICIPATION

society have had on political participation is one such conditioning factor. The making and manipulating of opinion and the introduction of television as a major factor in political campaigning are phenomena the consequences of which are probably not yet fully felt. Modern communications techniques—primarily television—have also introduced new complexities into the traditional role of the press in government.

Money has always been an important commodity in a competitive political process. The new techniques of communications, however, have upped the ante considerably. The advantages the unequal distribution of money available for political campaigns and lobbying confer on some at the expense of others is an obvious factor conditioning political participation.

Political participation takes on meaning from the ideas and opinions expressed by people on the whole range of subjects of relevance to government. The extent to which freedom of political expression encourages that exchange of controversial views which makes for health in a self-governing society is a measure of its vitality and confidence. Where society and government, however, discourage and punish dissent, it is a mark, not of overconfidence, but of timidity and fear. To the extent that freedom of political expression is unduly restricted or denied, the political participation of some citizens is substantially disadvantaged.

How Decisions Are Made   But how does political participation and the conditions under which it is exercised relate to the activity of governmental institutions and officials? What impact do the actions of people have on what government does and how it does it? What are the many processes whereby rules are fashioned for the governing of American society, and how do they work? Government, of course, does not make all the rules. Other social institutions—such as churches, universities, trade associations, and labor unions—also make rules. But rules laid down by governmental institutions have the ultimate sanction of legitimately applied force behind them. The processes that produce the authoritative rules constitute that aspect of the political system where the actions of the rulers are in large measure responses to the political activity of the members of society.

In any analysis of how these processes work it soon becomes apparent that one of the obvious characteristics of the American political system is its vast dispersion of power. Power is widely diffused in political parties, in Congress, in the presidency, in the bureaucracy, and even in the courts. Dispersing power was a response to the conditions of the last quarter of the eighteenth century, when American political institutions were forged. And it is not alone in the national government that power is dispersed; nation and states and cities and towns and counties also share power. An understanding of the historical origins and meaning of the devices which sought to disperse power is essential to an appreciation of contemporary American government.

But what of today? How sound are political institutions and principles, largely of eighteenth-century vintage, in today's vastly more complicated world, where the United States sits at the pinnacle of economic and military might? Although it may be granted that there is a remarkable stability in our political institutions, conceding at the same time that they have undergone great modification, the question must still be asked: how well suited are they to a wholly different national environment? Can America close the gap between ideal and practice? Can America learn to be powerful but not arrogant? Can America solve its racial dilemma? Can America make its cities fit places for humans to live? When such questions are asked, they suggest an agenda of as yet unresolved political problems.

Chapter 2 The Voter

The traditions of democratic theory, as well as common sense, dictate that a study of American government start with the individual citizen. A theme that is practically universal in Western political literature is that the state and government exist for the individual. Statements to this effect abound in the classics of the American political heritage: the Declaration of Independence, the Gettysburg Address, the Four Freedoms of Franklin Roosevelt.

If government exists for the individual, it gains legitimacy when it rests on the consent of the governed. In modern, complex societies, the way in which consent can most readily be expressed is through some process of choosing public officials. Elections have come to be regarded as the hallmark of a democratic political system and voting is the one political act which most people engage in with the greatest frequency and significance.

THE VOTER

In the United States, hundreds of thousands of elections take place each year. The importance of the offices that are filled varies considerably, for elections are held not only to choose the president of the United States and the members of Congress, but also local officials such as county clerks and even municipal dogcatchers, with a host of other state and local officials in between. But the fact that many election contests concern comparatively trivial offices does not detract from the symbolic importance of voting. For most citizens never perceive their role as participants in the political process as clearly as when they are casting their ballots.

Despite the obvious importance of voting and elections, the Constitution says little about how public officials are to be chosen. Interestingly enough, the one election that it does describe in some detail—that of the president and vice-president—bears little resemblance today to what was originally intended. As early as 1804, the complex arrangements which the framers of the Constitution devised for electing the president and vice-president were drastically modified by constitutional amendment.[1] Even a reading of the text of the amendment, however, does not prepare one for the way in which the electoral college has functioned, and certainly not for the presidential primaries and nominating conventions that are now taken for granted. Nowhere in the entire Constitution is there to be found any mention of political parties, which in practice perform such a vital function in elections at all levels. In reality, elections are more a product of historical development than of constitutional prescription.

The Right to Vote   The Constitution in no way recognized the principle of universal suffrage. Today recognition has come, at least in principle, but only after a series of struggles to enlarge the circle of those who would have a say in the political process.

During the colonial period, neither women nor slaves could vote, and property qualifications, although easily met in many cases, were widespread, and religious and racial restrictions were often imposed as well. Although the delegates to the Constitutional Convention did nothing to broaden the franchise, the obstacles to voting gradually

---

[1] Major provisions of Article II in the original Constitution were superseded by the Twelfth Amendment. An even more radical revision is contemplated by the proposed Twenty-sixth Amendment.

POLITICAL PARTICIPATION

began to disappear. First to go were the religious qualifications; property requirements held on somewhat tenaciously, but were almost completely wiped out by the triumph of Jacksonian democracy after 1828. The Fifteenth Amendment, ratified in 1870, was intended to guarantee the suffrage of the freedmen.[2] The last section of the amendment gave Congress power to enforce this prohibition through legislation, which it did during the Reconstruction period. The legislation it enacted and the occupation of the South by federal troops made it possible for Negroes to vote in great numbers for a time. But after the troops were withdrawn, the story of the disenfranchisement of Black Americans by a combination of violent methods of intimidation and legal restrictions began. At first, the activities of the Ku Klux Klan served as the chief means of undoing the constitutional promise of the Fifteenth Amendment. Beginning in 1890, ingenious constitutional and statutory devices were developed in the Southern states to make permanent the disenfranchisement already well accomplished.

Mississippi led the way with a new constitution adopted in 1890. A poll tax was imposed, along with a literacy test, to become effective in 1892. This seemingly innocent test was, in fact, designed to frustrate those Blacks who could afford, or who would dare, to pay the poll tax. An alternative to the test was a requirement that a potential voter demonstrate an "understanding" of any portion of the state constitution. The Negro was effectively barred by a strict enforcement of the provision against him, while it was conveniently ignored against equally ill-informed whites.

Grandfather clauses were the next product of the inventive minds who were determined to contrive means to bar the poor and ignorant Negro from voting while the white citizen in the same condition remained unaffected. Louisiana was the first state to adopt such a clause when, in 1898, it granted the right to vote to anyone who had been eligible to vote on January 1, 1866, or the son or grandson of a person so eligible, regardless of property or literacy requirements. In Alabama, a constitutional provision permitting persons (and their descendants) who had fought in the Revolutionary War to vote accomplished much the same result.

The mood of the South was perhaps most candidly stated by a Virginia state senator, who later would become a United States senator,

---

[2] "The right of citizens of the United States to vote shall not be denied or abridged by the United States or by any State on Account of race, color, or previous condition of servitude."

Carter Glass. In addressing a state constitutional convention meeting in the summer of 1901, Glass proclaimed that its main purpose was:

> Discrimination: Why that is precisely what we propose; that, exactly, is what this convention was elected for—to discriminate to the very extremity of permissible action under the limitations of the Federal Constitution, with a view to the elimination of every Negro voter who can be gotten rid of, legally, without materially impairing the numerical strength of the white electorate.[3]

Beginning in 1915, a series of Supreme Court decisions extending over four decades eventually nullified the determined ingenuity of the South. The grandfather clause was the first technique of discrimination struck down,[4] only to be succeeded by the white primary. By the 1920s the South was already a solid one-party area, so that all that remained was to exclude Black citizens from participating in Democratic party primaries. This practice was not invalidated until 1944.[5]

Southern devices aimed at disenfranchising Negroes had already accomplished their goal, however. Along with formal means, such as the white primary and unfairly administered literacy tests, economic and personal intimidation had reduced Black suffrage in the South to negligible proportions. More than Supreme Court decisions were needed to restore the promise of the Fifteenth Amendment.

It now became the task of Congress to supply the legislative machinery and sanctions to induce the Southern states to make the franchise a reality for all citizens. The growing significance of the Negro vote in big Northern cities in states with large electoral votes added political muscle to the demands made in Congress for the passage of civil rights legislation. In 1957 Congress made a modest start. Especially noteworthy was the creation of the Commission on Civil Rights, authorized to conduct investigations and gather data on all kinds of interferences with civil rights. The commission became instrumental in publicizing to the American public the plight of Blacks, Mexican-Americans, Puerto Ricans, and Indians in their struggle to achieve equality in the enjoyment of their civil rights.

Experience soon showed the inadequacies of the mild law of 1957. In 1960 another fight over a civil rights bill ensued. The measure finally enacted provided for voting referees to be appointed by the federal

---

[3] Paul Lewinson, *Race, Class and Party* (New York: Grosset & Dunlop, 1965), p. 86.
[4] Guinn v. United States, 238 U.S. 347 (1915).
[5] Smith v. Allwright, 321 U.S. 649 (1944).

government; their function was to register Negro voters in those areas where a pattern of discrimination had been found to exist. Four years later, a more comprehensive civil rights bill was enacted, including a provision which dealt with discriminatory administration of literacy tests. In 1964, as well, the Twenty-fourth Amendment was ratified by the requisite number of states. This amendment prohibited states from denying any person the right to vote because of failure to pay a poll tax. At the time of ratification, only five Southern states had a poll tax requirement so that the effect of the amendment was not momentous.

None of these measures was deemed adequate to the task of overcoming the impact of a century of systematic exclusion of Blacks from the Southern political process. In 1965 civil rights forces again mustered their strength. The outcome, after a Southern filibuster had been broken for the second time in as many years, was the Voting Rights Act of 1965. This law was a comprehensive and complex measure aimed at the heart of the Negro voting problem. The major feature of the act was the provisions permitting the appointment of federal voting examiners who were empowered to pass on the qualifications of a potential voter. The examiner could then order a local election official to permit a qualified individual to vote in all elections, federal, state, and local.

Examiners could be appointed by the United States Civil Service Commission upon a determination by the attorney general that literacy tests had been used as a qualification for voting on November 1, 1964. When such a finding was made, the use of such tests was to be suspended. Examiners could also be appointed if the director of the census determined that less than 50 percent of the eligible voters in a state or political subdivision thereof had registered or actually voted in the 1964 presidential election.

The act also took note of the inadequacies of the Twenty-fourth Amendment, which had prohibited poll taxes only in federal elections, by asserting that such taxes as used in certain states denied or abridged the right to vote. Congress also directed the attorney general to challenge in the federal courts poll taxes or any similar device used to prevent persons from voting in any kind of election. One of the most far-reaching provisions of the act was a requirement that any new voting laws passed by a state covered under the legislation be approved either by the attorney general or a federal court.

In late 1965, the United States Supreme Court granted South Carolina permission to file an original suit against the United States, contesting the constitutionality of the act. Eight hours of oral argument, an unusually lengthy period since normally only two hours are granted, took place in January, 1966. The importance of the case was demonstrated by the filing of *amicus curiae* (friend of the court) briefs by some twenty Northern and Western states. Five Southern states joined South Carolina in opposing the act.

The Southern states concentrated their attack on the provision permitting the suspension of literacy tests and the automatic "triggering" formulas used in the act. Congress lacked power, it was argued, under the Fifteenth Amendment to do this; and, under Article 1, Section 2, of the Constitution, the states were to determine the qualifications of voters. Objections were also raised against the requirement of submitting state statutes dealing with voting regulations to the attorney general of the United States, or to a special three-judge federal court sitting in the District of Columbia, for approval.

On March 7, the decision of the Supreme Court dismissing the suit by South Carolina was handed down. Writing for the Court, then Chief Justice Earl Warren rejected all the arguments made against the constitutionality of the act. The matter was put succinctly when he said:

> After enduring nearly a century of widespread resistance to the 15th Amendment, Congress has marshalled an array of potent weapons against the evil, with authority in the Attorney General to employ them effectively.[6]

Although he admitted that submission of state legislation to the attorney general was an "uncommon" device, the Chief Justice held that it was in response to "unique circumstances." It was on this aspect of the law that Associate Justice Hugo L. Black dissented from the otherwise unanimous decision.

The combination of Supreme Court decisions and congressional legislation over the last twenty-five years has begun to translate the promise of the Fifteenth Amendment into a reality for the Black voter, especially in the South. Within a few months after the passage of the 1965 act, almost 100,000 Negroes had been registered in five states in the deep South. Three years later, in the spring of 1968, the number of registered Blacks in eleven Southern states had risen by nearly 650,000.[7] This increase in registration was reflected in actual voting in the 1968

---

[6] South Carolina v. Katzenbach, 383 U.S. 301 (1966).
[7] Data from U. S. Commission on Civil Rights, *The Voting Rights Act . . . The First Months* (Washington: G.P.O., 1965), pp. 53–67, and *Revolution in Civil Rights* (Washington: Congressional Quarterly, Inc., 1968), p. 115.

election. According to a survey by the Bureau of the Census, the proportion of the nonwhite voting-age population in the South that actually went to the polls rose from 44 percent in 1964 to 51.4 percent four years later.[8]

Several months after the Nixon administration assumed power, Attorney General John N. Mitchell proposed that the provisions of the Voting Rights Act, which was scheduled to expire in 1970, be extended to the entire nation. Civil Rights organizations interpreted this as a concession to the South for the electoral support it provided Nixon in 1968. The storm of criticism was echoed in Congress. The chairman of the House Judiciary Committee, Emanuel Celler of New York, as well as ranking Republican William McCulloch of Ohio, expressed strong sentiment for simply continuing the act in its present form. Opposition centered around administration proposals that would have softened enforcement especially the plan to drop the requirement for approval of new voter legislation.

Woman Suffrage

The struggle for the right to vote by Black citizens is only part of their larger quest for a more equitable place in the political, economic, and social life of the nation. In many ways, the struggle by women throughout most of the nineteenth century and on into this century is comparable. Treated in several respects as though they were slaves, at least as far as their legal status in the eyes of the common law, women fought for the right to vote as they also fought for recognition as equal members of society along with men.

Changes in the legal status of women came about in the nineteenth century, but acquiring the right to vote proved a somewhat more difficult task. There were great fears that by giving women the vote, they would become morally tainted with the corruption of politics. Other objections were perhaps not so noble but nonetheless entertained. Corporations were apprehensive about woman suffrage because it would add to the vote of the working class. The liquor interests were also concerned lest the "dry" forces be reinforced.

The battle waged by the women was accompanied by militancy and, on occasion, by violence and official suppression. In the second decade

---

[8] *New York Times,* 1 January 1969, p. 43.

of this century, the suffragettes came under the militant leadership of Alice Paul, who did not disdain such tactics as picketing the White House to dramatize the demands of the fairer sex. In early 1917, a line of pickets paraded daily before 1600 Pennsylvania Avenue and, naturally, attracted headlines in papers throughout the country.

As officialdom is so often wont to do, it could not ignore the visitors at the most important address in the nation. Finally, after six months, the demonstrators were arrested for "obstructing traffic." Called before the bar of justice, the women remained defiant. They went off to jail, only to provoke a stream of protests from all over the country directed at the president and congressmen.

The House of Representatives responded in early 1918 by approving an amendment to the Constitution. But the Senate proved to be strictly a man's world, as the proposal fell short of the necessary two-thirds vote. Undaunted, the suffragettes staged a massive demonstration before the White House. Speakers were arrested; those jailed went on hunger strikes before conscience-stricken prison officials released them. Together with a relentless propaganda campaign throughout the nation, the desired effect was achieved. President Wilson was won over to the cause and was able to exert enough pressure on Democratic senators to produce the needed majority in the Senate in 1919.

Ratification followed quickly as three fourths of the state legislatures agreed to this important constitutional change by August, 1920. The victory by the suffragettes climaxed a battle a century long. During that time they had steadily worn down resistance in individual states so that by the time the movement reached its peak in 1914, some eleven states, all in the West, had already granted suffrage. But the big prize was the one achieved in 1920 when the Nineteenth Amendment became part of the Constitution.

The struggles of the Black American and of women, in many respects similar, demonstrate that gaining access to the political process is not always an easy task. Entrenched political forces, prejudices against race or sex, and attachment to tradition are all obstacles which have to be overcome. Although reason and persuasion are helpful, militancy, dedication, violence, and martyrdom have on occasion served as necessary lubricants.

Making the Vote Equal Possessing the right to vote is one thing; having that vote count the same as the next man's (or woman's) is quite another story. The problem of the inequality of the vote arises from the changing patterns of where Americans choose or find it necessary to live. Rural-agricultural America of 1800 had become, by 1950, urban-suburban industrial America.

In the nineteenth century, particularly during the era of Jacksonian democracy, the principle of equal representation based on population was widely accepted in the United States. To be effective in practice, such a principle requires that legislative districts be constantly adjusted to take account of changing population patterns. By 1920, the urban population of the United States had surpassed the rural population. Even before this time, entrenched political forces had begun to resist the implications of direct, population-based representation.

In the first half of the century, beginning in 1900, three factors produced gross malapportionment that came to characterize most of the states by the fifties. Some states simply refused to reapportion their legislatures, even though required to do so by their constitutions. Others experienced such drastic population shifts to the cities that once quite fair constitutional provisions became grossly discriminatory. A third group of a few states actually changed their constitutions in order to introduce inequitable representation, usually by including factors other than population.[9]

By 1960 a crisis in malapportionment had developed. Adding to the complexity of the problem had been the post-World War II population growth in the suburbs. The suburbs were the most poorly represented areas of all, since central cities were growing at a slower rate or even declining in population.

The population figures for some electoral districts dramatize the absurdly unjust discriminations which existed. California presented the extreme, where in 1962, the 6,038,771 people of Los Angeles County had one state senator, whereas a senatorial district in the Sierra Nevada Mountains had a population of only 14,294, with also one senator. The ratio between these two districts was 422:5. New Hampshire presented the spectacle of one lower house district with only three people, whereas its most populous district had 4,330, a ratio of 1,443:3![10]

---

[9] See Royce Hanson, *The Political Thicket* (Englewood Cliffs, N.J.: Prentice-Hall, 1966), pp. 15–16.

[10] Data are from Glendon Schubert, ed., *Reapportionment* (New York: Charles Scribner, 1965), pp. 80–82.

When put in terms of the individual urban or suburban voter, it often would mean that the vote of the citizen from the country-side would be worth many times his own. Even in the most fairly apportioned states, the vote of the rural dweller would be worth anywhere from twice to five times that of the urban-suburban resident. In the most poorly apportioned states, it might be worth forty, fifty, or even one hundred times as much.

The tenacity of those benefiting from barnyard government bore out words written by the noted political journalist and critic, H. L. Mencken, a quarter of a century earlier:

> The yokels hang on because old apportionments give them unfair advantages. The vote of a malarious peasant in the lower Eastern Shore [of Maryland] counts as much as the votes of twelve Baltimoreans. But that can't last. It is not only unjust and undemocratic; it is absurd.[11]

Absurd though it might be, thirty years and more were to pass from the time Mencken wrote in 1928 until something was done in Maryland and elsewhere. One of the most formidable obstacles was a Supreme Court decision of 1946, widely interpreted as holding that questions of legislative apportionment were not susceptible to judicial determination and therefore beyond the scope of the jurisdiction of the federal courts.[12]

In that decision, Justice Felix Frankfurter characterized the issue of malapportionment as a "political thicket." This view of the matter, however, was shared by only two other justices of the seven who decided the case.[13] The three dissenting members of the Court argued forcefully that inequality of the vote was, indeed, a denial of equal protection of the law under the Fourteenth Amendment. One Justice, Wiley Rutledge, although disagreeing with Frankfurter, felt that under the particular circumstances of the case judicial intervention would not be appropriate. Thus, by a vote of 4 to 3, those challenging malapportionment lost their case.

When carefully read, the several opinions of the justices added up to the proposition that malapportionment was indeed an issue over

---

[11] Malcolm Moos, ed., *H. L. Mencken on Politics: A Carnival of Buncombe* (New York: Vintage Books, 1960), p. 164.
[12] Colegrove v. Green, 328 U.S. 549 (1946).
[13] The Court was short by two members at the time because Justice Robert Jackson was in Nuremberg, Germany, as chief United States prosecutor in the Nazi war crime trials, and the new Chief Justice, Fred Vinson, appointed following the death of Harlan Stone, had not yet taken his seat.

which the federal courts could exercise jurisdiction. But, as is often the case, decisions of the Supreme Court are deliberately or unintentionally misconstrued by lower courts, lawyers, and journalists. That this was the situation with the *Colegrove* decision became clear over the ensuing decade.

The Courts Enter the Thicket

The Supreme Court itself, many state courts, and state legislatures all cited the *Colegrove* doctrine as a bar to judicial relief for those suffering from malapportionment. By 1962, there had been changes in personnel on the Supreme Court, and the degree of the evil of urban-suburban underrepresentation was clearly obvious to even the most casual observer of the American political scene. These factors, together with extensive criticism of the decision in law school journals, brought about the climate for another look at the problem.

A case originating in Tennessee finally became the vehicle for change. No reapportionment had taken place in that state since 1901, even though required by the state constitution. Gross disparities existed. They were most pithily summed up by the then Mayor of Nashville, Ben West, in describing a rural Tennessee county:

> It has 8,611 cows, 4,739 pigs and horses, 3,948 people and one state representative. Nashville's county had 381,412 people in 1950—and seven state representatives, meaning that each representative spoke for 54,487 people, but not, of course, for as many cows, horses and pigs.[14]

On March 25, 1962, The Supreme Court handed down its historic decision in *Baker* v. *Carr*.[15] Justice William J. Brennan wrote the opinion of the Court in which five other members joined. Without expressly overruling *Colegrove* v. *Green*, Brennan held that the earlier case actually supported federal court jurisdiction in reapportionment matters. The Court's opinion did not give much in the way of guidelines as to how fair apportionment must be to meet the requirements of the equal protection clause of the Fourteenth Amendment. Nevertheless, the log

[14] Quoted in "Unrepresentatives" (an editorial), *The New Republic,* 29 January 1962, p. 4.
[15] 369 U.S. 186 (1962).

jam had been broken, and in the ensuing months a host of cases were filed, challenging existing apportionments.

Justice Frankfurter wrote a lengthy dissenting opinion, joined by Justice Harlan, in which he predicted that the decision would create a "mathematical quagmire" for the courts. To Frankfurter, the majority was simply, and unjustifiably, supporting one theory of representation in preference to others. But Supreme Court decisions usually do give support to a particular point of view on controversial issues and naturally invite the wrath of those who happen to disagree with its philosophy, whether it concerns economics, slavery, segregation, or apportionment.

One Man, One Vote The underlying premise of the Supreme Court decision in the *Baker* case was the proposition that each citizen's vote ought to count as much as every other citizen's, no more, no less. Such a premise was clearly articulated in a case decided a year later involving a challenge to Georgia's county unit vote system, another ancient device for preserving rural control. In holding the system invalid, Justice William O. Douglas wrote that

> the conception of political equality from the Declaration of Independence, to Lincoln's Gettysburg Address, to the Fifteenth, Seventeenth, and Nineteenth Amendments can mean only one thing—one person, one vote.[16]

In a case involving congressional districts (*Baker* v. *Carr* had concerned state legislative districts) the Court required the one-man, one-vote standard.[17] It did so, however, on the basis of Article I of the Constitution, which, in Section 2, simply says that the members of the House of Representatives shall be chosen by the *people* of the several states. The question of whether the same standard would apply under the equal protection clause of the Fourteenth Amendment was thus left open.

The answer was not long in forthcoming. A few months later, six cases involving several reapportionment issues were decided. To most

---

[16] Gray v. Sanders, 372 U.S. 368, 381 (1963). Although Douglas used the phrase "one person, one vote," the "one man, one vote" version quickly became fixed in popular usage.
[17] Wesberry v. Sanders, 376 U.S. 1 (1964).

observers, the Court's answer came as no surprise. The notion of the equality of the vote was emphatically upheld as Chief Justice Warren wrote that "legislators represent people, not trees or acres."

Not only was the one-man, one-vote concept thus endorsed, but it was also held to apply to both houses of a state legislature. Prior to this decision, many states had made a desperate effort to preserve the dominance of rural interests in the upper houses of their legislatures. They had argued that their senates were similar to the United States Senate, where population was not a factor. But history was clearly against this contention and the Court rejected it.[18]

The full effect of this genuine revolution in the political makeup of state legislatures and local governing bodies may not be felt until this decade or later. Although it is difficult to foretell the shape of things to come it is clear that reapportionment will not only affect state politics. After the 1970 census, state legislatures will have to redraw congressional district boundaries, and those under the control of urban-suburban interests will naturally draw them to their own best advantage.

Long-standing inequities in congressional districts will undoubtedly be erased, and the long-time advantage the agricultural-rural areas of the nation have enjoyed in the lower house of Congress will disappear. What will replace it, however, and the resulting outcomes in public policy, will be determined by the kinds of issues that will face Congress. The winner in the reapportionment battle has been, for the most part, the suburban voter. If such a voter reacts to the problem of America's Black cities by supporting policies which only tighten the white noose around the Black inner city, it will be the city voter who will still be the loser—as he was before the apportionment revolution. And the rural-agricultural voter, over whose loss of power so many tears have been shed, more than likely will find safety in an alliance with his suburban brethren.

The Nonvoter

That people have struggled in the streets or in the courthouse to secure the right to vote might seem to indicate that Americans put a high

---

[18] Reynolds v. Sims, 377 U.S. 533 (1964). This case involved Alabama. Other cases decided that day concerned New York, Maryland, Virginia, Delaware, and Colorado. A few years later, the "one-man, one-vote" principle was extended to local governments in Avery v. Midland County, 390 U.S. 474 (1968).

premium on this most basic of all political acts. Yet the startling reality is otherwise. Barely more than three out of every five Americans chose to exercise the franchise in the 1968 presidential election. Out of a voting-age population of about 120 million, some 73 million, or 60.8 percent, went to the polls to choose between Richard Nixon, Hubert Humphrey, and George Wallace. This percentage represented a decline over the previous two elections when the highest office in the land was at stake. Another close contest in which Nixon had been involved—the 1960 contest with John F. Kennedy—had brought out 63.2 percent of the persons old enough to vote. But in 1964, when Johnson defeated Goldwater, the percentage slipped to 62.1 percent.[19]

Almost a century ago, in the election of 1876, nearly 86 percent of the electorate voted. Since that time, the figure has declined, not steadily, but in zigzag fashion. A low point was reached in the 1920 and 1924 presidential contests when only about 44 percent went to the polls, undoubtedly reflecting a slow start by the females in the enjoyment of their newly won right.

The spirited contest in 1928, in which Governor Alfred E. Smith of New York made a bid to become the first Catholic elected to the presidency, raised the turnout to around 52 percent. Increases in participation during the tenure of Franklin Roosevelt reached a peak of just under 60 percent in 1940. Decline set in again in 1944; and, in 1948, barely more than half (51.5 percent) of the electorate bothered to vote. There was a sharp jump (to 62.2 percent) in 1952, as General Eisenhower led the Republicans back to power after twenty years.

When compared with voter participation in European democracies, America does not come off well. In Italy, the turnout for national elections customarily tops 90 percent; in Denmark, in 1960 almost 86 percent went to the polls. West Germany has participation figures ranging from 78.5 to 87.8 percent in recent years and Canadian participation is normally about 80 percent.

To some extent, such gross comparisons are misleading, for there are extensive variations from state to state in the percentage of eligible voters who actually vote. In the past, very low voter turnout in the South dragged down the nationwide average. In the 1964 presidential election, for example, a mere 33 percent of the voting-age population in Mississippi voted for president. In six other Southern states, the turnout was less than half of those eligible to vote. Even these low

[19] *Congressional Quarterly,* Weekly Report 50 (13 December 1968): 3278.

figures represented a considerable increase over 1960 when Kennedy's Catholicism undoubtedly hurt him in the South with otherwise Democratic voters. By contrast, seventeen Northern and Western states exceeded 70 percent in 1964 and twenty-eight had done so in 1960.

The 1968 election presented a quite different pattern. Increased Negro voting, on the one hand, and the attractiveness of George Wallace, on the other hand, produced a much larger voter turnout in the South. Only three states fell below 50 percent: Georgia (44.1 percent), South Carolina (45.8 percent), and Texas (49 percent), although in each instance these figures represented gains over 1964. Mississippi no longer was the Southern laggard, recording a turnout of 50 percent of the voters. Increased voting in the South meant only one thing: much less voter interest and turnout in the North. No less than thirty-one Northern and Western states experienced a decline in the percentage of eligible voters who actually voted. In 1968 only nine states outside of the South recorded in excess of 70 percent. It is indeed ironical that lessening interest in the North occurs at a time when the problem of nonvoting in the South shows signs of improvement.

It is difficult to assess the causes of the decline of voter interest in the North. The issues of Vietnam and law and order appeared to stir voters, and the presence of George Wallace as a possible spoiler should have resulted in greater voter interest in the 1968 election.

Whatever the reasons may be for the drop-off in interest, and regardless of regional variations, the stark fact remains that millions of American citizens simply do not vote. The picture becomes even darker when voter turnout in off-year elections is examined. Even though a full House of Representatives and one third of the Senate is elected in these years, the highest turnout since 1920 was recorded in 1966 when just under 50 percent voted—still only half of the eligible electorate! More distressing yet are figures for local elections, school bond issues, and the like. In many cases, not more than a third of the voters bother to come out even when questions which may have an immediate and direct impact on their lives are at stake.

Nonvoting persists in the face of elaborate efforts to convince the qualified citizen that he should exercise his franchise. Before every election, he is admonished by the mass media that it is his civic duty to vote. He is nagged, wheedled, and cajoled. Appeals are made both to his patriotic impulses ("We are lucky to live in a country where free elections are held.") and to his self-interest ("If you remain home, don't complain later about what the government does"). Civic organizations vie with party workers in offering to transport him to the polls and even provide a babysitter if necessary. Still, people stay home in droves.

Reasons for Nonvoting What accounts for the fact that so few Americans vote? A major factor is the whole system of residency and registration requirements. The introduction of registration requirements at the end of the nineteenth century has been suggested as an explanation for the decline in voter turnout over the years.[20] This study, based on 1960 voting data from 104 of the largest cities, indicated that as such requirements began to be liberalized around 1924 turnout rose. Although there is no question that registration procedures are a deterrent to voting, the explanation offered in this analysis fails to account for the decline since 1960 in voter turnout in the North when it is increasing in the South.

The precise relationship between registration and voting may not be fully understood. It is clear, however, that procedures for registration which are inconvenient and time-consuming for the voter, and which may require him to register three or four months prior to the election, do cut down the potential voting electorate. Nor is a voter, once registered, necessarily relieved of the obligation in future years, for some states require periodic re-registration. In states or cities where there is a lack of party competition, the necessity for re-registration often works to the advantage of entrenched political organizations which benefit from relatively low voter turnout.

Even when special efforts are made to get people to register, the results may be less than satisfying. During August, 1968, when interest in the 1968 election was heightened by the Republican and Democratic conventions held that month, New York City mounted a special drive to get its poor and minority slum citizens registered. Although the goal was originally set at 50,000 new registrants, officials who conducted the drive in conjunction with neighborhood and community action groups felt satisfied that 17,000 voters had been added to the rolls, most of them people who never before had been reached by the political process.[21]

---

[20] Stanley Kelley, Jr., Richard E. Ayres, and William G. Bowen, "Registration and Voting: Putting First Things First," *American Political Science Review* 61 (June 1967): 374.
[21] *New York Times,* 31 August 1968, p. 9.

Another factor accounting for nonvoting is residence requirements. Some five and one-half million Americans could not vote in 1968 because they had not satisfied the residence requirements of their states.[22] Residence requirements, of course, make considerable sense when, for example, they are employed in a gubernatorial election to keep individuals from the polls who have not lived in a state long enough to become conversant with the dominant issues. Similarly, there is obvious justification for these requirements when they are used to prevent newcomers to a city from helping to choose the mayor. But it is not so easy to devise justification for residence requirements which prevent one from voting in a presidential election just because he has moved across state lines. Some states even provide that an individual cannot vote if he has done nothing more than move from one address in the state to another within a few months of the election.

The impact of residence requirements has increased drastically in recent decades, for the population is becoming increasingly mobile. Today, some twenty million Americans move each year, making the problem of residence requirements more acute. Some states have moved to lessen residence requirements and more may be induced to follow suit. A Supreme Court decision in the spring of 1969 invalidating one-year residence requirements for welfare eligibility suggests that the rationale for similar requirements for voting has been undercut. Certainly a requirement of thirty days residence in a state ought to be adequate for voting for president.

Permanent registration and the elimination, or at least the modification, of residence requirements are only two of the reforms that have been suggested to encourage a larger number of persons to vote. Other proposals are for more accessible polling places, longer voting hours, simplified procedures for absentee balloting, and the more widespread use of the short ballot in place of a ballot that is so cluttered with names of candidates for minor offices that it is an ordeal to plow through.

Other reasons account for nonvoting. Persons may be ill at home, hospitalized, or in mental institutions; they may be out of town and have neglected to request an absentee ballot; they may be convicted felons stripped of their voting rights.

In 1968, it was estimated that nearly forty-seven million persons of voting age failed to cast a ballot. Of these some four million were either

---

[22] Republican National Committee, Research Division, *The 1968 Elections* (Washington: Republican National Committee, 1969), p. 251.

aliens, prisoners, or inmates of mental institutions and another five and one-half million were disenfranchised because of residence requirements. Another seven million were sick or disabled, three million were away from home, three million said they could not leave their jobs, and one million failed to obtain absentee ballots.[23] Even after all these legal and other excuses, some twenty-five million persons did not choose to exercise their right to vote in 1968.

Voter Apathy Why are there some twenty-five million Americans who do not vote even when the contest is for the highest office in the land? Studies of nonvoting have produced a variety of explanations, largely psychological or sociological.

Politics, it has been said, is but one of many kinds of social activity in which the individual engages. His work, his family, his church, baseball, television and vacations all compete for his time. In an affluent society, all but a few (even though the few may number in the millions) enjoy economic security. Unemployment insurance, health plans, Medicare, social security, and pensions relieve many of the worries his ancestors, who were immigrants, experienced half a century or a century ago.

Affluence has permitted a large portion of the population to afford greatly increased leisure. Such time becomes filled, not with civic attention to the issues of the day, but with those activities perceived by the individual as constituting the good life. At one time, political campaigns were a major source of entertainment as candidates visited the small hamlets of rural America. Parades, picnics, and courthouse torchlight speeches were the chief means of reaching the voter. Today, billboards and television can do the jobs more quickly.

But more than merely affluence and the development of mass media account for the large number of nonvoters. The fact that nonvoting is significantly correlated with low socioeconomic status and with low educational achievement indicates that something deeper is involved.

The citizen who does not go to the polls on election day is likely to be from a low-income group; be a Black American; be a woman; have little education and be an unskilled worker or subsistence farmer; and

[23] Republican National Committee, *The 1968 Elections*, pp. 247, 249, based on data from the Gallup poll.

be fairly young (between twenty-one and thirty-five). These are obviously overlapping characteristics, and the more they are associated with any one individual, the less likely he or she is to vote.[24]

It is these kinds of persons who most often display feelings of alienation from the world of politics. They have little sense of counting for anything in terms of what they can do, or what influence their vote will have on candidates or issues. When asked about their feelings toward politics, such people are likely to respond, as did the wife of a worker in a Pittsburgh factory: "It doesn't make any difference [which party wins] to me. I'm not interested in stuff like that. I don't listen to nothing; I don't even read about politics in the paper."[25]

According to a Gallup poll taken after the 1968 election, fifteen million people who had registered did not vote, and another ten million could have registered but did not.[26] Most of these undoubtedly fit the general socioeconomic description of the nonvoter, but at least some were probably highly intelligent, as well as affluent citizens, who simply perceived little choice in candidates or issues in 1968.

Surprisingly enough, not all students of American politics are troubled by the large number of nonvoters, their socioeconomic characteristics, and the views they take of the political system. Some argue that nonvoting bespeaks a contented citizenry; if people were really dissatisfied with conditions, they would not be boycotting elections. Others have gone still further, asserting that society would be rent by violent cleavages if the dispossessed and disinherited became politically involved. Those who make this argument cite the example of several European countries, where participation in voting is high but where instability is chronic.

"Apathy," according to one commentator, "is probably good for the political system in that it is conducive to overall stability."[27] Since lower status groups are composed of people who are said to profess

---

[24] A great deal of data has been amassed in the last twenty years on voting behavior. The Survey Research Center at the University of Michigan is the largest source of such data. See Angus Campbell et al., *The Voter Decides* (Evanston, Ill.: Row, Peterson, 1954), and Angus Campbell et al., *The American Voter* (New York: John Wiley, 1960). See also Seymour Martin Lipset, *Political Man* (Garden City, N.Y.: Doubleday, 1960). Much of the data is summarized in Lester W. Milbrath, *Political Participation* (Chicago: Rand McNally, 1965). Voting behavior is dealt with further in Chapter 3.

[25] Quoted in V. O. Key, *Public Opinion and American Democracy* (New York: Alfred A. Knopf, 1961), p. 189.

[26] *Congressional Quarterly, Weekly Report 50* (13 December 1968): 3278.

[27] Lewis A. Froman, Jr., *Congressmen and Their Constituencies* (Chicago: Rand McNally, 1963), p. 49.

nondemocratic values, the fact that they do not vote in large numbers is viewed favorably, according to this argument.[28]

But to write off so casually such large numbers of American citizens puts the patriotic rhetoric of political speeches and civics textbooks under a cloud of suspicion. Rather than dismissing such people from the political system, is not the vital question: Why so many with such feelings? Rather than being a pillar of stability, is not this mass of nonvoters ". . . the soft underbelly of the system"? Is this not ". . . the *sickness* of democracy"? [29]

---

[28] Ibid., pp. 48–49; 122–23.
[29] E. E. Schattschneider, *The Semi-Sovereign People* (New York: Holt, Rinehart, and Winston, 1960), p. 104. Emphasis in original.

Chapter 3 Political Behavior and Public Opinion

The ideal of the rational, educated citizen has played a large role in democratic theory. If democracy is to work and survive, the argument has been, every citizen must receive an adequate education. He must be actively interested in issues and candidates. He must inform himself of these and, after careful, deliberate, and intelligent judgment, make choices which reflect a concern, not just for himself, but for others and the political community at large.

Somewhat overdrawn, perhaps, but nevertheless this is the kind of ideal often talked about in civics education. In the last twenty-five years or so, the disciplines of political science, psychology, and sociology have taken greater interest in the actual behavior of political man. Through the study of election results and through the use of interviews to determine people's attitudes on issues and on candidates a vast amount of data has been developed about these matters.

Much of the data concerning political behavior are derived from survey research using sampling techniques. Based on probability theory in statistics, samples are drawn which are a representative cross-section of the American population. Survey data are invariably subject to some sampling error and therefore should be interpreted with caution and never regarded as expressing absolute truths about political behavior. An understanding of behavioral data, in spite of its limitations, is nevertheless needed if relatively reliable knowledge is to replace mere hunches, which are usually only projections of one's own world.

The body of behavioral data calls into serious question the conventional expectations of the role the individual plays in the political system. A sharp gulf exists between the findings of behavioral investigation and the premises of traditional democratic theory. For the image of political man that has emerged is anything but the rational man of idyllic democracy. We already know that a significant portion of the citizenry plays little or no role in the political process. But even among those who do vote, a variety of nonrational, irrational, or emotional, along with rational, factors operate to determine the outcome of the voting decision.

Why People Vote

When an individual has rather deep feelings of futility toward the political world, he is likely to be a nonvoter. He not only fails to engage in this relatively simple activity, but he also probably shuts himself off from all stimuli coming from that world. The Pittsburgh housewife quoted in Chapter 2 is undoubtedly such a person.

Feelings of futility about what an individual can do to affect the choice of candidates or the outcome of policies vary widely. Some people will feel helpless about all issues and candidates and policies all of the time. Others will experience such feelings about only some issues, candidates, or policies, and different times and circumstances will have an impact. Even persons in high office and influential positions may express an attitude of futility over some issues. In an interview in September, 1966, the Chairman of the Senate Foreign Relations Committee, J. W. Fulbright, Democrat of Arkansas, expressed apprehension over China's probable involvement in the war in Vietnam if the policy of escalation of the United States continued. "I wish," he said, "I could do something to keep us from heading into a world war, but I don't know what to do."[1]

When a person does not shut himself off completely from the political environment, his most likely political act will be to vote. In making this decision, whether it comes months or a few days before an election, the individual has probably responded to a combination of factors. For one, his feeling of political efficacy (the opposite of futility) is somewhat high. In the 1956 election, nine out of ten of those with the highest sense of efficacy voted. But only slightly more than half of those with the lowest such feelings failed to vote.[2]

For some people, however, a feeling of having an impact on the outcome of an election is not necessary. Such persons may vote merely out of a sense of civic duty; they may believe that voting is a citizen's responsibility that must be discharged. As with political efficacy, a high sense of civic duty produces a high degree of probability that the individual will vote, while the reverse is equally true.[3] In many cases, these two characteristics are related, and where the one exists so also is the other likely to be present.

Factors Affecting Voting Behavior

Whether an individual will have a high or low sense of political efficacy or of civic duty will depend on a variety of socioeconomic factors. For both measures, there is a distinct relationship between low income, low educational level, minority status, and female sex, on the one hand, and low scores as to efficacy and civic duty, on the other hand. Only one out of ten persons with an income of less than $2,000 was likely to have a high degree of political efficacy, whereas almost four out of ten would have low scores. Almost the reverse would be true, however, of persons with incomes of $5,000 and over. Nearly half of the Negroes would have a low sense of political efficacy, whereas only one out of five whites would share similar feelings.

Although half of those with a college education have a high sense of political efficacy, only 15 percent of those with a grade-school edu-

---

[1] Jack Bell, "Fulbright Feels China Will Enter Expanded War," *The Sacramento Bee*, 25 September 1966.
[2] Angus Campbell et al., *The American Voter* (New York: John Wiley, 1960), p. 105.
[3] Ibid., p. 106.

cation feel similarly. Four out of ten professional and managerial people rank high, whereas among unskilled workers only 15 percent rank high. And though the differences are small, men generally have a higher sense of political efficacy than do women.[4]

Sense of Involvement   More immediate reasons may motivate a citizen to vote. Political efficacy and civic duty operate over the long term of the political life of the individual. There may be fluctuations from time to time, but generally such attitudes are fairly stable.[5] The impending election, interest in the campaign, and concern over its outcome operate more directly on the decision to vote.

When a particular election campaign arouses considerable interest in a voter, he is much more apt to cast his ballot than one who becomes only mildly concerned. Closely related to this factor is a very deep commitment to a particular result in the election. If the outcome makes little difference to a person, he is much less likely to vote than one who cares very much.[6]

The more immediate motivations act in conjunction with the longer term psychological traits of the voter. A very strong concern about the result of a particular election may bring to the polls the individual who ordinarily disdains politics. Although the chances may be slim that such will occur, it is nevertheless important to recognize that only a few thousand such cases may well be decisive in some elections.

Partisan Preferences   Once an individual has decided to vote in an election, the next problem he faces is choosing among candidates. In most cases this will mean making a choice among parties, because it is these organizations which put candidates forward. Although this is the general rule in presidential, congressional, state gubernatorial, and legislative elections, there are hundreds of local contests, judgeship elections, and school board elec-

---
[4] Angus Campbell et al., *The Voter Decides* (Evanston, Ill.: Row, Peterson, 1954), p. 191, Table A–2. Although income levels have risen since these data were collected in the early fifties, subsequent studies indicate that these patterns of behavior persist.
[5] Campbell et al., *The American Voter*, pp. 103–04.
[6] Ibid., pp. 102–04.

tions which may be nonpartisan with no party organization involved. Primary elections, in which the voter chooses from several candidates of the same party to determine which one will represent the party on the general election ballot, also do not involve the party organization, at least on the surface.

But in many elections the voter, in fact, does express a choice among (or between) parties. For most citizens such a choice is a relatively easy one; the voter is most likely to vote the way his father voted. The influence of family on the offspring's party preference is the most pervasive factor of all as far as party identification is concerned. Where both parents have supported the same party and have been somewhat active politically, three out of four of such children will share the same partisan preference, although not necessarily similar views on issues. When neither parent has had much interest in politics, the tendency of their offspring to choose the same party is lessened. If the parents were not consistently partisan, the children of such homes are more likely to call themselves independent.[7]

Once formed, a partisan attachment is likely to endure. Two out of three voters will, over the space of several presidential elections, still be voting for the party of their original choice. And more than half of the voting electorate has consistently supported the same party.[8]

Socioeconomic Factors

Although parental influence has considerable bearing on the choice of party identification, a number of other factors are associated with the makeup of the individual voter. The family environment quite often reflects a variety of socioeconomic factors which simply reinforce the inherited party preference. Thus, a Negro is likely to be of the same party as his parents, not solely because of this relationship but because Negroes as a group have a somewhat distinct party preference. The son of a midwestern Protestant farmer will probably be a Republican if his father is one, but also because the socioeconomic grouping reinforces the family influence.

The region of the country in which a voter lives; the place where he works; the kind of work he does; his color, religion, and ethnic background; his age; his sex—all of these factors, in complicated ways,

[7] Ibid., pp. 146–48; figures derived from Table 7–1, p. 147.
[8] Ibid., p. 148.

POLITICAL BEHAVIOR AND PUBLIC OPINION

will have a strong bearing on the choice of party made by the citizen. How these various factors operated to divide the electorate in the past three presidential elections is shown in the table which follows.

TABLE 1. How the Electorate Voted, 1960, 1964, and 1968 Presidential Elections

Voting Group	1968 D	1968 R	1968 W	1964 D	1964 R	1960 D	1960 R
Total Electorate	43%	43.4%	13.6%	61%	39%	50.1%	49.9%
Men	41	43	16	60	40	52	48
Women	45	43	12	62	38	49	51
White	38	47	15	59	41	49	51
Non-white	85	12	3	94	6	68	32
College	37	54	9	52	48	39	61
High School	42	43	15	62	38	52	48
Grade School	52	33	15	66	34	55	45
Prof. and Bus.	34	56	10	54	46	42	58
White Collar	41	47	12	57	43	48	52
Manual	50	35	15	71	29	60	40
Farmers	29	51	20	53	47	48	52
Under 30	47	38	15	64	36	54	46
30–49 Years	44	41	15	63	37	54	46
50 Years and Older	41	47	12	59	41	46	54
Protestants	35	49	16	55	45	38	62
Catholics	59	33	8	76	24	78	22

Source: Republican National Committee, Research Division, *The 1968 Elections* (Washington: Republican National Committee, 1969), p. 217, based on data from the Gallup poll.

Shifts within these major population groupings in each of these elections demonstrate the fluidity of the American electorate. Nevertheless, the kinds of support enjoyed by each of the major parties is revealed. The Democratic party draws its support largely from those with less education, from those in the least skilled jobs, from those who are nonwhite, from those who are Catholic, and from those who live in the central city. Voters who are white, Protestant, older, in more prestigious and better-paying jobs, better educated, and who live in the suburbs are the sources of Republican strength.

Individual and Group Voting Behavior

The demographic and socioeconomic characteristics of the American electorate are only guides as to how members of these groups are likely to vote. They cannot predict that any particular citizen will vote for the party for which other members of his group are voting. Over time, the composition of the major parties has changed and is changing, reflecting the shifting loyalties of various groups.[9] It is not correct, moreover, to regard the data of group voting behavior as meaning that all Catholics are Democrats or that all college-educated professional people are Republicans.

In the 1964 election, for example, according to the table, only 29 percent of manual workers were reported to have voted for Goldwater. But more than 16.5 million such workers voted, which means that some 4.8 million votes of the 27 million Republican total came from this source. Thus, almost one fifth of the Goldwater vote was supplied by manual workers. And, even though 11.8 million of these workers voted for Johnson, this number was only slightly more than one fourth of the total Democratic vote.[10]

Voting behavior is both a social phenomenon and an individual activity. Inherited party preference and socioeconomic status predispose a voter in one partisan direction or the other. But other factors, of more immediate influence, intervene and may have more causal significance as to which party or candidate a voter will support in any particular election. The voter's response to a candidate's personality, his perception (or misperception) of the candidate's stand on issues, and his feeling about the importance of certain issues to his own self-interest are some of the many factors which go into the complex psychological process of a voter making his ballot decisions. The voter's own personality may well be a crucial factor, and there are many often conflicting theories which attempt to explain this phenomenon.

Candidate Personality

"I Like Ike" was more than a mere campaign slogan. It reflected a widespread public feeling in 1952 that General Dwight D. Eisenhower had

---

[9] See Chapter 5.
[10] Percentage figures based on data in U.S. Bureau of the Census, *Current Population Reports*, series P-20: No. 143, "Voter Participation in the National Elections: 1964" (Washington: Government Printing Office, 1965), Table 5. (Actual percentages would be 17.7 and 27.3, respectively.)

the kind of personality and character suitable for a man in the White House. This type of popular response to a candidate's personality, so sharply evident in the 1952 and 1956 elections, is, for many voters, a decisive factor in their voting decision. The voter who claims that he votes for "the man, rather than for a party" is also indicating the drawing power of a personality.

Any number of factors about a candidate may appeal to the voter: how the candidate looks; his appearance of sincerity; his professions of religious belief. Survey data show that voters, when asked in 1952 and 1956 what they thought about Eisenhower, most often mentioned his nice personality and that they simply liked him. Other positive references to his personal qualities included his integrity and ideals and his sincerity.

In 1952 the most frequent unfavorable comment about Eisenhower related to his experience as a military man. By 1956, this objection had largely disappeared. In neither year was there any appreciable degree of unfavorable impressions about Eisenhower's personal qualities. Adlai Stevenson, however, engendered much more dislike or distrust when it came to these same qualities. Some thought him insincere and of low integrity; others simply did not like him. Many held against him the fact that he had been divorced. The largest unfavorable comment related to his manner of speaking and his tendency to joke too much. All these negative responses increased from 1952 to 1956.[11]

In different ways, personality factors again operated in 1960. John F. Kennedy's youthful image and sense of enthusiasm attracted many younger voters to the Democratic side. Although difficult to measure in numbers, Richard Nixon's makeup difficulties for the first of the television debates during the 1960 campaign were undoubtedly a damaging blow to his chances. So much of the public received such a negative image of Nixon that his press secretary was forced to issue a statement that the candidate was, in fact, "in excellent health and looks good in person."[12]

The contest in 1964 was between an incumbent president, who gave the appearance of calm and cool judgment in the making of crucial decisions about the nation's involvement in Vietnam, and his opponent,

[11] Based on Campbell et al., *The American Voter*, pp. 54–59, Tables 3–12 through 3–15.
[12] Quoted in Earl Mazo et al., *The Great Debates* (Santa Barbara, Calif.: Center for the Study of Democratic Institutions, 1962), p. 3. Mr. Mazo went on to comment that the "debates were practically as much a duel between make-up artists and technical directors as a contest for the Presidency of the United States." Ibid.

who seemed to convey the image of a man ready to shoot from the hip and damn the consequences. Subsequent events, however, demonstrated that campaign imagery may be just that and have little relation to the reality of personality. In 1968 the major personality interest was provided not by the two major party candidates, but by George Wallace. Nixon conveyed a remarkably restrained and untroubled image in contrast with that of the frenzy generated by his Democratic rival who was trying for a come-from-behind victory. Neither candidate, however, aroused much enthusiasm among a substantial portion of the electorate according to public opinion surveys.

Perception of the Issues   During a campaign, the candidate's personality is only one factor. The voter is also influenced by how he feels about the issues on which the parties or the candidates have taken positions. A major obstacle confronting the voter, however, is the tendency of the American political campaign to blur whatever issues might exist.[13] Even where rather clear differences between parties or candidates do emerge, the voter's lack of familiarity with the issues or his misperception of them are factors coloring his ultimate choices.

Even when a voter is aware of an issue, he may misperceive the role it is playing in a campaign. His attraction to a particular candidate can result in the voter actually believing that his candidate stands for something quite the opposite of the candidate's real position. Such was the case during the 1948 election. Many Republicans who themselves believed in price control, then a major point of controversy between the candidates, thought that Dewey also favored such controls, although he was clearly against them.[14]

The Uncommitted Voter   Most voting decisions will represent some combination of all of these factors. For many voters, an allegiance to one party generally prevails. Those with a fairly strong party identification are more likely to approve

---

[13] See Chapter 5 on political parties.
[14] Bernard R. Berelson et al., *Voting* (Chicago: University of Chicago Press, 1954), p. 220.

of the party's candidate and his position on the issues. For those who only weakly identify with a party, candidate personality or issue preferences play a more decisive role.

Many voters express no attachment to either party, and are sometimes referred to as independents. It is difficult to calculate the number of such voters because political analysts do not always agree on the definition of an independent. It may range from 10 to 20 percent of the electorate—anywhere from ten to twenty million or more voters!

One notion of the independent—often held by those people who so identify themselves—is that he is the voter who most closely resembles the rational political man. Rather than slavishly following a party and its line, he carefully evaluates the candidates' qualifications, investigates the issues, and makes his choice on an objective and rational basis. A counternotion—entertained by many behavioral analysts—sees the independent in quite a contrasting light. Compared to strong partisans, he is said to be less informed, less interested, and more confused.

No doubt some of each kind are represented among the class of voters denominated as independents, and it is among such voters that a great deal of switching between parties takes place. Of more significance than their personality, however, is the impact such uncommitted voters can have on any particular election. Whatever the reasons —rational or irrational or some mixture thereof—the existence of such a swing vote lends an enigmatic quality to elections and accounts for the ever-changing coalitions which combine to upset the existing dominant party.

In 1932 large numbers of voters who had never before voted Democratic gave their support to Roosevelt. Eisenhower's two victories were made possible by the shift of many who had been Democratic voters for twenty years to the Republican side. And in 1964 millions of Republicans crossed over to support Johnson, in part accounting for his landslide victory.

Each succeeding presidential election is necessarily different from the preceding one. Every four years millions have attained the age of twenty-one (or the lower age of eligibility permitted in some states). In 1968 there were twelve million citizens who had reached voting age since 1964.[15] Many, not having previously voted although eligible, are induced to vote either by the force of a candidate's personality or the press of a particular issue. Others will have had an uneven record of

[15] Republican National Committee, *The 1968 Elections,* p. 251, based on U.S. Bureau of Census data.

participation; they may have voted in some previous elections, but have sat out others.

The new voters, together with those who shift from party to party, regularly or perhaps only once or twice during their voting lives, represent somewhere between 20 and 40 percent of the electorate, varying from election to election.[16] To a greater extent than those who stick with the same party, the new and shifting voter is more likely to be swayed by his assessment of the performance of the party in power.

Some elections present the voter with a dilemma. A fairly strong party identification may nevertheless come into conflict with an equally strong attachment to a candidate of the other party. In such cases the voter may split his ticket—vote for most of the candidates of his traditional party but cross over and support an appealing candidate running on the opposition slate. Such was the case in both 1952 and 1956, when large numbers of Democrats, many in the South, supported Eisenhower for president but voted their usual way at the congressional, state, or local level.

Even more prone to splitting his ticket is the voter who thinks of himself as an independent. The rational independent may do so in the belief that it is the man and what he stands for that counts rather than the party. On the other hand the indifferent, uninformed voter may support some opposition candidates for a variety of less rational reasons. Such lack of concern can also result in a thoughtless casting of a straight party ticket, whereas some voters, with strong political motivations, deliberately vote a straight ticket to maximize their party's position.

Other kinds of dilemmas may confront the voter. A basic disagreement may arise between the party's or candidate's position and that of the voter himself, relating to a particular issue. In some instances, the voter may decide not to vote at all, or to split his ticket in some way. Other cross pressures may induce nonvoting. Intense partisan conflict between husband and wife may be resolved by both partners receding from their political involvement. Traditional attachment to the Republican cause gave many the choice in 1964 of repudiating a strong emotional appeal of the party or of supporting a candidate who seemed himself to have turned his back on much of what the Republican party had previously stood for. There must have been many such voters

[16] V. O. Key, Jr., *The Responsible Electorate* (Cambridge: The Belknap Press of Harvard University Press, 1966), pp. 16–22 and Table 2.3, p. 20.

among the almost seven million who failed to support the Republican ticket in 1964 as compared with 1960.

The data of voting behavior represents an exercise in the mass analysis of how people respond politically. It is an attempt to say that, given certain characteristics, a person is likely to act in a certain way. But there are always those persons whose particular combination of personality and socioeconomic characteristics defy any attempt at prediction.

To the outside observer, a voter's behavior may often seem irrational and often inexplicable. But to that voter himself, his choice may have a rationality all its own. The American voter has come in for some sharply critical commentary in recent years. If he is expected to live up to the ideal of the rational political man, he might well appear to be a fool. But such an expectation imposes qualifications which only an infinitesimal few in any society are likely to meet.

Perhaps too much attention is devoted to the erratic behavior of the electorate and not enough concern is directed at the political system. Might it not be that voters behave "about as rationally and responsibly as we should expect, given the clarity of the alternatives presented . . . and the character of the information available." [17]

Political Attitudes

The way a citizen votes is only the final act in a long process of confrontation with the political world. To understand more fully the place and role of the individual in the political system, we also need to know something about the way he acquires his attitudes and beliefs about government and public policy. It is on the basis of such attitudes and beliefs that opinions are formed. These, in turn, influence political behavior, the way the citizen votes, and the way he responds to governmental policy.

The political attitudes and beliefs of the citizen begin to take shape early in his life. Ideas about politics, like religious beliefs, are first learned in the home. The school situation quickly becomes a reinforcing factor. Many youngsters, in fact, up to the age of nine or ten, have difficulty in disassociating God from country,[18] as do some organiza-

[17] Ibid., p. 7.
[18] See the study by David Easton and Robert D. Hess, "The Child's Political World," *Midwest Journal of Political Science* 6 (August 1962): 238–39.

tions, composed of adults, which have as their motto *pro deo et patria*.

Learning to salute the flag, singing the "Star Spangled Banner," and discussing such national heroes as George Washington or Abraham Lincoln—all are activities designed to develop and instill in the child sentiments of affection for and belief in the political system. There are compelling societal reasons why, in some form or another, the child is given a civic education. For it is through such exposure to positive sentiments about their country that children come to accept government and to accord legitimacy to the role it plays in society.

It is this positive orientation to one's country—patriotism—which is appealed to, not only when people are asked to pay taxes, for instance, but also more significantly when men are asked to risk their lives in war for their country. But ordinary, everyday living itself would be chaotic and near impossible if, at some time in their lives, people were not taught to obey the policeman, the teacher, or the many symbols of authority frequently encountered.

Even before the entry of the United States into World War II, the Supreme Court refused to interfere with the requirement of saluting the flag imposed on Pennsylvania school children. Two youngsters of the Jehovah's Witnesses faith refused to take part in the exercise because it was in violation of their religious beliefs. Faced with this conflict, the Court, with only one dissent, held the state's interest in promoting love of country and national cohesion paramount. "The ultimate foundation of a free society," wrote Justice Frankfurter, "is the binding tie of cohesive sentiment." [19]

In three years, three justices had changed their minds and two new justices had come to the Court; the decision was reversed (6 to 3).[20] Nonetheless, the *Gobitis* opinion is suggestive of the keen need felt by members of a society that the young develop the appropriate feelings about their country.

Both family and school play important roles in the process of political socialization. But often, the civic education of the school runs sharply counter to the attitudes to which the child is exposed in the home environment. The children of low-income families, of minority status, and living in the slums of the city or in rural poverty are not likely to find much correspondence between the reality of existence and the positive things taught them about country. Where the parents express feelings

[19] Minersville School District v. Gobitis, 310 U.S. 586, 596 (1940).
[20] West Virginia State Board of Education v. Barnette, 319 U.S. 624 (1943).

of being outside the political mainstream, where a low sense of political involvement and efficacy is communicated, it would be unusual for the offspring not to share such attitudes.

Although the family is the first of the many social units to play a role in the socialization process, the child is presented with differing environments as he develops. Not only the school but also peer groups are important to the adolescent. Marrying often brings the person into contact with a different environment, as does the job situation.

Studies have shown, for example, that wives are more likely to succumb to their husband's political outlook than vice versa, when each comes into the marriage with different attitudes. Moving into a different part of the country may well induce a change in attitudes, as the desire to be accepted exerts a conforming pressure. Upward mobility, so characteristic of the economic progress of many American families, is still another factor which may change the earlier attitudes.[21]

Although the adult population often entertains cynical attitudes toward politics, children tend to have positive feelings about such activity. They sense the importance of political figures—such as the president or the mayor of their community—and view these persons more favorably than do their parents. As the child approaches adolescence, however, he seems to assume more adult attitudes. The more he identifies with the adult world, the more his ideas about politics begin to take on some of the cynical qualities communicated by his elders. Perceptions of social class or minority status are undoubtedly influencing factors. So, too, is the impact of the mass media. The conflict between the earlier positive learning and the later exposure to political realism often creates an ambiguity in political attitudes.

Nevertheless, the earlier attitudes have been found by researchers to have considerable staying power. It is in the preadolescent stage of development that many children develop an identification with one of the major political parties—a choice which will persist and be the single most important factor in later voting behavior.[22]

---

[21] These and other studies are discussed in Richard E. Dawson and Kenneth Prewitt, *Political Socialization* (Boston: Little, Brown, 1969).
[22] See Fred I. Greenstein, *Children and Politics* (New Haven: Yale University Press, 1965), pp. 71–75.

Public Opinion By the time a child becomes an adult, he enters a political world—if he does so at all—not totally unknown. But the development, shaping, and changing of attitudes does not abruptly stop upon reaching voting age. Through the remaining years of political life, the individual is normally deluged by a multitude of political stimuli, all seeking to make him respond in a particular way. The generality of his attitudes has to be turned into specific opinions on issues of public policy and on specific candidates for public office.

The hallmark of a democratic system is said to be the rulers' responsiveness to public opinion. The rhetoric of legislators, mayors, presidents, and governors echoes the creed. It would be a simple matter if public opinion were in the same category as votes, then mere counting would suffice. It is the very amorphous quality of public opinion, however, which has made it one of the most used—but least understood—words in the vocabulary of politics.

The term public opinion is not new, although the attempts to define it more precisely are of recent vintage. Although Plato and Aristotle wrote of the opinions of the masses and of the significance of this to the state, systematic attempts to deal with public opinion date from around the middle of the eighteenth century. In the nineteenth century, the role of public opinion in American democracy was noted and discussed by two foreign observers. Both Alexis de Tocqueville, a Frenchman, and James Bryce, an Englishman, devoted considerable attention to the subject in their now famous studies.[23] Within the last twenty-five years there have been any number of books and articles on public opinion, with almost as many definitions.

In a more general sense, public opinion may refer to most any problem or issue that conceivably could exist in a society. Whether the American League is better than the National League may be a subject about which millions of baseball fans have an opinion. Whether women's skirts should be well above or just below the knees may likewise elicit opinions from the general public. But the kind of public opinion normally of interest to the observer of politics and government consists of "those opinions held by private persons which governments find it prudent to heed."[24]

---

[23] Alexis de Tocqueville, *Democracy in America*, 1835, and James Bryce, *The American Commonwealth*, 1889.
[24] V. O. Key, Jr., *Public Opinion and American Democracy* (New York: Alfred A. Knopf, 1961), p. 14.

Although this definition may lack some of the technical precision often insisted upon by purists, it has the undeniable virtue of focusing on the relation between public opinion and government. It thus excludes those opinions which may convulse the nation until the point at which such become the subject of governmental concern.

Characteristics of Public Opinion

About some things, most everyone will have an opinion. But on certain subjects, very few will have any notion whatever of the existence of the thing about which they are asked. The level of information of most Americans on subjects of current political interest varies widely. When something has dragged on for a number of years, such as the war in Vietnam, great numbers of Americans will not only have heard of it but also will have opinions on it. If, however, a sudden coup should take place in a relatively new African nation, for example, many people would never even become aware of the incident. And those that did would probably have little or no idea where the country was.

Early in the Nixon administration, to cite an example dealing with a specific issue, the ABM (antiballistic missile) system began to shape up as a major test for the new President. The ABM proposal was first offered and discussed in the Johnson administration, and President Nixon decided to go ahead with it in a modified form. Events leading up to the presentation of Nixon's ABM plan were widely reported in the media as was the actual plan itself. Two weeks after President Nixon submitted his proposal to Congress, a Gallup poll found that 31 percent of a national sample had not heard or read about the ABM program.[25]

The major difficulty in the use of the term public opinion is the word public. If the public is taken to mean all adult members of the society, rarely if ever does such a conglomerate entity exist or does it have an opinion. Much more likely is the existence of a multitude of subpublics, or special publics—each a fraction of the total public—which, on different issues, does develop opinions.

When the Federal Communications Commission, for example, announces it is contemplating a change in the technical requirements for television broadcasting equipment, the interested public would prob-

---

[25] *New York Times*, 6 April 1969, p. 35.

ably consist of the manufacturers of such equipment and the station owners and engineering executives, perhaps three or four thousand persons. But were the Commission to suggest that broadcasters devote less time to televising football and baseball and show more ballet and live drama on Saturday and Sunday afternoons, the public concerned would probably number thirty or forty million.

Even when an issue calls into existence or mobilizes a public, the membership is likely to hold varying opinions. The ascertainment of opinion would be relatively easy if all that were required was a simple answer of "agree" or "disagree." When people were asked to express their opinions on the way President Johnson was handling the war in Vietnam, large percentages of unfavorable responses were often recorded. But those who disapproved often did so for widely divergent reasons. Some were expressing their unhappiness with the war, United States involvement in it, and the President's policy of escalation. Others, however, felt he was not escalating enough, so as to bring the United States quick victory.

On any given issue on which a public does have an opinion, the intensity with which the opinion is held is of importance so far as when government will find it prudent to take heed. The great number of political controversies which compete for an individual's attention necessarily means that he will be selective. As to many issues, no opinion, or a weakly held one, may develop. But as to those of most concern to his own self-interest, an intensely held opinion is more likely.

Opinion Formation Many of the same factors that affect voting behavior also operate to shape opinions. Voting is, in a sense, merely the physical act which follows the formation of an opinion. The voter may have decided that Eisenhower was a better qualified man in 1952 than Stevenson, in which case his opinion about the candidate would have been of prime importance. Or, in 1960, a voter may have felt that the Democrats would do more for the working man; here the opinion about the party may have been decisive.

In each of the cases mentioned, the opinion formed was in all probability not a mere reaction to what was occurring in 1952 or 1960. Events over a preceding period, perhaps of four, eight, or even twenty years, together with attitudes developed over a similar span, more than likely produced the opinion which determined the vote. Some social scientists have likened this process to what a funnel does to something passing through it. The distance from the larger opening to the smaller exit of the funnel represents a period of time. A host of factors over time combine to produce a particular opinion at a given time, election day, for example.[26]

Opinions are not necessarily specific. An individual forms opinions not only near election day on specific candidates, but also continuously on public policy issues as he becomes aware of them. He is also likely to have a more or less continuous opinion about one of the major political parties because this is why he chooses to identify with that party.

Opinions are closely related to attitudes but can be thought of as being somewhat more specific. This relationship is important to the formation of opinion because it is on the basis of the more general attitudes that the individual forms opinion responses. Thus, opinions are being shaped at an early age as attitudes are developing. The same factors that foster attitudes—family, school, church, and peer group—have a similar effect on opinions.

As the child nears the voting age, he is increasingly called upon to express opinions. In high school and college, matters of public concern are frequently discussed, not only in the classroom but also in the informal atmosphere of peer group. For the many who quit high school and attempt to get jobs, or for those who are forced into the ranks of the unemployed, opinion formation is more directly related to livelihood.

Whether the youngster goes on to complete high school or seeks work upon graduation, or whether he or she goes on to college, will be an important determinant of the kinds of opinions formed. Educational level and socioeconomic status are closely related. As these have an impact on the rate of voter turnout and on the citizen's sense of civic duty and sense of political efficacy, so do they bear on the kinds of opinions held by persons in different income groups and occupational skills.

---

[26] See Angus Campbell et al., *The American Voter* (New York: John Wiley, 1960), pp. 24–32, for a discussion of what they have called "The Funnel of Causality."

Communication and Opinions

That opinions are related to the environment in which the individual moves indicates that it is through exposure to the opinions of others that his own are formed. The factory, the office, the grange meeting, the church, the family, the local pub—in short, all of the social groups with which a person has contact—bear heavily on opinion formation. They do so because they serve as the media for the transmission and dissemination of ideas about public questions on the basis of which opinions are formed.

These smaller groupings tend to be more selective in the messages they transmit. But there are other sources of communications which aim for much larger audiences; these are the mass media: radio and television, mass circulation magazines, and metropolitan newspapers.

None of these sources, of course, concentrates exclusively on transmitting political messages. The grange meeting dispenses technical information about crops; the minister's sermon strives to impart moral ideas. The newspapers carry recipes and advice on finances and health. Much of radio and television purportedly is entertainment. Yet all of these media are available for and are made use of for political communication.

Were the formation of opinion spontaneous, the role of the different kinds of media in transmitting political messages would not be of much importance. But within each subpublic which becomes aware of some issue confronting it, there are likely to be many who have no opinion at all or, perhaps, a weakly held one. To activate the many inattentive members of the group requires a considerable expenditure of energy on the part of the small number who do have an opinion and hold it with intensity.

When this has to be done on a large scale—where the subpublic is almost, in fact, the entire public (as with, for example, the war in Vietnam)—the effort will be through media reaching millions. Thus does the president resort to nationwide television speeches or press conferences which will receive similar coverage in newspapers and on television. But on many hundreds of public policy issues, the subpublics will be much smaller and opinion communication under such circumstances more likely that of person to person.

In these situations, there is often an inequality of opinions or, to use the Orwellian formula, some opinions are more equal than others. The shop steward, the office manager, the preacher and the teacher, or the respected citizens of a small community are likely to be opinion leaders. Those that listen to them and form their opinions on the basis of what the leaders say are opinion followers.

And it is often the case that in speaking out on public issues, political leaders deliver cues which provide the basis for subsequent opinion formation. Although a person may have no opinion on raising taxes in a time of inflation, when the president of the party with which he strongly identifies announces his stand on the matter, that is the position his listener will undoubtedly adopt. Or, if the leader of the minority party in the Senate proclaims his distaste for an administration bill, that is the cue for like-minded partisans to announce their opposition.

Public Opinion and Public Policy In a very real sense, the study of American politics must inevitably focus on the relation between the opinions of various publics and what congressmen, bureaucrats, judges, and other decision-makers do. Many of the chapters which follow are concerned with this problem in a variety of different contexts. Other institutions of the political process to which the citizen relates—interest groups, political parties, and the press—are means of ascertaining what opinions exist and to what extent they should be followed.

On some issues of public policy there is a close correspondence between what a particular public wants and what government does. On others, there is little discernible relation between opinion and action. The processes whereby decisions are made is of prime importance, for, if they are structured in a way to frustrate some kinds of opinion while facilitating others, the kinds of decisions made will obviously vary.

Voting is one way in which the opinions of the public are translated into action. But the choices made at elections are usually preferences for people as officials, rather than for specific public policies. People may vote for a candidate because he promises a better break for the working man. But how this is to be achieved is quite another matter, and one on which those that supported the candidate may well disagree.

Other Forms of Political Activity

Voting, however, is not the only means whereby the citizen relates to his government. It is the one political act in which more people will engage with greater frequency and thus be the most significant act for many. But there are other ways for the individual to count for something in the political process.

Unfortunately, the more involved and the more committed political activity becomes, the fewer people will be found engaged in it. Voting only requires the physical exertion of getting to the polling place and then either marking a paper ballot or pulling down levers on a voting machine. Other forms of participation may require greater physical effort, more challenging intellectual efforts, or financial support.

For one thing, the citizen may try to persuade others to vote for the candidate whom he favors. He may help to bring his man to public attention by wearing a campaign button, displaying a bumper sticker on his car, or exhibiting a picture of the candidate in his living room window. Beyond such public shows of preference, he may help lubricate the campaign machinery of his candidate by making campaign contributions.

The citizen may choose to involve himself more personally and directly in political campaigns. For some, this involvement will not go beyond attendance at political meetings or rallies. For others, however, it will mean a large investment of time and effort in a political organization. Such organizational participation is most prevalent at the local level. From the ranks of such persons comes the manpower for essential tasks such as canvassing precincts and wards to stimulate interest in the candidate and to urge his passive supporters to become active in the campaign. It is such political activists who are eventually named precinct captains and county chairmen, and perhaps later on the party's nominees for elective office.

Since only about three fifths of the electorate turns out to vote in presidential elections, it should not be surprising that even a smaller fraction of the population engages in the other forms of political action. At best, not more than 10 percent of Americans engage in other forms of political participation besides voting. As many as this number may make contributions to parties or candidates; perhaps as many as 7 percent may attend political meetings or rallies, whereas only 2 or 3 percent actually belong to a political club or organization.[27] Another

---

[27] Based on data in Dan Nimmo and Thomas D. Ungs, *American Political Patterns*, 2d ed. (Boston: Little, Brown, 1969), p. 135.

estimate numbers those who are intense political activists as no more than 1 percent of the adult population.[28]

As with voter turnout, socioeconomic factors are closely related to the extent of political activity. In part, the extent to which one participates in political activity is a function of the amount of leisure time he has. Poor people are simply too burdened with the problem of sheer economic survival to have any time to spare. In addition, it is the poor who have come to feel alienated from the society. Many of the poor are also Black, and to many of them America is of, by and for whites. It is run, as they see it, by a power structure from which they are entirely excluded—a white power structure. Increased awareness of their plight has convinced many that there must be Black power, too.

But, even for those Negroes who do not analyze American society so pessimistically, effective participation in politics is extremely difficult, especially if participation is defined in broader terms than mere voting. The kind of organization that is necessary to exert an influence on the political process is anything but easy for a group whose members have been educated in inferior schools and forced into menial and low-paying jobs. The kind of pressure activity that comes naturally to affluent white interest groups has been far more difficult as far as Negroes are concerned. A similar situation exists for other segments of the population such as migrant workers, Mexican-Americans, and the poor in Appalachia.

Political Demonstrations In 1964 Congress enacted the most far-reaching civil rights bill since Reconstruction.[29] It was intended to insure equal accommodations to the traveling public in motels and restaurants and to eliminate job discrimination, among other objectives. But it passed largely because of the development by Black people and their white allies of an entirely new mode of political participation. Though lacking money, sophisticated organization, and access to the conventional channels of political influence, Negroes began to make use of one of the few resources available to them: their numbers. The campaign of direct action on

---

[28] Hugh A. Bone, *American Politics and the Party System*, 3rd ed. (New York: McGraw-Hill, 1965), p. 533.
[29] There had been two civil rights acts passed earlier, in 1957 and 1960, but the importance of their provisions was negligible. See Daniel M. Berman, *A Bill Becomes Law: Congress Enacts Civil Rights Legislation*, 2d ed. (New York: Macmillan, 1966).

which they embarked often made use of their very bodies—in sit-ins, for example, and in other kinds of demonstrations of all types. These tactics dramatized the grievances of Black Americans and compelled the white community of the nation to come to grips with the segregated system that they much preferred to ignore.

The demonstrations on behalf of civil rights can be viewed as a creative and inventive device that made it possible for individuals, otherwise lacking the conventional means, to become more potent in having an impact on the political process. The usefulness of the demonstration as a political weapon became obvious in the movement to end the war in Vietnam. Peace marches, such as in New York and San Francisco in the spring of 1967 and the massive confrontation at the Pentagon in the fall of that same year, helped to focus public opinion on the war. Individual and collective acts of defiance or resistance to the draft in the form of burning draft cards or of destroying records—whatever people's reactions might have been—showed the intensity of the dissenters' feelings.

Such unconventional political tactics were resorted to by those who felt they could no longer affect the course of events by traditional means. But even those who might disdain such tactics were undoubtedly influenced in their thinking on the war. The 1968 presidential primary campaign of Senator Eugene McCarthy helped to translate unconventional political opposition to the war into respectable and acceptable opposition. Whether the antiwar movement and McCarthy's strong showing in the New Hampshire primary against President Johnson was the direct or even indirect cause of Johnson's decision not to stand for reelection may never be ascertained. Nonetheless, although the war did not end as a consequence, the political end had come into sight for the man whom many in the antiwar movement held primarily responsible for it.

Demonstrations have not been the exclusive province of radical or Black groups. Mothers in New Orleans have demonstrated against integration of schools as have mothers in some Northern cities. The gun lobby has on occasion used very vocal and demonstrative means to convince local governing bodies not to enact gun registration regulations. Students unsympathetic to the demands of other student groups have engaged in counterdemonstrations. Clearly demonstrations, and even violent tactics, are means of political participation. The increasing frequency of their use, however, does not really represent a new phenomenon in American politics.[30] Their use represents, as it has in other eras of American history, the perception of the dissidents that the normal political processes are inadequately representative and responsive.

---

[30] See Arthur Schlesinger, Jr., *Violence: America in the Sixties* (New York: Signet Books, 1968), esp. "Violence as an American Way of Life," pp. 30–40. A full-scale historical analysis of the subject was undertaken in a staff study for the National Commission on the Causes and Prevention of Violence: Hugh Davis Graham and Ted Robert Gurr, *Violence in America* (New York: Bantam Books, 1969).

Chapter 4 The Pressure of Interests

The existence of interest groups in American politics has long been recognized. Even before the Constitution was ratified, James Madison developed a theory about the role of such groups that has never been equaled in perceptiveness and insight. Madison recognized that in any free society special groups would exist to promote the interests of their members. The major problem of government, he said, was to maintain a checkrein on these interest groups, which he called "factions." At the same time, he acknowledged that their activities would be a part of "the necessary and ordinary operations of government."[1]

Although Madison feared what powerful interest groups might do if they were neither counterbalanced by other interest groups nor checked by government, he was more apprehensive of a society in which interest groups did not exist. For he saw that liberty and factions were the two

---

[1] Clinton Rossiter, ed., *The Federalist Papers* (New York: The New American Library, 1961), No. 10, p. 79.

sides of a single coin and that a society in which interest groups did not exist would necessarily also be a society in which liberty did not exist.

Economic Interests Like Karl Marx in the following century, Madison emphasized the divisions in society that grow out of economic factors. It is the unequal distribution of property, he said, which is "the most common and durable source of factions." Those who owned property would constitute a group quite distinct from the propertyless. Similarly, there would be anything but an identity of interest between creditors and debtors. There would also be "a landed interest, a manufacturing interest, a mercantile interest, a moneyed interest," and many, many more.[2]

Madison was describing the late eighteenth-century American society that he knew. It was a far simpler American society than the one that exists today. Then a largely rural and agricultural nation, the United States today is an urban society with a vastly complicated social and economic structure. There has, of course, been a corresponding increase in the number of interest groups, their proliferation encouraged by the constantly increasing specialization of economic tasks that is characteristic of modern industrial nations. So far has this specialization gone that today organized groups like the Grinding Wheel Institute, Hack and Band Saw Association of America, Waxed Paper Institute, Rubber Heel and Sole Institute, American Gear Manufacturers Association, and The Linen and Lace Paper Institute represent only a sample of the myriad of specialized economic interests.

Economic interest, however, is not the only basis upon which organizations may be formed. Any set of common interests may stimulate the creation of an organized group. Since the United States is characterized not only by an industrial complexity but also by an ethnic, religious, and racial heterogeneity, there are literally thousands of noneconomic interest groups mirroring the intricate variety of social relations that characterize contemporary American society.

[2] Ibid., p. 79.

The Big Three—Business, Agriculture, and Labor

It is, however, the economic interest groups that are the most numerous. These include labor unions, both local and national, trade associations, and national business organizations like the United States Chamber of Commerce and the National Association of Manufacturers. Although it is these latter national organizations that are the best known groups in the business community, the smaller specialized organizations exert a considerable impact on the governmental process. They generally steer clear of national policy questions that do not directly affect them, but when their self-interest is involved they quickly spring to life. Since their interests are narrow and specialized, they attract comparatively little public attention. Yet, in obtaining tax concessions for themselves from Congress or in persuading administrative agencies to make rulings that are favorable to them, they are often even more effective than the better known national business organizations.

The narrow range of their interests frequently brings competing business groups into conflict with each other. Importers are arrayed against exporters, coal interests against the oil companies, and the short-line railroads against the long-haul regional systems. A large-scale organization such as the Chamber of Commerce of the United States frequently decides not to take any position on an important legislative issue because its state and local members may be hopelessly split on the stand that should be adopted.

Diversity and conflict also characterize a second set of economic interest groups, that is, those in the field of agriculture. The three general farm organizations—The American Farm Bureau Federation, the National Grange, and the National Farmers Union—represent entirely different groups of farmers. The cleavage between those who operate family farms and those who operate what are called factories in the field is too great to be bridged by a single organization as are divisions along regional lines. Moreover, there are hundreds of smaller organizations which represent even more specialized agricultural interests. These include commodity groups such as the National Apple Institute and the National Wool Growers Association.

Just as businessmen and farmers are highly organized, so also are workers. About fifteen million workers are members of unions that belong to the American Federation of Labor-Congress of Industrial Organizations (AFL-CIO). In reality, the AFL-CIO is a union of unions, composed as it is of some 135 national unions representing workers in every conceivable trade and occupation. As might be expected, there is more diversity than unity in such a conglomerate organization. The split is especially pronounced between the older craft unions, representing workers who do a particular job (carpenters, plumbers), and the newer industrial unions, which represent all the workers in a given production process (automobile workers, steel workers). So serious is the antagonism between these two groups that the uneasy marriage consummated between them in 1955 through the merger of the AFL (craft unions) and the CIO (industrial unions) seems in constant danger of falling apart. A major break in the solidity of the AFL-CIO did occur in 1968 when the United Auto Workers, one of the largest of the CIO unions, was suspended by the AFL-CIO for not paying its dues to the federation; the UAW later withdrew and in 1969 formed, with the Teamsters, the Alliance for Labor Action. The break was engineered by Walter Reuther, head of the UAW, who, for a long time, had been unhappy with George Meany's leadership of the AFL-CIO. Meany, as might be expected, was a product of the old American Federation of Labor.

The largest union in the United States, the International Brotherhood of Teamsters,[3] has remained outside the AFL-CIO since its expulsion from the merged labor federation in 1957 on the ground that it was dominated by racketeers. Another of the largest unions, the United Mine Workers, showed its contempt for the leadership of the AFL-CIO by declining to apply for membership. Also outside the federation are some forty million workers whose companies have still not been organized by labor unions. There are, in fact, twice as many unorganized workers as there are union members, and the spirited organizing drives of the 1930s seem to be a thing of the past. A notable exception has been the struggle led by Cesar Chavez to organize farm workers in California.

Another group of unions has come into prominence in recent years as the number of public employees has grown. Several organizations represent the different types of postal workers. Others—principally the National Federation of Federal Employees and the American Federation of Government Employees—represent many of the more than two million workers employed by the national government. The American Federation of State, County, and Municipal Employees speaks for many workers at those levels of government.

[3] In most cases, the use of the word international in the names of many essentially national union organizations simply reflects the existence of locals in Canada.

The Professionals In addition to these three broad categories, there are many other powerful interest groups. Some of them insist that their concerns are not economic at all but professional instead. The American Medical Association, for example, never tires of insisting that it is a professional organization, intent only on maintaining and elevating the standards of the medical profession. In the long fight it waged against Medicare and against earlier efforts to enact national health insurance legislation, it purported to base its opposition on exclusively professional grounds. A health care plan financed by the government, it said, would impair the doctor-patient relationship and would undermine the very practice of medicine. It was not difficult, however, to perceive that the doctors were at least as much interested in quite a different subject: protecting their advantageous economic position in society.

Although defeated on the Medicare issue, the AMA was able to demonstrate in 1969 that it still had some political clout. The group was credited with blocking the appointment of a Boston doctor, John Knowles, who was the choice of Secretary of Health, Education and Welfare Robert Finch to be an assistant secretary with responsibility over the health programs of the nation. AMA's political action arm had made substantial contributions to many members of Congress, mostly Republican, in the 1968 campaign. It felt that one of the names it had submitted for consideration for the post should have been nominated; it won its point.

The American Bar Association is another of the powerful professional interest groups. Tocqueville was one of the earliest observers to remark on the crucial role played by lawyers in politics. In a chapter devoted to the "Causes Which Mitigate the Tyranny of the Majority in the United States," he perceived that "lawyers, as a body, form the most powerful, if not the only, counterpoise to the democratic element." [4]

Subsequent events have demonstrated the accuracy of Tocqueville's remark. In the last quarter of the nineteenth century, it was partly through the newly organized ABA (1878) that notions of *laissez-faire* economics came to be accepted doctrines of American constitutional law. In the fight in 1937 over the packing of the Supreme Court, no organization was more vociferous in its opposition than the ABA. In the fifties it backed the Bricker Amendment, which would have seriously tied the hands of the president and the secretary of state in the

---

[4] Alexis de Tocqueville, *Democracy in America*, vol. 1 (New York: Vintage Books, 1945), p. 288.

conduct of relations with foreign nations. In addition, in the fifties, the ABA often showed hostility to decisions of the Supreme Court although such positions provoked dissension within the organization.

Like the AMA, the ABA frequently espouses what are ostensibly professional interests. Yet, even so, economic concerns, not only of the organized bar but also of its clientele, are not far from the surface. Its interest in the kinds of judges selected for appointment to the lower federal courts, in which its influence has been increasing, is related to the concern of the ABA that judges make decisions in greater conformity with the values held by the organized bar.[5]

The number of professional associations is limited only by the number of occupations which are called professional. These run the gamut from the American Society of Agricultural Engineers to the Professional Convention Management Association. Many of these organizations almost never have political interests. But on occasion their membership will become quite active in a political issue, as did the American Institute of Architects in opposing the extension of the east front of the Capitol building in Washington. The AIA, together with other groups, was unable to block this historical surgery, but is now engaged in attacking the pending proposal to alter the Capitol's west front.

Although many professional associations represent people engaged in private industry or in different educational specialties, quite a large number are composed of persons working for government at some level. Thus do the American Association of State Highway Officials, the National Association of Insurance Commissioners, and the National Association of Attorneys General serve as the groups through which the common interests and problems of these officials are expressed.

The public character of such organizations is indicative of the importance of a whole set of other interest groups which have had considerable influence on public policy in recent years. Such groups like to refer to their organizations as public interest groups (PIGS) because they represent public entities—cities or counties, for example. Some of the more prominent and active public interest groups are the Conference of Mayors of the United States, the National Association of Counties, and the National League of Cities. They have been in the forefront of recent and largely successful efforts to divert an increasing share of the federal budget to such programs as urban renewal and mass transportation. Indicative of the impact of such interests in fed-

[5] Joel B. Grossman, *Lawyers and Judges* (New York: John Wiley, 1965).

eral policymaking was the creation, in 1965, of another Cabinet-level department—the Department of Housing and Urban Development.

Cities and states are not content, however, to have their interests represented by such organizations. To look out for their special interests, many cities and states maintain an office in Washington staffed by representatives, which they prefer to call themselves rather than lobbyists. Even a few of the large universities, such as the University of California, have Washington offices because federal assistance for research contracts has become so important in their operations. In this respect, governmental entities and universities are only emulating large corporations, which for years have had lobbying staffs in Washington to watch out for their legislative, administrative, and government contract interests.

For the representation of economic interests, a large number of lobbyist entrepreneurs exist in Washington. These are usually law firms which handle lobbying activities as they do their ordinary legal business. Many such firms represent small clients with relatively insignificant interests, which nevertheless need, in the eyes of the client, this kind of service. But some men have made Washington reputations, and fortunes, by representing some of America's corporate giants both in legal and legislative matters. Such former presidential intimates as Tommy Corcoran, James Rowe, and Clark Clifford, who succeeded Robert McNamara as Secretary of Defense in the Johnson administration, are perhaps noted examples. In this group must also be included former Supreme Court Justice Abe Fortas, whose reputation as a political entrepreneur helped to heighten the clamor for his resignation in the spring of 1969.

Noneconomic Interests There are, however, some pressure groups which do not have an economic or self-interest base. Persons who join the American Civil Liberties Union, for example, do not generally anticipate that their right to speak will be threatened, or that they will ever be defendants in criminal cases. Their motive in joining the organization is a belief that the maintenance of individual freedom furthers the public interest. Similarly, it has been observed that the members of the American League to

Abolish Capital Punishment *"obviously do not expect to be hanged"*;[6] they form a pressure group simply because they oppose the death penalty on general principles that have nothing to do with economic self-interest. But such idealistic groups, each campaigning for what it believes to be the common interest, are vastly outnumbered by groups that use the term public interest as nothing but a euphemism for what will benefit them.

In addition to interests that are organized along fundamentally economic lines, there are a wide variety of other groups—ethnic, religious, and racial. There are also veterans' and patriotic groups, as well as organizations of horticulturalists, bird lovers, atheists, school principals, college professors, and almost every other conceivable grouping of human beings. All in all, there are thousands of national interest groups in the United States and hundreds of thousands of local interest groups. Clearly, we are a nation of organizers and organizations.

A Nation of Joiners? But are we also a nation of joiners? The statistics seem to compel a negative answer to this question. Between a third and a half of the adult population does not belong to a single group.[7] Even if membership in voluntary organizations runs as high as 65 percent of the adult population, only about 35 percent belongs to groups which sometimes take positions on political issues.[8]

Some people, of course, belong to several organizations, perhaps a dozen or more. Usually these are the same people whose rate of participation in elections is high and who are the most politically active. But in the main there is a wide gap between the eagerness of relatively few Americans to create groups and the disinclination of great numbers of their fellow citizens to join them. Americans may not really be such incorrigible joiners after all.

The fact that the joiners are relatively few in number and that these

---

[6] E. E. Schattschneider, *The Semi-Sovereign People* (New York: Holt, Rinehart, and Winston, 1960), p. 26. Italics in original.

[7] See Murray Hausknecht, *The Joiners* (New York: The Bedminster Press, 1962), p. 23; Robert E. Lane, *Political Life* (New York: The Free Press, 1959), p. 75; and Gabriel Almond and Sidney Verba, *The Civic Culture* (Boston: Little, Brown, 1965), p. 246.

[8] Dan Nimmo and Thomas D. Ungs, *American Political Patterns*, 2d ed. (Boston: Little, Brown, 1969), p. 135.

for the most part are the same people who are active in politics is of considerable consequence, for it gives to the interest group structure a distinctly middle- and upper-class bias that is anything but representative of the society at large. Even those organizations which purport to represent the lower classes are often run by persons who are respected and economically successful. The National Association for the Advancement of Colored People, for example, had until recently a considerable white membership, and white leadership as well. It is small wonder that a trenchant critic of American politics has written of the "bias of the pressure system" in the United States.[9]

The Leaders and the Led   This factor at once raises the question of whether organized groups in the United States are generally representative of their own membership and whether that membership has a powerful voice in determining policy. On the surface, at least, many interest groups are organized in such a way that they appear to provide for democratic decision-making. The AFL-CIO, for instance, has a system for electing delegates to its all-important national convention. The convention, however, is so large and unwieldy that control by a small oligarchy is virtually inevitable. Much the same could be said of the American Farm Bureau Federation, which does not even permit its members to elect convention delegates directly. Instead, they vote only for delegates to a state convention, which in turn selects those who will go to the national convention. Another example is provided by the United States Chamber of Commerce, where the national convention is also ostensibly the policymaking organ. Although the delegates to the convention are chosen in democratic fashion by the local chambers of commerce all over the country, it is not the convention but rather the Chamber's board of directors which is the locus of power both in the formulation of policy and in the election of officers.

Large-scale interest groups, in other words, behave much the same way as social organizations generally. The mass membership is usually reduced merely to ratifying the choices already made by the leadership, which consists of a small minority of members with the time, money, and inclination to take on the responsibilities involved. When the rank

[9] "Scope and Bias of the Pressure System" is the title of Chapter 2 in Schattschneider, *The Semi-sovereign People.*

and file of such an organization is encouraged to speak its mind, it is usually only a thundering endorsement of what the leadership has already decided.

The larger the organization and the more complex the problems with which it deals, the greater the likelihood that effective leadership will be concentrated in a few hands. Sometimes the effective leadership is not exercised by the elected officers at all, but rather by permanent members of the organization's staff. Especially if there is a high rate of turnover in the elected leadership, officers will be compelled to lean heavily on the permanent and full-time staff. This tendency may be so highly developed that the organization's course is really set not by the elected president and his fellow officers, but rather by an executive director and other staff members, such as research specialists, lawyers, and public relations experts, equally unaccountable to the membership.

Even in such situations, of course, the leadership of an organization must be careful not to diverge so far from the wishes of the members that a revolt will take place. The leadership group may well try to guard against the dire possibility that it will be supplanted by trying to influence the attitudes of its members. To inculcate the opinions that are considered appropriate and to evoke the actions that are considered desirable, the national headquarters of a group often bombards the members with as many communications and publications as its budget will allow. Typically, there will be a magazine of some kind that is sent to all members—*The Mortgage Broker,* for example, for those who belong to the Mortgage Bankers Association of America; *Nation's Agriculture,* for members of the American Farm Bureau Federation; and *Nation's Business,* for members of the Chamber of Commerce. The affluence of groups such as these makes it possible for the magazines to be highly professional products, containing entertainment features and articles of general interest as well as the inevitable discussions of political policy questions. Groups with more meager resources than these may have to settle for a considerably simpler format, but even a two-page mimeographed newsletter may suffice to inform the constituency of what the top leadership is thinking and doing.

POLITICAL PARTICIPATION

Mobilizing Grass-roots Support

The techniques employed by pressure groups to influence public policy consist not only of efforts to influence policymakers directly by means of lobbying, but also attempts to influence public opinion at the grass roots. Concern for the mobilization of public opinion is a relatively recent phenomenon in the development of interest group techniques. In the old days, pressure groups preferred the simpler method of dealing directly with legislators. They found this to be the least expensive method, even when, as was often the case, outright bribery was used to collect votes. Since money was passed without any real effort at concealment in the lobbies of legislative chambers, both in state capitals and in Washington, the term lobbyist came into use to describe individuals who operated in this manner. It was only after a number of congressional investigations and exposures in the press as well had pilloried the lobbyists and the organizations they represented that pressure groups began to shift to new and more subtle tactics, including the manipulation of public opinion. Today instances of outright bribery, or at least those that the public eventually learns about, are very few. At least in Congress, the days when votes were exchanged for "party girls" and hundred-dollar bills are gone forever. As one former congressman put it, the "practice of having legislators . . . embraced in the toils of the harlot is still in vogue at the seat of many state governments but has been practically abandoned in Washington, D. C." [10]

Occasionally, of course, something will happen to cast doubt on the theory that the old lobby is entirely extinct. In 1956, for example, Senator Francis Case (R., S. Dak.), who had not yet taken a position on a pending natural gas bill, made a dramatic announcement on the Senate floor: an oil company lobbyist had just attempted to give him $2,500, supposedly to assist him in his reelection campaign. Case declared that in the circumstances he would not vote at all on the bill, and the transparent attempt to purchase his vote was greeted with loud public indignation. For the most part, however, the new lobby disdains such overt manifestations of seeking influence. Funneling money to legislators is still important but the new lobby has learned how and when to give campaign contributions so as to avoid the kind of *faux pas* made in the Case affair.

[10] V. O. Key, Jr., *Politics, Parties, and Pressure Groups*, 5th ed. (New York: Thomas Y. Crowell, 1964), p. 137, note 16, quoting *Congressional Record*, 29 June 1950, p. A5076.

The new lobby prides itself on working in the open and on behaving with complete propriety. And there is indeed little question that its efforts to condition public opinion are constitutionally immune to attack, since they are protected by the First Amendment's guaranty that the right to petition for redress of grievances shall not be abridged.

One of the forms taken by pressure-group activities at the grass roots is the development of a program to create a generally favorable climate of opinion for the organization and its aims. Such programs are commonly carried out by organizations that are subject to government regulations and by organizations desirous of governmental assistance. Similarly, large organizations spend considerable sums on institutional advertising in newspapers and, especially, in magazines. Such advertising is not necessarily designed to generate public support for any current legislative aim of the organization, but rather to create in the public mind a favorable general impression of the organization and what it stands for. The privately owned power companies, for example, spent millions of dollars circulating a picture of a little boy fishing in a creek, with a caption indicating that he was engaging in free enterprise, just as the companies were. The hope, of course, was that the favorable image of the little boy would rub off on the gigantic companies. For much the same purpose, groups such as the American Association of Railroads or the National Association of Manufacturers prepare so-called educational material for distribution in the public schools, always insisting, of course, that they are not engaged in the indoctrination of the young.

Only the most well-heeled organizations can afford the expenditures involved in such generalized campaigns. Those that can afford them, however, view the expenditures as a worthwhile investment, providing them with a reservoir of goodwill that can be tapped when specific policy goals are sought.

The Public Relations Campaign

But most interest groups are more concerned with immediate matters, such as the defeat of legislation before Congress. Like the groups that engage in institutional advertising, these organizations often make use of the services of public relations experts. Typically, a public relations firm that is retained for such a purpose will try to persuade the general public that what is at stake is the welfare of the country at large and not the selfish interests of the individual organization.

One of the most elaborate campaigns of this kind in recent years was the one waged by the American Medical Association against all forms of national health insurance. In 1948, after the election victory of President Harry S Truman, the AMA was gravely concerned that the time might be ripe for the proponents of what it liked to call socialized medicine to make their bid. To combat any such effort, the organization levied an assessment of $25.00 on each of its 140,000 members. The money that was collected, it said, would be used to educate the American public on the progress that American medicine had made and on the necessity of assuring the continued high quality of medical care.[11]

The money was not to be spent by amateurs. The AMA retained a high-powered California public relations firm, Whitaker and Baxter, which had been involved three years earlier in a successful campaign to block a proposal by Governor Earl Warren for a statewide health insurance program. The firm employed the same Madison Avenue tactics that had conditioned Americans to shudder at the mention of "pink toothbrush" and "B.O." to produce the same negative reflex action against what the AMA called socialized medicine. It also persuaded doctors all over the country to double as propagandists, distributing literature in their waiting rooms and asking patients directly to urge their congressmen to oppose the legislation on national health care. Since patients tend to rank their doctor with their minister at the same high level of authority and selflessness, it was not surprising that an avalanche of letters descended on Congress. In addition, Whitaker and Baxter brought a multitude of other organizations into the fight. It could report by the end of 1949 that 1,829 organizations had gone on record in opposition to compulsory health insurance. By 1952 the number had grown to more than 8,000.[12] So successful were the firm's tactics that the health insurance legislation never even came to a vote in Congress.

But there is a high price tag on this kind of massive public relations campaign. In 1949 and 1950, the AMA spent almost $3 million on lobbying alone.[13] From 1949 to 1964, no other organization in the

---

[11] Stanley Kelley, Jr., *Professional Public Relations and Political Power* (Baltimore: Johns Hopkins Press, 1966), p. 67.
[12] Ibid., p. 81.
[13] These were the figures reported by the AMA itself in accordance with the provisions of the Federal Regulation of Lobbying Act of 1946.

country spent as much on its lobbying activities in any single year as the AMA did in each of the years 1949 and 1950.[14] In 1964 and 1965 money was again ladled out in large quantities to defeat the bill providing medical care for the aged. This time there were even spot announcements on television and radio, as well as advertisements in newspapers and in the mass circulation magazines such as *Life, Reader's Digest,* and the *Saturday Evening Post*. The AMA, however, was fighting a losing battle. The Goldwater debacle in 1964 had dragged so many Republicans to defeat that there were an almost record numbers of liberal Democrats in Congress.[15]

Had it not been for this chance circumstance, the AMA would undoubtedly have been successful once again. Moreover, the AMA's defeat in 1965 was hardly crushing. Since only the elderly are covered by Medicare, the United States remains the only advanced nation in the world without a comprehensive program of tax-supported health insurance. The public-relations approach is therefore now considered a tried and true technique of lobbying.

Campaign Contributions: Legalized Bribery?

Another and more ancient technique employed by pressure groups is the making of campaign contributions to candidates for public office who are favorably disposed to the organization's cause or who might be persuaded to become so. With campaign costs soaring in recent years, candidates have become increasingly dependent on large contributions from prosperous groups, except in constituencies where there is no effective opposition. Contributors with an interest in governmental programs are not at all reluctant to part with their money to facilitate access to the formulators of governmental policy and to create a favorable atmosphere in which legislative matters may be discussed.

The laws against bribery leave this area untouched. The late Senator

---

[14] *Legislators and the Lobbyists* (Washington: Congressional Quarterly Service, 1965), p. 76.

[15] The terms liberal and conservative are used many times in this book. In other contexts, the words can mean a variety of things. Here, they are intended simply to describe opposing attitudes on the proper role of the national government. The liberal is one who ordinarily does not view with dismay the use of federal power and money for the amelioration of economic and social inequality, whereas the conservative often tends to think that such a recourse is usually unnecessary and perhaps dangerous. Exceptions to these general tendencies abound.

Richard L. Neuberger (D., Ore.) could never understand why this should be so. He explained:

> If [my wife] Maurine or I ever would take one hundred dollars in cash behind the locked door of a hotel room to cast our vote for or against a specific legislative bill, we would be guilty of receiving a bribe. . . . But if, at the next election, we accept not one hundred dollars in cash but one thousand dollars in a check from the same donor, it is all perfectly legal, providing the check is made out to the Neuberger-for-Election Committee.[16]

Neuberger referred to the kind of situation he was describing as a twilight zone between bribery and legitimate campaign contributions. The danger, of course, is that if a gift is large enough, a Congressman will hesitate to say no when the donor later seeks support for legislation to benefit the selfish interests he represents. Courage bordering on foolhardiness will be required to turn him away.

The problem of campaign contributions by interest groups was once again highlighted during the summer of 1968. A bill to increase the permissible size and weight of trucks using the interstate highway system had passed the Senate earlier in the year with little notice. By summer, opponents of the measure—principally, the American Automobile Association—had mobilized considerable opposition to the bill. They were aided by disclosures that the American Trucking Association, chief advocate of the legislation, had made contributions totaling nearly $30,000 to certain members on key committees which had jurisdiction over bills of interest to the truckers. Specifically, eleven of thirteen Democrats on the House Public Works Committee, which had favorably reported the bill passed by the Senate, as well as the second- and third-ranking Republican members, had received contributions ranging from $500 to $3,000.[17] The adverse publicity was enough to kill the bill, at least for the time being; many members were apparently reluctant to take sides on the issue just before an election.[18]

Information on campaign contributions by interest groups is difficult to come by. Federal law prohibits contributions by corporations and labor unions. But such restrictions are so ambiguously drawn and enforcement so lax that they are easily circumvented, and what is reported is probably just a fraction of the actual picture of campaign giving. The

---

[16] Frank Church, "Campaign Money—How Much? From Whom?" *New York Times Magazine*, 26 August 1962, p. 67. Church is a Democratic senator from Idaho.
[17] *Congressional Quarterly, Weekly Report 31* (2 August 1968): 2076.
[18] Ibid., *40*, Oct. 4, p. 2674.

financial involvement of labor unions is much more open than that of the corporations. Most union money is expended through organizations like the AFL-CIO's Committee on Political Education (COPE).

Business interest groups, however, apparently do not make open contributions to candidates or political committees. Instead, individual officers of corporations or trade associations make personal campaign gifts. For example, during the 1952 presidential campaign, the officers or directors of no less than twenty-two of the large oil companies gave more than $300,000 to Republican candidates or campaign committees.[19]

Other Forms of Campaign Help

Both corporations and unions have found it easy to circumvent the law. A corporation will place campaign workers on its payroll, or permit long-distance telephone charges and the expenses of television productions to be billed to its account. It may lend a company plane to a candidate or send campaign literature for him. It may provide him with billboard space, furniture, and office equipment, and make its postage meters available. It does not even violate the law if it conducts a propaganda campaign to influence an election, or if it assigns corporation personnel to perform campaign duty.

Unions, too, have contrived to play an important part in elections while remaining in technical compliance with the law. Toward this end, for example, the Committee on Political Education (COPE) was created by the AFL-CIO. For, although the law prohibits a union from using its members' dues to make political contributions, the prohibition does not apply to an organization that depends on voluntary donations from union members. Despite the difficulty of building a sizable campaign war chest by soliciting individual contributions, COPE has been remarkably successful in keeping alive the influence of organized labor on congressional elections. The unions themselves, moreover, have not had to remain entirely aloof from election campaigns, for a 1948 decision of the United States Supreme Court held that the law is not violated when a labor organization spends money to publish and distribute issues of a union newspaper containing endorsements of congressional

[19] Alexander Heard, *The Costs of Democracy* (Chapel Hill: University of North Carolina Press, 1960), p. 106.

candidates.[20] This ruling stimulated the extensive use of the labor press in campaigns. Unions are also free to publish and distribute the voting records of congressmen, and to conduct voter registration drives. Such drives, and also the efforts made by unions to get out the votes, are especially important because historically the rate of nonvoting among working men has been much higher than among professionals and business people.

Such campaign contributions, direct and indirect, make many public officials substantially beholden to interest groups. Where a single such group completely dominates a constituency, that one group may literally own the official. Where there is a multiplicity of organized interests, a successful candidate has more than likely received contributions from several groups. Although no one can claim to own him, he is at the same time indebted to all.

The great bulk of campaign contributions constitutes investment in the future goodwill of the recipient. When an interest group feels it necessary to call on a congressman for support, there is usually no need to remind him of what the group has done for him in the past and of what it is in a position to do for him in the future. There is a tacit understanding about such things. The group has made contributions in the past and can be counted on again; all it wants is cooperation to the extent that it can be given. In most relationships between a pressure group and a congressman, there is never any real question about cooperation since there is probably a mutuality of interests to begin with.

Lobbying Administrators Different techniques must be resorted to when an interest group wants to influence a policymaker who is not an elected official. Almost all officials in the executive branch of the federal government are in this category because they hold office either by virtue of appointment or because they are career civil servants. In such a situation, any talk of campaign contributions would, of course, be entirely irrelevant. Substitute means of persuasion, however, have been found.

One way in which influence may be exerted on executive officials is to revive a practice often associated with the old lobby: providing

[20] United States v. CIO, 335 U.S. 106 (1948).

lavish entertainment for the formulators of public policy. A transparent example of this technique was provided by the Martin Company, at a time when it had defense contracts worth hundreds of millions of dollars, but wanted still more. The company provided a full weekend of recreation for twenty-six active-duty officers at a retreat in the Bahamas. The company chairman, when he was questioned by a congressional committee about the weekend idyll, defended the propriety of what the company had done. "A man could neither operate nor compete effectively," he said, "unless he had a close personal relationship."[21] This is a familiar explanation provided by government contractors when their function as entertainers is revealed.

Defense contractors, who run such an active entertainment lobby, take advantage of their right to deduct the expense from their taxable income. They also list as ordinary and necessary expenses the money required to purchase advertising space in magazines to explain the superiority of the military hardware that they produce. During the controversy over the Nike-Zeus antimissile system several years ago, an entire issue of the magazine *Army,* the official journal of the Association of the U. S. Army, was devoted to the subject. The prime contractor for Nike-Zeus, the Western Electric Company, bought full-page advertisements in the issue, and eight of the company's subcontractors also purchased space. Significantly, the same issue of *Army* also carried a map showing that the Nike-Zeus program would result in the spending of $410 million by the government in no fewer than thirty-seven states. Congressmen and their military-dependent constituencies are always interested in pork-barrel projects; the day after the appearance of the magazine, the argument on behalf of Western Electric started to be echoed by a number of senators and representatives.[22]

Military-Industrial Complex It is, in fact, the vast defense expenditures of the United States that have created perhaps the most awesome representation of interests in American history. Upon leaving office in early 1961, President Eisenhower warned against the relationship between the defense establishment and private industry. Noting that this conjunction of interests was new in

[21] Quoted in *Legislators and the Lobbyists,* p. 25.
[22] Douglass Cater, *Power in Washington* (New York: Random House, 1964), p. 41.

the American experience, he spoke of its "grave implications." He cautioned that "we must guard against the acquisition of unwarranted influence, whether sought or unsought, by the military-industrial complex. The potential for the disastrous use of misplaced power exists and will persist." [23] A day later, at his final press conference, Eisenhower reiterated his view in describing widespread advertising by military manufacturers as "almost an insidious penetration of our minds that the only thing this country is engaged in is weaponry and missiles." [24]

A decade later, the military-industrial complex is even more awesome, a consequence of the war in Vietnam and the seemingly insatiable appetite of weaponry planners to produce increasingly more sophisticated weapons systems. In ten years military contract awards nearly doubled, from $22.5 billion to $42.3 billion.[25] Much of this expense, of course, was for the war in Vietnam but the controversy over the large slice military spending takes out of the budget was renewed after President Nixon proposed his ABM (antiballistic missile) plan in 1969 at an initial cost of almost $7 billion. In that same year, total military spending was estimated at $78 billion. The impact such spending has on the American economy is enormous. Military spending, for example, on contracts and payrolls provided in fiscal year 1968 more than 10 percent of personal income in some eighteen states.[26]

A House investigation conducted in 1959 revealed that over 1,400 retired officers above the rank of major (261 of them generals or admirals) were employed by the leading 100 defense contractors.[27] Ten years later, Senator William Proxmire (D., Wisc.) published figures in the *Congressional Record* showing that the 100 leading contractors (not necessarily the same ones as in 1959) now employed 2,072 retired officers of the rank of colonel (or navy captain) and above.[28] Moreover, the top ten contractors had more than tripled the number of such officers working for them, from 372 in 1959 to 1,065 in 1969.

Although the extent of the relationship between the military and industry in terms of money and men can be easily documented, it is more difficult to assess the impact one has on the other. Senator Prox-

---

[23] Quoted in *Legislators and the Lobbyists*, p. 23.
[24] Ibid.
[25] *U.S. News and World Report*, 21 April 1969, p. 61.
[26] Ibid., p. 62.
[27] *Legislators and the Lobbyists*, p. 25.
[28] *Congressional Record*, 24 March 1969, p. S3073. Proxmire's data showed that in 1959 officers with the rank of colonel or above employed by the 100 leading contractors numbered 721, so there had been an increase of almost 200 percent.

mire disclaimed any intention of charging that his evidence demonstrated a conspiracy; but, he said, "the danger to the public interest is that these firms and the former officers they employ have a community of interest with the military itself."[29] Executives of the industry, as might be expected, did not share Proxmire's apprehension. One said that as long as we are in business and the government "tells us it needs military equipment, we would be remiss as a good corporate citizen if we didn't try to supply that need."[30]

The finger of blame cannot be wholly placed on industry. In the end, the civilians in the Office of the Secretary of Defense make the major decisions on new weapons systems needs. In a sense this may preserve the historic concept of civilian control of the military. But the heart of the problem may well be that the civilians brought into the Pentagon either share the uncritical acceptance of most Americans for more and more defense, or quickly become embued with an orientation toward defense.

The problem is perhaps best illustrated by President Nixon's choice of the two men he appointed to head the defense establishment. As Secretary of Defense, he chose Melvin Laird, who, before his appointment had been for some years the ranking minority member of the Defense Appropriations subcommittee of the House Appropriations Committee. For Deputy Secretary of Defense, Mr. Nixon designated David C. Packard, President of Hewlett-Packard Company, a large West Coast electronics manufacturer selling millions of dollars worth of components to prime defense contractors.

Lobbying tactics are also sometimes used by pressure groups that have no American constituency at all. Lobbyists who represent foreign governments are a case in point. A subject in which such lobbyists have been extremely interested in recent years is United States sugar legislation, which allows certain nations to sell sugar in this country at prices which are considerably higher than the world market price. In 1962, after the United States stopped importing sugar from Cuba, other producing countries exerted themselves strenuously in an effort to increase their share of the American market. In order to persuade Congress to act on their behalf, Mexican sugar interests retained a highly influential lawyer, Oscar L. Chapman, who had been Secretary of the Interior in the Truman administration. A former Assistant Secretary of Labor under Eisenhower, Rocco Siciliano, spoke for El Salvador, and a

[29] Ibid., p. S3074.
[30] *U.S. News and World Report,* 21 April 1969, p. 63.

former general counsel of the Department of Agriculture presented the case for the Nationalist Government of China. Lobbying by foreign governments is not new. In 1955, the Trujillo regime provided a trip with expenses paid to the Dominican Republic for members and staff assistants of the House Agriculture Committee only a few weeks before hearings were scheduled to begin on sugar legislation.[31]

Former Congressmen as Lobbyists

Retention of a former congressman as a lobbyist is a common tactic not only of foreign interests but of domestic pressure groups as well. Former Senate Majority Leader, Scott Lucas (D., Ill.), who became a full-time legislative representative after he left Congress, knew well why he was a valuable asset to the firm that employed him. "I can see almost anybody in the Senate almost any time," he said. "The Senate is a club and you're a member until you die, even if you get defeated for reelection." [32] In addition to Lucas, almost one hundred other former congressmen have worked as lobbyists in recent years. One of the many privileges they have enjoyed is the right to communicate directly with their former colleagues on the floor of the house in which they served.

Another former Democratic Senator—Earl Clements of Kentucky—became the effective spokesman for the tobacco industry in its fight to resist controls on advertising imposed by the Federal Trade Commission. As head of the Tobacco Institute, Clements, by virtue of his former associations in Congress, had little difficulty in rallying support for a bill which almost completely reversed a policy adopted by the commission. The FTC had issued a regulation requiring a health warning not only on cigarette packages but also in all cigarette advertising. The legislation, passed in 1965, prohibited the FTC from taking any action about health warnings in cigarette advertising for a period of four years. Clements' potency as a lobbyist was also enhanced by his close personal relationship to the President at that time, Lyndon Johnson. The two had been friends as fellow senators, and they remained so after Clements' defeat in 1956 when the Kentuckian became staff director of the Senate Demo-

---

[31] For a discussion of sugar lobbying, see Daniel M. Berman and Robert A. Heineman, "Lobbying by Foreign Governments on the Sugar Act Amendments of 1962," *Law and Contemporary Problems 28* (Spring 1963): pp. 416–27.

[32] *Congressional Record,* 10 October 1962, p. 21743.

cratic Campaign Committee. Clements' daughter also served as a personal secretary to Mrs. Johnson.[33]

Lobbyists and Congressmen Lobbyists have still another way of establishing a close relationship with congressmen: making themselves useful, or even indispensable, to the men whom they want to influence. Congressmen are forever complaining that they are provided with too little staff assistance and that they need more help from men who know both subject matter and the techniques of legislative politics. Lobbyists are delighted to step into the breach. Certainly there can be no doubt that they fill the congressmen's specifications. If they are earning their salaries, they know everything there is to know about the legislative subjects that concern their principal. Because this is so, the lobbyist is in a position to provide facts and figures, suggestions for questions that should be asked at committee hearings, and even the drafts of tailor-made speeches for the congressman's use. When a question of mutual interest is up for legislative consideration, the lobbyist may well be provided with a desk in the already crowded suite of the member.

Such a cozy relationship is entirely normal in a political system in which congressmen, like lobbyists, represent individuals and groups that want to get certain things done. It would, in fact, be strange if a legislator from an agricultural district in which the major crop was soybeans did not look upon the lobbyist for the American Soybean Association as a friend and ally. In such circumstances, the congressman sees the efforts of the lobbyist not as pressure, but, rather, as helpful assistance, as the following quote indicates:

> And then there are, of course, the lobbyists who agree with me. Now I believe in the fair trade laws. I was born over a [retail] store and raised in one. The [retailers] don't have to pressure me into seeing things their way. If anything, I'm lobbying them, telling them to get on the ball. And when their man comes around to see me, I don't think of him as a lobbyist with an ax to grind but as a man with sound judgment and good will.[34]

[33] For a detailed account of the cigarette controversy, see A. Lee Fritschler, *Smoking and Politics: Policymaking and the Federal Bureaucracy* (New York: Appleton-Century-Crofts, 1969).

[34] Donald R. Matthews, *U.S. Senators and Their World* (Chapel Hill: University of North Carolina Press, 1960), p. 178.

POLITICAL PARTICIPATION

The fact that congressmen use lobbyists quite as much as lobbyists use congressmen indicates that pressure and influence flow in both directions. Lobbyists, for example, may be used by a congressman to bring pressure on his own colleagues when additional support is needed on some bill that he is interested in promoting. Or the lobbyist may help drum up support in the constituency when the congressman is under pressure from powerful colleagues to cast a vote that will be unpopular back home.

The lobbyist-congressman relationship will thus more often be amicable and even intimate than hostile and antagonistic. Most lobbying, in fact, takes place among those who are friendly to begin with. The lobbyist for a free trade group writes off a legislator who is adamantly opposed to lowering tariffs and spends his time in what he considers to be more profitable pursuits: keeping his friends in line and courting those who are not strongly committed to either side.

Are Lobbies Effective?

How successful are the techniques of the new lobby? Neither congressmen nor officials in the executive agencies will readily admit that they are influenced by lobbying. They will readily acknowledge that they meet with lobbyists, listen to them, and often cooperate with them, but they maintain stoutly that no action of theirs was ever dictated by outside pressure. When they have acted in accordance with the urgings of a lobbyist, they insist that this was the way the constituency wanted it anyway, or, perhaps, that this is what the public interest required.

Lobbyists, on the other hand, have a less modest view of their effectiveness. Although they may not boast publicly about what they have accomplished, the impression that they convey to their employers is that they are great movers and shapers indeed. Of course, such an estimate of effectiveness may well stem from the lobbyist's desire to justify his efforts to the organization that pays his salary and also the other expenses of the campaign he conducts. Thus he is inclined to take credit for many things that almost certainly would have happened without his intervention. He may even spend a considerable portion of his time—and therefore of his organization's money—describing his brilliant, if sometimes entirely mythical, feats.

It can therefore be seen that both the lobbyist and those whom he lobbies are not the most trustworthy sources for information about the effectiveness of pressure-group activity in Washington. Doubtless the truth lies somewhere in between the extravagant claims and the self-righteous denials.

Lobbyists often score their greatest victories when the groups they represent want to obstruct or delay legislation. A group defending the status quo derives benefit from the sheer cumbersomeness of the legislative process in Congress. Its task is relatively easy because there are so many junctures at which a negative decision will doom a bill. Congressional procedures, in fact, are so formidable that they might well have been devised by men who hated the thought that legislation would ever be enacted. Although proponents of a bill must win every match, the opposition often requires only a single victory. Thus lobbies do not find it difficult to administer one defeat after another to presidents who champion ambitious legislative programs. Not that the lobbies can perform deeds of magic. Thanks to Senator Goldwater, the Democrats had such large majorities in Congress after the election of 1964 that it was almost child's play for President Johnson to win approval of the measures he favored. In 1966, however, the Republicans recouped many of the seats they had lost, and, with the parties more evenly aligned in Congress, the lobbyists once again racked up notable successes in their fight against Great Society legislation.

It is true that on many issues that arouse nationwide attention, the lobbies working on both sides often tend to cancel each other out. But, when legislation has a lower level of visibility, lobbyists for a particular point of view are in their element. For example, take the tax bill that was enacted in the closing hours of the Eighty-ninth Congress. As originally proposed by the administration, the measure had only a single purpose: to encourage the investment of foreign capital in the United States. On the floor of the Senate, however, no fewer than twenty-five amendments were tacked on, hardly any of them dealing with the principal subject matter of the bill. One amendment reduced the excise tax on hearses by 30 percent. Another increased the depletion allowances on the clay that is used in sewer pipes, and on clam shells and oyster shells. There were so many giveaway amendments of this type, all pushed through by high-powered lobbying, that opponents derided the measure as a "Christmas tree bill."

The victory for the lobbies was so open and brazen that there was some speculation about a possible veto by President Johnson. But President Johnson had a particular fondness for one amendment that had been written into the bill: a provision allowing individual taxpayers to earmark part of their income tax for a fund from which the major parties could finance their presidential campaigns. Since the president has no item veto, it was impossible to preserve the provision on financing presidential campaigns while turning thumbs down on the "Christmas tree" parts of the bill. Mr. Johnson decided to sign the measure, obviously influenced by the realization that the section on campaign finance would be of greater benefit to the Democrats, who generally find it more difficult to raise campaign money than do Republicans.[35] The lobbies got what they wanted.

In other instances it is difficult to account for the success or lack of success of a lobbying effort. The automobile industry mounted a massive campaign against the legislation dealing with automobile safety but could not prevent its passage. Undoubtedly, widespread public interest in the matter as well as the evidence developed by the bill's proponents convinced congressmen of its need. On the other hand, a massive lobbying campaign in the wake of the assassination of Senator Robert Kennedy failed to get really effective gun control legislation through Congress. A strong counteroffensive by the gun lobby stirred just as much of an emotional reaction.

A box score of successes chalked up by lobbies would not necessarily shed much light on their effectiveness. For much of the time, groups have little or no opposition and serve as interested allies of decision-making bodies. Such is the case extensively in the relation of interest groups with administrative agencies. As often as not, a mutuality of interests exists to the point where what the lobby does is perceived not as pressure but as cooperation.

Even if the question of the effectiveness of lobbies could be satisfactorily answered, the problem of assessing their role in the political process would still remain. No effective argument can be made that interest groups are an illegitimate part of American politics. Not only does the First Amendment of the Constitution guarantee the right to petition for redress of grievances, but interest groups also provide a kind of representation difficult to achieve under a strictly geographical system. As long as a multitude of interests exists in society, some way to voice their demands is useful and is needed.

---

[35] The following year, there were second thoughts in Congress about the provision on financing campaigns, and after a long struggle the action of the preceding year was nullified. See Chapter 5.

Supplementary Representation

The system of formal representation, although it reflects people as the basic unit, rests on a geographic basis. Each representative or senator is elected from a specific piece of territory, be it a congressional district or a state. Although some of these areas may be homogeneous enough to contain only a few special interests, most of them will contain within their boundaries a considerable number of such interests. Yet the geographical system of representation means that the congressman is intended to be the spokesman in the national legislature for all the various interests in his area. Obviously this can never be so. Some of the interests will be too insignificant numerically for him to worry about. These interests will therefore go unrepresented. Other interests will be in conflict with one another or with his own conscientious position. Obviously he cannot, no matter how hard he tries, represent them all. Some of the groups will in effect be deprived of a voice at the seat of government.

But the existence of organized groups and the lobbies that work for them in Washington provides what is in effect a supplementary system of representation. The group to which an otherwise unrepresented individual belongs will see to it that his interests are not neglected in the nation's capital. It may not be strong enough to bring his own congressman around to his point of view but it will have the ear of other legislators as well as of officials in the executive branch, and will therefore be able to provide, at the very least, a forum for the expression of the individual's position.

Implicit in any such defense of the present system, however, is the assumption that all interests in our society are fairly represented and thus that unreasonable demands by any group will always run up against effective opposition. Such an assumption is open to question, however, for an interest that is not organized can make little headway against one that is, and a group without money cannot effectively oppose one that is affluent.

An expert on pressure groups has pointed out how one-sided the struggle can be between a highly organized group and a largely unorganized group: "The lobbyists for electrical utilities . . . are eternally on the job; the lobbyists for the consumers of this monopolistic service are ordinarily conspicuous by their absence." [36] The fact that consumers—and many other interests as well—are not organized at all,

---

[36] Key, *Politics, Parties, and Pressure Groups*, p. 150.

POLITICAL PARTICIPATION

or poorly organized, is of critical significance, for it means that the system of pressure politics has no self-regulating mechanism to keep it fair, balanced, and equitable. Under such conditions, no invisible hand can possibly assure the existence of universal symmetry, or even of a tolerable equilibrium.

As might be expected, a high degree of organization is found most frequently among groups with money. The poor man—whether for lack of time, lack of sophistication, or lack of group consciousness—is not much of a joiner. And even when he does become a member of an organization, the resources of that group will normally be far too meager to support lobbying activities, especially on the national scene, for when public attitudes have to be formed, changed, or simply mobilized, expenditures of millions of dollars may be required.

It is certain that such an unequal situation will continue to exist for a long time to come, and that powerful pressure groups will retain a disproportionate influence in the formulation of policy. The question remains, however, whether the abuses, if not also the inequities, of the present system are being adequately dealt with.

Regulation of Lobbying Not until 1946 did Congress choose to pass any legislation at all to discourage lobbying abuses. Before then, it had never moved to do more than conduct investigations of lobbying. During the Wilson administration, a select committee produced sixty volumes of testimony on the lobbying tactics employed by the National Association of Manufacturers. Two decades later, a spectacular investigation was conducted by a special committee under the chairmanship of Senator (later Supreme Court Justice) Hugo L. Black (D., Ala.) into the unscrupulous efforts that lobbies had made to defeat legislation for regulating public utility holding companies.[37] But although both of these investigations commanded much public attention, neither resulted in any general legislation to regulate lobbying.[38] There might have been no compre-

---

[37] One revelation by Black's committee was a particular sensation: companies that wanted to insulate themselves against regulation had inspired the sending of thousands of bogus telegrams to congressmen.

[38] There were, however, instances in which Congress dealt with lobbying in specified areas. In 1935, Congress passed legislation requiring the lobbyists of public utilities holding companies to register with the Securities and Exchange Commission; it acted in a similar fashion in the Merchant Marine Act of 1936. And in 1938 the agents of foreign governments were required to register with the Department of Justice.

THE PRESSURE OF INTERESTS

hensive legislation in 1946, either, had it not been for President Truman. As a senator, Mr. Truman had been chairman of a special war investigating committee, which had learned a great deal about the methods used by pressure groups. Upon assuming the presidency, he took the lead in urging Congress to eradicate what he considered to be a serious threat to its integrity. The result was the Federal Regulation of Lobbying Act of 1946.[39]

Despite the title of the act, the provisions in the statute did not amount to regulation of any kind, partly because of a fear in Congress that regulation might raise serious questions under the First Amendment. Rather, the law was based on the principle of compulsory registration of lobbies and lobbyists. The hope was that the dangers represented by lobbying could largely be eliminated by compelling the lobbies to operate under public scrutiny. Accordingly, the provisions of the act were not punitive in character. Instead, they merely required both the lobbies and the lobbyists to place certain information about their activities on the public record.

Interest groups were to keep detailed records of the contributions received and the expenditures made. These records were to form the basis of quarterly reports that were to be filed with the Clerk of the House of Representatives. Every report would list the names of any persons who had contributed $500 or more to the organization on a single occasion together with the total amount that each had contributed during the entire calendar year. It would also contain information on expenditures: the identity of anyone who had been paid more than $10 by the lobby, and the purposes for which such expenditures had been paid.

Registration and disclosure were the requirements imposed on the individual lobbyists who represented a pressure group. The registration would have to be accomplished before the lobbyist even began his work. In sworn statements filed with the Clerk of the House and the Secretary of the Senate, he would have to identify himself and his employer and answer questions about the duration of his employment, his salary, and his expense allowance. Once he had registered, he would be bound by only a single requirement. Every three months, he would have to file a sworn statement with information on certain matters: the receipts and expenditures that his work had entailed; the identity of those to whom he had paid money; the purposes of such

---

[39] The act was actually only a single section of the omnibus Legislative Reorganization Act of 1946.

payments; the names of publications in which he had caused to be published any articles or editorials; and the proposed legislation in which he was interested. The information furnished by the lobbyist, like that which was provided by his organization, would, it was thought, be brought to the attention of members of Congress through publication in the *Congressional Record.*

The requirement that reports be printed in the *Congressional Record* has turned out not to have much practical meaning because of the limited readership of that publication. One group of readers of the *Record,* the congressmen and their staffs, is undoubtedly aware of much of the lobbying that is taking place under their very noses. Another group of readers is composed of the lobbyists themselves, who likewise benefit little from exposure of their own activities. Since the public readership of the *Record* is small, the only other source on which it can depend is the press to bring the most significant registration statements to public attention, but a reporter would have to do a considerable amount of research to uncover the real significance of the reports—and there are pathetically few who are both willing to do the necessary digging and also allowed by their papers to devote sufficient time to the task. The only publication that regularly reprints the registration information is the privately published *Congressional Quarterly: Weekly Report,* which has a small, though influential, circulation, consisting largely of congressmen, lobbyists, and newspapers.

This is not the only criticism that can be made of the act. For, weak as the reporting requirement was, it was sapped still further by an all-important exemption that appeared in the statute. This exemption was implicit in the law's statement that the reporting requirement applied only to an organization "the *principal* purpose of which" was to affect legislation, or one that collected money "to be used *principally*" for legislative purposes (emphasis added). This loophole enabled many organizations that were exerting a powerful effect on congressional legislation to escape the reporting requirement on the ground that their *principal* purpose had nothing to do with lobbying, since their efforts to influence legislation were merely incidental to other purposes. On this theory, an organization as powerful as the National Association of Manufacturers does not feel compelled to comply with the provisions of the act.

Another major defect in the act was its implicit assumption that the only target of lobbying groups is Congress. Completely overlooked was the fact that pressure groups spend vast sums to influence the decisions of the administrative and regulatory agencies whose actions are as important to them as those of Congress. The law, moreover, failed to cover efforts to influence congressional staff members. And, even with respect to those organizations which indisputably were obligated to register, no authority was given to the Clerk of the House or the Secretary of the Senate to inquire into the accuracy of the reports filed and to refer any false statements to the Department of Justice for criminal prosecution.

Weak as the law was, it was still too strong to suit the lobbies, and legal action was instituted to have its provisions invalidated. The major contention was that the right to lobby is completely insulated from congressional action by the provisions of the First Amendment. A district court, impressed by the argument, ruled that the law was indeed invalid because it abridged the constitutional freedoms of speech, assembly, and press. Upon appeal, the Supreme Court reversed this decision, but it saved the statute from unconstitutionality only by a drastically narrow construction of its provisions. In an opinion by Chief Justice Warren, the Court held that a person could be subject to the law's provisions only if he had tried to influence Congress by direct communication with its members. According to the Court, indirect lobbying—such as attempts to stir up grass-roots sentiment in order to generate pressure on Congress—could not be the subject of restrictive legislation.[40] Whatever its legal merits, the Supreme Court decision was a grievous blow at the lobbying act, for indirect methods are often precisely those that are preferred by the pressure groups. In 1962, for instance, the AMA spent $7 million to defeat Medicare. Of that amount, no more than 3 percent was used for direct lobbying. Because of the Supreme Court decision, only that relatively insignificant portion of the money disbursed by the AMA had to be accounted for.

It is unlikely that the Supreme Court will ever change its mind about lobbying and the First Amendment. Even the three justices who dissented in the 1954 case disagreed with the majority only because they would have gone further and declared the law to be a flat violation of the Constitution, instead of saving it by interpreting its provisions restrictively. Although it is true that the public's right to petition for redress of grievances needs to remain unfettered, also at stake is the same public's right to be free from manipulation. The ingenuity of lawyers, so skillful in punching loopholes in the lobbying law, might better be directed toward devising means to accomplish such an end.

[40] United States v. Harriss, 347 U.S. 612, 623 (1954).

The law, as interpreted, gives the impression that lobbying is regulated when, in fact, it is not. As a consequence, demands have arisen from time to time for new congressional action. The reaction of Congress to these suggestions has been unenthusiastic, to say the least. If anything, Congress has shown more solicitude for lobbying, as when, in 1962, legislation was enacted to provide tax advantages to business groups engaged in lobbying. Under the new law, such groups could deduct lobbying expenses from their capital income as long as the expenses were incurred for the purpose of influencing legislation of direct interest to the group. Although the expenses of lobbying at the grass roots are not deductible, the costs of every conceivable type of direct lobbying are: appearances before committees, communications with members of Congress, and even personal contacts with them. Moreover, the dues that are paid to organizations engaged in lobbying are now also tax deductible. Ironically, the legislation discriminated against the groups that could least afford such discrimination—those trying to defend the general interest. The corporate taxpayer can deduct dues paid to the National Association of Manufacturers because the NAM represents its particular economic interest, but an individual who belongs to a group such as the Friends Committee on National Legislation can take no deduction precisely because he had not joined for self-interested economic reasons.

In 1966 the Senate overcame traditional congressional reluctance to offend powerful pressure groups and voted to strengthen the 1946 registration statute. It acted on the recommendation of the new Joint Committee on the Organization of Congress—the first such committee created in twenty years. In accordance with the suggestions of the joint committee, the Senate added teeth to the 1946 law by requiring that lobbying registration reports be filed, not with the Clerk of the House and the Secretary of the Senate, who were powerless to do anything with them, but with the General Accounting Office, a congressional investigative agency, which was specifically authorized by the legislation to communicate to the Department of Justice any suspected infractions of the law. The Senate also extended the coverage of the bill to a wider range of organizations.

As in 1946, the lobbying provisions were part of a larger congressional reform package. Opposition in the House was directed at the lobbying changes, as well as at other reforms. House members are generally more vulnerable to organized pressures because one or two interests may dominate their smaller constituencies. Senators, on the other hand, usually represent such a variety of interests that they can more easily balance off competing groups. Whatever the specific objections of individual House members might have been, the House Rules Committee failed to take action on the Senate bill, thus killing it, at least for the Ninetieth Congress.

Executive Lobbying Although the laws affecting lobbying by private groups remain weak, there is one type of lobbying against which there is a forthright statutory prohibition. The law flatly forbids both officers and employees of the executive branch to use appropriated funds for the purpose of lobbying.[41] Yet the unambiguous wording of this statute is blithely ignored both in the White House and in the executive departments and agencies, all of which make use of many of the same lobbying techniques that are the stock-in-trade of private pressure organizations. This is understandable since any effort at enforcement of the provision against lobbying would have to come from the executive branch, which is by definition the offending party. But congressmen have become so dependent on executive lobbying, as well as lobbyists representing interest groups, that the practice flourishes.

Only when the law is flouted in a particularly flagrant manner do congressmen register any serious protest. One such incident took place in 1962, with the Secretary of Health, Education, and Welfare, Anthony C. Celebrezze, as the culprit. Celebrezze's offense was that his department had used $3,562 of public funds to send congressmen telegrams urging them to support an administration bill. His action created a storm on Capitol Hill, and Celebrezze was prevailed upon to issue what he himself referred to as "specific instructions that this procedure shall not be repeated." [42] In a policymaking process where the executive and bureaucracy have become such an integral part of the legislative process, the statute, in any event, is wholly unrealistic.

To a foreign observer of American politics, it seems strange that in the United States the executive branch must resort to the use of pressure tactics to promote its legislative program. For, in countries that are governed in accordance with parliamentary principles, it is taken for granted that the legislature will not obstruct the program of the party

[41] 41 Stat. 68, 18 U.S.C. 1913.
[42] Daniel M. Berman, *In Congress Assembled* (New York: Macmillan, 1964), p. 91.

in which the voters have expressed their confidence. The American system, however, does not operate on the basis of such principles, and here a president who wants his bills enacted must quite literally stoop to conquer.

Lobbying by the executive branch goes under the name of legislative liaison. There are legislative-liaison officials in each of the executive departments and agencies and also in the White House itself. Far from being offended at this arrangement, congressmen are pleased with it because the liaison officers help them handle requests from constituents, provide valuable information on pending legislation, and also try to help the member obtain special federal projects for his district. But, in the pressure system, no services are provided without charge, and in time the congressman learns that executive officials have kept careful track of the obligations he has incurred. He may receive a telephone call from an official in the Department of Defense who had recently given his tentative approval to the awarding of a major government contract to a company in the congressman's district: "The Administration would very much appreciate your support when the amendments to the farm bill come up for a vote next week." In such circumstances, a freshman congressman may well conclude that his hearing is playing tricks on him, or that the three martinis he had at lunch were even more potent than he had realized. For why on earth should the Department of Defense be interested in a farm bill? Under the same circumstances, the veteran member of Congress will understand immediately what is afoot. The coordination of legislative-liaison information in the executive branch had led to the conclusion that the one man in government in the best position to pressure him at the moment is the official whose final approval is still being awaited with bated breath by the congressman.

The White House Lobby Such a combined operation in the executive branch requires a high degree of organization and planning. Although executive lobbying is by no means a purely recent phenomenon, it was not until President Kennedy took office that it was placed on a systematic and coordinated basis. In command of the operation was Lawrence F. O'Brien, later to be named postmaster general by President Johnson. When a particular

THE PRESSURE OF INTERESTS

legislative struggle was in the offing, O'Brien and his men would select as their target the often small group of uncommitted members on the committee or subcommittee whose support might mean the difference between victory or defeat for the administration's bill. The campaign to win such members over might involve promises of defense contracts, new federal buildings or installations, or presidential patronage. To one who might be afraid that supporting the administration would hurt him in his constituency, the White House emissary would try to convince the member that his fears were unfounded.

Often O'Brien's men were able to reach a meeting of the minds with congressmen in an atmosphere of friendship and good will. Only when sweet reasonableness produced no results did they resort to threats and strong-arm methods. The most extreme sanction they could impose was to eliminate a congressman from consideration when patronage jobs were available and when favors were requested of the White House. A blacklisted member would be dead as far as the White House was concerned. He would find every office in the executive branch ignoring his requests for services, whether substantial or petty.

To assist them in their work, O'Brien and his cohorts maintained an exhaustive card index that provided up-to-date information about every member's needs, interests, whims—and, of course, voting record. The index enabled the O'Brien staff to apply indirect pressure on congressmen. A close personal friend, for example, might be persuaded to telephone a representative to offer advice about how he should vote on a pending amendment, or an old political crony might mention how happy he would be if a certain bill never emerged from committee. This kind of intercession often indicated that the card index had come through again.

Another technique of the Kennedy administration was the judicious use of patronage. O'Brien's exact title, "Special Assistant to the President for Congressional Relations and *Personnel*" (emphasis added), was a candid admission of the extent to which the White House used patronage to obtain support in Congress. President Johnson, while keeping O'Brien on as his head of legislative liaison, made him postmaster general, thus giving him another title historically redolent of jobs and boodle. Far more than did his predecessor, Mr. Johnson played a personal role in legislative battles, telephoning members of the House and Senate directly to solicit their support on bills and even summoning them individually to the White House for what came to be known as the Johnson treatment, a judicious blend of softsoap, appeals to patriotism, tearful pleading, and the more familiar presidential promises and threats.

On becoming president, Richard Nixon showed no inclination to downgrade the importance of executive lobbying. Although he refrained from emulating the styles of either of his two predecessors, he chose as one of his chief congressional liaison men Bryce Harlow, who had developed considerable skill in this role in the Eisenhower administration.

Well-developed legislative liaison machinery already exists when a new president takes office. The armed services have had for years their own offices on Capitol Hill so that their legislative-liaison specialists could be close at hand to the relevant committees—literally just a few feet away from the committee hearing rooms and staff offices. And most major departments have staffs whose principal function is lobbying Congress, often with an assistant secretary in charge.

A smoothly functioning executive lobbying operation is no guarantee of success for a president. For all the effort of the Kennedy White House lobby the results were meager indeed. And it is by no means certain that Johnson overly benefited from using his famed personal brand of persuasion. His most productive years, in terms of legislative output, were the two following his overwhelming victory in 1964 which carried in unusually large Democratic majorities in Congress.

The Pressure System and Democratic Government

The pressure system, then, dominates almost every aspect of politics in Washington.[43] Only rarely is governmental action the product of a debate between opposing concepts of the public welfare. Rather, policymaking commonly results from a struggle between pressure groups, both private and public. For better or for worse, this is the essential nature of the process of government in the United States. Yet, when looked at from the standpoint of the individual citizen's participation in the making of public policy decisions that will affect him, the pressure system leaves much to be desired. For millions of such individuals, it provides little in the way of meaningful representation and participation in the political process.

[43] Interest representation in policymaking by the courts is discussed in Chapter 12.

A system of representation so heavily dependent on economic resources, or on the number of members a group can claim, or on the conventional wisdoms embodied in the group's claims cannot provide the means for participation by virtue of its exclusiveness. One indication of the system's failure to provide meaningful participation is its inability to accommodate the claims of the poor and the Black. Because they are poorly organized, devoid of the financial means and organizational skills, and fighting against entrenched privilege, such groups have not found the system of interest representation functional.

Chapter 5 Political Parties

Although political parties are taken for granted today as an essential part of the political system, they are not even mentioned in the Constitution. The framers expected, or at any rate hoped, that the new government they were creating could function effectively without political parties and the divisiveness associated with them. Yet, choice between competing groups of leaders is basic to a democratic system. Many ways could undoubtedly be devised that would produce groups of leaders who could then contend for the public's approval. History has largely dispensed with the need for innovation, however, because it has produced political parties as the means whereby such choices are made.

Those who wrote the Constitution had actually had scant experience with political parties. In colonial times, the selection of candidates to run for public office was made not by political parties but by influential individuals. Since few people could satisfy the qualifications for voting, political leadership was the monopoly of a small minority, who clustered in merely transitory groupings of admirers around a particular leader—more personality cults than political parties.

But, as the restrictions on voting were eliminated one by one, the size of the electorate expanded, and political leaders found that new conditions created the need for a new approach to the problem of establishing rapport with potential voters. Even George Washington, when he ran for a seat in the Virginia House of Burgesses, had felt constrained "to arrange for an appetizing outlay of rum, punch, wine, cider-royal, and beer to please the varied tastes and win the votes of electors in his district." [1] But, although Washington was willing to provide the alcoholic equivalent of bread and circuses to attract voters to his banner, he could never reconcile himself to the idea that political parties might be a far preferable device for organizing the electorate. Prominent in the catalog of evils that he warned his countrymen against in his farewell address was "the baneful effects of the spirit of party generally." [2]

The party spirit, however, was already well advanced long before Washington left office. It began with reservations in Congress about what were considered to be the pro-British implications of Washington's foreign policy. During the bitter struggle in 1795 over whether or not the Senate should ratify the treaty that John Jay had negotiated with the British on behalf of the Washington administration, the opposition snowballed and started to take organized form. In 1796, which was a presidential election year, the opposition was sufficiently well organized to wage a fight against appropriating the funds that were needed to implement some of the provisions of the Jay treaty. With Thomas Jefferson as their leader, the opponents of the treaty went on to make a strong bid for the presidency in the same year. Although their attempt was unsuccessful, the groundwork had been laid for a new and powerful Republican party to challenge the Federalists for control of the national government.

Partisan conflict increased in intensity during the next four years. By 1800, it was impossible to conceal the fact that the framers' grand design of a government free from the spirit of party was a shambles. The Federalist party and the Republican party each went so far as to organize support in the various states for those candidates for the electoral col-

---

[1] William N. Chambers, *Political Parties in a New Nation* (New York: Oxford University Press, 1963), p. 4.
[2] Henry Steele Commager, *Documents of American History,* vol. 1, 7th ed. (New York: Appleton-Century-Crofts, 1963), p. 172.

lege who pledged themselves to vote for the presidential and vice-presidential nominees of the party: Thomas Jefferson and Aaron Burr for the Republicans, and John Adams and Charles Pinckney for the Federalists. A majority of the winning electors were pledged to the Republican candidates, and Jefferson was inaugurated President the following February.[3]

The drama of the conflict in the election of 1800 brought home to the people of the young nation that it does make a difference who is in power. It does make a difference who wins. In the American experience, this has been the single most important reason for the development of political parties. For it is through such institutions that the electorate can be organized and can thus make its choice as to who should control. In other countries, parties may be formed for other reasons; even in the United States, some political parties have risen for purposes other than control. But, by and large, the history—and function—of American political parties has been to win elections in order to control the elective offices of government.

The Two-party System

But why a two-party system? So well entrenched has the two-party system become in the United States that few question the reasons for its existence. In respect to party system, the United States differs from many other countries of the world, where three, four, or more parties may

---

[3] The voting in the electoral college exposed a serious flaw that had developed in the constitutional system for electing a president and vice-president. Since the framers had not envisaged the establishment of political parties, it had not occurred to them that members of the electoral college would be pledged to support particular candidates. They had therefore not provided that each elector, when casting his ballot for the two men whom he preferred, should designate one of them as his choice for the presidency and the other as his choice for the vice-presidency. The elector was simply to vote for two men, without indicating any preference between them. The name which appeared on a majority of the ballots would be president and the runner-up, vice-president. But the appearance of pledged electors created a tragicomic situation that no one had anticipated: a tie between the Republican candidates, Jefferson and Burr, since each elector who had voted for one of them had also voted for the other. The tie vote meant that the president would have to be elected by the House of Representatives, as provided in the Constitution. Burr, an ambitious self-seeker with no political scruples, engaged in a series of Machiavellian maneuvers aimed at winning the office for himself. Alexander Hamilton, however, decided that an unsavory character such as Burr was an even greater threat to the nation than a radical democrat such as Jefferson, and he rounded up enough votes in the House to make Jefferson president. In 1804, the states ratified a constitutional amendment—the Twelfth—to prevent such a situation from arising again. Under the terms of the amendment, each elector would indicate separately his choice for president and his choice for vice-president.

regularly battle for control of government. Both institutional and historical reasons account for the development and persistence of the two-party system.

Foremost among these is the method ordained for electing the president—the one national elective office provided for in the Constitution. It is necessary for a presidential candidate to try to win an absolute majority in the electoral college, for only in that way can he be elected without throwing the presidential contest into the House of Representatives. Thus there is only scant motivation for a small party wedded to a narrow ideology to go to the expense of running a presidential candidate. Even if its nominee should win a respectable percentage of the popular vote, he might still end up without a single electoral vote, because in each state the candidate with the largest number of popular votes wins all the electoral votes, and the runners-up are left with nothing.

If a third-party candidate should manage to capture a number of electoral votes by winning several states, these votes will ordinarily do him no good. Only where the electoral vote is relatively evenly split between his major party opponents would a third-party candidate have an opportunity of playing the role of a spoiler by requiring the choice to be made in the House of Representatives. This was perhaps the major objective of George Wallace in 1968 and he came close enough to throw a scare into the nation. One consequence was the most serious examination of the electoral college system ever undertaken and the strong possibility of a Constitutional amendment emerged.

Thus the tendency on the national scene has been for two political parties to exist, each attempting to appeal to a large segment of the electorate to command a majority in the electoral college. Public attention is focused on the two largest parties, each with some chance of pasting together a winning coalition.

The system of the winner taking all, which discourages the development of national third parties, also operates at other levels of the political system, and always with the same effect. Each state has but one governor, for example, and each congressional district no more than a single representative. Moreover, though each state has two senators, they are ordinarily elected in different years; and, even when the two of them are elected simultaneously because the death of an incumbent has created a vacancy, two separate contests are held.

History also played its part early in the days of the new republic in creating two parties. Although some attribute this to those who were anti-Constitution as opposed to those who favored the new system, it was the split over the Washington administration's pro-British foreign policy and its economic implications which sparked the first efforts at party opposition. By 1796, as it became obvious that Republicans were seriously challenging Federalists for control, people talked, as they had not done before, "about voting for or against this or that party candidate on the basis of their stands on the [Jay] treaty." [4]

The electoral system by itself might not create a two-party system. But, when this kind of system operated on the historical origins of two parties early contending for control, it certainly had the effect of reinforcing the maintenance of two major parties. There have been times, of course, when one major party dominated for considerable periods. The Democratic party, which is the name by which the Jeffersonian Republican party soon came to be called, held the presidency with only occasional interruptions from 1800 to 1860. The Federalist party soon died out, to be replaced by the Whig party, which managed to win two contests for president: William Henry Harrison (1840) and Zachary Taylor (1848). Both were war heroes.

Slavery and sectionalism brought about a major realignment of the party system; and, from the eve of the Civil War until 1932, the new Republican party (little ideological relation to the early Republicans) was dominant. The only successful Democrats during this long period were Grover Cleveland (two nonconsecutive terms, 1884 and 1892) and Woodrow Wilson (1912 and 1916). Since Franklin Roosevelt's first victory in 1932, it had been the Democrats who had managed, with the exception of General Dwight Eisenhower (1952 and 1956), a virtual monopoly on the White House until Richard Nixon's success in 1968.

Even during these lengthy periods of one-party control, the second contending party has not often been so overwhelmingly crushed that it at least could not summon the courage to do battle. And, even when capturing the White House seemed a formidable task, the second party has on occasion been able to win a majority in one or the other, or sometimes both Houses of Congress. At the local level, also, the major party temporarily in eclipse nationally may have a strong position in different parts of the country. All through the period of post-Civil War Republican ascendancy, the Democrats had a stranglehold on the South, which only now shows some signs of weakening. For most of the period from 1932 to the present, the Republicans, although out of

[4] Chambers, *Political Parties in a New Nation*, p. 116.

power nationally, have been very much in power particularly in the Middle West, until recently in parts of New England, and increasingly in suburban areas.

The cycles of party dominance thus demonstrate that, nationally, even the second major party may go for long periods without the fruits of a presidential victory. It is little wonder, then, that third or fourth parties have not been able to maintain themselves for very long in the face of certain starvation in the presidential contest. The historical development of two-party competition has thus been reinforced by the characteristics of the electoral system. The very fact that the two-party system has been in existence for so long increases the likelihood that it will persist for many years to come. Americans have simply become accustomed to thinking of it as a permanent feature of their political life. It is, in short, fully endowed with the sanctity of tradition. The phrase, the two-party system, strikes a responsive chord in American hearts. At least that seemed to be the assumption in 1964, when many Republican congressional candidates, fearful that Senator Goldwater at the head of their ticket might also drag them down to defeat, appealed to voters to split their ballots and thus help to preserve the two-party system. And in 1968 Richard Nixon refused to share a public debate forum with his two major opponents on the ground that inclusion of George Wallace would be a threat to the two-party system.

The very existence of two major parties, and the fact that they normally monopolize the presidential contest, provides a ready reference point for the stream of young people who each year become eligible as new voters. Where the choice of political party realistically presents a person with the option of identifying either as a Democrat or as a Republican, the two-party expectation is enhanced. Habit strongly conditions behavior. For over a century, the battle has been between Republicans and Democrats with only few and fleeting exceptions.

The existence of only two major parties has important consequences for the political system. Since each of the parties is, by its very nature, oriented to win, its concern with ideology and program is often subordinated to the goal of electoral success. The parties generally are pragmatic in approach; when a party forsakes pragmatism for ideology, its fate is likely to be that which befell the Republicans under Goldwater in 1964. The rejection of ideology is not so much a matter of philosophical choice as it is a matter of political necessity. Simply stated, there is no room for losers. The electoral system in this sense has strongly shaped the American political style.

POLITICAL PARTICIPATION

Decentralization of the Parties

When Americans speak of the Democratic and Republican parties, they are usually referring to the *national* parties, and they are thinking in terms of presidential campaigns. But, apart from their campaign role every four years, the national parties as entities exist only in an illusory sense. What do exist are hundreds of state and local Republican and Democratic party organizations. It is these which, when they win office, are in control of the bone and sinew of a political party through the thousands of jobs and favorable public policy advantages with which the party in power can reward its faithful followers. Although the drama of presidential politics usually commands the center of the stage, the local and state party organizations function on a full-time basis, instead of just once every four years. These groups organize for the elections that may mean little to outsiders but are of supreme importance to the people who live in a given locality. The way they are organized, and even their very existence, are keyed not to the election of a president but to the election of city councilmen, state superintendents of schools, sheriffs, district attorneys, probate judges, and county surveyors. These party organizations, indeed, exist for the purpose of organizing elections and filling public offices. In their individual bailiwicks, they may be far more important, and they certainly seem far more real, than the national parties.

It is these state and local organizations which enter into a kind of uneasy alliance every four years to perform still another function: to try to elect a president of the United States. It is the aim of winning the presidency that motivates the temporary establishment of a pattern of cooperation and coexistence that binds together countless local parties. Only after an elaborate process of coalescing has taken place every four years do recognizable national parties emerge. In reality, the national Democratic and Republican parties are not parties at all, but, rather, party systems.

Under such circumstances, ideology is in practical terms self-defeating for a party that intends making a serious effort to win the presidency. For, if a party is to stand a chance to win, it must be all things to all men lest it alienate one or another of the groups that have banded together in a political grand alliance. Hardheaded party leaders never let themselves forget a fact that is plain for all to see: neither of the parties is a harmonious grouping of like-minded individuals. Otherwise, it would not be necessary to use labels such as "Southern Democrats" or "moderate Republicans" to distinguish these Democrats and these

Republicans from other Democrats and other Republicans. The lure of the presidential prize is normally strong enough to overcome the natural tensions that exist among the subcoalitional elements.

Sometimes, of course, the tensions are simply too great to be overcome, even for the sake of establishing a united front for a presidential campaign. In 1912, for example, the wing of the Republican party led by Theodore Roosevelt found itself unable to subordinate its policies and principles to the goal of Republican victory. Unsuccessful in their effort to secure the Republican nomination for Roosevelt, these elements bolted and founded a party of their own, the Progressive party. The new third party, which gave its nomination to Roosevelt, fell short of an electoral victory, but it had the satisfaction of drawing off enough votes from the Republican candidate, William Howard Taft, to guarantee the election of his Democratic opponent, Woodrow Wilson. The lesson for parties oriented to win was clear: ideological rigidity may drive important elements out of the party and thus create the likelihood of defeat at the polls.

Not that defeat under such circumstances is absolutely inevitable. When the opposition party, too, is programmatically rigid or tactically inept, the other party may be able to take defections in its stride and win anyway. Precisely that happened in 1924, when the followers of Robert M. LaFollette abandoned the Republican party and formed a new Progressive party. The LaFollette Progressives attracted almost 5 million votes, but still the Republican candidate whom they had wanted to defeat, Calvin Coolidge, won the election. Similarly, the Democrats in 1948 suffered a double defection: Henry Wallace, one of the most prominent New Dealers, led a revolt from the left, and Strom Thurmond, Governor of South Carolina,[5] sparked a right-wing walkout from the Democratic National Convention over the issue of civil rights. Both Wallace and Thurmond ran for the presidency; Wallace as the Progressive party candidate and Thurmond as leader of the States' Rights party. Nonetheless, the convention nominee, Harry S Truman, won over the Republican candidate, Thomas E. Dewey.

These deviations from the traditional coalescing power of the two major parties were relatively minor aberrations compared with the unprecedented stress put on the two-party system in 1968. The Wallace candidacy attracted growing numbers—both Republicans and Democrats—who no longer could be induced to stay within the moderate

---

[5] Thurmond later became a senator and still later switched parties. In 1968, he was a key backer of Richard Nixon at the Republican convention.

and comfortable middle both parties had tried to preempt (with the exception of 1964) since the end of World War II. But, for the Democrats, the strain on that party occasioned by the emotions aroused by the war in Vietnam was even greater. To many long-time Democrats, the Johnson administration's war policy had been a disaster. In Humphrey they saw little more than affirmation of such a policy with not much hope for change. With the alternatives of Nixon and Wallace equally unacceptable, many Democrats, who otherwise would have been in Humphrey's corner, gave him either lukewarm support or none at all.

1968, in fact, may have been one of those landmark years in American political history; it may have marked the end of an era and the beginning of a new coalescing process. In this light, 1964, rather than being viewed as an exception, was perhaps the opening signal. If history is any guide, the two-party system will reassert itself, perhaps encompassing a realignment of major groups in the country. But it is also possible that, at least for a time, a third party will persist in its effort to displace one of the major parties.

Certainly the feat of George Wallace getting on the ballot in fifty states (only in the District of Columbia was the Wallace organization, the American Independent Party, not on the ballot) should not be underestimated. The ability to qualify for a place on the ballot in the face of restrictions in many states aimed at third parties demonstrated that the Wallace phenomenon was not strictly regional. And the popular vote he received supports this viewpoint: 48.5 percent of the total national Wallace vote came from states outside the South.[6] Neither did Wallace find it too difficult to tap the necessary financial support to mount a national campaign, although not on the same scale as the major parties.

Party Membership Organizing a national coalition of state and local parties requires more than simply welding together party organizations. This would amount to mobilizing only a rather small portion of the total potential electorate. A political party must be distinguished from the voters which it may succeed in attracting to support its candidates. Political parties in the

---

[6] Republican National Committee, Research Division, *The 1968 Elections* (Washington: Republican National Committee, 1969), p. 233.

United States are distinctly open organizations. (Although generally true, there is, of course, the fact that the Democratic parties in the South have been in the past and, to a considerable extent still continue to be, open only to whites.) Membership, as such, in a political party is quite different from church membership or Rotary Club membership. If a person is asked, "To which political party do you belong?" he may reply, "I'm a Republican." Except for a small fraction of the electorate, however, this probably means no more than that the person votes for, or identifies with, the Republican party.

There are few card-carrying members of political parties, simply because there is no special means of identifying party adherents except for the fact that people show up at party meetings regularly. One generally becomes active in a political party not through any formal process of joining but, rather, by merely beginning to take part in its continuing activities. In many towns and cities there is no party organization of any consequence in which one could become active even if the desire were present. In other communities, only one party may have any organizational form. Even where there is party organization, it may lie moribund until the stimulus of an election galvanizes it into activity.

For those individuals who become active, the primary focus is at the local level. The initiate will attend precinct meetings, canvass voters, distribute literature at the polls, and the like. The diligent worker earns the gratitude of his colleagues, and in time this gratitude may take the form of election to party office or even nomination to public office. Not all officers and nominees, of course, start at so low a level and with such menial tasks. Persons who have established community reputations may be invited into a party organization to start at the top, even in the role of candidate. Either way, those who come to exercise influence within a political party usually do so because they can command support of a following—either within the party or outside it.

Once a person with political ambitions establishes a local base, he may very well decide to branch out into wider fields. If he is talented—and the measure of talent is success—he may achieve prominence at the county level or at the level of the congressional district. In time, he may run for office; and, if he demonstrates an ability to win, his potential for even wider influence will be enhanced. This is the winnowing process by which statewide party leaders come to the fore, often going on, from a position as United States senator or governor, to become important national political figures.

Not all candidates for statewide or even national office travel this particular route. Those who do not, however, are usually granted exceptional status only because it is believed they have extraordinary ability to attract votes. In 1952, the Republicans gave their hearts to Senator Robert A. Taft of Ohio at their national convention, but they gave their votes to General Eisenhower because they thought that he had a better chance of winning. In 1960, the Democrats cheered Adlai Stevenson, but he was a two-time loser, and they chose to nominate John F. Kennedy. The same kind of practical thinking can shape political decisions at the state level. The Republicans in California ignored all the party faithful who had a claim on their gubernatorial nomination in 1966 and selected a motion picture actor, Ronald Reagan, because they wanted to win. More frequently, however, the parties look within their own ranks for a potential winner. Only when such a person is not to be found are they inclined to look elsewhere.

But success as a party leader within a state is reserved for a very few; even fewer succeed on the national scene. Political parties, although led by such people, do not consist solely of them. The source of party organizational strength rests in the numbers of people who can be enlisted in one capacity or another as party workers, and the percentage of the electorate involved in such activity is very low.

Political parties are thus composed of a core of leaders, activist supporters, and the nonactive members who identify with a party and more or less regularly support its candidates by voting for them at the polls. At the same time, parties are anything but fixed structures. A party, as one writer has described it, is "porous." Because it relies "on votes as the arithmetic of power," it is open "at its base, sides and apex."[7] A party is constantly in search of new voters and new candidates to attract those voters.

The cycle of party fortunes, on the presidential level, has been for the most part dependent on the ability of one of the major parties to bring about a different coalitional alignment productive of success. As V. O. Key, Jr., has put it: "If a party is to govern, it must bring into mutually advantageous alliances an aggregate of interests powerful enough to win a presidential election."[8] This statement suggests that it is not so much the party organizations which have to be coalesced as

---

[7] Samuel J. Eldersveld, *Political Parties: A Behavioral Analysis* (Chicago: Rand McNally, 1964), p. 5.

[8] V. O. Key, Jr., *Politics, Parties, and Pressure Groups,* 5th ed. (New York: Thomas Y. Crowell, 1964), p. 178.

that voters with interests must be appealed to. The party systems, in effect, become conglomerations of interest groups.

Party Differences Since a national party must attract to its banner a wide spectrum of individuals and interests, the welcome mat is always out in front of its door. Exclusiveness is a luxury that it cannot afford. Only at their peril will the Republicans write off votes from the workingman, or the Democrats, votes from the businessman. Unwilling to take such chances, each party tries to make its umbrella big enough to provide shelter for as many interests as possible in order to build a winning coalition. Important consequences inevitably follow. The two parties are both moderate. They feel that they must be because they must encompass not only the disparate party organizations of which they are composed but also because they must attract support from a broad spectrum of the popular electorate. Because they are both moderate, the national parties generally do not find themselves too far apart on issues. By appealing essentially to the same segments of the electorate, they often sound alike and look alike. Thus, in recent years they have been in fundamental agreement on issues that would have provided the basis for a major difference of opinion under any other political system. There has not been any basic disagreement between the parties on either the welfare state or American foreign policy.

This is true, of course, only when the national parties are operating in the context of presidential politics. Many local Republican party organizations undoubtedly look with dismay on the creeping socialism of the welfare state. They would be joined by equally disgruntled Democrats. And both local and state party officeholders and their followers, Republican as well as Democrat, can be found dissenting from positions taken by their national spokesmen on civil rights, Vietnam, and other issues.

Nonetheless, there are basic differences between the Democratic and Republican national party systems. Each can be said to have a distinctive center of gravity, and, although the parties overlap each other, their orientation and direction are somewhat dissimilar. For the Democrats, the center of gravity is liberal, and there is a positive attitude toward federal programs. For the Republicans, the center of gravity is conservative, and there is a pronounced antipathy to programs developed or administered in Washington. Yet these differences are not profound, for in both parties conservatives and liberals can be found among both leaders and followers.

The broad, and therefore moderate, nature of the two major parties is reflected in their national platforms, which statements of purpose are hammered out every fourth year at the nominating convention for the presidency. Although the platforms appear to be statements of party ideology, they are in reality something quite different: a calculated attempt to make the party acceptable to enough interests in the society to provide a winning combination of electoral votes. Democrats and Republicans alike promise good things and good times to every conceivable group. Later, excuses can be concocted for the party's failure to follow through on its promises; but right now, all other considerations must be subordinated to the winning of an election. Thus, in a normal presidential year, the two party platforms will be very much alike. There are differences in detail and in emphasis, but often these, too, are obscured through verbal legerdemain. Party platforms are essentially exercises in calculated ambiguity. For those who seek ideological precision, they are frustrating documents indeed.

Choosing Presidential Candidates

Similar considerations apply in the choice of a party's presidential candidate. As the platform must embody the conflicting ideals and aspirations of the heterogeneous groups to which the party must make its appeal, so too must its candidate be one capable of attracting wide support: support, not only from the party faithful, but also from those less partisanly committed. Candidates, then, must be well within the middle of their own party spectrum.

Only once in recent times, at the Republican National Convention in 1964, did one of the major parties repudiate the basic character of coalition politics and opt instead for ideological purity. The ideology was conservatism, the candidate was Senator Barry M. Goldwater, and the motto might well have been "He'd rather be right than President." The men behind Mr. Goldwater will probably be remembered longest for the dismally bad advice they gave their candidate about how to win the presidential election. They deserve, however, to be remembered for something quite different. That is, they put themselves in a position to control the convention and obtain the nomination for their leader.

Their efforts provide a textbook example of how to win a presidential nomination and how to lose a presidential election.

The campaign for the nomination was pursued on every front and that meant campaigning for delegates in a variety of ways, depending on the process of delegate selection prevailing in the different states. Some states provide by law that national convention delegates be chosen by party conventions, either at the local level or on a statewide basis. Conventions are generally made to order for party stalwarts to control, and the Goldwater people, as the most active party workers, found them entirely to their liking.[9] In other states, the law provided for presidential primaries instead of party conventions. In some of these states, there was a direct confrontation between delegates pledged to Goldwater and delegates pledged to one or another of his opponents. In others, there was a sort of popularity contest: voters would note their preference for the presidential nomination, and the winning delegate might be compelled by law to give his support on the first convention ballot to the candidate who came out ahead. Goldwater's supporters carefully selected those primaries in which he could put his best foot forward. They chose well, and Goldwater's victory in the California primary over Governor Nelson Rockefeller of New York not only added to his delegate strength but also was of considerable psychological significance, since it showed that he could attract large numbers of voters in a big state that was rich in electoral votes.

By the time the convention was called to order, it was already too late for his opponents to unite behind an alternative candidate. Even before the nominating speeches began, the convention showed its partiality to Goldwater by refusing to accept a platform plank rejecting the support of extremist organizations such as the John Birch Society and the Ku Klux Klan, and also by declining to strengthen the civil rights plank approved by the platform committee. Against this background, the nomination of Goldwater, when it came, was a distinct anticlimax.

Almost immediately Goldwater made it clear that he would not wage the usual kind of presidential campaign, calculated to appeal to broad masses of the electorate. In the speech in which he accepted the nomination of the convention, he specifically repudiated the concepts

---

[9] Mr. Goldwater had friends in party organizations throughout the country, for, as chairman of the Republican Senatorial Campaign Committee, he had appeared at party functions across the land to speak for Republican candidates and to raise money on their behalf.

of moderation, which had traditionally been the hallmark of presidential campaigns. "Extremism in the defense of liberty is no vice," he said. "Moderation in the pursuit of justice is no virtue." Moreover, the candidate for vice-president whom he selected,[10] Congressman William Miller of New York, was as conservative as Goldwater, although the usual practice is to strive for at least some degree of ideological balance on the national ticket.

The acceptance speech and the selection of Miller as candidate for vice-president established the keynote for the entire Goldwater campaign. The party was quite literally transformed from a broad, inclusive, and moderate coalition into a narrow, exclusive, and somewhat extremist sect. The results were predictable: utter disaster for the party and its candidates.

In 1968, an entirely different situation prevailed. The candidacy of George Wallace, and a third party, had already opened an outlet for conservatives in both parties. For well over a year before the Republican National Convention met, Richard Nixon had sold himself to party organizations as the solid, moderate choice of the party. His nomination was simply a reaffirmation on the part of Republicans that moderation was the path to electoral success. On the Democratic side, those who disagreed so strongly with their own party's failures, especially Vietnam, initially rallied behind Senator Eugene McCarthy. And, until Senator Robert Kennedy was cut down by an assassin, other disaffected Democrats saw him as the party's strongest challenger. But it was Vice-President Humphrey, as heir to national leadership of the on-going party organizations in the states, who in the end represented the more moderate—and thus presumably safer—course for the Democrats.

Undisciplined Parties In the 1964 campaign, many Republicans running for Congress, as well as some who were candidates for state and local offices, disassociated themselves from Goldwater lest his unpopularity rub off on them. In 1968, many Democrats made similar attempts to separate themselves on the war issue from Humphrey. Although this kind of outright break with the standard-bearer of the party is highly unusual, it was made

[10] Technically, the convention nominates the vice-presidential candidate, but it will always accept the recommendation of its presidential candidate.

possible by a constant and quite normal aspect of the political system: the decentralization of the two major parties. Except for the presidential and vice-presidential nominees, candidates normally look for support not to the national party but to the local, congressional, and statewide organizations that they have either captured or built on their own.

Each candidate runs his own campaign, often quite independently of what the national party is doing and saying. If the facts of political life in the particular locality necessitate repudiation of the national platform, or even repudiation of the presidential candidate of the party, the candidate can be expected to do what must be done. Moreover, the fact that he is beholden not to the national party organization but, rather, to the local party unit means that such repudiation can be accomplished with impunity. Southern Democrats have thumbed their noses at the national party for years. There is little that the national party can do to punish such recalcitrance. Party members in Congress may choose to retaliate although such action is rare. In 1965, however, two Southern Congressmen, John Bell Williams of Mississippi and Albert Watson of South Carolina, were stripped of their committee seniority for their defection to the Goldwater cause during the 1964 election. The same fate fell to Representative John Rarick of Louisiana for supporting Wallace in 1968.

Candidates feel free to go it alone largely because they do not depend for the financing of their campaigns on the national party. Campaign war chests consist largely of money raised by the individual candidate himself from businessmen, interest groups, party activists, and also, to a lesser extent, from the rank and file in the constituency where he is running. A candidate therefore feels no sense of gratitude to the national party. Rather, he is much more likely to attribute his success to his own skill and to the loyalty and hard work of those around him. The result is a party system stubbornly resistant to discipline, with successful congressional candidates often paying only lip service to the president's wishes, even when he is of their party.

Certainly, the national party is entirely irrelevant to a congressional candidate from a safe district. In such districts, where one party dominates, the organization on which the incumbent depends is often higly personal and always remote from national direction. Since only one party is strong in the district, the incumbent has nothing to fear from the general election. It is the primary election that may pose a threat to his continuance in office, and the national parties steer clear of any involvement in primaries lest they end up backing a losing candidate thus diminishing their influence in the locality even further.

The isolation of Senate and House races from the contest for the presidency does not, however, mean that the national party organization is uninterested in the outcome of such races. Quite the opposite is the case, for the national party wants as many of its congressional candidates to be successful as possible. The party in control of the White House knows that the greater its majority is in Congress, the greater the likelihood that the president will have at least a fair chance of being able to implement his program.

Because of this shared interest, it is possible to discern in almost any election year the development of a complex network of relationships providing at least a communications mechanism for national, state, and local party organizations. This applies in off-year elections as well as in the years when a president is elected, for the party in control of the White House wants to counteract the tendency of voters to turn against the president's party in midterm elections, while the party out of power wants to reinforce this tendency as much as possible.[11]

The coordinating function of the national party is generally performed outside the public's view. The only official party organ that has a high level of visibility, especially since the advent of television, is the national nominating convention. It is through the use of this device that the major parties have selected their presidential and vice-presidential candidates ever since the early 1830s. Prior to that time, the practice was for each party's members in Congress to caucus every four years for the purpose of choosing candidates for the presidency and vice-presidency. The use of this method meant that there was no popular participation in the nomination process. The caucus device, therefore, smacked of aristocracy and was thus wholly incompatible with the rising tide of democracy that crested with the election of Andrew Jackson in 1828. "King Caucus" was promptly dethroned, and the nominating convention developed to take its place.

---

[11] On only three occasions in the last hundred years has the party out of power failed to improve its position in Congress in an off-year election. In 1966, for example, the Republicans gained forty-seven seats in the House and three in the Senate.

The Nominating Conventions

As is so often the case in American political history, a wide gap develops between the spirit in which an institution was created and the way it evolves in practice over time. The national party convention is a notable example of this rule. Although it originally sprang from a democratic urge, it is today a visible demonstration of the frustration of the democratic process. Had not television made the national convention public property, its shortcomings might have gone unnoticed for much longer. Increasingly, however, the stage-managed character of the conventions has come under attack: the interminable, boring speeches; the individual theatrics engaged in by delegates conscious of publicity and seeking recognition back home; the obvious, well-planned, unspontaneous demonstrations on behalf of those placed in nomination. During the 1968 Republican convention, the total time for nominating and seconding speeches and demonstrations involving twelve candidates consumed nine hours and eighteen minutes.[12]

This languid display apparently convinced the Democrats to do something about their own show, scheduled for later in the month. All three major candidates—Humphrey, McCarthy, and Senator George McGovern—suggested that organized demonstrations on behalf of the candidates be eliminated. Although the convention managers complied, delegates still managed to mount demonstrations of a sort.

But these small concessions to decency and decorum are responses merely to surface problems and hardly get to the basic maladies afflicting the conventions. For the conventions are, in fact, only the last stage in the process of selecting the party nominees, and it is the entire process which is under question.

The choice of presidential nominees under the present system is largely under the control of the 10 percent or so who can be considered party activists. Whom they choose, however, may have little relation to the preferences of the vast numbers whose only association with political parties is to vote for the candidates those parties select. It is true that several states have presidential primaries, but there is much variation in them and frequently they do not even match contenders for the nomination so that the value of primaries is questionable.

In 1968, for example, only in the first of the primaries—in New Hampshire, where George Romney provided opposition—did Richard

---

[12] *Congressional Quarterly, Weekly Report* 33 (16 August 1968): 2179.

Nixon face a genuine challenge. And the eventual winner for the Democrats, Hubert Humphrey, did not enter a single primary. Even when a candidate does win a primary, he may find that the state's convention delegation is composed of many others who become delegates by virtue of holding party offices, or because they are chosen by state party conventions which may be held in addition to the primary.

The convention, which is supposed to be the forum in which the party chooses its candidate, turns out, in fact, to be no contest at all. Not since 1952 has either party had a genuine struggle for the nomination. In that year, it took the Democrats three ballots to select Adlai Stevenson; and, although General Eisenhower won on the first Republican ballot, it was a relatively narrow victory, 595–500, over Senator Robert A. Taft of Ohio. Since that time, the convention winners have been those who have built up an insurmountable lead through long and arduous cultivation of the party activists who generally wind up as convention delegates. Neither the primaries nor the open give-and-take among delegates at the convention seems to be a significant factor.

That a national convention gives the appearance of being such a contrived instrument of choice was dramatically reflected by both of the parties in 1968. Richard Nixon's triumph was smoothly engineered and almost flawless, to the point where it became dull. By contrast, the chaotic Democratic convention illustrated in a different way the control exercised by those in charge of a convention. The symbolic barbed wire surrounding the convention site, the treatment of delegates and reporters on the floor, and the autocratic handling of the gavel were but a few of the realities of the Chicago debacle which made a mockery of this intended exercise in democratic choice.

Perhaps the wounds done to the major parties by the 1964 Republican and 1968 Democratic conventions are only transitory. Certainly the Republican presidential victory in 1968 shows how much can change in the space of four years. Most likely the Democrats will survive their convention trauma and narrow electoral defeat of 1968. One benefit that might emerge from the Democratic debacle is extensive party reform, particularly in the manner of choosing delegates. Responding to the bad image which Chicago created, the newly designated Democratic National Chairman, Senator Fred Harris of Oklahoma, appointed two committees early in 1969 to make a thorough study of the whole structure of the party with an eye toward effectuating greater participation in the machinery of choosing candidates and developing a platform.

Extensive reform, however, runs squarely into the decentralized nature of the party system. The organization of political parties as well as the methods of choosing convention delegates is almost entirely a creature of state laws. Thus, even if the Democratic party's national organs can agree on reform measures, the task of getting changes in state law presents a formidable task.

The National Committees Although the national parties are on public display primarily through their nominating conventions, mechanisms have been developed that make the parties on-going institutions during the remainder of the quadrennial cycle. The task of keeping the two parties alive between conventions falls to the Democratic and Republican National Committees.

The two national committees are organized on somewhat different bases. On the Democratic National Committee, there is equality of representation among the states and territorial possessions (such as Guam and the Virgin Islands); each is permitted to place two members on the national committee of 110. For many years, the Republicans used a similar system, but in 1952 they decided to depart from the principle of equality and award bonus seats on the national committee to states that had in the last election succeeded in placing Republicans in office.

Both parties, however, use the same method for choosing the national committee members from the various states. At the national convention every four years, each state delegation caucuses to select that state's two members. Since the powers of the national committee are few, it is often the case that the most powerful political leaders in the state have no desire to be elected to the national committee. The choice, therefore, often falls on individuals whom the state party wishes to honor—a heavy contributor, for example, or one who has worked especially hard to advance the party's fortunes.

Those who are elected to the national committee need not invest a great deal of time in their work since the committee meets only about four times a year. Probably the most important function that it performs is to make the arrangements for the next national convention. It will, for one thing, choose the site for the convention. At times this is a matter of considerable substantive significance as it undoubtedly was in the Democrat's choice of Chicago in 1968. There may be widespread support in a particular city for one or another of the potential presidential nominees, and holding the convention in that city could therefore be psychologically advantageous to that man. Because almost every city has its own political coloration, there will often be considerable infighting in the national committee over the decision on the convention site. In addition, the national committee recommends to the convention a slate of temporary and permanent officers.[13] This power, too, may sometimes be used with telling effect, for choosing people who are identified with one of the men being considered for the presidential nomination may have an impact on what the convention decides.

Aside from helping to make the arrangements for the next convention, the national committee performs only one other function, the election of its own national chairman. Just as the national committee is supposed to be able to act for the party between conventions, so, too, does the national chairman represent the party between meetings of the national committee. This, however, is a grandiose view of the national chairman's role when his party has won the presidency. In that event, it is the president and not the national chairman who is acknowledged to be the leader and spokesman of the party. The national chairman, in fact, will scrupulously refrain from publicly expressing an opinion on policy matters, clearing even his most innocuous statements with the White House. With policy matters in the hands of the president, the national chairman simply does the work of a presidential assistant for party matters such as organization and patronage. And when a president himself is political enough to be interested in such matters, the national chairman may become nothing more than a figurehead. That is precisely what happened with the Democratic National Chairman, John W. Bailey, during the administrations of Presidents Kennedy and Johnson.

The national chairman of an out party has a somewhat better chance to assert himself. Still, if his party is badly split, he, too, may decide to confine his attention to organizational matters. In the aftermath of the Goldwater debacle, for instance, with the future orientation of the Republican party a matter of considerable doubt, the National Chairman, Ray Bliss, functioned exclusively as a technician, trying to rebuild the party organizationally and leaving ideology to others.

Although the national chairman is elected by the national committee,

[13] Two sets of officers, temporary and permanent, are chosen in order to double the number of opportunities for exposing party figures to public view.

this procedure usually amounts to nothing more than the ratification of a decision made elsewhere. For each party invariably follows the custom of allowing its presidential nominee to choose his own national chairman and, in effect, impose his choice on the national committee. The man selected by the presidential nominee will serve at least until election day and perhaps beyond. Only when an election goes particularly badly, as did the election in 1964 for the Republicans, will pressure build up for the replacement of the national chairman. The anti-Goldwater Republicans in 1964 vented their rage on Chairman Dean Burch, a zealot in the conservative cause. After Burch had been forced out of office, the national committee, for the first time in many years, had a free hand in designating his successor, since there was no party leader who was strong enough nationally to dictate its choice. Having had enough of ideologists for awhile, the committee settled on Mr. Bliss, whose only philosophy was Republican victory. Having successfully brought the party back from its low point in 1964, Bliss was rewarded for his 1968 effort by being forced out of the chairmanship. There were those who felt Mr. Bliss was too much of a technician.

Permanent Party Organizations

Although national chairmen come and national chairmen go, there is a factor that makes for at least some stability in the organization of each national party. For, during the past two or three decades, a full-time professional party bureaucracy has developed in each of the parties under the national chairman. This bureaucracy consists of the highly professional staff people who serve in the headquarters of the respective national committees in Washington. They include experts in public relations, propaganda, and public-opinion polling, as well as specialists in fund raising and in organizational work. Most of the professionals stay in their jobs long enough to accumulate considerable expertise. Only a narrowly sectarian national chairman will insist on cleaning out all the old-timers and staffing the headquarters only with true believers. Inevitably this means a serious loss of effectiveness and, later on, the painful beginnings of a fresh effort to reestablish a truly professional staff. The new emphasis on permanence of headquarters staff reflects the realization that it is virtually impossible to start from scratch every four years and build an efficient national party organization.

POLITICAL PARTICIPATION

There was a time when only a skeleton staff would be maintained at the national committee for three and one-half years of the four-year presidential cycle. Only when the election campaign was actually in the offing would the staff mushroom in size. This tendency has by no means been entirely overcome, and there are still many in both parties who think of presidential campaigning as a part-time job. But the trend is distinctly in the direction of full-time work aimed at creating a positive party image, learning as much as possible about what motivates the electorate and nonstop organizational work to pump life into local party organizations, many of which become virtually moribund between elections.

This new development in party organization has resulted in nationalizing the American party system to a certain extent. Nevertheless, many impediments must be overcome if the parties are truly to become national in anything but name. One major factor that helps preserve decentralized and locally oriented parties is that national party organs —the national committee, the national chairman, and the national headquarters—have no coercive powers. They can neither dictate the choice of candidates nor use financial pressure to influence either policy or tactics at the local level. Until the national party can enforce a certain basic loyalty to the principles of its program, the essential nature of the party system will remain unchanged, with the real levers of political power outside the reach of the national party.

The centralization of party operations is further impeded by the existence of separate campaign organizations for a party's members in the House and Senate. The primary purpose of the congressional and senatorial campaign committees is to raise money for the financing of reelection campaigns by incumbents. Congressmen want to preserve them for precisely the reason that some of the nationally minded party leaders want to abolish them: they free representatives and senators from dependence on presidential favor when the party is in power. Congressional campaign committees, as a matter of fact, originated as the result of strain between President Andrew Johnson and the so-called radicals who dominated the Republican party in Congress during his term of office. For fear that President Johnson would use the power of the national party to help crush their reelection hopes, the radicals organized their own campaign committee to assist them in the 1866 election. Before long, the Democrats in Congress chose to emulate the Republicans. Campaign committees were at first concerned only with House elections; members of the Senate did not yet face the problem of appealing to a popular electorate since their selection was still in the hands of the state legislatures.[14] When the Seventeenth Amendment introduced the popular election of senators in 1913, it was only a matter of time before senatorial campaign committees were created.[15] Today, as in 1866, the congressional campaign committees act with considerable independence of the national parties. Their function is to work for the election to House and Senate of as many party members as possible.

The fact that the congressional campaign committees have a separate existence from the national committees is a reminder that the route to election for representative or senator is likely to be quite different from the course that must be pursued by a presidential candidate. In the one case, local constituencies and interests are paramount; for a presidential candidate, a national electorate has to be cultivated. This quite real separation of interests is perhaps much more significant than the constitutional separation of powers. A trenchant student of American politics believes that it actually results in something akin to a four-party system, with the Democrats and Republicans each split into a presidential party and a congressional party.[16]

Periodically attempts are made to bridge the gap between presidential politics, oriented to a national constituency, and congressional politics, oriented to local constituencies. After the Democratic party suffered its second consecutive defeat at the hands of Mr. Eisenhower, National Chairman Paul Butler inspired the creation of the Democratic Advisory Council, which would serve as the unified voice of the party. The council was to include among its members prominent Democrats oriented to the White House such as former President Truman, Eleanor Roosevelt, and Adlai Stevenson, who had twice been the party's presidential candidate. Seats on the council would be reserved as well for the seven principal leaders of the congressional party, including Sam Rayburn, Speaker of the House, and Lyndon Johnson, Majority Leader of the Senate. Rayburn and Johnson, however, declined to serve, and the other congressional leaders followed suit. None of them wanted to lend their support to an organization that would doubtless press them to respond more to the programmatic preference of voters in the North, and less to those of the Southern wing, which was so powerful in the

---

[14] Article I, Section 3.
[15] V. O. Key, *Politics, Parties, and Pressure Groups*, p. 324.
[16] James MacGregor Burns, *The Deadlock of Democracy: Four-Party Politics in America* (Englewood Cliffs, N.J.: Prentice-Hall, 1952).

congressional party. Thus the advisory council was reduced to acting as spokesman not for the Democratic party as a whole, but only for those who were nationally oriented and presidentially inclined members of the party. When Mr. Kennedy was elected President in 1960, the council formally dissolved.

The Republicans have been no more successful than the Democrats in unifying their congressional and presidential wings. In 1962, President Eisenhower brought together about 150 party leaders at his Gettysburg farm to announce the establishment of an All-Republican Conference. The idea was that the party should speak between its conventions through an organization which would include Republican officeholders of both the past and present, as well as the party's current candidates for office. The Republican leaders in Congress, however, Senator Everett McKinley Dirksen and Congressman Charles A. Halleck, took a dim view of the conference, fearing that it would be dominated by the presidential wing of the party. Because of their reservations, the first meeting of the conference was also its last. A second attempt to bring together the two wings of the party was made in 1965. The mechanism this time was the Republican Coordinating Committee, consisting of party leaders from both sides of the presidential-congressional divide: Mr. Eisenhower, all former Republican presidential nominees, the House and Senate leadership, the Republican national chairman, and representatives from both the Republican Governors' Association and the Republican State Legislators' Association. The congressional leadership chose not to boycott the coordinating committee, and cooperated in the preparation of several position papers on domestic and foreign issues. Documents on which agreement could be reached between Mr. Goldwater and liberal Republicans were, however, innocuous at best, and the long-range effects of the coordinating committee were no more impressive than those of the All-Republican Conference.

The Parties and Participation

The major characteristics of the American party system—decentralization and lack of discipline—seriously impede the ability of political parties to perform the national function of providing a viable and meaningful choice of candidates and platforms to the American electorate. The system, as it has evolved, does little toward providing the individual citizen with a meaningful relationship to the political processes of developing policy alternatives and the choice inherent in the availability of alternatives.

Nor does the party system, although it has the potential, serve adequately as a means of individual participation. Only when parties are perceived as meaningful vehicles of translating individual interests into political results will people in large numbers turn to parties and give of their time and money. And this will come about only when parties play more decisive roles than they presently do in developing public policies. Thus on two levels—the collective as well as the individual—the American party system, especially as it operates in conjunction with national politics, is less than satisfactory.

The self-satisfaction of Americans with the two-party system may in reality be an exercise in self-delusion. If we have become accustomed to believing that the vast differences inherent in the American social and economic structure can somehow be contained within two broadly based but uneasy coalitions, the Wallace phenomenon of 1968 should give us pause. Rather than creating moderation and thus affording stability, the two-party system may simply have served to mask for too long greater social cleavages than we had thought possible. Pent up for too long, and attenuated by the rapid rush of events, basic social, economic, and racial problems—all intertwined—now overflow the channels artificially forced on them by a two-party system.

The major political institutions of participation—interest groups and political parties—serve well only a small fraction of the body politic. For the rest, they do little to close the vast psychological chasm between the citizen and his government. Beyond the inadequacies of these institutions, moreover, lie other factors—money, communications, and the climate of political expression—which further condition the viability of our mechanisms of political participation. It may be that the modern industrial-technological society is not conducive to meaningful participation and representation within either an interest group or party framework. The answer may lie in the creation of entirely new institutions and mechanisms for participation and representation. American political ingenuity needs to be turned to such a creative task unrestrained by the sacredness of the two-party system.

Part Two

The Political Process: Conditioning Factors

Chapter 6 The Media, Public Relations, and the Political Process

One of the fastest growing industries in the United States today is the communications industry. Americans, like people in the other highly industrialized nations, seem as hungry for information as those in the underdeveloped countries are for food. Television is becoming increasingly ubiquitous, the motion picture business is booming, the advent of paperbacks has created a vast new market for books, and, although consolidations rather than new ventures have recently characterized the newspaper and magazine fields, journalistic publications still command an enormous readership.

Although the communications media devote far more time and attention to entertainment than to public affairs, it is difficult to exaggerate their impact on popular attitudes. For even the most inane comic strip or television program serves to inculcate or at least to reinforce certain social, or antisocial, values. Although the author may have no didactic purposes in mind, he may nonetheless inadvertently be teaching certain lessons—that war is a glorious field of human endeavor, for example, or that obedience to law is in the individual's self-interest because crime does not pay. It is not merely from thoughtful expositions of social problems that individuals are exposed to social attitudes.

The communication of both fact and ideas is, of course, essential for any government, whatever its form may be. One-man rule or one-party rule would be ineffective unless means existed to transmit the decisions of policymakers to those who are to implement them and to those who will be affected by them. In a democratic society, where decision-makers are, at least in theory, supposed to be guided by what the people want, communication is of even greater importance. It is the means through which political leaders may inform themselves about the needs and desires of the people they rule, and it is the means also by which individuals learn about the policies of their government.

In times past, the tools of communication have been confined to word-of-mouth and printing. In modern times, however, there has been a veritable revolution in communications, making it possible for the first time in history to communicate simultaneously with large numbers of people all over the nation and even now all over the world. Moreover, the medium of television possesses a kind of immediacy that involves the audience more directly than any other process of one-way communications has been able to do.[1]

The revolution in communications technology has had a pronounced effect on the political system and the individual's relation to it. The impact may be discerned in fields such as these: relations between government and the mass media; campaigns by pressure groups—and by government as well—to mobilize and manipulate public sentiment; and the use of manipulative techniques in political campaigns.

The Magic Tube   In recent years, television has replaced newspapers as the primary source of news for most Americans. This is a factor of considerable significance because Americans generally are less critical of what they see on television than they are of what they read in the papers. Surveys have

---

[1] For a pioneering analysis of television's impact, see Marshal McLuhan, *Understanding Media* (New York: McGraw-Hill, 1964).

shown that people consider television far more reliable and creditable than newspapers.[2] It seems that for many Americans there is considerable truth to the old adages that seeing is believing and one picture is worth a thousand words.

The credibility of television endows the medium with enormous potential for affecting the political process. At first, television news programs attempted to emulate the impartiality of news presentation supposedly practiced by newspapers. But, as the national network news programs were personalized—with Huntley and Brinkley and with Walter Cronkite—interpretative reporting became the vogue. During coverage of the 1968 election night, there was considerable editorializing in favor of abolishing the electoral college as the specter of George Wallace as a spoiler was the main topic of discussion.

Documentaries, another form of television news, are even doctored. An ABC network show, "Presidential Decision Making," on which Senator Robert Kennedy participated, was criticized for staging portions of what was thought by the television audience to be actually happening. A Chicago station's presentation of a pot party at Northwestern University, as part of a documentary on marijuana, was later found to have been staged. The very selection of topics, whether on straight news programs or specials, invests in the network news staffs considerable influence in affecting the political diet of many Americans.

Yet the question of whether television news programs are biased can be examined on quite another level. Even when television stations try to remain impartial, the result is often programs dominated by presentations of the government's point of view. For much of the news that is carried emanates from Washington, and of that quantity only a small amount consists of hard news: the passage of a bill by Congress, a decision by the Supreme Court, a ruling by an administrative agency, or the death of a political leader. The rest is largely opinion—the secretary of defense or the secretary of state assuring the American people that things are going well in Southeast Asia, or the president telling a news conference that the American economy is fundamentally sound. By acting as a transmission belt for the statements of governmental officials, television presents opinion in the guise of news—not

---

[2] Bernard Rubin, *Political Television* (Belmont, Calif.: Wadsworth, 1967), p. 3, citing data from studies conducted for the Television Information Office. The sponsorship of the studies should be cause for a bit of skepticism; studies commissioned by newspaper interests present a contrary picture.

necessarily its own opinion, to be sure, but nonetheless opinion. The very attempt at impartiality in itself contributes to the presentation of the status quo and the government's point of view.

Newspapers are not basically different in this respect. Their editors and publishers never tire of explaining self-righteously that the expression of opinion is confined to the editorial page, never seeping through to the news pages. Many of them do not even permit a reporter to cast any doubt on an official statement that is known as a certainty to be entirely false because such interpretive reporting might seem like the mere exposition of personal opinion. Washington officials, therefore, often find that it is not difficult to make the media function as an extension of their public relations operations. As long as the front page expresses their point of view, they could not care less what appears on the editorial page, which has a comparatively insignificant readership.

Never was the dilemma better illustrated than in the early 1950s, when Senator Joseph R. McCarthy of Wisconsin was waging his campaign to persuade the American people that their most cherished institutions were riddled with Communists. The more sensational—and the more mendacious—the charges that McCarthy made, the more publicity both he and the charges received. The mere fact that a United States senator had called someone a Communist was considered headline news, even though he might not offer a shred of evidence to buttress the allegation. Although there might be denunciations of his tactics on the editorial pages, the news pages belonged to him, and they were the important ones. On those pages, his grossest defamations were reported without any intimation that there was little reason to take them seriously. Thanks to the press, McCarthy became one of the most powerful men in America. Defamations that no newspaper could print on its own without risk of a ruinous libel judgment could now be carried with impunity, since statements made by congressmen in their official capacity are privileged against legal action, and the privilege extends also to those who report what they said.

If indeed the mass media were responsible for McCarthy's phenomenal rise, they were also responsible for his precipitous fall. Not always, however, can the communications media so effectively, if fortuitously, compensate for the damage they do by disseminating self-serving official statements as news. More typically, the press in effect makes its facilities available to government, and government makes full use of the opportunity to instill the attitudes that it considers proper in the American people.

The Press and Vietnam Such was the case with reporting on Vietnam, at least until 1963. In that year, a group of reporters in Saigon began filing dispatches that were not at all in accord with what Washington was saying about the South Vietnamese government of Ngo Dinh Diem. In contrast with what American officials were saying, the reporters drew a portrait of Diem as an arbitrary despot whose tyrannical tendencies were limited only by his incompetence. Popular feeling against Diem was dangerously high, said the reporters, and the National Liberation Front could not have asked for a more perfect symbol of the government against which they were rallying popular opposition. The administration, however, was unswerving in its continued support of Diem. The reporter whose articles cast the greatest doubt on the wisdom of this policy was David Halberstam because his newspaper, *The New York Times,* is the most influential in the country. So upset was the administration at Halberstam's refutation of its version of events that President Kennedy actually went so far as to intercede with the publisher of *The Times* in an effort to have the reporter withdrawn from Vietnam. Halberstam might be too close to the story and too involved in it, the president suggested; was it perhaps time for him to be given another assignment? The publisher chose to stand by his reporter. The *Times,* he told Kennedy, was quite satisfied with Halberstam's present assignment and had no intention of changing it.[3] Halberstam later won a Pulitzer prize for his reporting from Vietnam.

Far less displeasing to the administration was the reaction of *Time* magazine to the stories on Vietnam filed by its correspondent, Charles Mohr, who saw the situation much as Halberstam did. When he was asked to prepare an exhaustive analysis of how the war was going, Mohr filed a story which began with the words, "The war in Vietnam is being lost." The story never saw the light of day. In its place appeared a highly optimistic assessment of the situation, concocted by staff writers in New York. Adding insult to injury, the managing editor of *Time* wrote an angry denunciation of the American press corps in Saigon, including, presumably, Mohr himself. The reporters who said that the war was going badly, said the editor, were chronic malcontents who never ventured into the Vietnam countryside, preferring instead

---

[3] Halberstam had been scheduled to take a vacation trip outside Vietnam but the publisher, Arthur Ochs Sulzberger, told him to stay there so as to avoid giving the impression that the *Times* was bowing to governmental pressure. David Halberstam, *The Making of a Quagmire* (New York: Random House, 1965), p. 268.

to huddle together at the bar of the Caravelle Hotel in Saigon, interviewing each other. This was too much for Mohr, who left the magazine and joined Halberstam on *The New York Times*.[4]

What the government resented most about reporters like Halberstam and Mohr was precisely what distinguished them as reporters: their instinctive tendency to relate the truth as they perceived it even when this might mean stepping on officials' toes. The government, on the other hand, seemed to think that their proper role was not as independent observers, but as members of a United States team for which the signals were called by officialdom. The team metaphor, in fact, was used by Admiral Harry Felt, commander of all American forces in the Pacific, when he became angered at a question put to him at a press conference by Malcolm Browne of the Associated Press. Felt snapped at Browne, "Why don't you get on the team?"[5] It is doubtful that the framers of the First Amendment had in mind a team effort linking press and government in a common endeavor. Rather, they saw the press as a valuable check on government. They anticipated, in fact, that government would react with hostility to the watchdog activities of the newspapers, and it was for that reason that they tried in the First Amendment to immunize the press against retaliation by government.

Critic or Handmaiden? The relationship between members of the press and government officials often seems closer to collusion than to antagonism. The lazy reporter learns quickly that life can be beautiful if he contents himself with rewriting government handouts. Not only is little effort required for such an endeavor, but also there is no risk of offending officials who may be fertile sources of news in the future. That is often the case in Washington, especially for reporters who are assigned to a comparatively narrow beat—those who cover a single department or agency of government, for example. In such situations, the reporter may not only be reluctant to file a story that contains material critical of one of his regular sources, but he may also be maneuvered into a position in which he is directly used by an agency official to accomplish certain policy purposes.

Considering the nature of the policy process in Washington, it is

[4] The pressures on reporters in Vietnam are discussed in ibid., pp. 269–274.
[5] Ibid., p. 72.

not surprising that government officials try to use reporters in much the same way that they seek to use the leaders of interest groups. The way that Washington functions, it is necessary to build support in many centers of power before new policies can be formulated or, even, old policies implemented. Since publicity is a major tool for the building of such support, the cooperative reporter can become an invaluable ally of the decision-makers, just as the interest group can also contribute to the mobilization of supporters and beneficiaries of a governmental program. Interestingly, both interest groups and the press have had the same label applied to them: the fourth branch of government. This designation carries an implicit recognition that both are integral parts of the political process.

One of the ways that officials use the press is for the purpose of floating trial balloons. A policymaker may, for instance, be hesitant about issuing a new set of regulations with respect to the procedures of his agency lest there be a public storm over his action. Faced with such a problem, he may call in a friendly reporter and disclose to him the new departure that he is contemplating. The reporter writes about this development, however, only on the condition that he not reveal the source of what he has learned. The information is imparted to him on a background basis. He may write that "the government is contemplating" the new policy, or that "officials are considering the desirability" of revamping certain programs. However he phrases it, the important thing is that he write the dispatch on his own responsibility without being able to name the official who has discussed the matter with him as the source of his information.

The reporter finds it hard to say no to such a proposition because that would mean giving up an opportunity to beat his competitors to the punch. From the point of view of the government official, there is everything to gain and absolutely nothing to lose from the background interview he has given. If publication of the story results in a furor over the possibility that the contemplated action will indeed be taken, the official knows that it would be a mistake to act and have to brave the wrath of his critics. If, on the other hand, his trial balloon is not shot down, he can feel free to go ahead as he desires.

There are many variations on the background device. At times the reporter may be told that he has permission to attribute the story, but only to anonymous high government officials or governmental sources. In time, the experienced newspaper reader will be able to decipher many of the code terms. He will understand that "a completely reliable source in the Defense Department" can only be the Secretary of Defense. "A high government official in an unparalleled position to understand the President's thinking" has to be the president himself. As long as his name is not used, however, the official has often succeeded in what he was trying to do. If absolute anonymity is desired, he may insist on no attribution at all.[6]

Newsmen have even served as unofficial emissaries for the government. John Scali, an ABC network reporter, took on the delicate mission of ascertaining Russia's probable response to the measures the Kennedy administration had devised to meet the Cuban missile crisis. As James Reston, *The New York Times* columnist, has said about foreign policy matters, "The diplomats are the unpaid stringers for the reporters, the reporters the unpaid tipsters for the diplomats."[7] Reporters are in every sense participants in the policymaking process, rather than mere observers.

This is hardly a recent development in American history. In the first tumultuous years after the ratification of the Constitution, newspapers were on the very firing line as the struggle between the Federalists and the Jeffersonians began. Leading Federalists often went so far as to finance the establishment of newspapers to serve as propaganda vehicles for their point of view. Alexander Hamilton, for example, helped set up the *Gazette of the United States* as an unofficial publicity arm of the Federalist leadership.[8] It was not long before the opposition, too, saw the necessity for a propaganda outlet, with Jefferson and Madison acting as midwives for the *National Gazette.* So slavish were these two newspapers in serving the parties that had financed their establishment that they were almost worthless as sources of news.

The Modern Newspaper   As with many other modern economic enterprises, the newspapers aim at a mass market, and the result, especially aggravated in recent years, has

[6] For an extended discussion of background conferences and the like, see Douglass Cater, *The Fourth Branch of Government* (New York: Vintage Books, 1965), pp. 129–40. At the time that he wrote his book, Cater was the Washington Bureau Chief of the magazine, *The Reporter.* He later resigned to become a special assistant to President Johnson, and thus he became qualified to be referred to in background stories as "a reliable White House source."

[7] James Reston, *The Artillery of the Press: Its Influence on American Foreign Policy* (New York: Harper and Row, 1967), p. 74.

[8] William N. Chambers, *Political Parties in a New Nation* (New York: Oxford University Press, 1963), p. 41.

been an orgy of concentration and almost monopolization. Today the population of the United States is double what it was in 1909. Yet the number of daily newspapers has shrunk by more than a third. A steadily growing number of cities are served by only a single newspaper. In just a few years, New York City witnessed the death of the *World-Telegram,* the *Sun,* the *Journal-American,* the *Daily Mirror,* and the highly respected *Herald Tribune*.[9] Today that city of eight million people has only two morning papers and one afternoon newspaper.

To a discouraging extent, newspapers are losing their individual character, relying increasingly on syndicated material. Soon they may reach the point where it will be possible to distinguish one from another only by reading reports of local crime, for in this field free enterprise still reigns supreme. In their efforts to attract a mass audience, the newspapers have come to emphasize entertainment features at the expense of news coverage. Their pages are crowded with comic strips, recipes, advice to the lovelorn, contest material, and other such significant bits of Americana. For every so-called drugstore in which it is difficult to find any drugs, there seems to be at least one newspaper in which news reports appear only when there is simply nothing else available to fill the empty space around the supermarket ads. And what news there is about national, not to mention international, politics is almost always not from the paper's own correspondent but, rather, from one of the major wire services, Associated Press or United Press International. Since the wire services send their news to thousands of papers with almost as many editorial points of view, they tend to avoid interpretive reporting and concentrate on simply relating events as they occur. These characteristics of wire service news are accentuated by the time pressure that AP and UPI place on their reporters, with the result that such reports often lack the perspective needed to understand events.

Only a few newspapers feel that they can afford a staff of reporters of their own to cover the major news areas of the nation. *The New York Times* is in a class by itself in the thoroughness of its political coverage, and extensive bureaus are also maintained in Washington by papers such as the *Milwaukee Journal* and *St. Louis Post-Dispatch.* A world of difference separates such newspapers, and those published in Washington, from most others, which either use their Capitol Hill

[9] Of the newspapers listed, the *World-Telegram, Journal-American,* and *Herald Tribune,* were themselves the products of consolidations.

reporters to provide news of exclusively local interest or else have no Washington correspondent at all.[10]

The increasing dependence of newspapers on syndicated material has vastly expanded the audience for the Washington columnists. Columnists like James Reston, Joseph Alsop, and, until his retirement, Walter Lippmann have a large readership for their opinion pieces. So do columnists like the team of Rowland Evans and Robert Novak whose speciality is the inside story; without peer in this regard was the late Drew Pearson. Although the inside columns are often exercises in creative writing, more frequently they reflect the point of view of someone in government who wants to get a certain version of events before the public. The power of these columnists is greatly feared in Washington, as well it might be. It was Pearson, for example, who brought down Senator Thomas J. Dodd of Connecticut through a long series of columns exhaustively documenting Dodd's financial manipulations, including his misuse of campaign funds.[11] Some of the most widely syndicated columns also appear in one or another of the daily newspapers published in Washington and, therefore, are part of the regular reading diet of government officials both high and low. Their impact on official thinking is considerable; in fact, such columns may have a greater impact on officialdom than on the reading public. In addition, they often serve to inform one set of government officials about the views of another set of government officials concerned with the same problem. So enormous is the governmental apparatus that without the communications links provided by the daily press, the instances of officials working at cross-purposes with each other would be even more numerous than they are today.

Just as the newspapers serve many of the purposes of the politician in office, television, too, can suit official purposes admirably. Weekend interview programs on television provide a highly effective communications device for government officials. The audience would be small indeed for a straight speech by the secretary of state. Provide a panel of inquiring newsmen, however, and there is enough drama and even combativeness to draw a respectable audience of viewers. All three

---

[10] A number of newspapers break away, at least to some extent, from complete reliance on AP and UPI by subscribing to the New York Times News Service or to the even more recent Times-Post Service, established by the *Los Angeles Times* and the *Washington Post*.

[11] Pearson obtained his material from two disaffected former employees of Dodd who took advantage of their access to the files in Dodd's office to copy thousands of incriminating documents.

major television networks provide precisely such a format for political interviews. The National Broadcasting Company has "Meet the Press," the Columbia Broadcasting System, "Face the Nation," and the American Broadcasting Company, "Issues and Answers." The politician is more than willing to put up with the barbed questions of reporters; that is a small price to pay for access to a national forum at no financial cost.

On the whole, there is a serious question as to whether the media effectively perform their role as a watchdog over governmental actions. It is true that the media's coverage of the war in Vietnam eventually helped to swing a large segment of public opinion against the Johnson administration's conduct of it. But a large share of credit for creating the credibility gap must be attributed to Johnson himself, who was so inept at handling the press. To the extent that the media fail in their role, the political process is deprived of an important balance wheel. The danger is not only that government often escapes criticism; the more basic fault is that the media do not provide an adequate level of intelligible information on the issues of public policy. The field is thus left open to those whose motivations are decidedly ones of self-interest: pressure groups and government officials and agencies.

The Rise of Public Relations

When government officials use the press to help condition popular attitudes, they are engaged in public relations. The term public relations and the concept it embodies are both of recent vintage. They appear to be inevitable adjuncts of the mass society, in which manipulation of human behavior and the engineering of consent have been elevated to the level of a science.

Business organizations were the first to make use of public relations techniques. In the first decade of this century, several large corporations began hiring men to help them put their best foot forward in the press. Prior to this time, the corporations had worked on the assumption that the less publicity they had, the better they could do their work. Secrecy was recognized as an ally. Now there was a sudden realization that publicity was a two-edged sword. Used judiciously, it could be a potent weapon in the corporate arsenal. A fever pitch of corporate activity was quickly reached. The gas and electric utilities became so conscious of public relations that in 1927 they were reported to have spent $25 million to $30 million for advertising alone.[12] Even at this early date, a variety of techniques that are still in common use today had already been developed. Speakers' bureaus made people available to clubs and other organizations to tell the industry's story; news releases and even prefabricated editorials were provided to the press; and, in an effort to head off proposals for public ownership of power facilities, money was paid to professors to write studies that embodied exclusively positive thinking about the utilities. Taking a cue from the utilities, the National Association of Manufacturers also began to place considerable emphasis on public relations. A director was hired to take charge of this phase of the NAM's work, and between 1933 and 1937 the amount spent for public relations rose from 7 percent of the NAM's budget to 55 percent.[13]

So great did business's demand for public relations people become that an entirely new vocation of skilled technicians came into being. Colleges and universities, whose educational programs were becoming more and more closely attuned to the needs of corporations, began offering courses in public relations side by side with courses in the liberal arts. Soon academic majors in public relations were also added. The new generation of public relations practitioners founded two professional organizations to represent their interests, the American Public Relations Association, in 1944, and the Public Relations Society of America, in 1948.

Government did not lag far behind industry in its appreciation of what the art of public relations might accomplish. The first field to which these arts were applied was wartime propaganda. During World War I, the Committee on Public Information was created to drum up support for the cause of the Allies. Many of the techniques of this committee, known as the Creel committee,[14] were also used in World War II by a new propaganda agency, the Office of War Information. Although the OWI was abolished at the end of the war, it was reincarnated during the cold war years as the United States Information Agency, which still remains in existence to expound the positions of the government and to attempt to create for the United States a favorable impression abroad. USIA, however, is forbidden to propagandize at home.

---

[12] Stanley Kelley, Jr., *Professional Public Relations and Political Power* (Baltimore: Johns Hopkins Press, 1966), pp. 9, 22.
[13] Ibid., pp. 23–24.
[14] After its chairman, George Creel.

Congress finds it easier to prevent the USIA from manipulating public opinion in the United States than to curb the public relations activities of governmental agencies that were not created with a propaganda purpose in mind. When it comes to agencies with a general governmental purpose, Congress seems to feel that it is caught on the horns of a dilemma. On the one hand, it recognizes that facilities must be available for agencies that are administering specific programs to respond to both public and congressional inquiries. It is ostensibly for that purpose that offices of public information, public affairs, and the like have been created. Yet, it is cognizant that these same offices are available to the administration for the quite different purpose of propagandizing. The unsatisfactory compromise under which it generally operates is to give the public information offices considerable leeway, pulling in the reins only when especially brazen behavior is revealed.

Engineering Consent The extensive use of public relations techniques by both interest groups and government means, as a student of this development has phrased it, that we have moved a long step away from "the concept of the consent of the governed to that of the engineering of consent." [15] The patron saint of public relations in the United States, Edward L. Bernays, understood, as far back as 1928, that the engineering of consent and the manipulation of opinion are the special skills of public relations men. Bernays wrote as follows about the concept, "the voice of the people," of which democratic political theorists have made so much:

> The voice of the people expresses the mind of the people, and that mind is made up for it by group leaders in whom it believes and by those persons who understand the manipulation of opinion. It is composed of inherited prejudices and symbols and clichés and verbal formulas supplied them by the leaders. Fortunately, the sincere and gifted politician is able, by the instrument of propaganda, to mold and form the will of the people.[16]

Bernays spoke about "the sincere and gifted politician." He did not explain, however, how the skills could be kept from the insincere and unscrupulous demagogues, petty tyrants, and tyrants who were not so

[15] Kelley, *Professional Public Relations*, p. 229.
[16] Edward L. Bernays, *Propaganda* (New York: Horace Liveright, 1928), p. 92.

petty. In actual fact, the techniques of public relations and mass manipulation have been of crucial importance to the most noisome dictatorships of the twentieth century.

The same techniques are available today, for money, to groups that want, for whatever reason, to shape the minds of people. Although the skills of the public relations practitioner may be applauded, his motives often bespeak an utter contempt for the people. During the course of one public relations campaign, such an attitude was well expressed in an interoffice memo. Having laid the groundwork for the campaign, said the memo, "now we are ready to decide which magazine should perpetrate it upon the defenseless public." [17]

Political Public Relations If public relations techniques have well served the purposes of both governmental officials and interest groups, they have been even more useful to candidates in political campaigns. This has introduced a new element of irrationality into a process that had never been distinguished for appeals to reason. Long before the advent of the public relations man and the advertising man, it was easy to see that election campaigns were not educational campaigns designed to inform the voter and thus increase the likelihood that he would choose well on election day. Instead, vote buying, intimidation, and all kinds of fraud were features of American elections from the very beginning. Elections, moreover, even when they were free of corruption, have hardly been sportsmanlike contests between candidates who wanted nothing more than to communicate their ideas to the electorate. Far from this, appeals to passion and prejudice and fear have been widely used. The development of mass media and the growth of the public relations industry have thus meant more of a quantitative change than a qualitative change, making possible the manipulation of voter opinion on a larger scale than ever before.

The manipulation of public opinion has, in fact, become institutionalized to a significant degree. Recent decades have even seen the sprouting of public relations firms that specialize in merchandising and packaging candidates. It is such firms which are expert at creating a favorable

---

[17] Quoted in Andrew Hacker, "Pressure Politics in Pennsylvania: The Truckers v. The Railroads," in Alan F. Westin, ed., *The Uses of Power* (New York: Harcourt, Brace, and World, 1962), pp. 324–76.

THE MEDIA, PUBLIC RELATIONS, AND THE POLITICAL PROCESS

image for the candidate—an image which only seldom bears any significant relationship to the reality. Such techniques, which are priced extremely high, were at first considered a luxury for all except presidential candidates. Today, however, they are used almost as a matter of course in any election contest where large numbers of voters must be reached and where the use of the mass media is therefore indispensable.

Off-year elections have become almost as much of a bonanza for public relations firms as presidential elections. In 1966, for example, Ronald Reagan won the governship of California with the help of a public relations firm, and Governor Nelson Rockefeller of New York was reelected with similar assistance. The services of the firm that represented Reagan were evidently available to the highest bidder, irrespective of political ideology. For the same company that promoted Reagan, a conservative, in 1966, had worked for a California liberal Republican, former Senator Thomas Kuchel, four years earlier. Ironically, the campaign manager of Kuchel's opponent in that election was none other than Ronald Reagan! Even more striking is the fact that the same firm, Spencer-Roberts, had gone so far as to call Reagan a "right-wing extremist" in 1964, when he was helping Senator Goldwater defeat Governor Rockefeller in the California presidential primary.[18]

In his attempt for reelection in 1966, Rockefeller also saw the need, as he had in the California presidential primary in 1964, for outside public relations talent. He hired a combination advertising and public relations firm called Jack Tinker & Partners, one of a group of similar concerns operating under the high-sounding name of Interpublic Group of Companies, Inc.[19] Among other triumphs, Tinker had been responsible for the catchy Alka-Seltzer commercials, which in 1965-66 had done so much to boost the sales of that product.

In 1968, another political public relations star was born in the person of Joe Napolitan, whom one writer has characterized as *"the complete professional."* [20] Unlike some others in the field, Napolitan does place ideology over money: "I work only for Democrats and only for Democrats I like." [21] The creative team rapidly assembled by Napolitan

---

[18] Jack Langguth, "Political Fun and Games in California," *New York Times Magazine,* 16 October 1966, p. 27.
[19] Tom Buckley, "The 3 Men Behind Rockefeller," *New York Times Magazine,* 30 October 1966, p. 137. Interpublic had handled the Goldwater campaign in 1964. Theodore H. White, *The Making of the President 1964* (New York: The New American Library, 1966), p. 383.
[20] Thomas J. Fleming, "Selling the Product Named Hubert Humphrey," *New York Times Magazine,* 13 October 1968, p. 47, italics in original.
[21] Quoted in ibid., p. 139.

following the Democratic convention in late August was the key factor in helping Humphrey close the large gap that existed in the early part of the campaign between him and Nixon. That Humphrey barely missed winning was more because of the divisiveness of the Democratic party, resulting from the Vietnam issue and the events in Chicago, than because of Napolitan's efforts.

Television and Political Campaigning

The public relations men who specialize in political campaigning find the transition from commercial advertising to political advertising not at all jarring. Most of them, in fact, learned the principles of opinion manipulation when they were helping to sell automobiles, cosmetics, and household nostrums to the American consumer. When asked how he felt about advertising a politician, one of Napolitan's men replied: "It's just like any other kind of product. . . . The candidate has his good points and his drawbacks. We try to put him in the best available light." [22] Sloganeering, indeed, is one of the standard practices perfected by public relations firms for the use of television during political campaigns. After coming to the conclusion that few besides those who are already committed to a candidate will choose to watch a political speech on television, the advertising and public relations advisers in the Eisenhower campaign of 1952 designed a promotional program that would emphasize spot announcements rather than set speeches. This approach had the advantage of allowing the candidate to slip up on television viewers when they were in pursuit of entertainment rather than political appeals. The metaphor of slip up, in fact, was employed by a public relations consultant to the Republican National Committee. Speaking of the problem of reaching those who are uninterested in politics, he said: "You have got to slip up on them through the broadcasting media. You have to catch them when they are looking or listening to something else, if you want to reach them at all." [23] Spot announcements and five-minute trailers are, of course, ideally suited to this purpose since, as the same consultant put it, the members of the television audience "have to listen before they can get up and switch them off."

[22] Ibid., p. 147.
[23] Address by Carrol Newton, of Batton, Barton, Durstine, and Osborn, to a meeting of Republican state chairmen, June 1958, quoted in Stanley Kelley, Jr., "Campaign Debates: Some Facts and Issues," *Public Opinion Quarterly* 26 (Fall 1962): 357.

Still another consideration was behind the decision to avoid lengthy television speeches by Mr. Eisenhower in 1952. Since such speeches are usually broadcast during the time normally occupied by the most popular entertainment programs, the audience may resent the disruption of the evening routine and take out the resentment on the candidate who has appeared, uninvited, in their living rooms. When one of the programs in the "I Love Lucy" series was cancelled to make room for a campaign address by Eisenhower's opponent, Adlai Stevenson, one irate viewer actually sent the following telegram to Stevenson: "I Like Ike and I Love Lucy. Drop dead." [24]

Ever since, the emphasis has been on the short, punchy, and commercial type of approach, rather than simply using television for the ordinary campaign speech. In 1964 the Democrats used an advertising agency which conceived some very hard-hitting spot announcements. While operating under general instructions from the Democratic high command to hit hard at Goldwater, the agency produced two spots which, although only shown once each because of the furor they raised, succeeded admirably in putting Goldwater on the defensive.

The first pictured a little girl joyfully plucking petals from a daisy; the film then faded through her eyes and showed a countdown of an atomic test. It concluded by dissolving into a mushroom cloud. The second commercial, broadcast ten days later, showed another little girl licking an ice cream cone. In the background could be heard a motherly voice intoning about strontium 90 and pointing out that Goldwater had been against the test ban treaty. A final creation, shown over and over during the campaign, pictured a social security card being torn in half.[25]

In 1968, the Nixon campaign featured, again and again, a five-minute show with film clips of the war in Vietnam and violence in American cities. Dubbed in, in calm, reassuring tones, was the voice of Nixon, giving some of the best lines from his Miami acceptance speech. One Humphrey spot featured a mother and her young baby. After expressing fear for the future of the child, the announcer recited the promises that Humphrey had made to set things right. At the end, the baby could be heard uttering a contented sigh.

Another spot advertisement of the Democrats sought to exploit what many considered to be one of Nixon's weak points—his selection of the

---

[24] Richard S. Salant, "The Television Debates: A Revolution That Deserves a Future," *Public Opinion Quarterly* 26 (Fall 1962): 342.
[25] White, *The Making of the President 1964*, p. 384.

relatively unknown Governor of Maryland, Spiro Agnew, as his running mate. Agnew had speedily developed a reputation for putting his foot in his mouth, which the press was quick to exploit. The commercial flashed on the screen read: "Agnew—for Vice President?" Laughter greeted the video question and, as it faded, the screen next showed these words: "This would be funny if it weren't so serious. . . ."

To critics who express doubt that complicated political issues can be compressed into five-minute, one-minute, or twenty-second spots, the answer has been that at least the unwilling, uninterested voter is being exposed to something. But, by playing to the weaknesses of the American electorate, the parties, the advertising agencies, and the networks are going a long way toward insuring that the voter will never be anything else. As Professor Kelley has said, "The rational interests of candidates and parties lead them to encourage irrationality in the electorate."[26]

Television Debates

The one major departure in the use of television during a major political campaign was the series of debates between Kennedy and Nixon in 1960. For, in bringing together the two adversaries, the tendency of voters to tune in on only friendly political telecasts was overcome. Because of the unusual character of the debates, a much greater audience was exposed to the two candidates than would have been the case normally. The average television audience for all four debates was measured at seventy-one million people.[27] And apparently the debates did have an impact on the voting. A survey by Elmo Roper reported that about 5 percent of the voters indicated that their final decision had been solely because of the debates. These voters split for Kennedy by about a three-to-one margin, resulting in a net gain of about a million and a half votes, far more than the 113,000 by which he won.[28]

Although there was considerable hesitation on the part of many to characterize the Kennedy-Nixon confrontations as genuine debates, it did represent some effort at giving the electorate a slightly more rational way of assessing the candidates. There was a widespread feel-

[26] For a general summary, see Stanley Kelley, Jr., *Political Campaigning* (Washington: The Brookings Institution, 1960), pp. 27–33.
[27] Salant, "The Television Debates," p. 338. The fact that all three networks carried the debates simultaneously undoubtedly was a factor.
[28] Ibid., p. 341.

ing at the time that similar debates would become a fixture of future presidential campaigns. At an early press conference, President Kennedy stated that he would debate in 1964.[29] Nixon said in 1962 that "debates between the Presidential candidates on television are a fixture, and in all the elections in the future we are going to have debates between the candidates."[30]

Such prophecy has not been borne out. In order to have the 1960 debates, Congress had suspended Section 315 of the Federal Communications Act. The provision of the act for equal time required that if one candidate received free television or radio time, all candidates would have to be treated similarly. This would have meant granting equal time to about a dozen of the minor presidential candidates, something the networks were loathe to do. But, when Congress again sought to suspend Section 315 for the 1964 election, an insurmountable obstacle was encountered.

Unlike President Kennedy, Lyndon Johnson was reported to have felt that the debate forum was not as suitable to him as were other means of reaching the public. Nevertheless, both Houses of Congress passed bills which would have suspended Section 315. Without publicly indicating his disapproval, President Johnson succeeded in getting the Democratic leadership in the Senate to sponsor a motion to table a conference report on the bill. A conference had become necessary because each House had passed a different bill. The tabling motion passed 44–41, with only Democrats in support.[31] In this way, any possibility of debates in 1964 was eliminated.

The American electorate was again deprived of a face-to-face confrontation of the major candidates in 1968. While Humphrey and Wallace were willing to engage in a three-way debate, Nixon remained adamant, claiming that to so dignify Wallace's candidacy would be to demean the two-party system. After a long delay, the House passed the necessary suspension of Section 315, but Republicans in the Senate threatened a minor filibuster at a point during the second week in October when both the Senate and the House were desperately trying to close up shop so that members could go home to campaign. Although Humphrey responded by offering to buy the television time (under such circumstances, Section 315 would have been inapplicable), Nixon

---

[29] Earl Mazo et al., *The Great Debates* (Santa Barbara, Calif.: Center for the Study of Democratic Institutions, 1962), p. 7.
[30] Quoted in ibid., p. 13.
[31] Congressional Quarterly Service, *Congressional Quarterly Almanac,* vol. XX (Washington Congressional Quarterly, Inc.), pp. 412–14.

steadfastly persisted in his refusal. The future of television debates—the expectation that they could contribute to raising the level of campaigns—remains very much in doubt.

News management, manipulation of opinion, and the use of public relations techniques in politics all bear heavily on the integrity of a modern democratic society. It may be that politics in a mass-culture, mass-media society in the nuclear age can be carried on in no other way. The realization that democracy in the town-meeting style is a long-lost myth can at least alert one to the role of communication in the political system—its implications and its dangers.

Chapter 7 Money and Politics

Since decisions made by government have important financial consequences for individuals and groups, it is only natural that those who are directly affected by public policies will try by every means to influence those policies in a direction favorable to themselves. The most effective methods for influencing governmental policy all involve the expenditure of money. The money may be used to help put a particular candidate in office and thus make him beholden to his benefactor. Or it may be spent for the purpose of generating pressures on governmental officials to make certain decisions rather than others. Either way, the problems presented for democracy are obvious. The traditional premise of democracy is that among the individuals who comprise a nation there should be equality of political power. It is this premise that underlay the Supreme Court's endorsement of the principle that electoral districts should be carved out on the basis of one man, one vote. The unequal distribution of wealth in our society, however, creates anything but equality with respect to the influence that various individuals can have on government, apart from casting a vote.

Those who put money into the political process, either as campaign contributions or for lobbying purposes, may well think of the funds they have parted with not as an expenditure, but, rather, as a prudent investment. Since it is through the political system that lucrative advantages are conferred and sizable economic resources distributed, the investment, if it is wisely made, can be expected to yield large dividends. The $300 million that was spent on all political campaigns in 1968, for instance, is an extremely small sum when compared with the nearly $300 billion spent by federal, state, and local governmental organizations in the same year.

The interrelationship of money and politics goes back a long way. Political entities as different from one another as ancient Rome, the republics of medieval Italy, and England all provide examples of the power and influence that money can buy; and, even in the Golden Age of Athenian democracy, elections were not entirely free from corruption.[1] In the United States, the first overt use of money to influence the course of politics evidently took the form of subsidizing newspapers to serve as vehicles of party propaganda. With the extension of the suffrage in many states after 1824, the amount of money needed to win an election increased as did the brazenness of the tactics employed to raise it. John Quincy Adams recorded an instance in which he was approached, while still President, to contribute to an election campaign in Kentucky in 1828. He noted a "proposition to me to contribute $5,000 or $10,000 to carry the election of a governor and legislature of Kentucky . . . by the circulation of newspapers, pamphlets, and handbills." According to Adams, the practice he described was already entirely commonplace.[2]

What makes the present situation different is the drastic increase in the amount of money that it takes to make a dent in the political system. It was relatively easy to do so as recently as 1912, when expenditures in the presidential election campaign, at least as officially reported, came to less than $3 million. That figure is strikingly low when com-

---

[1] Louise Overacker, *Money in Elections* (New York: Macmillan, 1932), pp. 5–19.
[2] Quoted in Jasper B. Shannon, *Money and Politics* (New York: Random House, 1959), p. 16.

pared with the nearly $35 million reported in 1964.[3] The growth of the electorate, new campaigning technology, and the astronomical cost of television time have combined to create an entirely new situation.

The Big Contributor Even when campaign costs were far lower than they are today, candidates were inclined to rely on a relatively small number of wealthy contributors, rather than to seek a large number of small contributions. In support of the presidential candidacy of James Buchanan in 1850, August Belmont, of the Rothschild banking interests, made a contribution of $10,000. So financially indispensable did he make himself to the newly organized Democratic National Committee that he was chosen to be its chairman.[4] No one has ever probably put it better than David Davis, a close adviser to Lincoln during the 1860 campaign and later appointed by Lincoln to the Supreme Court: *"Men work better with money in hand. . . . I believe in God's Providence in this Election, but at the same time we should keep our powder dry."* [5]

The narrow base of political contributions persists to this day. More than half of the money raised by party committees operating at the national level consists of contributions of $500 or more. In 1964, there were about 10,000 people in this category [6]—a minuscule portion, indeed, of an electorate that totaled 110 million persons.

The major political parties, moreover, do not seem overly concerned about this state of affairs. Quite to the contrary, there have been entirely new approaches to party fund raising that put even greater emphasis than before on large contributions. The most celebrated innovation along these lines was the creation by the Democratic party, during the Kennedy administration, of the so-called President's Club. There was only a single qualification for membership in the club: a $1,000 contribution to the Democratic party. By 1964, fully 4,000 persons had chosen to join. Some undoubtedly were influenced by the fact that

---

[3] Based on figures in *Congress and the Nation, 1945–1964* (Washington: Congressional Quarterly Service, 1965), p. 1536, and Herbert E. Alexander, *Financing the 1964 Election* (Princeton: Citizens' Research Foundation, 1966), p. 8. Nearly $40 million in spending was reported for the 1968 presidential election.
[4] Shannon, *Money and Politics,* p. 21.
[5] Quoted in ibid., p. 23, italics in original.
[6] Alexander, *Financing the 1964 Election,* p. 86.

members of the President's Club had been wined and dined in the past at White House parties and, also, given policy briefings by high-level administration officials. But snob appeal may not have been the only attraction, at least to those who were involved in business dealings with the federal government. No doubt many of them joined on the assumption, or at least with the hope, that they were making a good investment. Not to be outdone, the Republicans formed their own Congressional Boosters Club. Although membership in this club, too, could be purchased only with a $1,000 check, the Republicans could not hope to raise nearly as much as the Democrats since the opposition party is never in as good a position to repay favors as the party in power.

Creation of the President's Club was not the only effort by the Democrats to fill their campaign coffers by taking advantage of the fact that they controlled the White House. For years both parties had been selling advertising space in the program books that they distributed at the national conventions. For some time, the cost of an ad had been $5,000 a page with most of the space purchased by large corporations which wanted to be remembered in days to come. In 1964, the Democrats raised the ante, boosting the price of an advertising page to $15,000. No evidence was adduced to show that the cost of printing convention program books had risen threefold. Rather, it seems clear that with Mr. Johnson in the White House and expected to remain there for at least four more years, the Democrats thought that corporations whose earnings depended largely on governmental actions would not choose to be penny-wise and pound-foolish. They were right: the advertisements brought in a total of $1½ million.

So successful was the venture, in fact, that the Democrats decided there was no reason to wait four years for the next national convention to issue another publication with abundant space for advertisements costing $15,000 a page. In late 1965, they issued a book under the title, *Toward An Age of Greatness*. The net profit was $900,000, earmarked for use in the 1966 congressional elections. Although federal law prohibits corporations from contributing to political campaigns, the possibility that a Democratic attorney general would file suit against corporations that had been persuaded by the Democratic party to provide financial support for Democratic candidates seemed remote, at best. It was no surprise, therefore, when the Department of Justice announced that it had come to the carefully considered conclusion that "the facts within our knowledge do not demonstrate a violation." Public reaction to the whole episode was, however, sharply unfavorable; and, in the face of biting attacks in the press, the Democrats decided that the money raised would not be used for campaign purposes, but for a bipartisan registration drive.[7] One may be certain, however, that this will not be the last of the efforts to provide government contractors with an opportunity to express their appreciation in a practical way.

Campaign Contributions: Ineffective Regulations

Attempts to diminish the impact of money on political campaigns are perennial in American politics. Yet there has been only a minimum of federal legislation on the subject. In 1907, Congress did prohibit corporations from contributing to the campaign funds of any candidates for federal office. The revelation two years earlier that the New York Life Insurance Company had given $48,000 to Theodore Roosevelt for his presidential campaign in 1904 had provided the impetus for this legislation, and the Senate committee that reported the measure could declare that the "evils of the use of money in connection with political elections are so generally recognized that [it is] unnecessary to make any arguments in favor of the general purpose of this measure."[8] The reformers, however, wanted to do more than merely exclude corporations from the field of campaign finance. They decided, therefore, to press for a statute that would compel public disclosure of campaign contributions, thus eliminating transactions under the table. The result of their agitation was the enactment in 1910 of another statute requiring that itemized statements of receipts and expenditures be filed within thirty days of an election by the treasurer of every political committee that operated in more than a single state. Since 1910, three other federal laws have been passed to deal with various aspects of the problem: the Corrupt Practices Act of 1925, the Hatch Act of 1940,[9]

---

[7] Ibid., p. 103.

[8] Quoted in James K. Pollock, Jr., *Party Campaign Funds* (New York: Alfred A. Knopf, 1926), p. 35.

[9] This statute is frequently referred to as the second Hatch Act because it took the form of amendments to an earlier statute that had also been introduced by Senator Hatch.

and the Taft-Hartley Act of 1947. This series of legislative enactments means that in federal elections the following provisions on campaign contributions and campaign spending are in force:

1. Both corporations and labor unions are prohibited from contributing money to political campaigns.
2. Campaign committees must make quarterly reports on the money they receive and the money they spend. Included in each report must be a listing of all persons who have contributed more than $100. No more than $3 million may be spent by any campaign committee in any one calendar year.
3. Candidates for seats in the House of Representatives may spend no more than $5,000 in their election campaigns, and the expenditures of candidates for the Senate may not exceed $25,000.
4. No individual may contribute more than $5,000 a year to any one campaign committee.
5. Civil servants may not be solicited for campaign contributions.

In addition to these federal regulations, forty-three states have their own statutes to regulate the financing of campaigns.[10] When taken together, the federal and state legislation on political finance seems to constitute an impressive effort to cope with the problem. The appearance, however, is almost entirely deceptive. For example, the $3-million limit on spending in presidential campaigns is easily avoided through the creation of a number of different committees, each of which is entitled to spend up to the statutory maximum. Moreover, the $5,000 limitation on individual contributions is also circumvented with no difficulty by having other members of the family make contributions or by making the maximum contribution to several different campaign committees. To make matters still worse, corporations may not be allowed to contribute to campaigns, but there is no law to prevent their executives from giving. And although labor unions may not make contributions, separate committees sponsored by labor, such as the AFL-CIO Committee on Political Education, can and do provide financial support to candidates they favor. Still another loophole is that candidates do not have to report the considerable amounts that they spend for personnel, traveling, and subsistence. Lastly, the ceilings on cam-

---

[10] Based on Herbert E. Alexander and Laura L. Denny, *Regulation of Political Finance* (Berkeley, Calif.: Institute of Governmental Studies, 1966, published jointly with the Citizens' Research Foundation, Princeton, New Jersey), pp. 41–47.

paign spending do not apply to primary elections. This is one of the gravest defects in the array of statutes, for, in safe constituencies and in one-party states, the primary election and not the general election is the one that counts, and it is therefore only in the primary campaign that large sums of money are spent. It is probably no exaggeration to conclude, as one scholar has done, that the restraining effect of the legislation is "purely illusory." [11] Legislators—both state and national —have demonstrated over the years little inclination to bite too hard the hands that feed them.

Certainly the laws that are on the books have not resulted in a reversal of the trend toward heavier and heavier campaign spending. In 1952, approximately $140 million was spent on political campaigns at all levels. This amount rose to $155 million in 1956, $175 million in 1960, an even $200 million in 1964, and $300 million in 1968, all figures being estimates, since exact costs are almost impossible to calculate.

There are some political leaders who are convinced that much of the money that is spent has little effect on the outcome of the election. This realization, however, seldom results in any agonizing reappraisal of campaign budgets. James A. Farley, former Chairman of the Democratic National Committee, once explained why this is so. "I know that half of what is spent is wasted," he said. "The only trouble is, I don't know which half." [12] The half that is not wasted often makes the difference between defeat and victory in congressional elections, not to mention municipal, county, and statewide elections. Presidential elections, however, present a somewhat more complicated picture. It seems that from 1904 through 1928, money was indeed the crucial factor, and the candidate who spent the most was invariably the winner.[13] But the correlation broke down completely in 1932, 1936, 1940, and 1944, for Franklin Roosevelt, in each of his four election victories, was heavily outspent by the Republicans. Likewise, Harry Truman won in 1948 though the Democratic campaign cost considerably less than that of the Republicans. Since that time, the party that spent more won in 1952, 1956, 1960, and 1968; the side that spent less winning in 1964. Thus it is safe to say that neither party can expect to win a presidential election solely on the basis of the amount of money it can raise and spend, for the right candidate at the right time may be more than

---

[11] V. O. Key, Jr., *Politics, Parties, and Pressure Groups*, 5th ed. (New York: Thomas Y. Crowell, 1964), p. 513.
[12] Philip M. Stern, "The Money in Politics," *Progressive* (July 1962): 15.
[13] Alexander Heard, *The Costs of Democracy* (Chapel Hill: The University of North Carolina Press, 1960), p. 17.

enough to make the difference. Yet neither party can overlook the fact that great sums of money are needed to mount the kinds of campaigns—given the costs of television—that party managers think are necessary.

The trend toward increasingly higher campaign expenditures also results in a natural selection of wealthy men as candidates. A large hurdle will already have been cleared if the candidate himself can give a big boost to his campaign chest. This factor is of even greater significance in elections for congressional or local officials. At these levels, with relatively small constituencies, a well-heeled candidate may, himself, be able to outspend what his opponent can manage to raise.

Spending Patterns Almost invariably, the Republican strategists have more money to work with than the Democrats do. The reason is simply the affinity of big businessmen and other wealthy individuals for the party that has long been referred to as the party of business. Only in recent years has the gap between the amounts spent by the two parties been narrowing, as a result of organized labor's fund-raising efforts, mostly on behalf of Democratic candidates. In 1960, the combined amount spent by the Democratic party and organized labor finally, for the first time, exceeded Republican financial expenditures. In 1964, however, the Republican predominance reasserted itself, and in 1968 the gap became even wider.

The big business bias of Republican contributors is borne out by the statistics covering individual contributors. Only in 1964—because of Johnson's efforts at reaching a consensus with the business community—have America's wealthiest families favored the Democrats. In 1960, there were some 95 persons who made total contributions in excess of $10,000; of these, 60 gave to Republicans and 35 to Democrats. But, in 1964, of the 130 large donors, 65 contributed to Democrats, 52 to Republicans, and 13 hedged their bet by supporting both parties. In dollar amounts, these contributions in the two election years were distributed as follows:

Year	Republicans	Democrats
1964	$ 900,000	$1,211,600
1960	1,000,000	470,000

MONEY AND POLITICS

In spite of the Democrats' better showing in 1964 among the rich, America's famed wealthy families still showed their traditional tenderness for the Republican cause. From the members of just twelve of these families, the amounts given were as follows: [14]

Year	Republicans	Democrats
1964	$445,280	$133,500
1960	545,510	78,850

The figures make it clear that what are vulgarly referred to as fat-cat contributors are by no means on the way out. Nor have programs initiated by the two national parties to broaden the base of campaign finance been very successful. The search continues for a satisfactory approach to the problem. In 1961, President Kennedy showed an interest in the problem by appointing a commission to study the financing of presidential elections. One year later, the commission issued its report. After noting the large sums that are expended in presidential campaigns and the dependence of the two parties on wealthy contributors, the report declared that the present situation was helping to create "widespread cynicism about the democratic system." [15]

The Need for Reform Recognizing that current laws are entirely inadequate to regulate the financing of campaigns, the commission recommended the enactment of entirely new legislation. Its considered conclusion was that the best way to encourage large numbers of people to make political contributions and thus dilute the influence of the few large donors was to hold out incentives to prospective contributors. For the poorest of them, the reward that it suggested would be a tax credit: half of any contribution up to $10 could be deducted from the taxes owed to the government.

[14] These and other campaign contribution data are drawn from the two studies by Herbert Alexander, *Financing the 1960 Election* and *Financing the 1964 Election*. Both were published by the Citizens' Research Foundation in Princeton, New Jersey, in 1962 and 1966, respectively. The twelve families' names are: duPont, Field, Ford, Harriman, Lehman, Mellon, Olin, Pew, Reynolds, Rockefeller, Vanderbilt, and Whitney.
[15] President's Commission on Campaign Costs, *Financing Presidential Campaigns* (Washington: Government Printing Office, 1962), p. 11.

For anyone wishing to contribute a larger amount (more than $10 but less than $1,000), the incentive would also be attractive, though not so generous as the one available to the little man: the contribution could not be deducted from taxes owed but, rather, from the income that would be subject to taxation. The commission proposed that this tax incentive program should go into effect at once. After an eight-year trial period, it suggested, another and more far-reaching procedure should be considered: federal matching grants for the first $10 of every political gift. The hope was that this program would increase the number of small contributors while at the same time rewarding handsomely the party that successfully scoured the countryside for them.

So little did the commission think of existing legal ceilings on campaign receipts and expenditures that it recommended repealing them in their entirety. On the theory that publicity has a cleansing and policing power, which is more effective than rigid limitation, it favored establishment of a reporting system with teeth. Creation of a central registry of election finance would be a prerequisite, it said, if the job were to be done properly.

The recommendations of the commission would obviously help to minimize the baleful influence that money continues to exercise on politics. President Kennedy said he was impressed by the report, and in both 1962 and 1963 he sent Congress legislation modeled after the proposals made by the commission. In addition to tax incentives, Mr. Kennedy recommended that regulation be extended to primary elections, and also that individual contributions be limited to $5,000 to one political committee or candidate, thus eliminating multiple contributions. In one respect, however, the Kennedy proposal fell short of genuine reform because there was no recommendation for effective enforcement of violations of the reporting requirement.

But the bill was still too strong for Congress. The Kennedy legislation was almost entirely ignored on Capitol Hill. Only a handful of congressmen seemed concerned about the moral implications of prevailing campaign practices. Several years later, however, a somewhat more favorable climate had developed on Capitol Hill. Public displeasure over the wrongdoings of Adam Clayton Powell in the House and Thomas Dodd in the Senate undoubtedly helped to generate some force behind campaign reform bills. As yet, only the Senate has been persuaded to act.

The response of the Senate was a measure passed late in 1967 incorporating some reforms that had been long sought, such as limiting individual contributions to $5,000, applying the rules to primary elections, and lifting the unrealistic ceiling on what campaign committees could expend. A House committee reported a similar bill in midsummer of 1968, with an even more desirable feature added. The reporting and policing under the House bill would be in the hands of a special elections commission. Under the Senate bill, the reporting would be to officials employed by Congress—the Secretary of the Senate and Clerk of the House—a situation not likely to induce the most rigorous enforcement of the rules. Inaction in the House, however, killed the bill, at least for the Ninetieth Congress, which adjourned in October, 1968.

In late 1967, a Senate committee also reported a bill which would have provided, for the first time, for public subsidization of political campaigns. Actually, this bill grew out of a law already enacted by Congress a year earlier. This was the legislation that gained the appellation, Christmas tree bill, because of all the tax giveaways that had been written into it at the behest of lobbyists. In keeping with the Christmas spirit, the author of the campaign proposal, Senator Russell Long of Louisiana, the assistant Democratic leader of the Senate, had proposed an entirely unexpected gift of many millions of dollars to the Democratic and Republican national committees.

The Long Amendment provided that individuals filing federal income tax returns could check a box on the form to indicate that they wanted $1.00 of their tax to go into a presidential election campaign fund. The money that was thus earmarked would be distributed equally to the political parties whose presidential candidate had obtained more than fifteen million votes in the last election—in short, the Democrats and Republicans. It was estimated that this could have resulted in a campaign fund of $60 million to be split by the two parties in 1968.

Basic objections to the Long Amendment were quickly voiced on the Senate floor. It was pointed out, for example, that the scheme would not mean that less money was spent on campaigns, but rather more, for the parties would continue beating the bushes for private contributions to supplement the public funds that they would be tapping. Thus the parties and their candidates would continue to be beholden to fat-cat contributors. Certainly the ordinary citizen who checked the box on the tax return would be deluding himself if he thought that now he would be on a par with members of the President's Club in having access to the White House. The little man, in fact, would not have made a contribution to his party at all but, rather, to both parties.

It was also pointed out that the scheme discriminated in an unconscionable way against minor parties. Such parties would be entitled to a share of the public funds only if they had polled in excess of five million votes in the last election—a total that no third party in American history had been able to reach, at least up to that time.[16] Even in the event that a third party could earn the right to some money from the fund, it would have to wait until the next presidential election four years later before it could collect.[17] And, as if to add insult to injury, it would then receive only $1.00 a vote for every vote in excess of five million. This attempted freezing out by legislation of any potential third party, and what amounted to the concomitant statutory establishment of a two-party system for all time to come, convinced some that not only was this patently unfair, but also that it was unconstitutional.

There were other objections, too, against the Long Amendment, including the argument that the projected fund would still leave members of Congress in the hands of wealthy contributors since it would be available only to presidential candidates. Yet the amendment went through the Senate with little debate and without any committee holding hearings on the proposal. The House, also without hearings, followed the lead of the Senate, and, only eighteen days after Long had persuaded the Finance Committee, of which he was chairman, to endorse his plan, the Long Amendment was on the way to the White House. The Democratic National Committee had all kinds of ideas about what it could do with all the money that would be made available to it in 1968, and President Johnson, who, at that time, was thought to be the certain Democratic candidate, affixed his signature to the bill with what was plainly a feeling of elation.[18]

But a few months later, when the next Congress convened, in January, 1967, there was anything but elation as its members began to appreciate the implications of what they had done. Democrats who had always stood for the principle that the president should not be able to push congressmen around just because they belonged to his party, had awakened to the realization that they might very well become just

---

[16] Senator Robert LaFollette had come the closest, when he received 4.8 million votes as the Progressive party candidate in 1924. The minor parties in 1948, Henry Wallace's Progressives and Strom Thurmond's States' Rights Democrats, polled fewer than three million votes between them.

[17] Thus, Wallace with ten million votes in 1968 would have had to wait until 1972 to share in the fund.

[18] Mr. Johnson was opposed to many of the special interest riders that had been attached to the bill at the behest of pressure groups but, faced with the choice of approving the whole bill or vetoing the whole bill, he did not hesitate very long.

so many tails on Lyndon Johnson's kite when the President came into the inheritance that the Long Amendment had provided for him. Republicans, too, had second thoughts about the desirability of so great a strengthening of their national party at the expense of its congressional representatives, not to mention the desirability of allowing the Democrats, who could hardly ever raise as much money as the opposition party from private sources, to share equally in such a gargantuan public fund.

The rather unusual upshot of some lengthy maneuvering occasioned by the second thoughts was a suspension of the provisions of the Long bill while a new approach was sought in committee. The result was a bill reported later in 1967, graciously named the Honest Election Law. It abandoned the income tax checkoff of the original Long Amendment and substituted in its place outright federal assistance; if further action had been taken on the bill, this would have amounted to about $14 million for each of the major presidential candidates. It also would have subsidized senatorial campaigns, ranging from $100,000 to $1,523,000, depending on the level of past voting in the particular state.

Also modified were other objectionable features of the original Long plan. The public funds could be used only if candidates agreed not to accept any private contributions from sixty days before to thirty days after the election. (The loopholes in this are obvious.) The minor party provisions were loosened somewhat by using as the minimum a percentage figure of 5 percent of the vote cast in a preceding election; this would have reduced the number needed to around three and one-half million. Still no third party, of course, would have qualified in 1968. But, had the bill ever become law, Wallace's American Independent Party could have received, after the election, forty cents for each vote cast. This would have amounted to some $3,720,000. If anything, the success of the third party in 1968 more than likely has insured that any similar bill will face even greater opposition in the future.

Increasing Costs at All Levels

Increasing spending at all levels is becoming a serious enough problem to warrant attention in the form of federal legislation that, operating in conjunction with state regulation, would effectively control the situation. In 1966, expenditures for gubernatorial, senatorial, and congressional offices indicated that these campaigns were costing more than ever before. Governor Rockefeller's campaign organization reported spending about $5 million in his successful effort to win a third term in New York.[19] California's gubernatorial campaign was estimated to have cost the two parties $8 million, although the officially reported totals came to under $5 million.

Even the average state assembly seat in California, representing about 250,000 people each, ran from $10,000 to $15,000, with several costing in excess of $30,000.[20] Under existing federal law, the maximum a United States senator is supposed to spend is $25,000. Yet one state senator in California reported spending $74,152![21]

Overall national spending by the two parties in 1966 for House and Senate contests amounted to almost $12 million. The Republicans outspent the Democrats by a ratio of nearly 2–1: $7.6 to $4.2 million. These figures do not include spending by state and local party groups or spending in primaries, which may be much more than in a general election. In Virginia, the two Democratic candidates for the Senate together reported expenditures of $110,000, whereas the two Republicans reported only $41,000. But in the July Democratic primary, the four candidates involved spent nearly $800,000, a record for Virginia.[22]

The rather minuscule senatorial expenses in Virginia reflect, in part, the relatively lower costs of campaigns in predominantly one-party states. For in a somewhat more competitive congressional district in the same state, the two candidates reported spending more than $200,000. Clive DuVal, the unsuccessful Democratic candidate in a northern Virginia district consisting largely of suburban communities of Washington, D.C., had expenditures of $127,666, while his opponent, Republican Joel Broyhill, spent $92,000.[23] As the Republican party becomes more competitive in the once solidly Democratic South, spending in that area can be expected to increase substantially.

---

[19] Richard L. Madden, "Rockefeller Campaign Cost About $5 Million," a *New York Times* news service dispatch reported in the *Sacramento Bee*, 30 November 1966.

[20] Richard Rodda, "Campaign Costs Top $9 Million," *Sacramento Bee*, 14 December 1966.

[21] Martin Smith, "GOP Candidates Outspent Democrats in Election Campaign," *Sacramento Bee*, 16 December 1966.

[22] *Washington Post*, 9 December 1966, p. B-4. There were two Senate races in Virginia in 1966, because earlier in the year Senator Harry F. Byrd had resigned and the Governor of Virginia appointed his son, Harry F. Byrd, Jr., to the vacancy. The new appointee then had to compete for the seat in the ensuing primary and general election.

[23] Richard Corrigan, "DuVal Spent a Record $127,666 in Losing Race," *Washington Post*, 8 December 1966, p. C-1.

1968 saw still another escalation in the costs of campaigning at all levels. It was estimated that some $25 million alone was spent by the various Republican and Democratic contenders for their respective parties' nominations. Rockefeller and Nixon each spent about $5 million. McCarthy's unsuccessful effort to win the Democratic nomination cost between $5 and $7 million. On the presidential election itself, the Democrats spent some $12 million while the Republicans' total was near $20 million. Wallace reported spending $6 million.

A number of factors contributes to spiraling campaign costs. Current campaign techniques utilizing expensive media like television and direct mail brochures place a heavy burden on each of the candidates to try to outdo each other. Increasing reliance on public opinion sampling undertaken by private polling organizations for candidates has raised campaign expenditures. The very length of campaigns adds to their cost. The normal campaign lasts from after Labor Day to election day, some two months. A shorter period might not only reduce expenses but might also, because of greater concentration of effort, be more effective in stimulating more people. Finally, primary elections increasingly add to the total cost of political campaigning. In competitive party areas, candidates find it necessary first to spend money to survive the primary, and then to give battle in the general election.

Some of the inequalities occasioned by uncontrolled spending could be lessened by comparatively mild reforms. Since the airwaves are public property, the networks could be required by law to provide candidates with television and radio time. Candidates for office at all levels could be given the franking privilege for at least one mailing to registered voters, a benefit now enjoyed only by incumbent congressmen. Such reforms, however, along with public subsidies to candidates, are not likely to appeal to incumbent lawmakers who perceive that money does make a difference.

Other Costs of Political Office

Although campaign outlays are high and getting higher, these are not the only expenses for which officeholders seek contributions. The costs of maintaining an office, especially at the national level, can also lead to dependence on political contributions, as the case of Senator Thomas Dodd, Democrat of Connecticut, showed. Charges were made in late 1965 that Dodd had been the recipient of cash gifts since 1961 totaling more than $100,000. These gifts had come from testimonial fund-raising dinners held not only to provide campaign funds, but also to bolster, according to Dodd's associates, "the Senator's sagging personal financial situation." It was further alleged that Dodd had treated these gifts as tax free and for this reason had not reported them as income.[24]

In October, 1966, the Senate ethics committee, to which the Dodd matter had been referred, reported that records indicated "that the Senator received on the order of $500,000 in political contributions, between 1961 and 1965, of which at least $200,000 was classified as 'personal gifts' to Dodd."[25] In April, 1967, the committee recommended that Dodd be censured for the misuse of political funds—and in June, by a vote of 92–5, the Senate did so order. The Dodd episode illustrates still another problem of money and politics, the extent of which may run well beyond the difficulties of a single senator. Although the censure may have made others more circumspect, it will not solve the basic problem.

The Bobby Baker scandal had led the Senate to create an ethics committee (Select Committee on Standards and Conduct) and the Powell case resulted in the House establishing a comparable body (Committee on Standards of Official Conduct). In the wake of the Dodd affair, both houses also provided for limited disclosure of their members' sources of income. But the requirements were such that only the most general kind of information can be made public; more detailed statements are kept confidential and are available to the committees if an investigation into alleged wrongdoing is undertaken. Much more experience with the disclosure requirements and the committees is needed to determine whether these limited steps will deal adequately with the problem of ethics in Congress.

Interest Group Spending   Although contributions to political campaigns provide the most dramatic example of the impact of money on the political process, there is an even more direct way in which men of means make their influence

---

[24] *Congressional Quarterly, Weekly Report* 16 (22 March 1966): 840.
[25] Richard Harwood, "Ethics Group to Delve Into Dodd's Finances," *Washington Post*, 27 October 1966, p. A-1.

felt: through pressure on governmental policymakers, wherever they are to be found.[26]

Not too much is known about the extent of interest group spending. The reporting provisions of the Federal Regulation of Lobbying Act do provide some figures, but only for spending at the national level. Moreover, this law has an impressive number of loopholes at least as interpreted by the courts. It applies, for instance, only to organizations whose principal purpose is to influence legislation. Moreover, it applies only to direct attempts to influence congressmen, not to the often more effective and more costly indirect lobbying methods such as the organization of public relations campaigns. And it applies only to attempts to influence Congress, not the administrators of executive agencies and the members of regulatory commissions, though these often make decisions of great moment.

Even a more serious problem is that lobbies may well be reporting lesser amounts than they are actually spending since there is no means provided by the 1946 law to check on the accuracy of what is reported. It is difficult to dismiss this suspicion because the amounts reported by lobbying groups are not only extremely low, considering the work they do, but also because the amounts reported seem to be getting smaller instead of larger with the passage of the years.

For the first few years that the law was in effect, the totals rose steadily, from $5.2 million in the first year to $10.3 million in 1950. In that year, however, an event occurred which seems to have convinced the lobbies that a new approach was in order. An investigation into lobbying by a select committee of the House of Representatives concluded that the spending which had been reported did "not begin to reflect all that is actually collected and spent in efforts to influence legislation." If the full truth were ever known, it added, "this Committee has little doubt that lobbying in all its ramifications would prove to be a billion dollar industry." [27] The publicity generated by this con-

---

[26] See Chapter 4 on interest groups. There is a kind of carry-over between the two modes of influencing public policy. This is true in the sense that officials of interest groups often turn up among those who make significant campaign contributions. For example, twenty-four directors or honorary directors of the American Petroleum Institute made contributions in 1964 totaling $75,000. Various officials of the National Association of Manufacturers, twenty-two in all, gave a total of $64,000, and seven officers or directors of the Chamber of Commerce contributed $7,200. Almost all this money went to Republican candidates and committees. Alexander, *Financing the 1964 Election*, pp. 91–92.

[27] Quoted in Belle Zeller, "Regulation of Pressure Groups and Lobbyists," in *Annals*

gressional investigation may have convinced interest groups to be more discreet about their reporting, for within two years the total they collectively reported had shrunk to $4.8 million, only half of what had been reported previously; nor have the reported totals risen much since that time.[28]

To the extent that the lobbying reports can be trusted, it seems that there are several organizations which are consistently the biggest spenders. The top three are the American Legion, the AFL-CIO, and the American Farm Bureau Federation. At times, however, these groups are surpassed by others who come into the picture briefly to promote or oppose a specific piece of legislation. The American Medical Association, for example, had never spent more than $50,000 in a single year until 1949, when its outlay suddenly shot up to $1.5 million, a sum that was almost exactly duplicated the following year. The reason for the spurt was the campaign to defeat the Truman administration's proposal for national health insurance. As soon as this goal had been accomplished, the level of spending by AMA dropped considerably, not to rise again to its former heights until 1965, when the battle against Medicare was waged.

If some groups greatly expand their activities in order to achieve specific purposes, there are others that actually come into existence to achieve certain specific goals. The Coordinating Committee for Fundamental American Freedoms, for instance, was organized to provide a rallying point for opponents of civil rights legislation in 1964. The half-million dollars that it spent came largely from the Mississippi State Sovereignty Commission, which in turn received its funds from the Mississippi state legislature.

The difficulties of determining with any degree of precision how much money is spent by lobbying groups are compounded when an effort is made to determine the amounts that are spent by large corporations to procure government contracts in the military and space fields. Since it must be presumed that the efforts are commensurate with the rewards that beckon, these efforts must be great indeed, since

---

of the *American Academy of Political and Social Science* 319 (September 1958): 100. This entire issue of the *Annals* was devoted to the subject of pressure groups and lobbying.

[28] From 1954 through 1964, the total reported hovered around the $4 million mark. In 1965, it rose to almost $5.5 million. In 1967, $4.7 million was reported and there was a slight decline to $4.3 million in 1968. For a complete analysis of yearly totals through 1964, see *Legislators and the Lobbyists* (Washington: Congressional Quarterly Service, 1965), pp. 31–47. More recent data may be found in the latest fall or spring *Congressional Quarterly Guide to Current American Government*.

the defense budget alone has now reached astronomical levels, in the neighborhood of $80 billion a year. Yet little is known specifically about the extent of contractor influence on the decisions of the Department of Defense or the National Aeronautics and Space Administration.[29]

Taxes and Politics Most of the money that is spent by individuals and interest groups for legislative lobbying is intended to influence Congress as it considers general measures that will have some incidental impact on the economic situation of the spender. There is, however, one type of lobbying that is in quite a different category: the attempt to obtain favorable provisions in tax legislation. It is a commonplace for tax laws to contain provisions that will single out a particular industry or a handful of companies for preferential treatment. Instances can even be found in which a single company or even one lone individual has been plucked from the common herd and given some tax advantage. Often such bonuses are tucked away in an obscure section of a highly complex piece of legislation and, to make detection even more difficult, are described in opaque technical language that only a tax lawyer can make sense of.[30] An outstanding example of a provision in the Internal Revenue Code that was tailor-made for just one person was the 1951 statute that was specifically written to save Louis B. Mayer, then head of Metro-Goldwyn-Mayer, a wopping $2 million in taxes.[31] Whatever money it cost Mr. Mayer to lobby this provision through Congress was obviously well spent.

Far more money than this, however, may be involved when the tax obligations of an entire industry are framed. The 27½ percent depletion allowance for oil producers is a prime example. A study by the Treasury Department revealed that, primarily because of this loophole, one oil firm with profits amounting to over $65 million in a six-year period not only paid no income taxes, but also actually received a $425,000 refund of taxes it had paid previously.[32]

---

[29] See the discussion of the military-industrial complex in Chapter 4.

[30] So complex are the tax laws that they have been described as "a remarkable essay in sustained obscurity," possessing "all the earmarks of a conspiracy in restraint of understanding." Quoted in Philip M. Stern, *The Great Treasury Raid* (New York: Random House, 1962), p. 285.

[31] Ibid., pp. 44–48.

[32] Ibid., p. 19.

THE POLITICAL PROCESS: CONDITIONING FACTORS

The depletion allowance has long been vehemently criticized; until recently, all attempts to repeal it or even modify it have been thwarted in Congress. In its successful campaign to protect its privileged tax position, the industry has benefited from the fact that some of the most powerful members of Congress—including the late Speaker Sam Rayburn, the late Senator Robert Kerr of Oklahoma, and most notably, the former Majority Leader of the Senate and former President of the United States, Lyndon B. Johnson—represented oil-producing areas. But oilmen have made their positions even more invulnerable by lubricating the election campaigns of friendly candidates. In 1952 and 1956 alone, officers and directors of oil companies made contributions of $650,000,[33] not including the amounts that were made available to congressional candidates in the oil-producing states.

Although the magnitude of such sums makes the political contributions of other corporate officers seem puny by comparison, oilmen have no monopoly on well-financed campaigns to influence tax legislation. Revealing facts about political contributions by savings and loan associations were placed on the record in the 1967 trial of Robert G. Baker, former Secretary of the Senate Majority and an intimate associate of Lyndon Johnson. Testimony indicated that the officers of several such associations in California had turned over some $100,000 to Mr. Baker in 1962 to help head off pending legislation that would have increased the taxes on their businesses. There was evidence at the trial that the contributions had been suggested by the Washington lobbyist for the United States Savings and Loan League and that the funds had been turned over to Mr. Baker. According to Mr. Baker, he passed the money on to Senator Kerr, Chairman of the Democratic Senatorial Campaign Committee, for distribution to other senators. The government charged that a large part of the funds had been diverted by Mr. Baker to his own personal use.[34]

There are more than a few instances of campaign contributions following hard on the heels of special tax legislation, or vice versa. One particularly obvious case centered around a change that Congress made in 1966 in a provision of the law on investment tax credits passed four years earlier. When it was originally enacted, the tax credit applied only to corporations doing business in the United States. The 1966 amendment extended coverage to firms operating in United States possessions or territories. A senator who has made a career of tax muckraking

---

[33] Heard, *The Costs of Democracy*, p. 106.
[34] *Washington Post*, 17 January 1967, p. A-1 and 20 January 1967, p. A-1.

learned from the Treasury Department that the amendment would apply to no other company in the United States except the Harvey Aluminum Company, which had a wholly owned subsidiary in the Virgin Islands. The Senator, John J. Williams (R., Del.), pointed out that Harvey Aluminum had purchased a $15,000 advertisement in the Democratic campaign book published in 1965 and that three officers of the company had each contributed the necessary $1,000 to become a member of the President's Club.[35]

Even where no overt campaign contribution is evident favorable tax treatment can be brought about through political influence. In 1961 several major companies were convicted and assessed heavy fines for fixing prices and rigging bids. Clark Clifford, prominent Washington attorney and a one-time adviser to President Truman, was successful in obtaining from the Internal Revenue Service a ruling which allowed his client, General Electric, to deduct the fines as a business expense in computing its corporate income taxes. Clifford was appointed by President Johnson in 1968 to succeed Robert McNamara as Secretary of Defense.

The interest of the Internal Revenue Service in taxes and politics acts both ways, however. What privileges the tax laws confer in general, the Internal Revenue Service can take away in particular cases. A case in point involved a leading conservationist organization, the Sierra Club of California. For years, the club had enjoyed tax-exempt status, in accordance with the policy laid down by Congress for educational and charitable institutions. Such status was important in two ways. First, it meant that the club had to pay no tax on the income it received. And second, it meant that individuals who made contributions to the club could deduct the amount from their taxable income.

The Sierra Club's difficulties with Internal Revenue Service began in 1966, when the club ran full-page advertisements in *The New York Times* and *The Washington Post* expressing opposition to pending legislation that would have authorized the construction of two dams on the Colorado River. In the advertisements, the club claimed that construction of the water project would inundate large portions of the Grand Canyon and thus deface one of the outstanding national scenic attractions in the country. Construction of the dams was a pet project of the banks, utilities, and irrigation districts which would benefit economically from the power to be generated, and the Sierra Club knew that

---

[35] *New York Times*, 27 October 1966, p. 46.

its advertisement would stir up a storm. It did not, however, anticipate the instant retaliation to which it was subjected.

The day after the advertisement appeared, the Internal Revenue Service warned supporters of the Sierra Club that their contributions might no longer be tax deductible, since an investigation was just beginning to determine whether the club was entitled to a continuation of its tax-exempt status. The threat had an immediate impact. According to the executive director of the Sierra Club, the IRS statement cost the club $125,000 in anticipated contributions in the next six months. When those six months had elapsed, Internal Revenue Service dropped the other shoe and announced that it had revoked the tax-exempt status of the club because of this attempt to influence the passage of legislation. An appeal was taken from the ruling, but, at least until the dispute was definitively settled, the club would be seriously hobbled, because of the falling off of contributions. Meanwhile, the interest groups on the other side, acting under the name of The Central Arizona Project Association were, of course, perfectly free to pursue their lobbying activities in favor of the construction of the dams. Not just that. The business concerns contributing to this lobbying effort could deduct their contributions from taxable income.[36] This kind of deduction has been available since 1962 for lobbying expenses that are incurred for the purpose of influencing legislation of direct financial interest to the taxpayer.

Another example of the involvement of the Internal Revenue Service in politics concerns the war in Vietnam. In 1965, supporters of the Johnson administration's policies organized a group called Affirmation: Vietnam. One of the organizers presented himself in person at the offices of IRS in Washington to request that the group be granted tax-exempt status so that it would be able to attract contributions more readily. Upon being told by Internal Revenue Service that applications for such status take from thirty to ninety days to process, the organizer reached an aide in the office of then Vice-President Humphrey, and within a matter of days a favorable ruling was issued by IRS. Tax officials admitted that someone in the vice-president's office had called about the application, but they denied that this had anything at all to do with the extraordinary speed of their action. Even if that is true, it is evident that an organization supporting administration policies finds it easier to

---

[36] The Central Arizona Project Association reported spending $117,300 on lobbying in 1966 and $78,867 in 1967. *Congressional Quarterly Guide to Current American Government* (Fall 1968), p. 117.

deal with Internal Revenue Service than one on the other side. After eighteen months, the Washington Peace Center, a group just as strongly opposed to American prosecution of the war in Vietnam as the other organization was in favor of it, was still waiting for IRS action on its application for tax-exempt status.[37]

Evidence of the interconnection between money and politics can thus be found almost wherever one looks in the American political process. It is difficult to deny that the presence of this influence raises serious questions about whether political equality is a meaningful concept in the political process or whether it exists only in theory. Reason, goodwill, and persuasion are all esteemed qualities of a democratic society. Standing alone, however, they seem incapable of articulating the demands of the members of the polity, or of converting these demands into public policies. Money is an indispensable added ingredient in the political system, and it is a factor that makes some decidedly more equal than others.

[37] *New York Times,* 13 February 1966, p. 7.

Chapter 8 Freedom of Political Expression

Participation in the political process would have only a hollow meaning without an atmosphere of free expression. The ways in which individuals and groups relate to the political process depends on the extent to which individuals are free to communicate information, ideas, and opinions to their government and to each other. Freedom of expression is thus not a luxury that the society can afford only in good times; it is, rather, a vital life fluid in the body politic of a democratic society.

The nation's commitment to freedom of expression is explicitly stated in the First Amendment to the Constitution:

> Congress shall make no law . . . abridging the freedom of speech, or of the press; or the right of the people peaceably to assemble, and to petition the Government for redress of grievances.

It is one thing, however, to state noble objectives; it is quite another thing for a society to live up to the demands placed on it by such commitments. On the whole, the history of freedom of political expression in the United States demonstrates that the ideal has often been sacrificed to expediency. Especially during periods of crisis, has the value of freedom of political expression been forced to give way.

The notion that there should be an explicit guarantee of protection for the freedom of public discussion was not accepted by the framers of the original Constitution. The lack of a bill of rights was one of the major arguments advanced by opponents of ratification. It was true that the Constitution in its original form did provide certain guarantees of civil liberties. The writ of *habeas corpus* was protected against suspension except in the case of rebellion or invasion when the public safety might require it. The right of trial by jury in criminal cases was guaranteed. The passage of bills of attainder or *ex post facto* laws was prohibited.[1]

These guarantees, however, did not succeed in dispelling the doubts that opponents had expressed, and the persistence of these doubts give rise to the possibility that the Constitution might not be ratified by the necessary number of states. To avert this outcome, the proponents of the Constitution capitulated on the issue and pledged that they would urge the very first Congress to propose to the states the ratification of a bill of rights in the form of amendments to the new Constitution. Only on this basis were some otherwise hesitant states induced to vote for ratification.

In accordance with the arrangement that had been agreed upon, the First Congress approved and submitted to the states a proposed bill of rights. Ten of the twelve amendments of which it was composed were promptly ratified and became a part of the Constitution in 1791, only three years after the ratification of the Constitution itself. Within a few years, however, the First Amendment concepts of free speech

---

[1] *Habeas corpus* protects an individual who is deprived of his freedom by compelling the governmental body which has custody over him to convince a court, when challenged, that the deprivation of freedom is legal. A bill of attainder is a legislative enactment determining that a particular individual is guilty of a crime. Trials were to be exclusively the business of courts. An *ex post facto* criminal law is one that retroactively makes conduct punishable, even though it had been entirely legal when committed. All three of these protections are contained in Article I, Section 9.

An additional protection involved the definition of treason and the requirements necessary to obtain a conviction. No one could be convicted of treason unless it was proved he had engaged "in levying War against [the United States], or in adhering to [its] Enemies, giving them Aid and Comfort." The proof would have to consist of testimony by two witnesses to the same overt act, or of a confession by the defendant in open court. (Article III, Section 3.)

and press were to be tested severely. As has been the case so often in our own century, the background of the assault on free expression was a crisis in foreign policy.

The Alien and Sedition Acts

The great controversy over foreign policy in the 1790s revolved around the issue of relations with France and Britain. The Federalists, who sympathized with Britain, did not allow the controversy to be resolved through the normal give-and-take of democratic political debate and decision-making. Convinced that the anti-Federalists, who were partial to France, were dominated by revolutionaries and French agents, they used their control of Congress to eliminate their influence and even suppress them entirely. To this end, the Alien and Sedition Laws were enacted in 1798. Of the two statutes, the Alien Law, which gave the president power to deport aliens, was the more narrowly drawn, for it applied only to enemy aliens, and it restricted use of the deportation power to time of war. In the Sedition Law, on the other hand, Congress painted with a broad brush. Here there was no talk about aliens or about wartime. The act was phrased in general terms and thus applied as much to citizens as to aliens, as much in peacetime as in time of war.

The Sedition Law made it a criminal offense to criticize the government if that criticism could be characterized as malicious, scandalous, or false. It was also made unlawful to excite "the hatred of the good people of the United States" against the president or either House of Congress. The provisions of the law applied to the spoken word as well as to written or printed matter. Whatever the mode of expression, stiff fines and long terms of imprisonment were provided.[2]

Some fifteen indictments were returned under the Sedition Law, and ten convictions resulted. Some of those who were sent to jail were editors of anti-Federalist newspapers. One had expressed the hope that the next time guns were fired in honor of the President, John Adams, one of the cannonballs would catch the president in the seat of the pants. Another editor was convicted for calling Adams "power mad." Even a member of Congress, Matthew Lyon, an anti-Federalist from Vermont, was handed a prison sentence. In addition, trials held

---

[2] James Morton Smith, *Freedom's Fetters: The Alien and Sedition Laws and American Civil Liberties* (Ithaca, N.Y.: Cornell University Press, 1956), p. 420.

under the act provided Federalist judges with a platform from which to blast away at those who sympathized with the egalitarian ideals of the French Revolution, and to expound their own views on political questions of the day.

In terms of their immediate impact, the Alien and Sedition Laws accomplished some good, from the standpoint of the Federalists. The mere enactment of the Alien Law had persuaded many foreigners, some of whom did indeed hold radical views, to leave the country voluntarily, and the jail sentences meted out under the Sedition Law at least removed some anti-Federalist opinion-makers from the public arena. Yet, if the Federalists had hoped that punishing a few would silence many more, that hope was frustrated. Criticism of the Adams administration, in fact, increased in intensity, and the critics now had a new misdeed to lay at the door of the Federalists: authorship of a statute that seemed to be cut from the same cloth as the hated English laws against seditious libel. Public opinion was so aroused that Jefferson and Madison were able to persuade the state legislatures of Virginia and Kentucky to pass strongly worded resolutions condemning the Alien and Sedition Laws and even going so far as to deny that the federal government had any right to enforce the laws in the two states. Although these Virginia and Kentucky resolutions were as much motivated by sentiments for states' rights as by concern for civil liberties, they were framed in language that amounted to an eloquent reaffirmation of the First Amendment. They certainly did the Federalists no good in the election of 1800.

Partly because of the odium that attached to them because of the Alien and Sedition Acts, the Federalists suffered a defeat of such magnitude in that election that their party was never again able to recover. The anti-Federalists captured both Houses of Congress, and Jefferson, who was their candidate, was elected president. One of President Jefferson's first acts was to pardon all those who were still in jail under the Sedition Act. Congress, too, made it clear that a new day was dawning, by passing legislation to remit the fines that had been paid.[3]

The Alien and Sedition Acts left a sufficiently bad taste so that Congress during the entire nineteenth century refrained from passing any legislation whatever that even appeared to violate the provisions of the

---

[3] Smith, *Freedom's Fetters*, p. 268. The Sedition Act had never been subjected to a constitutional test because the Federalists who manned the judiciary would not permit the defendants to challenge the law itself. Alfred H. Kelly and Winfred A. Harbison, *The American Constitution*, 3d ed. (New York: W. W. Norton, 1963), p. 198.

First Amendment on freedom of expression. Not that there were no abridgements of free speech in that century. In the pre-Civil War years, abolitionists took their very lives into their hands when they ventured into the South to preach their doctrines. During the Civil War itself, repression appeared on the other side, with efforts both by President Lincoln and by the military authorities to stamp out pro-Confederacy sentiment in the North. Also, during the last quarter of the century, industrial strikes often resulted in attempts on the part of employers and those who spoke for them in government to make it dangerous to espouse radical economic and political ideas.

World War I

Yet it was not until World War I that there was any real repetition of the kind of statutory suppression that was embodied in the Sedition Law of 1798. First, in 1917, came the Espionage Act, and then, the following year, the Sedition Act of 1918 was passed. Like its 1798 namesake, the Sedition Act of 1918 was largely concerned with the expression of political opinions. Among other things, the act made it a crime to use words calculated to bring into disrepute the Constitution, the flag, or the form of government of the United States. It also proscribed statements calculated to interfere with military conscription or obstruct the sale of war bonds. Even advocating that others commit any of these seditious acts was made punishable.

Many prosecutions were brought under the Sedition Act and under the Espionage Act of the previous year. With both judges and juries in the grip of patriotic passion, there were long prison sentences for people whose crimes consisted of no more than stating that war was contrary to the teachings of Jesus Christ, or that raising taxes on the rich would be a more equitable way of financing the war than the floating of bonds. That little concern was shown for the principle of free expression was perhaps best epitomized by one judge's statement that freedom of speech means the protection of "criticism which is made friendly to the government, friendly to the war, friendly to the policies of the government." [4]

So slowly did the wheels of justice turn that none of the convictions

---

[4] Judge Van Valkenburgh, in U.S. v. Rose Pastor Stokes, as quoted in Zechariah Chafee, Jr., *Free Speech in the United States* (Cambridge: Harvard University Press, 1948), p. 37.

came before the Supreme Court for review until 1919 after the war was already over. At that point, as a student of free speech has remarked, the most that the justices could do was to "lock the doors after the Liberty Bell [had been] stolen."[5] As it turned out, the members of the Court were not even willing to do that much.

The first case involving a constitutional challenge to the 1917 and 1918 statutes came in *Schenck* v. *United States*.[6] Schenck and others had been convicted for mailing circulars to potential draftees urging them to refuse induction. They claimed that punishing them for mere verbal expressions was an abridgement of free speech and therefore a violation of the First Amendment. The Supreme Court disagreed. Its opinion, written by Justice Oliver Wendell Holmes, has become a landmark in American law.

Clear and Present Danger In his opinion, Justice Holmes contributed a new phrase to the vocabulary of constitutional jurisprudence: "clear and present danger." In every case, said Holmes, words that the government wanted to punish would have to be considered with due regard for the circumstances in which they had been uttered. The very same statement might be punishable in one context, though completely privileged in another. In every case, the test should be whether the words, in the context of the circumstances, had created a "clear and present danger" that evils might come about which Congress had the constitutional power to prevent. As applied to the *Schenck* case, this meant that the Court had to decide whether the antidraft circulars, mailed to prospective conscripts during a time of war, had created a "clear and present danger" that conscription would be impeded and the war effort hampered. Holmes, together with all his colleagues on the Supreme Court, concluded that Schenck and the other defendants had indeed created such a danger. As a consequence, their conviction was affirmed.

It cannot be denied that Holmes tried to develop a formula that would keep curtailment of free expression to a bare minimum. The danger created by an utterance would have to be "clear and present," not merely hypothetical. Yet, subsequent events have proved that even if Holmes made only a tiny pinprick in the First Amendment, there were

[5] Ibid., p. 37.
[6] 249 U.S. 47 (1919).

others standing by to expand the minute aperture into a gaping hole. Moreover, in arriving at his conclusion that exceptions to the rule of the First Amendment were permissible, Holmes placed his faith in a highly dubious analogy. "The most stringent protection of free speech," he said, "would not protect a man in falsely shouting fire in a theater and causing a panic."

The Holmes analogy deals with a matter of the physical world and with the senses, which are presumably subject to empirical verification. But the realm of political and economic ideas is not so susceptible of proof; it remains in the uncertain world of opinion. Moreover, Holmes qualified the act of shouting with the word "falsely"; the assumption must be that if a man actually saw a fire and shouted, yet caused a panic, he would go unpunished. When a man exclaims political, economic, or social heresy, however, who can judge that what he says is "false"? Although Holmes may not have intended it, the essence of the notion he spawned has become the fact that the crime is not that the individual has said anything at all, but the particular substantive content of what he has said or printed.

A further difficulty inherent in the "clear and present danger" test is that it is, like most formulas made by judges, highly subjective. The outcome of its application depends on the particular circumstances of a case and the peculiar attitudes and beliefs of the judge or judges attempting to apply the test. That even the same group of men can differ was demonstrated a short time later when the same Court applied the test and Holmes found himself in disagreement with his brethren. The case [7] involved a conviction under the Sedition Act of 1918. The defendants had been convicted for urging munitions workers to strike in order to protest the use of American troops to thwart the Russian Revolution. When a majority of his colleagues on the Supreme Court found that the convictions had to be affirmed under his "clear and present danger" test, Holmes was alarmed. He could see no danger here except in what the Court had done. Had the defendants really posed any serious threat when they threw some leaflets containing their views out of a window and onto the street? Holmes thought not. This is what he said:

> when men have realized that time has upset many fighting faiths, they may come to believe even more than they believe the very foundations of their own conduct that the ultimate good desired is better reached by

[7] Abrams v. United States, 250 U.S. 616 (1919).

free trade in ideas—that the best test of truth is the power of the thought to get itself accepted in the competition of the market, and that truth is the only ground upon which their wishes safely can be carried out. That at any rate is the theory of our Constitution. It is an experiment, as all life is an experiment. Every year if not every day we have to wager our salvation upon some prophecy based upon imperfect knowledge. While that experiment is part of our system I think that we should be eternally vigilant against attempts to check the expression of opinions that we loathe and believe to be fraught with death, unless they so imminently threaten immediate interference with the lawful and pressing purposes of the law that an immediate check is required to save the country.[8]

The Red Scare

Holmes' dissent, in which Justice Louis D. Brandeis concurred, contained libertarian language that ranks with the best in John Milton's *Areopagitica* and John Stuart Mill's *On Liberty*. But the majority of the Supreme Court was merely reflecting the temper of the times. The immediate postwar period had generated a mood of hysteria against unorthodox beliefs and the chief victims were great numbers of aliens. Attorney General A. Mitchell Palmer, an appointee of President Wilson, led this fight against the "Red" threat. In one single night, in a series of raids in thirty-three different cities, more than four thousand persons alleged to be Communists or other brands of radicals were arrested.[9]

Citizens as well as aliens were caught in this indiscriminate net, and such legal niceties as arrest warrants were dispensed with. Meeting halls, homes, and any other places where the suspected people might be were raided. The purpose of the raids was to round up the suspected aliens for deportation, and hundreds were expelled without semblance of a fair proceeding.[10] Palmer, not content with this, and, even though he was opposed in his methods by others in the Wilson administration and by some in Congress, issued dire warnings of a revolutionary plot set for May 1, 1920. Although May Day went by without incident, the National Guard had been called out and the entire New York City police force had been put on 24-hour duty.[11]

[8] Ibid., p. 630.
[9] Robert K. Murray, *Red Scare, A Study of National Hysteria, 1919–1920* (New York: McGraw-Hill, 1964), p. 213.
[10] Ibid., pp. 213–17.
[11] Ibid., pp. 252–53.

Although the mood of the country cooled somewhat as it returned to normalcy, the problem of the First Amendment and state legislation aimed at subversive activity eventually confronted the Supreme Court. At issue was the constitutionality of a New York statute enacted in 1902 as a reaction to the assassination of President McKinley by an anarchist in the preceding year. It made it a crime to advocate that organized government be overthrown by force or violence. Under this statute, an indictment was obtained against Benjamin Gitlow, a left-wing Socialist,[12] for publishing a manifesto which, it was claimed, was an incitement to the forcible overthrow that the state legislature had prohibited. Gitlow's trial resulted in a conviction, and it was this conviction which the Supreme Court was asked to review. Gitlow urged that his conviction be reversed on the ground that the statute was an unconstitutional abridgement of free speech. The Supreme Court, however, rejected this argument and left the conviction standing.[13]

Justice Edward T. Sanford, who wrote the opinion in the *Gitlow* case, reduced the "clear and present danger" test to a shadow of its former self. Holmes had wanted to leave it to the jury in each case to decide whether the utterance complained of had created the danger that an evil that Congress could act against would take place. But as Justice Sanford interpreted the principle, a state legislature could in effect take this question out of the hands of the jury and itself decide that a certain type of utterance created a "clear and present danger" that a certain evil would occur. That, said Sanford, was exactly what the state legislature in New York had done. It had determined that a certain class of utterances—those containing advocacy of the violent overthrow of government—possessed a dangerous tendency, and it had therefore banned them. Thus the only question that the jury had to decide was whether Gitlow in fact had made the statement that the prosecution had attributed to him. Only on this point did the state have to offer evidence. There was no need for evidence on whether the utterance had, in fact, created any danger, since the state legislature had already resolved that question.

What was left of the First Amendment in the wake of the Sanford decision was not clear. For all that a state legislature would have to do in the future to exempt itself from the prohibition against abridging free speech would be to declare that the kind of statement that it

---

[12] Gitlow later became a leader of the Communist party, and still later a renegade from the party and a government informer.
[13] Gitlow v. New York, 268 U.S. 652 (1925).

wanted to outlaw had a dangerous tendency. It would not be very different from outlawing U-turns upon a finding that they often caused traffic accidents. A motorist accused of violating such a law could not offer evidence that the particular U-turn he made caused no danger to anyone since the day was clear, the road was straight, his eyesight was excellent, and he could see that there was no other car within miles in either direction. The only way he could win an acquittal was to prove that he had not made the turn at all. Against a decision that left the "clear and present danger" test in such a shambles, Holmes, and Brandeis with him, had no alternative but to register emphatic dissent.

There was one respect, however, in which the decision in the *Gitlow* case advanced the cause of free expression. For until this case was decided, the First Amendment had been looked upon only as a restriction on Congress, not on the state legislatures. The wording of the amendment ("*Congress* shall make no law . . .") [14] had dictated this interpretation, and so had the historical context in which the amendment was proposed and adopted. It had, in fact, never occurred to those who pressed for the Bill of Rights that the states might become oppressive and abridge individual freedom. What they were worried about at the time was the new national government. There was thus no constitutional limitation on the power of a state to restrict freedom of expression.[15]

But the events leading up to the Civil War had demonstrated that the states can pose at least as much of a threat to individual liberty as the national government can, and in the aftermath of that war the Constitution was amended to provide the protection that had not been available before against oppressive state actions. One of the post-Civil War amendments, the Fourteenth, contained such spacious language that some contended it had been meant to afford individuals the same protection against oppressive state practices that the Bill of Rights conferred with respect to oppressive federal practices.[16] Accordingly, legal

[14] Emphasis added.

[15] Any doubt that still remained about whether the Bill of Rights applied to the states was resolved by the Supreme Court in 1833. The Court had to decide whether a portion of the Fifth Amendment had to be respected by the states or only by Congress. Since the Fifth Amendment, unlike the First, does not mention Congress, speaking, rather, in general terms, the question was a substantial one. The Court's decision, however, was that no portion of the Bill of Rights had any applicability to the states. Barron v. Baltimore, 7 Pet. 243 (1833).

[16] Particularly relevant were the following words in the amendment: "No State shall make or enforce any law which shall abridge the privileges or immunities of citizens of the United States; nor shall any State deprive any person of life, liberty, or property, without due process of law. . . ."

counsel for Mr. Gitlow argued that the New York state statute should be judged against the same First Amendment criterion that would have applied had the law been an act of Congress. It was an audacious argument, for just three years earlier the Court had denied that there is any obligation on the states "to confer upon those within their jurisdiction . . . the right of free speech." [17] The Court, however, disregarded the precedent, and made this momentous pronouncement:

> For present purposes we may and do assume that freedom of speech and of the press—which are protected by the First Amendment from abridgment by Congress—are among the fundamental personal rights and "liberties" protected by the due process clause of the Fourteenth Amendment from impairment by the states.

In a sense, of course, this was a hollow victory for Gitlow, since his conviction was affirmed anyway. It was also a somewhat hollow victory for free expression, since the "dangerous tendency" test propounded by Justice Sanford made it easy for either the states or the federal government to abridge with impunity those utterances which were considered unsafe. But the holding did become a precedent for many later decisions that took a more generous view of freedom of speech and of the press. It also hastened the incorporation of more and more Bill of Rights guarantees into the Fourteenth Amendment.[18]

The War Against the Communist Party

The New York statute under which Gitlow was prosecuted later became the model for a federal antisedition act. In 1940, a few months after the start of World War II, Congress passed the first federal antisedition law since World War I. This law, known as the Smith Act, made it a crime to teach or advocate the overthrow of the government of the United States, or any state, by force or violence. It also prohibited the organization of any group to teach or advocate violent overthrow, or even mere membership in such a group. In addition, there was a catch-all conspiracy section, making it just as serious a crime to discuss plans for doing any or all of these things.

---

[17] Prudential Insurance Company v. Cheek, 259 U.S. 530 (1922).
[18] As a result of a line of decisions over the last decade, there are today only a few provisions in the Bill of Rights that do not restrict the states in the same way that they restrict the federal government.

FREEDOM OF POLITICAL EXPRESSION

At the time that the Smith Act was being debated in Congress, its opponents pointed out that although the statute used the words "overthrow of the government . . . by force or violence" over and over again, it was not subversive *acts* with which the legislation was concerned. The real targets of the law, it was said, were at least one step removed from any attempt to overthrow the government, for what people were being forbidden to do was to *teach and advocate,* to *organize,* and to *belong to an organization.* In this view, the conspiracy section was the most dangerous of all, since it could be used to punish those who were planning at some future time, not to attempt violent overthrow but simply to teach or advocate it, or— even further removed from the realm of action—to organize or join a group that taught and advocated it.

It was precisely this conspiracy section which was used as the basis for the conviction of eleven top leaders of the Communist party in a lengthy trial concluded in 1949. The defendants lost an appeal of their conviction in the United States Court of Appeals, and fared no better when they carried their case to the Supreme Court. Speaking through Chief Justice Fred M. Vinson, the Court declined to accept the argument that there had been any violation of the defendants' First Amendment rights. Although the six justices in the majority claimed to be applying the "clear and present danger" test, they were really using a rewording of the Holmes formula that had been suggested by Judge Learned Hand, of the United States Court of Appeals for the Second Circuit, in first affirming the convictions of the eleven Communists. Hand had said: "In each case [courts] must ask whether the gravity of the 'evil,' discounted by its improbability, justifies such invasion of free speech as is necessary to avoid the danger." [19]

The Hand formula and its adoption by the Supreme Court meant that "grave and probable" had replaced "clear and present," thus substantially reducing the burden of proof that the government would have to carry in order to justify the suppression of dissent. Had the government been compelled to prove acts amounting to a "clear and present danger," it is unlikely that it could have done so. The defendants had not been accused of a single overt action aimed at bringing down the government. No blueprint or plan for sabotage had formed any part of the evidence in the government's case; nor were the defendants even accused of teaching or advocating overthrow of the government,

[19] Quoted in Dennis v. United States, 341 U.S. 494 (1951).

or sabotage. Their crime was nothing more than that they had *conspired* to teach and advocate the revolutionary doctrines espoused by Marx, Engels, Lenin, and Stalin. As Justice William O. Douglas said in a dissenting opinion, "we deal here with speech alone." [20]

The hysteria of the McCarthy era had so clouded the air, however, that there was practically no public understanding of this point. Many were under the impression that the Communists had been convicted of trying to overthrow the government, although there was certainly no member of the Supreme Court who labored under this misapprehension. Yet, even federal judges, though insulated from political pressures by life tenure, are not always immune from the influence of public attitudes. Justice Hugo L. Black, who joined Justice Douglas in dissent, evidently thought that precisely this had been responsible for the Court's action in upholding the convictions of the eleven Communists. "There is hope," he said, "that in calmer times, when present pressures, passions, and fears subside, this or some later Court will restore the First Amendment liberties to the high preferred place where they belong in a free society." [21]

Six years later, the Court did, in fact, move toward a realization of the hope that Justice Black had expressed. Although it declined to go so far as to invalidate the Smith Act outright, it reversed the convictions of fourteen lower-echelon Communists and, in so doing, ruled that the government, in prosecuting Smith Act cases, would have to prove more than mere abstract advocacy of revolution; actual advocacy of revolutionary acts would have to be shown.[22] It is always hazardous to speculate about the reasons for such a reversal by the Supreme Court. It is probably relevant, however, that the McCarthy era had ended and that public excitement over Communism had diminished somewhat. There had also been changes in the Court's membership. Chief Justice Vinson had died, and his successor, Earl Warren, had little sympathy with legislation infringing freedom of expression. In addition, two of Vinson's allies in the 1951 decision were also gone from the Court.[23]

Although the Supreme Court's decision in this case all but destroyed the effectiveness of the Smith Act, the government had another arrow in its sling: prosecutions under the Internal Security Act of 1950. In this act, Congress had established machinery for compelling the Commu-

---

[20] Ibid., p. 584.
[21] Ibid., p. 581.
[22] Yates v. United States, 354 U.S. 298 (1957).
[23] Justice Robert H. Jackson had been succeeded by John Marshall Harlan, and Justice Sherman Minton by William J. Brennan, Jr.

nist party, as well as its front organizations, to register with the federal government. In its registration statement, the party would, among other things, have to list the names of all its members, thus subjecting them to all sorts of pressures in a society that was not overly fond of Communists. As if that were not enough, innumerable legal disabilities would attach to members of the party. They could not, for example, apply for a passport, or accept employment in a defense plant, or even apply for a scholarship financed with federal funds. In the event that the party refused to obey a final order to register, it would subject itself to a fine of $100,000 for every day that it persisted in its refusal.

Fighting to preserve its right to continue functioning without governmental harassment, the party appealed to the federal courts to invalidate the Internal Security Act. The principal argument it made was that the act violated the First Amendment by restricting freedom of speech, press, and assembly. Never in history had the Supreme Court struck down an act of Congress under the First Amendment, and the Court declined to do so in this case. But the party was more successful with another of the constitutional arguments that it made: that requiring Communists to register would violate the Fifth Amendment by compelling them to incriminate themselves, since membership in the Communist party had been made a crime by the Smith Act. When the United States Court of Appeals for the District of Columbia threw out the government's case on this basis,[24] the Supreme Court declined to disturb, or even to review, its decision.[25] Then, in a series of decisions, the Court dealt with other provisions of the Internal Security Act, invalidating one section after another.[26] So complete was the judicial evisceration of the act that the Subversive Activities Control Board, the administrative agency established to label organizations as Communist, was left with virtually nothing to do, and membership on the board became a $26,000 a year sinecure.[27]

[24] 331 F. 2d 807 (1963).
[25] 377 U.S. 968 (1964).
[26] See, for example, Aptheker v. Secretary of State, 378 U.S. 500 (1964), and Albertson v. Subversive Activities Control Board, 382 U.S. 70 (1965).
[27] The term sinecure was widely used to describe membership on the board after it was disclosed that President Johnson had appointed to the board a 29-year-old accountant whose only qualification seemed to be that he had married a presidential secretary who was a particular presidential favorite. Soon after taking office, President Nixon nominated Otto Otepka for a vacancy on the board. Otepka, a former State Department security officer, had fallen from grace during the previous administration for leaking secret information to a Senate committee. His friends on Capitol Hill, particularly Senator Dirksen, now sought to reward Otepka by getting Mr. Nixon to appoint him to the job which now paid $36,000.

A Climate of Fear   In the post-World War II period, the campaign against alleged subversion was by no means confined to the enforcement of sedition statutes. Many other aspects of governmental action, both national and state, made it risky, especially in the 1950s, to voice any radical opinions. Loyalty oaths and legislative investigations became a regular feature of American life, as did attempts to bar left-wingers from employment in industry and even in schools and colleges. Individuals who might have made important contributions to government chose careers outside the public service to avoid subjecting themselves to the awkwardness and embarrassment of a field check by the Federal Bureau of Investigation, involving the questioning of their friends, neighbors, and associates about intimate details of their personal life and their political activities.

With the executive and legislative branches vying with each other to prove their anti-Communist zealousness, it fell to the courts to preserve the First Amendment from the depredations being made against it. During the most intense years of the cold war, however, there was never a majority on the Supreme Court that was willing to tackle the issue head on. Rather, the justices contented themselves with trying to eliminate some of the grossest violations of individual rights and to introduce at least a modicum of fairness in the procedures being employed. And even this niggling effort brought down an avalanche of denunciation and invective on the heads of the justices, even including a demand for the impeachment of former Chief Justice Warren.[28]

The reluctance of a majority on the Court to challenge the political branches of the government directly on the subject of free expression and free association was evident in a series of decisions concerning the House Committee on Un-American Activities. The committee operated under a broad mandate to investigate the "objects of un-American propaganda activities in the United States," as well as "propaganda that . . . attacks the principle of the form of government as guaranteed by our Constitution. . . ." In addition, it was one of the three committees in the House that had been given the power to issue subpoenas to compel the presence of an unwilling witness and to insist, under threat of punishment, that he answer its questions and produce records it wanted.

In one hearing after another, the committee had subpoenaed unfriendly witnesses and pilloried them for the political beliefs and activ-

---

[28] Anti-Warren sentiment was especially strong in the South, attributable to the Chief Justice's 1954 opinion invalidating racial segregation in the public schools.

ities that it imputed to them. When subjected to questioning about their politics, many witnesses declined to reply, invoking the protection of the Fifth Amendment, which says that in a criminal case—and a congressional investigation can lead to criminal prosecution—no person shall be compelled "to be a witness against himself. . . ." Against these witnesses, the committee could take no action, though the simple fact that one had been compelled to appear before a body with the term un-American in its title was often enough to assure dismissal from one's employment and ostracism by one's friends. Some witnesses declined to make use of the Fifth Amendment, claiming instead that the committee was precluded by the First Amendment from subjecting them to an inquisition about their politics. Against such witnesses, the committee did have a weapon. It would certify to the House as a whole that contempt of Congress had been committed, and thus set in motion a series of events that would culminate in a criminal prosecution by the Department of Justice. The Supreme Court became involved when it was asked to review convictions obtained in these cases.

It was in 1957 that the Supreme Court for the first time reversed the contempt conviction of a witness who had declined to answer questions of the committee. In a scathing opinion by Chief Justice Warren, the Court referred deprecatingly to the authorizing resolution under which the committee operated. "Who can define the meaning of 'un-American' "? it asked. "What is that single, solitary 'principle of the form of government as guaranteed by our Constitution' "? Chief Justice Warren conceded that the power of Congress to investigate is broad. But, he cautioned, the investigative power "cannot be inflated into a general power to expose where the predominant result can only be an invasion of the private rights of individuals."[29] Since the committee had made no effort to compensate for the deficiencies of its authorizing resolution by informing witnesses of how its questions were serving a valid legislative purpose, the Court held that contempt had not been committed when one witness declined to provide answers.

The sharp language employed by Chief Justice Warren made it seem that the Court would subject to the most critical scrutiny all future contempt-of-Congress convictions that related to the Un-American Activities Committee. The impression was heightened by the fact that only one member of the Court[30] dissented from the majority decision. The checkered career of the committee was far from over, however. A

---

[29] Watkins v. United States, 354 U.S. 178 (1957).
[30] Justice Tom Clark, who had been Attorney General in the Truman administration.

change in the personnel of the Court and a switch in the votes of two justices who had been on the majority side in the earlier case combined to give the committee a new lease on life only two years later. With Chief Justice Warren now forced into dissent, a 5-to-4 majority affirmed the conviction of a professor who had been uncooperative with the committee.[31] The Court relied on what it called a balancing of the interest of the committee in obtaining information from the witness against the witness's interest in exercising his First Amendment rights.

The balancing test rests on the assumption that the First Amendment, despite its categorical and unqualified wording, should not be interpreted as conferring an absolute right to freedom of expression. Instead, the right that it did confer should be weighed against the equally important right of the government to protect itself. When the balance was struck in that particular way, with the interest of a single individual placed on one side of the scales and the interests of all society on the other, the result was seldom a happy one for the individual.

Justice Black was a vigorous critic of the majority's position. The framers of the Amendment, he said, had themselves done all the balancing that they intended to be done, confident that absolute freedom of expression was less dangerous to society than any authorization, however slight, of repression. Thus Black's fundamental position was that in free-speech cases, there was no place at all for using the balancing technique. If the Court disagreed with him, he hoped—usually in vain—that it would not balance the rights of an individual against the rights of society, but rather two rights of society against each other: the right to receive the benefits of free discussion against the right to protect the internal security of the nation.

Vietnam: The Antiwar Movement

As the war in Vietnam became more and more the central issue in the sixties, new problems of free expression arose. Wars always seem to breed efforts to suppress dissent, and in this respect Vietnam was no different from the nation's previous wars. What was different was the magnitude and intensity of the dissent to be suppressed. To begin with, Vietnam was an unpopular war, with impor-

---

[31] Barenblatt v. United States, 360 U.S. 110 (1959).

tant segments of the public resenting the absence of clear-cut goals, the absence of any immediate prospects of either victory or peace, and the credibility gap for which the Johnson administration was blamed. With a great deal of the opposition to the war concentrated among the young, another factor came into play: the extent to which the direct-action tactics of the civil rights movement had made an impression on the generation of students that had been snapped out of the lethargy of the cold war years by the inspiration of the Blacks' campaign for "Freedom Now." The civil rights movement had resorted to defiance of established authority when it concluded that this authority was illegitimate since it represented only the white community. Another justification for the breaking of a law was the conscientious conclusion that the law violated basic precepts of morality and therefore lacked any authority.

This was precisely the reasoning of many in the peace movement. It was said that a president who had been elected on a peace platform and had then turned around to adopt the war platform of his opponent had swindled the voters and thereby forfeited any claim to their loyalty. It was also said that even a legitimate government could not compel its citizens to participate in an atrocious war of aggression in which the principal victims were women and children.

Not all who accepted this chain of reasoning were led to outright defiance of the government through acts of civil disobedience. Many could legitimately be considered conscientious objectors, and were willing to comply with the legal procedures that are set down to obtain the appropriate Selective Service classification. Others did whatever they could to evade the draft without actually defying it—feigning illness, maneuvering to obtain occupational deferments, or taking refuge in the universities. The great legal questions, however, were posed not by these actions but rather by the actions of others who positively sought ways to demonstrate their opposition not only to the draft but also to the war in general.

One dramatic way for a draft-age youth to demonstrate his opposition to the war was by destroying his Selective Service Classification Card. The method became especially popular after August, 1965, when Congress made the destruction of one's draft card a criminal offense, thus increasing manifold the symbolic value of such an action. When the number of draft-card burnings did, indeed, increase, the Department of Justice instituted several prosecutions under the new law. Although convictions were the result in the ensuing trials, in one case the statute enacted by Congress in 1965 was held unconstitutional by one United States court of appeals.[32]

The Supreme Court showed no disposition to challenge the power of Congress to provide for conscription and the means to insure its workability. Chief Justice Warren wrote a strong defense of the power of Congress, dismissing the alleged infringement on the First Amendment right of expression as merely incidental.[33] Only Justice Douglas resisted the majority tide by urging that even though O'Brien had not pressed the point, the validity of conscription in the absence of a declaration of war by Congress should be settled.[34]

Where no direct challenge to the power of Congress was involved, those trying to show their opposition to the draft fared better than draft-card burners. A number of students at the University of Michigan had participated in an antiwar demonstration outside the offices of the local draft board in Ann Arbor. Evidently the students had broken no law because they were not arrested and no legal action was taken against them. Their names, however, were forwarded to their own local draft boards, with the result that some of them lost their student deferments and were placed in the classification 1-A. The government was not at all united in its reaction to these events. On the one hand, General Lewis B. Hershey, national director of the Selective Service System, felt that the local boards had acted within their powers. As Hershey saw it, the students could not threaten to disrupt the work of the local board in Ann Arbor and then expect to be granted special privileges by the Selective Service System. The Department of Justice, on the other hand, viewed the situation in an entirely different light, declaring publicly that the machinery of the Selective Service System should not be used for punitive purposes. It was therefore entirely satisfied when the Court of Appeals for the Second Circuit found in

---

[32] Each of the eleven courts of appeals has jurisdiction over one of the judicial circuits into which the country is divided. When contrary decisions are handed down by different courts of appeals, this conflict must be resolved by the Supreme Court, especially when one court of appeals has invalidated an act of Congress.

[33] United States v. O'Brien, 391 U.S. 367 (1968).

[34] On the same day as the O'Brien decision, the Court denied writs of *certiorari* in two cases which, according to Douglas, raised a constitutional issue never before decided: whether the draft is valid during peacetime. In both cases Douglas dissented from the denial of *certiorari*. Holmes v. United States, 391 U.S. 936, and Hart v. United States, 391 U.S. 956. *Certiorari* is one of the two major ways in which litigants, unhappy with a lower court decision (usually a United States court of appeals or a state highest court), request the Supreme Court to review such a decision. The granting of the writ, which has the effect of bringing the case before the Supreme Court, is entirely discretionary and requires the vote of four of the nine Justices.

favor of the young men without, however, handing down a sweeping ruling that might have cast doubt on the finality of local board classifications in ordinary cases.

But the government's most dramatic attempt to suppress antiwar activities came when it obtained indictments in early 1968 for draft resistance against the famous baby doctor and author, Benjamin Spock, and four others.[35] After a four-week trial, four of the five were found guilty (Raskin was acquitted) by a federal court jury in Boston. On the government side, it was hoped that this show of force would reduce the widespread evasion and defiance of the draft which had built up to a peak during the fall of 1967. Rather than being distressed by the indictments, those in the antiwar movement saw it as an opportunity to air in a court of law their charges that the war in Vietnam was illegal.

The presiding judge, however, refused to allow the defendants to introduce evidence about the illegality of American conduct of the war. The accused were thus deprived of their chief defense: that advocating refusal to participate in the war was in fact legal because the war itself was illegal. What the defendants hoped to show was that they were advocating refusal to do an illegal act.

Judging from the renewed wave of draft-card burnings in the fall of 1968, it seemed clear that the government's aim to lessen resistance to the draft had not been successful. In fact, by the end of 1968, offenses against the Selective Service System had become the third most frequent federal crime. It remained to be seen, also, whether the convictions would stand on appeal. Initially the U.S. Court of Appeals for the First Circuit was the court to review the case. It decided in July of 1969 that the convictions of all the defendants had to be reversed but said that the government could retry Coffin and Goodman if it could meet a higher standard of proof in establishing specific intent to commit a crime. The decision fell far short of vindicating the First Amendment freedom of expression of the defendants. One judge dissented precisely on this basis, saying further that the Constitution barred application of conspiracy to the facts in the case.

Even before the decision had been rendered, the government, evidently enamored of the conspiracy approach to suppress dissent, had indicted several persons who, it alleged, had organized the demon-

---

[35] Charged along with Spock for conspiracy to aid and abet draft resistance were William Sloane Coffin, an active opponent of the war and a chaplain at Yale University; Marcus Raskin, a one-time White House Office adviser to President Kennedy; Mitchell Goodman, an author; and Michael Ferber, a Harvard graduate student.

strations in Chicago during the 1968 Democratic National Convention. The decision of the Court of Appeals in Boston, however, indicated that the government would have to try even harder if it hoped to be successful.

Although opposition to the war in Vietnam has severely tested the resiliency of the First Amendment, developments in other areas have actually extended the protection offered freedom of expression. Perhaps most notably, the Court has been solicitous of the right to criticize the conduct of public officials. The Court demonstrated this solicitude by making it extremely difficult for any official to recover damages in an action for libel. In such a suit, the Court ruled, it would not suffice for the official to establish that the charges made against him were false. He would also have to prove that they had been made maliciously and with reckless disregard of the truth.[36] Any other conclusion, the Court feared, would have acted to inhibit private citizens and the press as well from the kind of robust, free discussion of public issues that is so close to the heart of the democratic process. So concerned were the justices about maintaining this kind of discussion that they were willing to leave public officials in a highly vulnerable position, subject to entirely baseless defamation and yet unable to proceed legally against it.

Business and the First Amendment

In other First Amendment cases, too, the justices have shown that they are reconciled to the fact that often a price must be paid for safeguarding the First Amendment. One of the most important of these was the case in which the Court interpreted away much of the coverage of the 1946 Federal Regulation of Lobbying Act in order to avoid raising grave First Amendment problems. In passing the law, Congress has said nothing to indicate that it was intended to apply only to those who contacted members of Congress directly. But the Court chose to construe the act to include only "lobbying in its commonly accepted sense—to direct communication with Members of Congress on pending or proposed Federal legislation." [37] It also meant that organizations engaged in grass-roots lobbying were now exempt from the registration requirements of the act.

[36] New York Times v. Sullivan, 376 U.S. 254 (1964). See also Garrison v. Louisiana, 379 U.S. 64 (1964).
[37] United States v. Harriss, 347 U.S. 612 (1954).

FREEDOM OF POLITICAL EXPRESSION

This was not the only instance in which the Supreme Court was willing to reconcile itself to a generally unsatisfactory situation in order to avoid any incursion, however slight, on the First Amendment. Another such instance involved a struggle between railroad and trucking interests in Pennsylvania over the legal limits on weights carried on the highway. When the railroads mounted a massive propaganda campaign to advance their cause, the truckers counterattacked with a legal suit under the antitrust statutes, claiming that the public relations activities of the railroads amounted to a conspiracy in restraint of trade.[38] The federal district judge who tried the case agreed and awarded the truckers a substantial monetary judgment; his decision was upheld by the U.S. Court of Appeals for the Third Circuit.

But to the Supreme Court the First Amendment issue lurking in the case loomed larger than it had for the courts below. This issue had been raised by the railroads, which claimed that their public relations campaign represented nothing more than an exercise of the right of petition. Although the members of the Supreme Court may not have been happy with the unfair means that the railroads had employed to discredit their competitors, they were even more concerned about maintaining the integrity of the First Amendment. As a consequence, they held unanimously that the district court and the court of appeals had misinterpreted the intent of Congress in the antitrust statutes. Any other conclusion would have raised serious constitutional questions.[39]

Public Employees: Rights of Expression

Although these cases indicate that the Supreme Court is zealous in keeping the political process open, at least where the explosive issue of internal security is not involved, there is one aspect of the problem that the Court seems reluctant to tackle in recent years: the right of public employees to participate in political activity. At the present time, this right exists only in a highly attenuated form. For Congress ordained, in the Hatch Acts of 1939 and 1940 that no federal employee may accept an active role in a political party or in

---

[38] The legal aspects of the case are analyzed in a comprehensive case study by Andrew Hacker, "Pressure Politics in Pennsylvania: The Truckers vs. the Railroads," in Alan F. Westin, ed., *The Uses of Power* (New York: Harcourt, Brace, and World, 1962), pp. 356–66.
[39] Eastern Railroad Presidents Conference v. Noerr Motor Freight, 365 U.S. 127 (1961).

an election campaign. In imposing this restriction, Congress acted out of the best of motives. What it wanted was to protect civil servants from pressure by the party in power to pay for their jobs with service to the party. Among many of those who are covered by the Hatch Act, however, there is a strong feeling that Congress, in enacting such a broad restriction to combat such a limited evil, had used an elephant gun where a flyswatter would have been more appropriate. In any event, they resent being reduced to the status of second-class citizens, and are not satisfied with the assurance that it is all for their own good.

The number of second-class citizens is by no means small. Some two million federal employees are included, as well as public employees at the state and local level if their jobs are financed in whole or in part by federal funds. In addition, so many states have chosen to emulate the example of Congress by passing "little Hatch Acts" that the total number of Americans whose political activity is circumscribed by one law or another comes to about ten million. Under such circumstances, it would be worthwhile for the Supreme Court to take a long, hard look at the functioning of the Hatch Act in its present-day setting. Although the Court would have to reverse a decision made in 1947 that the law is a legitimate use of the power of Congress to protect the impartiality and integrity of the public service,[40] the auguries are not unfavorable for reconsideration of its previous decision. For one thing, none of the justices who subscribed to the 1947 decision is still on the Court, while Justices Black and Douglas, who dissented, continue to serve. In addition, one of the most respected state supreme courts in the nation, the California Supreme Court, invalidated a state law that prohibited public employees from participating in election campaigns.[41] This decision may well be an indication of how the United States Supreme Court will react when an appropriate case under the Hatch Act comes before it.

It is clear that in the years ahead many new questions about the dimensions of political expression and dissent will be posed. Although courts will frequently be called upon to provide the answers, the most important factor in the long run will be the willingness of society at large to recognize the social usefulness of free speech.

The omens are by no means all favorable. For although Americans

[40] United Public Workers v. Mitchell, 330 U.S. 75 (1947).
[41] The California court recognized that, as the number of persons employed by government rises, "the necessity of preserving for them the maximum practicable right to participate in the political life of the republic grows. . . ." Bagley v. Washington Township Hospital District, 55 Cal. Rptr. 401 (1966).

are abstractly devoted to free speech, they tend to take a dim view of people who exercise the right to espouse unpopular positions. It is such ambivalence which makes it possible to favor denying the right to speak to Communists even while adhering to a belief in freedom of speech generally.[42]

An entire nation, moreover, should not thrust such a burden for maintaining the viability of free expression as it does on the courts, and especially on the Supreme Court. In many instances this simply amounts to a legislative body passing the buck to judges to make the often unpopular decision to uphold the rights of minorities. The more a nation becomes accustomed to avoiding responsibility, the easier does it become to disparage the importance of the freedoms of the First Amendment. And even though the judicial organs may play a necessary and key role in *protecting* freedom of expression, the function of government should not be solely negative. As one writer has recognized, the "natural balance of forces in society today tends to be weighted against individual expression." Such conditions, he continues, demand that "in a modern democratic society . . . a deliberate, affirmative, and even aggressive effort be made to support the system of free expression.[43]

A great deal is at stake because none of the ways in which the citizen relates to his government can be very meaningful if free expression cannot be practiced without fear of retaliation. In obtaining information on which candidates or which party to vote for, in framing one's ideas about the political system, in identifying with an occupational or ethnic or religious or fraternal group, or in playing a minor role in a political party organization—individuals are engaged in the great discourse which is the stuff of free government. The meaning of a free society is that even people who dissent on the most basic questions should be permitted to proselytize and organize for the acceptance of their views, however extreme these views may be. There is much wisdom in these words by a great philosopher of free expression: "To be afraid of ideas, any ideas, is to be unfit for self-government." [44]

---

[42] James W. Prothro and Charles M. Grigg, "Fundamental Principles of Democracy: Bases of Agreement and Disagreement," *Journal of Politics* 22 (May 1960): 276.

[43] Thomas I. Emerson, *Toward a General Theory of the First Amendment* (New York: Vintage Books, 1967), p. 115.

[44] Alexander Meiklejohn, *Political Freedom* (New York: Harper and Row, 1960), p. 28.

Part Three

The Policymaking Process

AN INTRODUCTORY NOTE

THE CONCEPT of representative government implies a certain kind of relationship between citizens and their government. At the very least, it implies that citizens are involved in the selection of those who will make governmental decisions, and that means are available to influence the decisions of those who have ben selected. Part I of this book has dealt with the variety and complexity of the relationships between citizens and their government. In Part II some of the factors that condition these relationships were considered. The focus now shifts to *who* the policymakers are and *how* they make decisions; in Part III, therefore, the concern is with the policymaking process.

A study of the policymaking process consists of more than a description of the three branches of government: the legislative, executive, and judicial. The reality of American government is far more complex than such a study would indicate. Neither is it much help to invent other, unofficial branches of government as tools of analysis, although at various times interest groups, the press, and the independent regulatory agencies have each been referred to as a fourth branch of government.

Since the policymaking process *is* a process, it is far preferable to analyze it as such. A process can be defined, in the simplest terms, "as a series of related events or acts over a period of time." [1] When looked at in this way, the policymaking process consists of a series of events or acts from the origination of ideas for public policy to the time when such ideas become effective as rules that govern or at least influence the behavior of both citizens and government.

---

[1] Robert E. Agger, Daniel Goldrich, and Bert E. Swanson, *The Rulers and the Ruled* (New York: John Wiley, 1964), p. 40.

Although defining the policymaking process may be a relatively simple task, describing it is not. For no single pattern characterizes the process; there is, in fact, no single process. It is more appropriate to think of the policymaking process as series of processes, the end result of which is the making of policy decisions.

One of these processes involves the origination of ideas for public policy. There are literally thousands of sources from which ideas spring about what government should do: individual citizens, organized interest groups, agencies in the bureaucracy, individual congressmen, staff members of congressional committees, heads of departments, and even the president. Conceiving of ideas is one thing; gaining support for their consideration by policymakers is quite another task. Thus an important part of the policymaking process is concerned with developing the policy agenda: what ideas will be given serious consideration.

Once adequate support is generated behind an idea for public policy, the focus shifts to *how* and *by whom* such an idea can be converted into effectively binding rules which guide individual or organizational behavior. All three of the major institutions (or branches) of governments are engaged in the process of making rules. Some rules may take the form of a law enacted by Congress; but many more rules, which are just as effective in guiding conduct, are made by executive agencies, by the president, or by the courts. Whether a rule emerges in the form of a law of Congress, or a regulation of an executive agency, or a decision of a court, depends on a variety of circumstances. And in each instance of rule-making different processes and different policymakers may be involved.

The notion of process implies, perhaps, a beginning and an end. But the policymaking process of American government is not so easily delimited. Much of what takes place from origination to rule-making occurs simultaneously rather than consecutively. What may seem to be the end of the process for a particular policy may only mark the beginning of another cycle, for the policymaking process follows few formal rules, and the forms that it takes vary with the circumstances. The process is open-ended and open-sided, at once a fascinating and frustrating object of study.

The policymaking process, moreover, fails to conform with the formal appearance suggested by the existence of three branches of government. Congress, it is true, does play the primary role in making laws; executive agencies do have the major responsibility for administering public policy. Of greater importance, however, to an understanding of the dynamics of the policymaking process is the notion of interdependence among the many rule-makers, no matter what institution or branch they may formally be members of.

A chairman of a congressional subcommittee, a lobbyist, and a bureau chief in a department may very well be linked in a subsystem, each representing his organization's interest in a particular policy area.[2] The policymaking process consists, in large part, of hundreds of such subsystems, each concerned with different policy areas: coal mining, barge shipping, juvenile delinquency, conservation, cable television, smoking, and so on and on, paralleling the myriad social and economic problems pushed on to the public policy agenda.

Under such a loosely structured system, describing the policymaking process in terms of legislative, executive, and judicial branches has limited utility. For the subsystems cut across institutional lines. Nonetheless, the existence of institutions of government does have significance, for their nature and functions condition the roles played by rule-makers in the policymaking process. In the subsequent chapters, stress is placed on the interaction among the institutions and actors in the policymaking process. Following a chapter on the origination of ideas for public policy and how they gain a place on the policy agenda, the policymaking process is viewed as a series of interactions; first, from the perspective of Congress, and then, from that of the presidency and bureaucracy. The concluding chapter in this part focuses on the courts as policymakers.

---

[2] The subsystem concept is developed in J. Leiper Freeman, *The Political Process: Executive Bureau—Legislative Committee Relations*, rev. ed. (New York: Random House, 1965).

Chapter 9 Formulating the Policy Agenda

Congress enacts a law increasing the depletion allowance on clam and oyster shells. In the same bill, it establishes a short-lived but revolutionary new method for the financing of presidential campaigns. . . . The President announces the cessation of all bombing of North Vietnam. . . . The Federal Communications Commission approves the merger of two giants in the communications industry, the International Telephone and Telegraph Corporation and the American Broadcasting Company. Later on, it votes to reconsider its action, after the Department of Justice has registered a strong objection. . . . The Secretary of the Interior announces that the administration no longer favors the building of two dams on the Colorado River. . . . A federal court of appeals in New York decides that local draft boards may not revoke the deferments of students for engaging in protest demonstrations against the Selective Service System. . . . The Supreme Court clears the way for the malapportioned state legislature of Georgia to select the governor of the state after no candidate in the general election succeeded in obtaining the absolute majority that the state constitution required.

Each of these events involved the making of public policy decisions and the settlement, however tentative, of a complex question with perhaps a long and intricate history. In many of these situations the policymakers had not been responsible for raising the question in the first place. Where, then, did the decisions originate? The answers reflect the diversity of a complex society, for in these examples the actions which set in motion the processes of policymaking ranged from those of individuals (draft demonstrators) to interest groups (clam and oyster producers) to business corporations (ITT and ABC).

In many cases, ideas for public policy originate outside of government. Groups and individuals engaged in economic activity or the pursuit of particular social goals frequently perceive that satisfaction of their claims can be realized in some form of governmental promotion or regulation. But, just as frequently, ideas for public policy germinate in the myriad agencies and offices and bureaus of the government itself, or from advisers to the president. Individual congressmen and congressional committees are also a source of policy ideas. And quite often, moreover, it may well be interrelated combinations of any of these groups or individuals, in government or outside government, which push forward the ideas.

The President as Prime Mover

Almost anyone may conceive of an idea to better government services or ameliorate some social injustice or solve a foreign policy dilemma. But the mere origination of an idea (even a good one) is far from a guarantee that it will ever receive serious consideration by policymakers. Gaining a place on the policy agenda is an essential first step in the policymaking process. In that regard the president has an unparalleled advantage. This is not so because the framers of the Constitution intended it that way.

There is, in fact, abundant evidence to the contrary. For, in 1787, there was widespread opposition to executive power because of the tyrannical actions which the colonists ascribed to George III and because of the autocratic policies of many colonial governors. As a consequence, some delegates to the Constitutional Convention pushed for a weak executive that would be largely subservient to the legislative power. Others went so far as to propose a plural executive in which there would be fragmentation rather than concentration of power.

But men like Alexander Hamilton favored a strong executive which could act with "energy and dispatch," and it is those who thought this way who would today be pleased with how things have worked out in practice. Not that the words of Article II of the Constitution, in which the powers of the president are described, made it inevitable that a strong executive would come to dominate the governmental process. It has been more a case of powers that were described in such an ambiguous way that energetic chief executives have been able to stretch them almost beyond recognition, and of limitations that were not set out explicitly.

The principal decision that resulted in the development of a strong executive concerned the method by which presidents would be elected. The question of choosing presidents precipitated one of the great controversies at the convention. At first the delegates registered their tentative approval of an arrangement by which the president would be elected by the legislature. They did this early in their deliberations by adopting the so-called Virginia plan as a basis for discussion. This plan, which had been drafted by James Madison, dealt with a number of important questions, including the basis of representation in Congress. But none of its provisions was more important than the one providing that the president would be elected by the two Houses of Congress. For if the convention had adhered to its original approval of this plan, the American system of government would probably have come to resemble the parliamentary system of England and other European countries. Ultimately, however, the delegates decided that the election of the president should not be in the hands of the legislature. Instead, the president was to be chosen independently, through the complex mechanism of the electoral college.

This decision was of enormous significance. It meant that the chief executive would not be dependent in any way on the legislature for his election, unless no candidate received a majority in the electoral college.[1] Instead, the president would have his own independent basis

---

[1] The adoption of the Twelfth Amendment after Jefferson had won out over Burr in the House of Representatives in 1801 drastically reduced the likelihood that this power would come into play very often. As it has turned out, only in 1825, when John Quincy Adams was elected, has the choice of a president been thrown into the House. The threat which the Wallace candidacy posed in 1968 made it appear quite possible that for the first time since the 1824 contest, the House might have to decide,

of power—and today, with the development of political parties and the growth of a mass electorate, that means the American people as a whole. It was, then, this decision of the convention that made the president, more than any other political institution, representative of the nation and responsive to it.

The development of presidential power, however, is not solely the product of choices made by the framers of the Constitution. At least as important, it has been presidents themselves, as individuals, who have made the office what it is today. It is the very presidents whom historians remember—men like Jefferson, Lincoln, Theodore Roosevelt, Wilson, and Franklin D. Roosevelt—who have expanded the powers of the presidential office not only for themselves but also for those who followed them.

Above all, this expansion has meant an effort to exert presidential leadership over Congress. It was ironic that this effort began with Jefferson, for the man who was to become the nation's third chief executive had preached the virtues of legislative preeminence before he himself assumed the presidential office. Once in that office, he became convinced of the necessity for presidential leadership over his own party in Congress. By working through trusted associates in positions of legislative leadership, Jefferson managed to exercise a degree of control over Congress that was not to be matched until the administration of Woodrow Wilson more than one hundred years later.

In this century, it was Wilson who concentrated first on developing the art of legislative leadership. Even before his inauguration, Wilson made known his conception of the relations of the president with Congress. The president, he wrote, must be "as much concerned with guidance of legislation as with just and orderly execution of law. . . ."[2] This characterization of the presidential role has proved remarkably farsighted. Times of stress—caused by rapid industrialization, the growth of population, economic depression, involvement in two major wars and two other exhausting conflicts, world power and responsibility—have indeed made the president the prime figure in setting the policy agenda.

The Constitution provides that the president "shall from time to time

---

if neither of the two major party candidates received a majority of the electoral votes. Fortunately, the nation was spared such an ordeal, but, unless the demand for reform of the anachronistic electoral college system is sustained and translated into constitutional amendment, the threat of chaos still hangs heavily.

[2] Quoted in Wilfred E. Binkley, *President and Congress*, 3rd ed. (New York: Vintage Books, 1962), p. 253.

give to the Congress Information of the State of the Union, and recommend to their Consideration such Measures as he shall judge necessary and expedient."[3] In modern times, these few simple words have become the basis for a veritable proliferation of messages from the president directed toward Congress. Taken all together, and accompanied by drafts of specific legislation, it is this flow from the president, constituting his program, which forms the principal agenda of public policy.

The Message Barrage   The opening of this presidential fusillade takes the form of the annual State of the Union Message. Usually delivered on the day (President Johnson began the practice of appearing in the evening, to gain a maximum television audience) Congress convenes early in January, the State of the Union address is general in tone. It summarizes past accomplishments and suggests new ideas for government policy.

Many of those ideas are later spelled out by the president in his budget message. Although the principal purpose of the budget message is to explain the specific spending proposals that the president is making for the next fiscal year,[4] the message has even greater significance. For, it not only discusses the general fiscal picture of the nation, but also indicates specific amounts that the president wants Congress to appropriate for different policy areas, such as defense and space or health and education. It also contains requests for new legislation, set forth now in far greater detail than the generalities contained in the State of the Union Message.

A third opportunity for the president to communicate formally with Congress has been available since 1946, when a statute was enacted requiring the submission of an annual economic report. This document, produced by the President's Council of Economic Advisers, attempts to assess the state of the national economy and forecast trends that can be expected in purchasing power, employment, and production. It also may contain recommendations for federal legislation to help achieve the goal of maximum employment set out in the 1946 statute.[5] Other

---
[3] Article II, Section 3.
[4] The fiscal year begins on July 1.
[5] It was in this statute, the Employment Act of 1946, that the Council of Economic Advisers was created.

legislation with direct economic consequences may be requested, or desirable economic practices may be suggested. The wage-price guidelines, for example, which both Presidents Kennedy and Johnson hoped would restrain business and labor, were announced and reiterated in successive economic reports.

Although the State of the Union Message, the budget message, and the economic report complete the first round of presidential communications to Congress, they are only the beginning of an incessant flow of messages from the White House to Capitol Hill. One after another, messages containing the details of a particular program recommended by the White House and accompanied by draft legislation are dispatched by the president. In just two months in 1967, for example, fourteen such messages, all calling for legislation, were sent to Congress by President Johnson. Among the topics dealt with were aid for the aged, consumer protection, crime, civil rights, selective service, foreign aid, poverty, health and education, air pollution, and child welfare.

A new president, especially of a different party, is somewhat handicapped in developing his policy agenda. President Nixon, however, soon dispelled any impression that there would be a letup in the message barrage. Some fourteen presidential messages were sent to Capitol Hill in the first 100 days after the inauguration, including his plans for an antiballistic missile system and major revisions in the budget developed by the previous administration. And on April 14, after being in office less than three months, Nixon sent a message to Congress outlining a whole series of major legislative proposals he intended to send to the Hill.

The messages and bills continue to pepper Congress through its entire session. Not all are expected to receive immediate attention. Those that do not will remain as reminders of what the president wants, and in succeeding years Congress will be prodded to act on them. The major tasks that the president wants Congress to perform are presented in this manner. So encyclopedic is the typical legislative program emanating from the White House and so detailed are the recommendations it embodies that Congress usually has time to consider little else.

A National Perspective   The president's role as the chief source of policy origination would have surprised most of the framers of the Constitution and dismayed many.

Even today there is considerable uneasiness over the growth of presidential initiative in developing public policy—both in domestic legislation and foreign policy. Yet Congress finds it difficult to wrest the initiative from the executive branch. With today's society and its problems growing increasingly complex, only the president and the executive agencies seem able to develop programs that deal on an integrated basis with vast constellations of issues. Congress appears institutionally incapable of perceiving program interrelationships. Although the committee system on which it relies has encouraged a helpful degree of specialization, there is no effective machinery for overall coordination. Committees may know all there is to know about particular pieces of legislation, but Congress as a whole lacks a coherent view of how the proposals would fit into a general blueprint for domestic policy and their relationship to foreign policy.

Although there is nothing inherent in the Constitution which makes this inevitable, a combination of circumstances have conspired to make it so. In the first place, it is the president, or, rather, those seeking the office, who must put together a national coalition of interests. To the extent that a candidate attempts to appeal to interests or groups which have important electoral strength, he makes himself responsive to the demands of such groups if elected. Thus the development of national political party systems aiming for the single national electoral prize has produced a nationally oriented president.

Quite unrelated to the development of the party system are two other factors, both fiscal in nature. As the end of the nineteenth century approached, the ability of the United States government to finance itself on the basis of tariff duties declined. A very modest income tax law enacted by Congress in 1894 was declared unconstitutional by the Supreme Court the following year. In 1913, the Sixteenth Amendment was ratified, authorizing "taxes on incomes from whatever source derived," thus greatly increasing the fiscal resources potential of the national government although relatively high tax rates did not become common until the 1930s. But, even before the passage of the income tax amendment, the growing expenditures of the national government had become a matter of concern, particularly to the business community. President Taft had appointed a commission to investigate the problem, and the concept of the executive budget which it recommended finally found congressional favor in 1921, with the passage of the Budget and Accounting Act.

Before this act was passed, the president had little opportunity to hammer out a systematic legislative or budget program to present to Congress. The individual executive departments would present their spending requests directly to congressional committees, knowing little and caring less about how much was being asked by other departments. The resulting chaos persuaded Congress to adopt the far-reaching reform of 1921. No longer were the executive agencies to be permitted to make their own individual decisions about how much money they would request from Congress. Now the president, and the president alone, would make appropriations requests on behalf of his administration as a whole.

The Budget: Instrument of Policy

By accepting the concept of an executive budget, Congress put the president in a position to become dominant in the most important of all policymaking processes: the development of the budget. And at the same time, Congress gave the president a major management tool to help him discharge his budgetary responsibility: the Bureau of the Budget. All that was necessary after the passage of the 1921 act was for the kind of situation to arise that called for the full utilization of the budgetary power. This came about with the great crash of 1929 and the ensuing depression. The rejection of *laissez-faire* economic thinking during the first administration of Franklin Roosevelt, from 1933 to 1937, greatly accelerated the government's involvement in domestic economic and social policy. In the years that followed, world war and cold war emphasized the close relationship between domestic and foreign policy on the one hand and economic and fiscal policy on the other.

Thus the budget of the United States is a major instrument of national policymaking. Far more than simply an economic document, it is also a political document, reflecting the level of support that the administration wants Congress to approve for different interests in the economy: agriculture, or health, or education. It also bears a significant relationship to the general economic activity of the nation, for a budget can be designed to stimulate the economy or to cool it off, whichever course of action seems to be the wiser one under the circumstances. In addition, the budget indicates what is to be the course of the nation's foreign and military policy. Other governments can draw the necessarily obvious conclusions when the budget calls for increased spending for missiles instead of strengthening the peace-keeping machinery of the United Nations.

Every program for which money is to be spent must first have been authorized in legislation passed by Congress. For some programs (benefits for veterans of World War I provide an example), this authorization has been provided years ago on a long-term basis. For other continuing programs, such as foreign aid or military construction, annual authorization bills must be passed by Congress before any money can be appropriated. And no new program—whether it be the war on poverty or assistance for urban transportation—can be funded before authorizing legislation is enacted.

The budget submitted by the president, then, consists of requests for both authorizing legislation (establishing new programs or sanctioning the continuance of old ones) and appropriations legislation (providing money for programs previously authorized). It is, in practice, one of the major expressions of his program as president, and provides Congress with its most substantial task. Yet, although the budget is the responsibility of the president, it represents the work and interests of a vast conglomeration of governmental agencies.[6] It is these agencies that originate many of the program ideas that eventually find their way into the president's budget.

The appropriate term for describing this congeries of organizations in the executive branch is bureaucracy. Although the term is often used disparagingly, its meaning is really free from a value judgment, signifying nothing more than a collection of bureaus. The bureaucratic system of organization simply reflects specialization of function—a technique that is by no means confined to government. Most large-scale industries, for example, are, for reasons of efficiency, organized as bureaucracies. So are many national religious organizations. Bureaucracy, in short, is simply a way of organizing complex social or economic—as well as political—activity. Thus the American Telephone & Telegraph Company, the University of California, the Roman Catholic Church, the Methodist Church, and the AFL-CIO are as much bureaucracies as is the United States government.

It is precisely because bureaucracy reflects specialization of function

---

[6] The agencies (the term is used generically) in the executive branch range from gigantic departments such as Defense (employing more than a million civilians), to middle-sized ones, such as Interior (about 65,000 employees), to much smaller ones, such as the Export-Import Bank (300 employees). More than two and one-half million persons are employed in the executive branch in a variety of organizations called departments, agencies, bureaus, offices, and commissions.

that the executive agencies are the prime source of ideas for public policy in the federal government. Who in government, for example, is likely to know more about the problems of marketing milk than the Dairy Division of the Agricultural Marketing Service of the Department of Agriculture? Or more about the need for more national parks than the National Park Service of the Department of the Interior? Or more about the kinds of research the government should support in anthropology than the Division of Social Sciences under the associate director for research of the National Science Foundation? Or more about the economic picture of the railroad industry than the Bureau of Rates and Practices of the Interstate Commerce Commission?

The list could be continued indefinitely and ultimately would include practically all the activities that Americans engage in, from the arts to zoology. The bureaucracy has grown this vast—in size and scope—in response to public demands either for governmental support of certain activities or for governmental regulation of other activities. The Social Security Administration is an example of promotional activity, whereas the Interstate Commerce Commission illustrates the regulatory motivation.

Many of the large, cabinet-level departments are really nothing more than collections of agencies or bureaus, each of which was originally created in response to the demand for either promotion or regulation. This fact actually applies to all of the present-day departments except for the first three, which were created during the administration of George Washington to perform the obvious governmental functions of defense, the conduct of foreign relations, and the financing of national programs. Otherwise, the departments are really holding companies that perform something of a coordinating function for subject-matter bureaus.

The two most recently established cabinet departments are prime examples. The creation of the Department of Housing and Urban Development (1965) did little more than upgrade the then existing Housing and Home Finance Agency, which had included the Urban Renewal Administration, the Public Housing Administration, and the Federal Housing Administration. In 1966, the Department of Transportation was created. But this, too, represented primarily a reshuffling of agencies already existing in the Department of Commerce and elsewhere. The Bureau of Public Roads, previously in Commerce, became the Federal Highway Administration, whereas the Federal Aviation Agency, created in 1958 as an independent agency, was brought within the new department as the Federal Aviation Administration.

Interest groups understand this fact of executive organization and, as a consequence, pay less attention to the broad-gauge departments and more to the narrow-gauge bureaus. The American Forestry Association or the Forest Products Research Society, for example, are likely to be more interested in the Forest Service of the Department of Agriculture than in the department as a whole. The same can be said of other specialized interest groups and their counterpart specialized agencies, wherever these happen to be located in the federal bureaucracy. It is out of the cross-fertilization that takes place between the interest group and the bureau that many initiatives for new or altered public policy originate. Commonly, the agency incorporates the idea into legislation and then tries to advance the legislation on the intricate and tortuous path toward becoming a part of the president's program.

With each of the myriad agencies trying to promote its own pet projects, many more ideas are pressed on the president than can possibly be accommodated within the budget. It is often political factors that determine which of the ideas will be incorporated into the president's program and which will be confined to oblivion or, at any rate, compelled to wait for another day. There is nothing surprising about the fact that the political element is so often decisive. A president and his staff are more likely to be receptive to suggestions that they think will benefit the fortunes of the president and his party. Such benefit is measured in terms of the impact of the program on those groups in the electorate which supported the president and his party and may do so again. To satisfy and solidify such support is the most important political yardstick.

Nor does this exercise usually raise a conflict between what is good for the president and his party and what is good for the country. Presidents invariably become convinced that what they think is best for the country is, in actuality, precisely that. Once having become so convinced, it is then the president's task to convince the country at large—or as much of it as will respond to him—as well as, in most cases, Congress. There are few absolute truths when it comes to desirable public policy. In such a situation, the essence of the president's political task is one of persuasion.

A second criterion employed by the president is an economic one. The president knows that it is useless to request the enactment of programs that will require more money to finance than Congress is willing to appropriate. In addition, he must take into account the impact of federal spending on the nation's economy. Even military and foreign policy recommendations cannot be evaluated apart from economic considerations. The abrupt abandonment of a certain weapons system may have a disastrous economic impact on the industry in a certain state, or the closing of an unnecessary shipyard may throw thousands of men out of work.

The President Needs Help

The political and economic considerations which the president must take into account in making his budgetary decisions are both varied and complex, and they must be applied to a staggering number of governmental programs. And the number of those programs is steadily growing. It is a task obviously beyond the capabilities of any single individual, one that requires extensive staff help. Certainly the members of the cabinet are not in the best position to assist for, although in theory they are supposed to be the loyal and cooperative advisers of the president in the discharge of his functions, the practice has been, and still remains, otherwise. For one thing, a president may have in his cabinet at least one or two individuals whom he might have selected primarily to satisfy a dissident faction in his party. Even when this is not so, cabinet members tend to see their responsibilities from a different perspective than the president. Inevitably they become the advocates and spokesmen for the agencies in their departments and those interest groups allied with them. Moreover, cabinet members are almost as much the creatures of Congress as they are of the president. Each of them, after all, has the responsibility of managing an organization created by Congress, and of running programs that are entirely dependent on Congress for their continuation and funds. Serving in such a dual capacity, cabinet members are buffeted about by too many pressures for them to serve effectively as completely trustworthy advisers to the president in fashioning the overall executive program.

The Budget and Accounting Act of 1921, however, provided the president with a highly effective tool to manage the budgeting process, in the form of the Bureau of the Budget. Yet, although the bureau helped the president keep his head above water right from the start, it did not

FORMULATING THE POLICY AGENDA

realize its full potential for almost twenty years. For during the period of the Great Depression, and during its aftermath as well, Franklin Roosevelt's New Deal spawned new federal agencies and programs at a faster rate than the bureau could effectively coordinate them. Recognizing the acuteness of the problem, Roosevelt appointed a three-man committee of political scientists to investigate the problem and make recommendations to him. This triumvirate, whose official title was the President's Committee on Administrative Management,[7] reported back to Roosevelt in 1937. The committee summarized its principal conclusion in a bit of eloquent understatement: "The President needs help." Its recommendations for providing this help were later translated into reality when Roosevelt used reorganization powers that Congress had granted him somewhat grudgingly to create the Executive Office of the President.

Today the Executive Office of the President is the president's good right arm in bringing some order out of the chaos that is the executive branch. It consists of a group of staff agencies, all of which perform coordinating functions. Perhaps the best known are the Bureau of the Budget and the White House Office. But there are others, as well: the National Security Council, the Council of Economic Advisers, the Office of Emergency Preparedness, the National Aeronautics and Space Council, and the Office of Science and Technology. Considering the extent to which the president leans on these agencies today for staff assistance, it is easy to forget how new the Executive Office of the President is. Although technically it came into existence in 1939, World War II prevented it from really coming to life, and it was not until 1945 that it began to assume its present importance.

Bureau of the Budget In the development of the president's budget, the Bureau of the Budget plays a key role. Headed by a director whose selection does not have to be confirmed by the Senate, the bureau consists of about 325 professionals. It is a highly trained staff—in law, economics, business administration, political science—with most holding at least one degree and about half possessing more than one. Members of the bureau work in an atmosphere of anonymity, little known to the general public, and

[7] It was more commonly referred to as the Brownlow Committee, after its chairman, Louis Brownlow. Its other two members were Luther Gulick and Charles E. Merriam.

have, over the years, developed a kind of *esprit de corps*. It is this attitude which accounts in large part for the bureau's ability to serve presidents of different parties and varying temperaments while only the very top layer of authority is changed as new administrations come to power, or as a director may resign.

In fulfilling its budgetary function, the bureau and its personnel reach deeply into the nooks and crannies of the bureaucracy. The budget analysts assigned to appraise the budgetary requests of the various departments and agencies serve as a kind of presidential alter ego, making the presence of the chief executive felt in countless places and in countless ways.

Under the elaborate system of central clearance in which the Bureau of the Budget participates, the budget submitted to Congress by the president takes almost a full year to produce. Ten months before the submission of the budget to Congress and sixteen months before the start of the fiscal year to which the budget applies, BOB personnel consult with representatives of the Treasury, Council of Economic Advisers, Federal Reserve Board, and perhaps the president himself to begin developing the basic assumptions on which the January budget will be built. Once guidelines have been established, the budget director holds exploratory talks with the heads of the various departments to learn in general terms about the programs for which they want to request funds. It is not unusual for all the members of the president's cabinet—as well as the heads of about eight other federal agencies—to make personal calls on the budget director to argue their cases. After this process has been completed, there is usually enough information to provide the basis for the establishment of tentative budgetary ceilings for each agency. Then the agencies are notified of these planning figures, and asked to prepare detailed analyses of the costs of their proposed programs.

Submission by the various agencies of their analyses means that the preliminaries are out of the way and the main event can begin. During the fall months, the Bureau of the Budget holds hearings at which each agency presents detailed justifications of its budgetary requests. The hearings are conducted by examiners who are thoroughly conversant with the respective agencies and their problems. When the examiners are done, the budget director makes his own review, working out the most difficult policy questions in consultation with the president. Then, section by section, the completed budget is approved by the president. After that, only the budget message remains to be prepared.

This complex budgetary mechanism allows the president to assert his views and his public policy inclinations over the chaotic and conflicting demands of the bureaucracy. It remains true that the source of most policy initiatives lies at the grass roots of the bureaucracy. As the policy development process works its way up the bureaucratic hierarchy, however, these policy initiatives are tempered by the more general and more nationally oriented views of the president.

A second major function of the bureau, legislative clearance, accomplishes much the same purpose for new legislation or for amendments to existing law. No agency proposal for legislation may be sent to Congress without first being sent to the Bureau of the Budget for clearance. The proposal will not likely see the light of day unless the bureau finds that it is in accord with the program of the president.

The legislative clearance function of the bureau extends well beyond the bills that agencies want Congress to consider. The practice has developed of having congressional committees submit all bills before them to the executive agencies which would be affected to obtain a recommendation. Bills that originated with the agencies themselves will, of course, have already run the gauntlet of review by the Bureau of the Budget. But for those that originate with congressmen, or with interest groups that have prevailed on a congressman, committee referral to an agency really means referral to the Bureau of the Budget. Thus presidential influence, exerted through the Bureau of the Budget, is brought to bear on all legislation considered in Congress.

White House Office Although the Bureau of the Budget, and especially its director, works closely with the president, the members of another component of the Executive Office of the President have an even more intimate relationship with the president. These are the individuals who make up the White House Office, the group of personal advisers to the president not only in his legislative role but in every other aspect of his work as well. Those members of the White House Office who participate in presidential speech writing, for example, are involved in some of the same process of screening legislative proposals submitted by the executive departments as is the Bureau of the Budget. For the drafting of a presidential address involves far more than a mere literary and stylistic effort. Far more important is the need for comprehensive information about what the executive departments want said and what they think should be left unsaid. It is a vital necessity also to assure that every part of the speech is cleared with all departments in the government that are concerned with the problem even tangentially.

Most presidents are compelled to lean heavily on the advice of those assistants who are on their immediate staff. The presidential assistant sees far more of the chief executive than the cabinet official does, for the simple reason that his office is located only a few feet away from the president's own, in the White House itself. Such an assistant's perception or interpretation of what cabinet officials want, and what they will settle for, often forms the basis of a presidential decision. Assistants to the president are in constant touch with congressmen and newspapermen, putting them in an excellent position to interpret for the president what is politically desirable and (not always the same thing) what is politically feasible. They are also a constant source of new ideas, especially those presidential assistants who are given an opportunity to become specialists in particular policy areas.

Some presidents lean on their staff assistants more than others do. President Eisenhower was frequently criticized for being too dependent on his staff, especially on Sherman Adams, a former governor of New Hampshire, who bore the title, Assistant to the President. Although no one had the same title during the Kennedy administration, Theodore Sorensen, the Special Counsel, was extremely active as an idea man and speech writer. Something of the same role was played for a while in the Johnson administration by William B. Moyers. In appointing his staff late in 1968, President Nixon was reported to want to avoid either one-man dominance or small-group control of his assistants.

Men such as Adams, Sorensen, and Moyers became celebrated public figures, their names constantly in the press and their work a continuing subject of newspaper comment. The same was true of James Hagerty, President Eisenhower's Press Secretary; Pierre Salinger, President Kennedy's Press Secretary; and McGeorge Bundy, President Johnson's Special Assistant for National Security Affairs. These men became public figures in their own right, and were able to use their White House positions as stepping-stones to better things. Hagerty became vice-president of the American Broadcasting Company; Bundy, president of the Ford Foundation; Jack Valenti, a Johnson special assistant, president of the Motion Picture Association of America; and Moyers, publisher of the New York suburban newspaper, *Newsday*. Of this group, only Adams went into retirement after leaving the White House, and the reason for that was obvious: he had left his position with President Eisenhower under fire because of disclosures that he had accepted expensive gifts from a Boston financier who had extensive dealings with the federal government.

The fame that such White House assistants have achieved would have appalled the first man who carried the title of Assistant to the President, Harry Hopkins, who served Franklin Roosevelt. In Hopkins' view, no one should serve as presidential assistant unless he had a passion for anonymity. He should, in effect, have no existence apart from his service to the president. Roosevelt clearly preferred assistants who matched Hopkins' description. His successors, on the other hand, have not been offended at the fact that their assistants have become public figures. This difference in presidential attitudes is indicative of the fact that there is no set way in which members of the White House are supposed to behave. Everything depends on the will, the temperament, and the preferences of the man they serve.

So close is the relationship between a White House assistant and the president that there is usually a wholesale turnover of personnel when a new chief executive is elected. This holds even when the same party continues in office. True, President Johnson asked the major White House assistants to stay on after the Kennedy assassination, and they agreed. But in time the extraordinary character of the president-staff assistant relationship asserted itself, and one by one the Kennedy men resigned. The White House staff as a whole, which had breathed the atmosphere of Harvard and Massachusetts during the Kennedy administration, became much more Texan in character. This distinct shift underlined the unstructured and intensely personal nature of the White House Office.

Even before President Nixon announced his cabinet, he had chosen his White House staff. With the exception of Bryce Harlow, who had served Eisenhower, the Nixon appointees were men he had come to know well, for the most part, as advisers in his successful quest for the presidency. And with many of his assistants coming from California, the Nixon choices also reflected the fact that he still had political roots deep in his native state.

Yet, in spite of the fluidity of personnel and flexibility in organization, the White House Office can be considered an integral aspect of the modern presidency, quite as much as of the Bureau of the Budget. Although no president is bound by Constitution or statute to have a White House Office (by contrast, the Bureau of the Budget is a creature of statute), no president could possibly fulfill his multiple responsibilities without one. The men of the White House Office serve, literally, as additional eyes, ears, mouth, brains, and hands of the president. With their assistance, he can begin to cope with the flood of intelligence pressing in on him for his attention and understanding. With their assistance, the president can begin to sort out the multitude of discordant voices, at home and abroad, which want the government to do this or that, or to stop doing something. In short, the White House Office plays a key and indispensable role in deciding what presidential policy should be. To the extent that his assistants can relieve him of the burden of decision-making can the president conserve his energy and brainpower to be able to make the really crucial decisions which, ultimately, no one else can make. In fulfilling this function of assisting the president to make decisions, very often White House Office staff members are called upon to mediate conflict between or among cabinet departments or other agencies.

The White House Office and the Bureau of the Budget do not exhaust the assistance available to the president in the origination of public policy. Other components of the Executive Office of the President, although not having the wide field that is open to White House staff or to Bureau of the Budget personnel, assist in more specialized areas. The Council of Economic Advisers, for example, provides the president with ready access to informed economic thinking. It is on the council that the president will depend for much of the information that he needs in shaping his economic program. It is the council, too, which prepares the economic report delivered by the president each year to Congress. But it is characteristic of the variety of presidential advice that the council is only one of many sources of policy ideas in the economic field. The director of the budget, the secretary of the treasury, the secretary of commerce, the secretary of labor, and also the chairman of the Federal Reserve Board, all provide the president with advice on economic affairs. Nor is all economic policy originated by the president. There is, for example, an agency that is almost entirely independent of the president, the Federal Reserve Board, which has the power to make decisions with a profound effect on monetary and fiscal policy and vast implications for the general state of the national economy. Nor is the board reluctant to make policy, even when its actions help cancel out others taken by the president. In late 1965, as the administration was trying to stimulate the economy, the board proceeded to raise interest rates to such an extent that a business slowdown ensued.

In foreign-policy formulation and execution, the National Security Council, also a part of the Executive Office of the President, plays an ambiguous role. Like the Bureau of the Budget and the Council of Economic Advisers, both of which were created by statute,[8] the National Security Council was the product of a congressional enactment, the National Security Act of 1947. But unlike these other components of the Executive Office of the President, the National Security Council is more like a miniature cabinet than a staff agency. Four of its five members, in fact, are in the cabinet: the president, vice-president, the secretary of state, and the secretary of defense. The only member not in the cabinet is the director of the Office of Emergency Preparedness.[9] Congress established the council with the thought in mind that it would help eliminate duplication and conflict between the Departments of State and Defense. With a staff at its command, the NSC, it was hoped, would serve as a coordinating and unifying agency. Only during the Eisenhower administration, however, did the council even approach this statutory ideal. Even then it was sometimes difficult to distinguish between an ordinary cabinet meeting and a National Security Council meeting, since Eisenhower initiated the practice of inviting to NSC's meetings other top men in his administration. Thus the typical National Security Council meeting often included officials such as the secretary of the treasury, the director of the Bureau of the Budget, the chairman of the Atomic Energy Commission, the chairman of the Joint Chiefs of Staff, and the director of the Central Intelligence Agency, the last two having status as advisory members.

During the Kennedy and Johnson regimes, the NSC was deliberately downgraded, and was used, if at all, primarily to embellish decisions already arrived at by the president. Even before his inauguration, however, Nixon anounced that the council would become the central decision-making instrument in foreign policy. Within the first 100 days of his administration, the new president had met with the National Security Council fifteen times.[10] In the past the fate of the National

---

[8] The Budget and Accounting Act of 1921, and the Employment Act of 1946, respectively.

[9] OEP is itself still another component of the Executive Office of the President, with responsibility for long-range planning to cope with a national emergency.

[10] Don Oberdorfer, "Nixon's First 100 Days," *Washington Post*, 27 April 1969, p. A-4.

Security Council had depended on the strength of the role assumed by the president's assistant for national security affairs. Both McGeorge Bundy, who served Kennedy and Johnson in this capacity, and Walt W. Rostow, who succeeded Bundy, were the dominant decision-makers on questions of foreign policy, especially Vietnam. But Mr. Nixon seemed to prefer both an effective National Security Council as well as a strong voice for his foreign affairs adviser. Chosen for this post was Henry A. Kissinger, who had already established a reputation in academic and governmental circles in foreign policy matters, and whose basic approach to a settlement in Vietnam became the Nixon administration's program.

Commissions and Task Forces

Although there are extensive mechanisms for policy development within the executive branch, circumstances may dictate reliance on sources outside the official family for new ideas. Two major devices have been used by presidents in recent years: task forces and commissions. A task force is normally an unofficial group of experts, often from outside government, which a president may name to study a particular policy area. After President Johnson's election in 1964, for example, he established a number of such task forces to seek new policy ideas. One of these produced a proposal for sharing federal tax revenues with the states, an idea later embraced by the Nixon administration. So, too, did President Nixon resort to the task force device in the period preceding his inauguration.

Commissions, on the other hand, are likely to be more official looking, with a number of public figures usually being named to them. The Warren Commission, appointed by Johnson in the wake of John Kennedy's assassination and headed by Chief Justice Earl Warren, was composed of senators and representatives. The Warren Commission, however, differed from most groups of this kind inasmuch as it was appointed, in effect, to determine whether Kennedy's alleged assassin had, in fact, been responsible and whether he acted alone. A more typical use of the presidential commission as a source of policy ideas was the one headed by the then Governor of Illinois, Otto Kerner. The Kerner Commission,[11] appointed by President Johnson, did produce

[11] Its official title was the National Advisory Commission on Civil Disorders.

many new ideas to help resolve the racial problem, but these were largely ignored by the president who had appointed it. The Presidential Commission on Law Enforcement and Administration of Justice, also appointed by President Johnson, had a somewhat greater impact on initiating public policy, as many of its recommendations found their way into a crime control bill enacted in 1968.

The commission device, although used extensively by President Johnson, has been employed by many chief executives. Its obvious appeal is as a means to rally support behind policy recommendations through the weight of big names—private and public. The form such commissions have taken has varied widely, and their record of success in influencing the course of public policy has been highly uneven.

The president, then, obtains information and policy ideas from a wide variety of sources. But it is his responsibility and his alone to mesh the demands of the bureaucracy and of interest groups into a program of his own. In this task, the White House Office and the Bureau of the Budget are of immense assistance to him.

The nature of the policy-originating process indicates that it is misleading to speak of the executive branch as if it were a monolith headed by the president. There is, in fact, considerable conflict between the president and his staff advisers, on the one hand, and, on the other hand, the bureaucracy out of which most ideas for policy percolate. Interaction among these divergent components of what is generally called the executive branch results in the setting of the major policy agenda of the nation. Although the president publicly claims credit for those ideas he wants to push, this propensity for image enhancement should not obscure the process of interaction that actually takes place.

Congressional Policy Initiatives

By no means, however, is the executive branch the exclusive source of policy ideas. Although the character of Congress has changed over the years, Congress has not completely abdicated to the executive its function of policy origination. Some initiatives in Congress emanate from individual senators or representatives. For the most part, these initiatives have a distinctly local orientation, or else they can easily be traced to pressure by an interest group. Often, in fact, the bills introduced by an individual member are not intended to initiate policy at all but instead to ingratiate the congressman with his constituents or with an interest group. If he is a member of the minority party in his house of Congress, there is little chance that his bill will ever be enacted, or even get to the floor, for that matter. Even if he is a member of the majority party, the support of the administration or at least the absence of its active opposition is essential if his introduction of the bill is to prove more than an empty gesture. Only about one thousand of the bills that are introduced become law and many of them are of little national importance. Yet, since congressmen so often are not interested in producing legislation but rather in improving their images and in strengthening their political positions back home, they continue introducing in the neighborhood of 20,000 bills during every two-year term of Congress.

Of the more serious policy ideas that originate in Congress, far more come from one or another of the committees than from individual members. An interest group which cannot prevail on the executive to support one of its legislative proposals may well decide to try its luck with a congressional committee. Like the agencies of the bureaucracy, the committees are organized along functional lines, so there is an agricultural committee in each house corresponding to the Department of Agriculture in the executive branch, a labor committee [12] to match the Department of Labor, and a commerce committee [13] parallel with the Department of Commerce, to name just a few. Each of these committees exercises continuing supervision of the activities of the executive agencies within their purview. From this continuing process of legislative oversight, often carried out by specialized subcommittees, many policy suggestions emerge.

Years of work on a congressional committee may provide sufficient expertise for a senior member to increase the likelihood that he will become the fountainhead of new ideas in the field of his specialization. It is through his position as a member of a committee, in fact, that an individual congressman is most likely to be responsible for the development of major legislative policy. Although such initiative will usually be in the domestic field, on occasion an impact can be made in the area of foreign relations. A prime example of initiative in foreign policy was the campaign by former Senator Mike Monroney (D., Oklahoma),

---

[12] The proper names of the committees that deal with labor legislation in the House and Senate are the Committee on Education and Labor and the Committee on Labor and Public Welfare, respectively.

[13] In the House, this committee is called the Committee on Interstate and Foreign Commerce.

in the late 1950s, for some increased means of financing development projects in the less advanced nations. Although he had to overcome lack of executive enthusiasm, he persisted, and eventually saw the United States endorse and participate in the creation of the International Development Association as an affiliate of the World Bank. Only after Monroney got the Senate to endorse the idea in the form of a resolution did the administration move to implement the idea.[14]

In the domestic area, a largely individual effort by the late Senator Estes Kefauver (D., Tenn.) resulted in getting a drug bill through Congress. The germination of the idea actually went back more than a decade before the bill finally became law in 1962. In February, 1951, a Washington attorney who was suffering from a sore throat sought help from his physician. With prescription in hand, the patient went to a drugstore where he was greeted with the staggering news that each of the prescribed pills cost fifty cents.

Upon complaining to his doctor, who admitted he had no idea of the high cost, two alternative drugs were suggested. But to the patient's dismay, these drugs were the same price. This attorney happened to be married to an economist who worked for the Federal Trade Commission. Her superior, John Blair, also an economist, agreed that the situation merited looking into. But after some initial fruitless inquiries by the staff of the FTC, the matter was dropped. With a change in 1953 to an administration not overly receptive to governmental interference in business affairs, any hope that the investigation would be pursued faded away.

Early in 1957, Kefauver became chairman of the Senate Judiciary Subcommittee on Antitrust and Monopoly. As one of his chief staff members, he hired John Blair, whom he had known since 1945. Later, in 1957, Blair hired as a member of the subcommittee staff the same woman, who was a Ph.D. economist and who had worked for him at the FTC. When casting about for new fields to investigate for monopolistic practices, Blair asked his old FTC associate for suggestions. Her response was the drug industry. It was by this chain of coincidences and circumstances that the investigation of the drug industry and the cost of drugs was launched. From it, five years later, the law emerged.[15]

[14] James A. Robinson, *The Monroney Resolution: Congressional Initiative in Foreign Policy Making*, Eagleton Institute, Cases in Practical Politics, No. 8 (New York: McGraw-Hill, 1960).
[15] Richard Harris has compiled an exciting and detailed chronicle. Some of it appeared first in *The New Yorker* magazine; although usually not regarded as such,

Not all ideas for policy begin in this way. All begin with people, of course, somewhere. But what differentiates the drug bill episode from other impulses for legislation is that no great or even discernible public demand existed for such legislation at the outset. Eventually, because of the Kefauver hearings on the bill, and particularly after the thalidomide scandal broke, the public was aroused and support was generated. The same could be said for the automobile safety laws Congress enacted in 1966. For years the highway death toll had been climbing. The horrors and costs of automobile accidents were obvious to everyone. Yet, the public appeared to be little concerned; and, if it was, its concern remained unorganized and inarticulate. As long ago as 1956, in a House committee hearing, witnesses had testified that construction and design features were an important factor in the death and injury totals.

Yet, most emphasis remained focused on driver training and safety. But with the publication in 1965 of a carefully researched book on engineering defects in automobiles—*Unsafe At Any Speed*—by Ralph Nader,[16] public attention was so aroused that in less than a year two major pieces of legislation resulted. Senators Abraham Ribicoff of Connecticut and Walter Mondale of Minnesota provided Nader with a platform in the Senate which helped considerably to publicize the problem. And eventually the administration, sensing the public's interest in car safety, swung behind the demand for legislation.

In a March, 1966, message on transportation, President Johnson asked for legislation giving the secretary of commerce authority to issue safety performance standards. Congress, over vigorous opposition from the auto industry, toughened the bill considerably, making the standards to be issued not guidelines but legal requirements. The auto safety episode shows that it is often difficult to ascertain precisely where the initiation for particular legislation began. In this case, the efforts of a single individual—a young Connecticut lawyer—seem to have been the catalyst for action. Not always, however, can the source of a policy idea be so easily identified.

An unusual form of legislative initiative occurred in 1968, when Congress enacted a 10 percent income tax surcharge. Although it had been sought by the administration for more than a year, there was con-

---

The New Yorker contains some of the best political reporting of any magazine. The entire history of the investigation and legislation is in Richard Harris, *The Real Voice* (New York: Macmillan, 1964).
[16] (New York: Grossman Publishers, 1965.)

siderable reluctance on Capitol Hill to grant the request. Finally, Congress agreed, but only after exacting from President Johnson a promise to make substantial budget cuts and to make recommendations for much needed general tax reform. Although President Johnson followed through on the first demand, shortly before his term expired he announced, with regard to the second demand, that he would not make such recommendations because the incoming Nixon administration should have the opportunity to present its own tax reform proposals.

Taking Credit Although the overwhelming dominance of the president's legislative program might seem to suggest that little policy initiative is forthcoming from Congress, this is primarily a problem of the disproportionate publicity given the chief executive. It seems to be one of the ironies of congressional life that ideas which sooner or later generate enough public support and thus become potential political plusses are taken over by the president for his program. A good example is Medicare. A public opinion poll of whose idea Medicare was might well show a substantial portion of opinion crediting former President Johnson with the legislation.

So much was made of the final triumph of Medicare in 1965 that it would not be surprising that the casual reader of newspapers or the television viewer might confuse credit for passage of the bill with credit for its origination. Yet, it was during the Eisenhower administration, a decade earlier, that Democratic Representative Amie Forand, of Rhode Island, first introduced legislation incorporating the social-security financing method which is the keystone of the concept of Medicare. Never pushed by Eisenhower, endorsed by Kennedy with only little luck because of the opposition of Wilbur Mills, Chairman of the House Ways and Means Committee, Medicare was an instant success in 1965 largely because Mills was induced to abandon his opposition.

Whether an idea for public policy seems to come from the president or from Congress, the case may often be that at bottom the real initiative has come from an interest group. Through their relationships with the specialized agencies of the bureaucracy or the specialized subcommittees of Congress, the role of interest groups in originating policy is truly ubiquitous. Such role may take the form of genuine origination or be in the nature of a counterattack. The latter was the basis, for example, of the American Medical Association's program entitled Eldercare. Introduced as an alternative to Medicare in 1964 and 1965, it became the rallying point for the opposition to the administration bill.

Many of the same pressure groups which try to generate new legislative policy demonstrate the same keen interest in influencing the initiation of administrative policy. For often Congress leaves a considerable degree of discretion to the administrative agency which it puts in charge of carrying out a new program. Thus an interest group may be able to regain from favorable administrative policymaking at least part of what it lost when legislation was enacted.

Agency Initiatives The occasions for such a second chance have grown increasingly numerous in recent years as the subjects with which federal legislation deals have become exceedingly complex. Even in the case of relatively simple legislation, a certain amount of administrative discretion is inevitable. Take the example of a common kind of statute, one which confers benefits upon a class of persons within the population. It is obviously necessary, when such legislation is passed, to devise some way of determining who the eligibles are and how they must apply for the benefits. When, for example, Congress passed legislation to provide federal loans for college students, it gave the Office of Education (in the Department of Health, Education, and Welfare) the authority to administer the funds. There was little in the legislation about how all this should be handled: what regulations should be issued, what procedures should be established for maintaining communication between the colleges and the disbursing authority; what types of forms and applications and records should be prescribed. It was up to the Office of Education to develop what amounted to a whole set of policies governing the administration of the program.

Such is almost always the case with laws passed by Congress, whether they deal with education, agriculture, the securities markets, or foreign aid. Congress works from the assumption that the agency which administers a program is in the best position to determine where inadequacies exist, where different procedures would be more effective, and where there are areas of need that were not originally anticipated. For this reason, it may devise general and even ambiguous directives to govern the work of the agency, instead of trying to spell out in minute detail all possible contingencies. Experience in running a program often results in an agency pushing for changes. Such was the case with the non-Communist affidavit Congress required of student loan recipients when it passed the NDEA Act. Because of this requirement, several leading colleges and universities refused to participate in the program, and HEW joined forces with them in urging repeal, which Congress did in 1962.

Frequently, however, it is not the agency which induces Congress to change its mind on how a program is to be administered, but rather Congress which does the inducing and the agency which beats a retreat. That is what happened when the Office of Economic Opportunity interpreted a provision of the act establishing the poverty program in a way that Congress did not like. In the statute, Congress had directed that antipoverty projects be formulated with the "maximum feasible participation" of the poor themselves. To OEO, this meant that the poor should be encouraged to establish their own indigenous organizations to develop proposals for how antipoverty funds could best be spent. But vesting control over funds in such groups was anathema to some big-city mayors who had seen the poverty program in terms of patronage and solidification of their own power and political organizations. Friendly congressmen were prevailed upon to join in the protests, and before long the pressure compelled OEO to execute a reversal and redirect its efforts along more conventional lines.

Just as policy initiatives frequently emanate from Congress, from executive departments, and from nondepartmental agencies such as OEO, they sometimes come from the so-called independent regulatory agencies, each of which exercises extensive powers in an economic field that Congress has placed under federal regulation. It was one of these agencies, the Federal Trade Commission, which made the first move to compel tobacco companies to place health warnings on cigarette packages and in cigarette advertising. The tobacco interests promptly moved in to persuade Congress that it should seize the initiative from the FTC and pass regulatory legislation that would not hurt the cigarette companies too much. Congress complied, requiring the companies to do no more than print a warning on the side of each cigarette package. There was no requirement that would put any crimp into the companies' multimillion-dollar advertising campaign aimed at new smokers. At least, however, the first tentative step had been taken in the direction of alerting the public to the evidence that cigarette smoking may cause lung cancer or heart disease. In the future, this extremely mild legislation might become the opening wedge to a serious federal effort to safeguard the public health against the threat posed by cigarette smoking. If that happens, the credit for initiating the legislation will clearly belong to the Federal Trade Commission.[17]

Another regulatory agency, the Federal Communications Commission, which licenses radio and television stations, became, in the mid-sixties, concerned with the loud volume of television commercials, after numerous complaints from the viewing public had been received. When it appeared that the FCC would hold hearings on the matter and might, if the evidence warranted, issue regulations on the subject, the networks and advertisers became concerned. Former Representative Oren Harris (D., Ark.), the chairman of the House Interstate and Foreign Commerce Committee, and often a friend of the broadcasting industry, let it be known that his committee would not favor such a move on the part of the FCC. This threat was sufficient to discourage the FCC. Whether or not the mere publicity generated helped to lessen the practices of loud commercials, the incident demonstrated the role of such a regulatory commission in taking the initiative in a sensitive policy area.

Court Decisions as Policy Initiatives

Although courts are generally regarded as having the last word in the policymaking process, quite often the last word takes the form of new policy origination. This can be true, of course, whether the courts are merely interpreting statutes or determining their constitutionality. Since the invalidation of a law normally requires a constitutional amendment to overcome the decision, this occurs less frequently. But what is perhaps the most significant of all amendments to the Constitution, the Sixteenth, authorizing Congress to levy an income tax without regard to apportionment and without regard to its source, came about this way. In 1895, the Supreme Court invalidated a relatively mild federal income tax; [18] eighteen years later, the Sixteenth Amendment was ratified.

---

[17] See the provocative study of the cigarette-labeling controversy, A. Lee Fritschler, *Smoking and Politics: Policymaking and the Federal Bureaucracy* (New York: Appleton-Century-Crofts, 1969).

[18] Pollock v. Farmers' Loan & Trust Company, 157 U.S 429 (1895).

FORMULATING THE POLICY AGENDA

In recent years, disaffection with Supreme Court decisions requiring the states to apportion their legislatures on the basis of "one man, one vote" and outlawing prayer in the public schools has prompted moves to overcome these rulings, thus far without success. Where the Supreme Court has, on the other hand, merely construed the meaning of a statute, Congress can remedy this by amending the law or enacting new legislation.

Until 1944 the operations of insurance companies had not been considered to be commerce within the meaning of the clause of the Constitution conferring on Congress the power "to regulate commerce . . . among the states." Under this interpretation, dating to 1869, states had been the prime instruments of regulating the insurance industry. Seventy-five years later, after vast changes in the economy and population of the country and in the insurance industry itself, the Supreme Court decided otherwise. The question was whether the Sherman Antitrust Act of 1890 applied to insurance companies. The Court decided that it did apply.[19]

The dissenting justices were not so much against the general proposition that the insurance business was indeed commerce; they urged, however, that such a major change in public policy—as the decision certainly was—should not be undertaken by the Supreme Court but by Congress. Responding to this cue, Congress enacted legislation the following year permitting continued state regulation and providing that the antitrust laws would be applicable only to the extent the states failed to regulate the insurance business.[20]

Congress is not always successful in overcoming decisions of the Supreme Court which have the effect of declaring new policy. In the post-World War II period, secretaries of state had developed a policy of denying passports to American citizens for alleged subversive activities or associations. After several challenges to this practice, the Court held, in 1958, that nothing in the various passport laws enacted by Congress conferred such authority on the secretary of state.[21] Since the decision rested on statutory rather than constitutional grounds, the Court left room for Congress to confer such authority if it so desired.

The Department of State immediately drafted legislation which would have accomplished this and had it introduced in Congress. Though there was considerable criticism directed at the Court for its

---

[19] United States v. South-Eastern Underwriters Association, 322 U.S. 533 (1944).
[20] Act of March 9, 1945, known as the McCarran-Ferguson Act.
[21] Kent v. Dulles, 357 U.S. 116 (1958).

passport decision and the Eisenhower administration backed the legislation, sufficient support for the bill was lacking. To this day, those in Congress who would like the secretary of state to have such power have been unable to muster adequate strength.

Sometimes even a single individual can take legal action that results in the initiation of new policy or the introduction of changes in existing policy. A major expansion of the rights of criminal defendants in state trials was brought about by a convict languishing in a Florida jail, through a handwritten and artless petition, at that. Clarence Earl Gideon was serving a five-year prison sentence on a charge of breaking into a poolroom with the intention of committing larceny. Gideon had been forced to represent himself at his trial because he had no money to retain a lawyer and the state had declined to provide him with legal counsel. There was nothing unusual about such a trial, for the Supreme Court had previously held that only in a capital case was a defendant automatically entitled to appointed counsel; in other cases, a lawyer would have to be provided only if special circumstances made it unlikely that a defendant could protect his own interests adequately.[22] Gideon asked the Court to overrule its earlier decision and reverse his conviction, for, he claimed, he had been deprived of his "liberty . . . without due process of law," in violation of the Fourteenth Amendment. The Supreme Court agreed to hear the case, and appointed one of the most brilliant lawyers in the nation, Abe Fortas, to argue the case for Gideon. Fortas, later to be appointed a justice of the Supreme Court, succeeded in convincing the Court to overturn Gideon's conviction and lay down a new constitutional rule: an indigent charged with a felony [23] would have to be provided with a lawyer.[24]

The reversal of the conviction meant that Gideon was entitled to a new trial with counsel. This time the result was acquittal instead of conviction—dramatic proof of how important a lawyer can be. Not only for Gideon, but for other criminal defendants as well, the ruling opened a new era, and in the field of constitutional law it precipitated considerable controversy. Later Supreme Court decisions expanded the rights of criminal defendants, and these decisions, in turn, precipitated a counterreaction: that too much leniency was being shown toward

---

[22] Betts v. Brady, 316 U.S. 455 (1942).
[23] A felony is usually defined as a crime for which the punishment is a prison sentence of more than a year.
[24] Gideon v. Wainwright, 372 U.S. 335 (1963). The history of the Gideon case is detailed in Anthony Lewis, *Gideon's Trumpet* (New York: Vintage Books, 1966).

FORMULATING THE POLICY AGENDA

criminals. Such charges became part of the law and order rhetoric and a major issue in the 1968 election.

The fact that the courts so often find themselves involved in the initiation of public policy makes it tempting for individuals and groups desirous of obtaining certain ends to make use of the judicial process for this purpose. Instances abound of organized efforts by interest groups to bring about significant changes in public policy through favorable court decisions. The legal initiatives of the National Association for the Advancement of Colored People are a case in point. More than thirty years ago, the NAACP began to resort to the courts when it realized how hopeless it was to expect that either Congress or the president would want to take up the cudgels for civil rights. The power of the South, both in Congress and in the Democratic party, was too great for that. The courts, however, were another matter, and within a few short years the legal basis for racial segregation had been swept away through judicial action. The high point for the NAACP came about in 1954 when the Supreme Court declared public school segregation a violation of the equal protection clause of the Fourteenth Amendment.[25] The school segregation decision was the culmination of a long legal struggle by the NAACP for a drastic revamping of public policy toward Negroes. At the same time, the decision represented only the beginning of a new struggle, still in progress today, for the effective implementation of the principles enunciated by the Supreme Court, not only in schools, but also in transportation, recreation, housing, and employment.[26]

It is evident from the examples cited that in the American political system initiative for new policy or for changes in existing policy can come from a wide array of sources. The dominance achieved by the president in the legislative process should not obscure the fact that the policymaking process as a whole is nonetheless wide open. Nor should it be forgotten that, although the president's legislative program has a preeminent position in the process, the program is a compound of ideas that originate from innumerable sources.

These sources lie not only within the bureaucracy, Congress, and the courts, but outside the formal structure of government as well. As

---

[25] Brown v. Board of Education, 347 U.S. 483 (1954), and Bolling v. Sharpe, 347 U.S. 497 (1954).

[26] The development of the *Brown* decision is examined as a study in the judicial process in Daniel M. Berman, *It Is So Ordered: The Supreme Court Rules on School Segregation* (New York: W. W. Norton, 1966).

THE POLICYMAKING PROCESS

a matter of fact, it is often difficult to make a meaningful distinction between governmental and nongovernmental sources of policy, for the difference between the two is more apparent than real. The organs of government are so closely connected with the interests in society to which they respond that it is realistic to look upon the political process as a single vast web of relationships between representatives of one sort or another and policymakers.

Once ideas for governmental policy, whatever their source, gain a place on the agenda, they must, to be effective, be converted into the laws, rules, regulations, and procedures which help govern the conduct of individuals, companies, and government officials. The wide spectrum of sources from which ideas for policy emerge suggests that this conversion process is equally diffuse. At the very least, it involves a complex system of relationships linking together congressmen, constituents, interest groups, the president and his staff agencies, members of the bureaucracy, and the courts.

Chapter 10 Policymaking: Focus on Congress

Public policy outcomes may take many forms: a law of Congress, an executive order of the president, rules promulgated by an executive agency, an order of a regulatory agency, or a court decision. Regardless of the form, there is a common purpose at the core of the policymaking process: converting ideas into public policy. This process of conversion results in laying down effectively binding courses of conduct for individuals or organizations: in short, the concern is with rule-making, no matter where such rules are made.

The political institutions engaged in rule-making have their own distinctive characteristics. They reflect different traditions and loyalties and represent divergent interests and constituencies. As a consequence, these institutions differ in their rule-making processes. These differences are important because they affect the nature and content of the rules and their impact on varying segments of society. In this sense the policymaking process cannot be studied apart from the institutions and the actors that participate in it. This chapter views the policymaking process from the perspective of Congress.

President vs. Congress Formally, perhaps, Congress is the chief maker of public policy as expressed in the laws enacted by that institution. But as the passing years of history have endowed the modern presidency with qualities of leadership and power that little resemble the institution created by the Constitution, so, too, has history infused Congress with institutional characterisics that bear importantly on its contemporary role in policymaking.

For both the president and Congress, one constant of American political history that has conditioned their respective roles is the continuing clash—or, at the very least, tension—that exists between Congress and the president. The president's role as chief legislator naturally brings him into a prominent position in the process of rule-making. It is not enough for him to formulate a program and legislative agenda. In a political culture where there is a high emphasis on performance, modern presidents have striven mightily to live up to such expectations. The phrase, "The President proposes but Congress disposes," although a simple description, is nonetheless an apt one. What it fails to emphasize, however, is that as much presidential effort goes into making Congress dispose as is exerted in proposing.

Much of the tension between the president and Congress arises, therefore, out of the propose and dispose roles of the two institutions. And nothing contributes more to this than the fact that the president and Congress represent two quite different constituencies. As the nationally elected chief executive, the president must try to weld a coalition of diverse interests across the nation. He must accomplish this in order to be reelected, and it is just as important that he accomplish it in order to succeed with his legislative program. With Congress, however, it is entirely different. Congress, in fact, preserves the very diversity out of which the president attempts to put together a national program simply because members of Congress represent less general interests than the president does.

The representative nature of each house of Congress makes it inevitable that this be so. From the start, members of the House of Representatives were intended to be emissaries sent by the people of the states to a national legislative body. The member, in other words, was expected to represent local interests. It is therefore only natural that, although the Constitution merely requires that a representative live in the state that elected him, the voters will seldom send to the House anyone who lives outside the boundaries of the district he wishes to represent. The dominant thinking seems to be that a member of the House cannot know his district well enough to represent its interests unless he makes his home in it.

Senators, too, were supposed to be emissaries, and even ambassadors, from their states. Indeed, they were at first chosen not through any process of popular election but, rather, by the state legislatures, as if to emphasize the fact that their job was to represent one sovereignty in the councils of another. Not until the Seventeenth Amendment was adopted in 1913 did the Constitution require that senators be popularly elected.[1] But this did not really alter the role of senators as representatives of their states. What it did change, in those cases where senators had previously been chosen by the legislature, was the nature of the electorate that a senator would have to face. The senator's political future would now depend on the will of a statewide electorate with that will no longer refined and sifted through the legislature. Thus the senator found himself in something of the same position as the representative. It was true, of course, that his constituency would be larger and he would have to seek a vote of confidence from it less frequently, but the overriding fact was that, like a member of the House of Representatives, he would speak directly for a popular constituency. Both houses of Congress, therefore, are composed of representatives whose political survival is tied to the wishes of the constituency they represent.

Localism

The nature of the American party system reinforces this local orientation of representatives and senators. Since a candidate for Congress is very much on his own in terms of organizational and financial support, he sees his victory at the polls as a product of his own making. Even when he has benefited from the fact that he ran on a ticket that was headed by a

---

[1] The constitutional amendment merely provided the capstone to an evolutionary process, for during the nineteenth century, many states initiated the practice of permitting their people to elect senators directly.

strong presidential candidate, he tends to attribute his success to local and state factors. Moreover, since the congressman is convinced that the voters do not want him to be a presidential "Yes man" or a party hack, he avoids tying himself tightly, at least in public, to any cause but that of his constituency.

A number of factors thus operate to ground the elected representative in the values of the geographical area he represents. There are thus 435 members of the House with as many constituency colorations. Each state's pair of senators, in addition, are in a class by themselves, and even the two senators from the same state may be far from peas in a pod. This is especially true if they are not of the same party. Or even if they are, they may be very different from each other in the way they perceive their constituency.

Congress is, therefore, a collection of locally oriented members whose primary focus must inevitably be on their constituency. In part this is so because the representative is usually so much a local product that it is natural for him to think the way his district thinks. Another factor is the congressman's perception of his self-interest. To a Congressman, self-interest means getting himself reelected. Whatever motives first move a man to run for Congress, once elected there is an almost irresistible impulse to strive for reelection. As one congressman put it, "Once you are here and it gets in your blood, there is no turning back." [2] A congressman who is stricken with "Potomac fever" cares little about the fact that his job is exhausting, the salary is barely sufficient to maintain one house in Washington and another back home, family life is disrupted, and it is seldom possible to make a really significant contribution to national policy.[3]

As congressmen come to appreciate the way in which the House and Senate operate, they recognize how little a freshman member can accomplish even if he works hard and is both intelligent and forceful. What is needed to be someone important is seniority, for it is on the basis of years of service that much of the power in Congress is allocated. To obtain seniority, of course, one must be reelected time and time again—every two years for a representative and every six years for a senator. It is to that end that the energies of members of Congress are devoted. Some crave the power that seniority will bring for its own

---

[2] Quoted in Charles L. Clapp, *The Congressman: His Work As He Sees It* (Garden City, N.Y.: Doubleday, 1964), p. 485.

[3] Ibid., pp. 474–85. Clapp was told about these disadvantages of the job of a congressman in an extensive series of interviews with members. Since these interview statements were made congressmen have seen fit to raise their salaries to $42,500.

sake. Others want to make a contribution to history, to help the little people who are their constituents, or to discharge a solemn duty.[4]

Continuation in office is thus highly dependent on activities related to one's constituency and these activities soon become an important aspect of the job. Congressmen are in a position to take advantage of the fact that, in an age when legislation is increasingly technical and complex, the average voter finds it difficult to evaluate the record that his representative is making on legislative issues. Faced with this problem, the voter is inclined to support the congressman who projects a favorable image by demonstrating interest in the individual constituent and by producing positive benefits for the constituency. As one representative expressed it: "The people back home don't know what's going on. Issues are not most important so far as the average voter is concerned. The image of the candidate plays a much greater role."[5]

Constituency Service This development has proceeded so far that today most of the combined time of a congressman and his staff assistants is devoted to constituency relations and image projection. There are many things that a congressman can do to establish a favorable image in his constituency. At one end of the scale is such a petty device as the sending of congratulatory notes to newlyweds and new parents. Those in the latter group will often also get a copy of *Infant Care,* the Government Printing Office's all-time best seller. Since a good many voters cannot give the name of either their representative or one of their senators, the congressman's hope is that the gift of a book, especially of one that has practical value, may at least establish familiarity with his name.

At the other end of the scale are those positive benefits which a member of Congress may help to obtain for his district or state: a flood control project, a new post office building, a defense contract, a new Veterans Administration hospital, the opening of a new army installation. Even when the truth is that the congressman had little or nothing to do with the particular event, every effort will be made to make it appear otherwise. If the congressman belongs to the president's party, for example, he will be entitled to announce the awarding of the de-

[4] Ibid., pp. 486–89.
[5] Ibid., p. 421.

fense contract, the establishment of the new military base, or the decision to build the new hospital, as if to imply that his efforts turned the trick.

Case Work   Most of the personal services that congressmen perform for their constituents are referred to, on Capitol Hill, as case work. This catchall title is supposed to cover any problem that a constituent may be having with the agencies in the federal bureaucracy. In devoting the time of his staff and occasionally his own time as well to case work, a congressman may be helping to rectify actual cases of bureaucratic injustice. More often, however, he is dealing with a constituent who is simply impatient with regular procedures, or with one who wants to add a congressional thumb to the scales on which his claim will be weighed. Perhaps a veteran may have been unfairly denied a benefit by the Veterans Administration; a local businessman may feel that the Small Business Administration has been unduly slow in passing on his loan application; the owner of an electronics plant may have little idea of how to deal with the Department of Defense.

Even when intervention by a congressman merely takes the form of a request for information, the implied pressure is clear, and even more so when the member is on a committee or subcommittee with jurisdiction over the agency. For such a committee or subcommittee can refuse to authorize important new programs, or investigate the agency for wrongdoing, or—in the case of an appropriations subcommittee—even withhold funds for the operation of the agency. So convinced are many congressmen that case work is an effective way of developing a favorable image that they welcome, and even invite, opportunities to be of service to their constituents even on matters that have nothing to do with government: locating a pair of scarce tickets to the Army-Navy game, or quashing a Washington tourist's parking ticket, or making a hotel reservation for a family planning to visit the nation's capital.

Most of the case work in a congressional office is not performed by the member himself but by staff assistants. Many problems can be dealt with in a routine manner with the staff assistant forwarding the constituent's letter to the executive agency that is involved and later incorporating the agency's reply into a letter to the constituent. It is not even necessary for the congressman to sign the letter personally; in many congressional offices, staff people are authorized to write the member's name for him as if he had signed it, and many offices even have automatic signature devices. But the constituent knows nothing about the impersonal manner in which his letter has been treated; even when the correspondence has availed him nothing, he is inclined to appreciate the mere attempt to help him.

A general picture drawn of more than five hundred individuals is bound to do injustice to many congressmen. Naturally, there are those in Congress who do not conform to the locally oriented, reelection-obsessed image. Nonetheless, the pull in this direction is strong, and it requires dedication as well as deftness to avoid the localism syndrome. By and large, representatives and senators are locally oriented in loyalties as well as attitudes. This is a factor which strongly conditions the policymaking process in Congress, and it is a factor which often proves frustrating to the president, whose constituency is national rather than local.

There Are Two Houses Further complicating the president's relations with Congress is the fact that he does not deal with a unicameral legislature but, rather, with two houses of Congress, which are quite diverse institutions at that. The House and Senate are two quite different cross sections of American interests, opinions, and prejudices, and each has its own distinctive history and traditions. The structure and procedures of the two houses, in fact, differ so radically from each other that in a very real sense it is misleading to talk of Congress as if it were a single entity. Moreover, each tends to go its separate way because there are relatively few points where the two must do business with each other. There is but one joint committee that can report bills: the Joint Committee on Atomic Energy.[6] Party leaders of each house meet together on occasion with the president in the White House. The only mechanism for bringing members of the House and Senate together more frequently is the conference committee system, requiring that a number of representatives and senators must meet together when one chamber is unwilling to accept

---

[6] A detailed study of this joint committee is contained in Harold P. Green and Alan Rosenthal, *Government of the Atom: The Integration of Powers* (New York: Atherton Press, 1963). Although without legislative power, the work of the Joint Economic Committee has some impact on congressional economic thinking.

the modifications that the other chamber has made in one of its bills. But this meeting ground is only for a few senior members of the legislative committees concerned and not the leadership of the two houses.

Even if more effective means existed for bringing the Houses of Congress together for greater cooperation, it would still be extremely difficult to engender a harmonious relationship because there is a basic rivalry between the two. The Senate is anxious to prove that it deserves to be called "the Upper House"; members of the House, however, persist in referring to the Senate simply as "the other body." The Senate also delights in its closer involvement in matters of foreign policy, another cause of resentment in the House. The Senate must ratify treaties made by the president and it also must confirm ambassadorial appointments. These functions confer on Senators, especially those who sit on its Foreign Relations Committee, opportunities for exposure to the public denied most House members. What is true in the area of foreign policy is also the case in other policy fields, although to a lesser extent. Many members of the House feel, whether justified or not, that although they do more work than members of the other body, Senators get the headlines.

In fact, there is considerable justification for the representatives' chagrin. House members do indeed have the opportunity to become highly skilled legislative technicians because they are not ordinarily permitted to serve on more than a single major committee. This allows them to develop a greater degree of expertise than senators, who often serve on two or three major committees and on two or more minor committees as well. As House members see it, this senatorial spread makes a member of the upper house a jack-of-all-trades—and a master of none.

The superior expertise of House members is especially evident in one of the most important aspects of Congress' work, the appropriations process. In the House, a member of the Appropriations Committee almost never sits on a second committee; devoting himself almost exclusively to matters of supply, he may eventually become a genuine expert, particularly in the subjects with which his subcommittee deals.[7] In the Senate, on the other hand, the smaller membership of the chamber means that it would be impossible to man all the standing committees without giving several assignments to each senator. The result is that the typical senator, serving as he does on a group

---

[7] One such subcommittee member, Melvin Laird, became the Secretary of Defense under Nixon.

of committees, almost always must spread himself thin. It is thus highly unlikely that he will ever become an expert in such an abstruse field as appropriations.

Because House action on appropriations bills often results in cutting funds requested for an executive agency, most hearings in the Senate are dominated by a campaign to restore money that has been eliminated. In effect, the Senate committee sits as something of a board of review, often agreeing to appeals by executive agencies for the restoration of funds denied them by the House.

House members express deep resentment at the prodigality of the Senate with the taxpayers' money. Senators respond with anger. They are convinced that in most cases the House is guilty of entirely hypocritical action when it cuts to the bone an appropriations request. As senators see it, this is the situation: because representatives act first on appropriations bills, they can make utterly unconscionable cuts in executive estimates, confident that the Senate can be counted on to put back the money which is needed. The House, they say, attempts to work both sides of the street. While relying on the Senate to cancel out cuts that would be damaging to the nation, it manages at the same time to establish a reputation as the only federal unit striving constantly to introduce economy into government.

Committees

Just as localism and rivalry between Senate and House are among the facts of life in Congress, so also is the most important aspect of congressional organization: the existence of powerful standing committees set up along specialized lines. Time has not diminished the accuracy of Woodrow Wilson's observation that "Congress in session is Congress on public exhibition, while Congress in its committee rooms is Congress at work."[8] Today, as in Wilson's time, the committee system is still the very core and essence of Congress. It is no exaggeration to say that it is in committee that legislation is really fashioned while the House or Senate as a whole must usually be content to do little but tinker.

The growth of congressional committees has largely paralleled the growth of the bureaucracy. In much the same way that demand for governmental services, on the one hand, or regulation, on the other

[8] Woodrow Wilson, *Congressional Government* (New York: Meridian Press, 1959), p. 69 (first published in 1885).

hand, has spawned executive agencies, so also has it resulted in the creation of congressional committees. For the most part, committees have been created to represent interests or activities of groups in society as these groups have become politically important. As a consequence, the number of committees in both houses grew to unmanageable proportions, so much so that in 1946 the number was sharply reduced. Today there are sixteen standing committees in the Senate, and twenty-one in the House, almost all of them interest oriented. But the tendency toward specialization of function has nonetheless been increasing in recent years, resulting in a vast proliferation of subcommittees. In the Eighty-ninth Congress (1955–66), there were 125 subcommittees in the House and 99 in the Senate,[9] each of the standing committees having spun off a number of satellites devoted to more and more narrow problems.

The example of the House Agriculture Committee is instructive. Agriculture is too broad a field to be represented in its entirety by a single committee. As a consequence, the House Agriculture Committee has created a number of subcommittees. Several of these correspond to the principal agricultural commodities: cotton, dairy products, livestock and feed grains, poultry, tobacco, and wheat. Others correspond to particular areas of interest in the agricultural community: conservation and credit, domestic marketing, family farms, research and extension.

Not that all committees in Congress have followed the principle of specialization as far as the House Agriculture Committee has done. The parallel committee in the Senate, for example, the Committee on Agriculture and Forestry—even its name differs from that of its counterpart in the House—has chosen to create no commodity subcommittees and only five subcommittees of any kind. It should not be thought, however, that there is universally a higher degree of specialization in the House than in the Senate. The Senate Judiciary Committee, for instance, had in 1969 fifteen subject matter subcommittees but House Judiciary had only seven.

By itself, specialization is not a vice. In practice, however, specialization in Congress has resulted in a dispersion of power that defies attempts at control either by the formal leadership of the two houses or by the president. The specialized committee system has, in effect,

---

[9] Lewis A. Froman, Jr., *The Congressional Process: Strategies, Rules, and Procedures* (Boston: Little, Brown, 1967), pp. 38, 105. In 1969 the comparable figures were 129 and 98.

created a multiplicity of competing centers of power: the elected party leadership and the automatically chosen (by the seniority rule) committee chairmen.

Because committees and subcommittees so often determine the fate of legislation in Congress, the majority party leadership, which works to advance the president's legislative program (if of the same party), often faces an uphill struggle. Although that leadership holds office by virtue of election by the members of the majority party in each chamber, it finds that at every step it must accommodate itself to the committee chairmen, whom Wilson described as petty barons who "may at will exercise an almost despotic sway within their shires. . . ."[10] Since these party leaders are not often in a position to help him or hurt him very much, the ordinary congressman feels only little compunction to disregard the party and its leaders; it is more important to him that he serve his constituents well and also stay in the good graces of committee chairmen. Thus party regularity in voting can be counted on only at the opening of a new Congress, when the House chooses its Speaker and when both chambers name members to the standing committees. When these decisions are made, Democrats vote as one man to give effect to what the majority has decided in caucus; so also do the Republicans. The result is straight party-line voting—normally for the first and last time in the course of a two-year Congress. For as soon as these preliminary organizational matters have been disposed of, the influence of party begins to diminish. This is not to say that the wishes of the party leadership have no bearing at all on the vote that a member casts. More often than not, especially when an issue is of no special concern to his constituency, the congressman receives neither advice nor pressure from any quarter and in such instances is happy to vote as the party leadership wishes him to. Thus, if one studies the roll-call votes cast by members of Congress on all issues, irrespective of their relevance to the concerns of the constituencies, one finds that party is actually the single most important factor in determining how members vote.

Such gross figures, however, can be seriously misleading. They lump together controversial issues with noncontroversial issues, foreign affairs with domestic affairs, and—most important of all—subjects of interest to the member's constituency and those about which the constituency could not care less. Even more important, studies of voting by roll call

[10] Wilson, *Congressional Government*, p. 76.

seem to be based upon the premise that the most important actions taken by a congressman are the roll-call votes that he casts. The fact is that such publicly recorded votes may be the least reliable indicator of a congressman's behavior. For such votes do not reflect the positions that the member has taken in subcommittee or committee; nor do they reflect, for members of the House of Representatives, the many unrecorded votes that are taken when proposed amendments to a bill are under consideration on the floor during Committee of the Whole proceedings. Yet such votes, which determine the shape that a bill will take when it is finally voted on, may be far more crucial in affecting public policy than the roll-call vote on final passage, which is often little more than a mere formality.

Representatives and senators have at least as much incentive to heed the wishes of committee chairmen as the urgings of elected leaders of the party. An individual congressman has much to lose by incurring the displeasure of a chairman, who can often decide the fate of legislation affecting the member's political future. Thus, faced with competing pressures from a committee chairman and from the party leadership, the chances are good that the member will turn his back on the party and do the bidding of the committee chairman; nor is it an unusual occurrence for such conflicting pressures to be brought to bear on congressmen. Party leadership, since it is elected, represents in general the diversity of the two parties that comprise each of the two houses. Committee leadership, by contrast, reflects the special-interest subject matter conferred on the committees.

Committee Chairmen Although the power of committee chairmen is sometimes exaggerated, they are still formidable cogs in the congressional policymaking machine. They occupy their seats of power because of the prime influence that committees exercise over legislation and because of the control they have over their committees. When hearings on a bill are held by a committee, it is the chairman who largely determines who will testify; it is he who also controls the time made available to witnesses and committee members. When his committee recommends enactment of a bill, the report it submits has ordinarily been drafted by a staff subject to his control. When a committee bill is being debated on the floor, the chairman is usually its manager, controlling half the time available for debate (the ranking, or senior, member of the minority controls the other half). And, when an effort is made to reconcile a committee bill passed by his house with a different version approved on the other side of the Capitol, he usually heads the conferees and has an important voice in deciding who they shall be as well.

Yet, although the power of a committee chairman is thus indeed imposing, rebellions against dictatorial chairmen occur often enough to remind those who head committees that they are dependent on the toleration of their members. By simple majority vote, for example, a committee can adopt rules limiting the power of the chairman to set dates for committee meetings and to hire staff assistants. It is often the case, however, that committee members, encouraged by party leaders, are perfectly willing to allow a chairman to rule dictatorially. The reason is simple: the existence of a tyrannical chairman provides both committee members and party leaders with an ideal method for evading responsibility when it seems advisable, for political reasons, not to bring a particular item of legislation to the floor. In such circumstances, the blame for obstructing the legislation can always be placed on the committee chairman.

Seniority System

Committee chairmen do not suffer unduly from the fact that they are sometimes made the scapegoat for congressional obstructionism. For almost all committee chairmen are politically untouchable: it is next to impossible to defeat them at the polls.[11] That, in fact, is why they became

[11] One committee chairman found that his colleagues were more of a problem than his constituents. Adam Clayton Powell, chairman of the House Committee on Education and Labor, was accused of misappropriating committee funds to his own use. A select committee, appointed by the Speaker of the House in 1966 to investigate the charges, recommended that Powell (who, since the committee reported, had been overwhelmingly reelected by his Harlem constituency) be seated but be censured and fined $40,000. A combination of Southern Democrats and Republicans rebelled against the leadership, which had endorsed the committee's proposal, and instead voted to exclude Powell from the House. Powell then brought suit against the House and, to the surprise of many, the Supreme Court, in the fall of 1968, agreed to review the lower court decision throwing out the case. Powell also won a second endorsement from the voters when they again returned him to the House in the 1968 election. His position was further strengthened when the Department of Justice decided, after a grand jury investigation, that the available evidence did not warrant criminal prosecution on the misappropriation charges. At the opening of the Ninety-first Congress in January, 1969, the House, after five hours of debate, voted to give Powell his seat but stripped him of his twenty-two years of seniority and fined him $25,000.

chairmen in the first place: constant reelection made them the majority party members with the longest period of continuous service on their respective committees. That is how the inflexible seniority system works. Intelligence, ability, or party regularity have nothing to do with the selection of a chairman. The only factor that counts is the ability to get reelected over and over again, provided only that one stays on the same committee. Since it takes many years for a member to earn a chairmanship, many chairmen are already advanced in years even before they take over the reins of a committee.

Old age, however, is not the only characteristic that many committee chairmen have in common. Much more important for the nation is the fact that almost all chairmen come from constituencies which are entirely under the domination of a single political party. The existence of the seniority system makes it extremely difficult for a member who is elected to Congress from a closely divided state or congressional district to succeed to the chairmanship of a committee. Because his constituency is so marginal, the chances that his tenure in Congress will be long and uninterrupted are slim indeed. More probably, the seat he occupies will shift back and forth at frequent intervals between the two parties, and the state or district will never send a congressman with enough continuous seniority to gain a committee chairmanship. In effect the constituency is penalized for a characteristic that is anything but blameworthy: the presence of two healthy and vigorous parties engaged in keen competition for votes. It is the lack of such competition which tends to result in chairmen who are less than responsive to new economic or social ideas and changes in national mood and direction. The consequence is a corps of committee chairmen often at odds with their national party and with the president, if both Congress and the White House are controlled by the same party.

Nevertheless, strong support for the seniority system is found in Congress, especially among senior members, who have either already become chairmen or else can see a chairmanship in their future. Junior members tend to be critical of the system though cynics point out that "the longer they are here, the more they like it." The principal argu-

---

Six months later, the Supreme Court vindicated Powell's position by holding that the action of the House was unconstitutional. But the Court did not intimate whether Powell would be able to collect his pay for the period of exclusion; this question would have to go back to the lower courts if Powell cared to pursue it, as he subsequently did.

ment that has been advanced in favor of the present system of selecting chairmen is that seniority is usually synonymous with experience, both in the subject matter of the committee and in the subtleties of the legislative process. Yet, no provision has been made for taking into account the experience that one may have obtained in the subject matter of the committee while in private industry, or in another government position, or in academic life. Nor does mere length of service on a committee automatically insure that a man who becomes a chairman will possess relevant and current knowledge.

It is also said in defense of the seniority system that it provides a mechanical procedure for selecting chairmen, thus avoiding the dissension and bitterness that would doubtless accompany any attempt to apply a less objective rule, or if the choice were made by election by members of the committee. Yet, other important offices in Congress, Speaker of the House and Senate majority leader, for instance, are posts filled by election without automatic regard for seniority. It is more than a little ironic that men who thrive on a diet of politics in most of their activities should shun the normal processes of competitive democracy when it comes to the question of selecting committee chairmen. As long as the system remains in effect, enormous power to advance or obstruct national legislation will continue to be exercised by representatives and senators who come from a single district or state and who are not in any sense accountable to the nation as a whole.

Subcommittee chairmen, as well, cannot be considered responsible to a nationwide constituency since, like the chairmen of their parent committees, they ordinarily fall heir to their positions by virtue of seniority. As a consequence, subcommittee chairmen often become powerful men in their own right and are among those in Congress with whom the president must come to terms. Until his death in 1966, John Fogarty, a Democratic representative little known outside his state of Rhode Island, exercised greater control over the nation's expenditures for research programs in the field of health than any other individual in the country, including the president. As chairman of the House appropriations subcommittee, which exercised jurisdiction over the Department of Health, Education, and Welfare, Fogarty became a champion of an agency in that department, the National Institutes of Health. He used his power to such effect that, although most House appropriations subcommittees were consistently cutting presidential requests for funds, Fogarty's subcommittee was just as consistently raising the amounts requested for the National Institutes of Health. Whether a Republican like Eisenhower was in the White House or a Democrat like Kennedy or Johnson, Fogarty, and NIH, could not be stopped.

Power Dispersed   Power is thus further dispersed throughout Congress not only because there are so many committee and subcommittee chairmen but also because many subcommittees themselves have become relatively autonomous policymaking bodies. It is these subminiature legislatures, because of their concern with a narrow area of legislation, that have now acquired the reputation for expertise. There is a tendency to defer to their knowledge and convictions on bills to which they have devoted detailed scrutiny. This tendency is considerably reinforced by the well-understood principle of reciprocity. Members of one subcommittee expect the members of the other subcommittees to respect their judgment. As a result, the full committee, which is made up of the members who also sit on the subcommittees, exercises minimal influence on the legislation produced by its subunits.[12] That members of a committee usually sit on two or three or even more subcommittees simply reinforces their tendency to defer to the judgment of other subcommittees.

How Congress makes policy is thus distinctly conditioned by these four principal institutional characteristics:

1. The local orientation most congressmen must retain and cultivate as a matter of survival.
2. The existence of two separate, somewhat jealous, and competitive houses.
3. The specialized, interest-oriented committee and subcommittee system.
4. The wide sharing of powers in the hands of committee and subcommittee chairmen and the elected party leadership.

It is this semichaotic scene that the president's program and, indeed, all legislation faces.

[12] See Richard Fenno, "The House Appropriations Committee as a Political System: The Problem of Integration," *American Political Science Review* 56 (June 1962): 316. Though Fenno's concern was with one committee, there is every reason to assume that reciprocity prevails to one degree or another in all committees in both houses. Many subcommittees, however, exercise far less power than do those of the House Appropriations Committee.

On the Road: Hearings Once a bill has been formally introduced into either house, it is referred to the appropriate subject matter committee. In most cases, within the committee it goes to the subcommittee having jurisdiction. For the vast majority of bills, this is the end of the road. For those bills that are part of the president's program and for those with considerable pressure behind them, hearings are scheduled.

The general purpose of hearings is to enable members of the subcommittee or committee to decide whether the bill should be advanced further toward enactment. Testimony from witnesses normally constitutes the evidence on which members base their judgment. But the legal terminology that is often used to describe congressional hearings does not necessarily mean that the committee is engaged in a dispassionate attempt to assemble all the facts and then decide whether the enactment of the bill is in the best interests of the nation. Although this may occasionally be true, more often the hearings can be looked upon as dramatic productions that are staged for the purpose of generating publicity and building support for the bill.[13] Certainly committee members do not constitute an impartial jury. Many of them, in fact, will have announced their position on the bill long before the hearings are held and will play an active role in trying to convert the committee to their way of thinking.

When hearings are held on administration bills, the primary witnesses will very often be representatives of the executive branch. If the bill is of great importance, leading members of the administration normally testify to underscore the interest of the president and also to arouse public support through maximum press coverage. Certainly the head of the department that would administer the legislation will appear, though an official of his rank will ordinarily confine himself to broad and general principles, leaving specifics to be dealt with by his subordinates. Other agencies that might also be affected by the legislation will usually be called upon to share their thinking with the committee, either in writing or in the form of oral testimony. An agency that is asked for comment on legislation never takes a position without first clearing its views with the Bureau of the Budget. The purpose is to obtain a certification that the opinions expressed are in accord with the program of the president.

Apart from administration witnesses, it is for the subcommittee or

---

[13] See, for example, Ralph K. Huitt, "The Congressional Committee: A Case Study," *American Political Science Review* 48 (June 1954): 340–65.

committee chairman to determine who will receive invitations to testify. He can, of course, use this power to good advantage to predetermine the kind of picture that the hearing will present. In most cases, however, he will allow testimony to be offered by the representatives of any organizations with a substantial interest in the bill under consideration. The result is that the typical hearing is dominated by testimony from spokesmen for pressure groups. Appearing before congressional committees and arranging for others to appear is, in fact, one of the principal tasks of a lobbyist. Spokesmen for the Chamber of Commerce, for example, may testify on as many as twenty-five separate occasions in a typical year and express opinions in writing an additional hundred times or so.

Still, this picture should not be overdrawn. Many hearings do succeed in eliciting information of value to the committee. In addition, hearings often furnish one of the earliest opportunities to ascertain what bargains can probably be struck. They also help provide a method for adjusting group conflicts, since any legislative action will win acceptance more readily if the impression can be created that "it has been arrived at 'in the right way,' [with] 'everyone' [having] had a chance to be heard." [14]

Marking Up

After the hearing stage, the subcommittee decides whether to advise the full committee to take favorable action on the legislation. In turn, the full committee meets to decide whether to recommend to the chamber as a whole "that the bill do pass." In both cases, such decisions are taken in an executive session from which press and public are normally excluded. It is during such sessions that the marking-up process takes place. This is the stage at which the committee discusses and votes on proposed amendments to the bill under consideration.

During the marking-up stage, the committee often leans heavily on its professional staff, whose members are generally permitted to attend executive sessions. Often staff assistants will know more about the legislation than some of the committee members. Although the quality of staff assistance varies from committee to committee, many profes-

---

[14] David B. Truman, *The Governmental Process* (New York: Alfred A. Knopf, 1951), p. 375.

sional staff members are highly qualified experts in the subject with which the committee deals.

Professional staff members are so important to most committees today that it is difficult to understand how Congress ever got along without them. Yet the fact is that not until 1946, when the Legislative Reorganization Act was passed, were any funds made available for anything but clerical help. The hope in 1946 was that professional committee staffs would help Congress narrow the gap in expertise that had developed between the legislative and executive branches. To a large extent, that hope has been fulfilled. Congressmen can now count on staff members to prepare background information for them in the form of staff studies, set up legislative and investigative hearings, prepare questions to be asked of witnesses, and even conduct the interrogation of witnesses. Even more important, staff assistants normally prepare the drafts that are used as the basis of the reports that accompany legislation to the floor after digesting the often voluminous testimony presented at hearings. Since the congressmen themselves are too busy to do such work, the chairman and ranking members usually are content to establish the basic direction of the report and let the staff take over at that point. In such a situation, it sometimes happens that the tail wags the dog with important, if subsidiary, policy questions decided by the committee staff.

When more extensive research assistance is desired, the facilities of the Legislative Reference Service are available on a nonpartisan basis to committees as well as to individual congressmen. The service, which is administratively a unit of the Library of Congress, was created in 1914 but it did not assume its present form until 1946, when Congress made an all-out effort to equip itself with the technical knowledge that it would need to supervise the executive agencies effectively. The Legislative Reference Service was placed on a permanent statutory basis and authorized to recruit a sizable professional staff. Today the service has a pool of more than 200 experts and an annual appropriation of some $2 million. Yet there is still a serious question as to whether its funds are sufficiently generous to handle the growing responsibilities that are thrust upon it.

Research is almost never a problem for two participants in the legislative process. Pressure groups are always in command of the information they need as is the administration. Armed with such information and with a thorough knowledge of committee members and their inclinations, the lobbyists who represent pressure groups are galvanized into activity when a bill of interest to them is in the process of being marked up. To gain concessions at this point is usually far easier than to wait until the bill has come to the floor. For at the committee or subcommittee level, perhaps only one or two congressmen need to be won over for the aims of the group to be achieved. If the lobbyists delayed mounting their campaign until floor debate was under way, it would be necessary to win over many more congressmen to their cause to achieve the same results and obtain helpful amendments to the bill under consideration.

White House Lobbying If pressure groups are usually intent on amending bills in committee, the administration is just as often concerned with fending off amendments that would weaken the bill it is sponsoring. It cannot always count on the support of the committee or subcommittee chairman in this effort even when the chairman has introduced its bill in his own name, for the introduction may have been little more than a courtesy to the president. Whether the chairman will actively resist crippling amendments will usually depend on his personal relations with the president or with other administration officials, or simply on his own independent judgment of whether the legislation is really desirable. Thus, on important bills, the administration launches a major campaign of its own to preserve the integrity of the legislation it has sponsored.[15]

Sometimes strategically placed committee members are approached by emissaries of the president or by subordinate executive officials. At other times, it is the president himself who communicates with the congressmen, either on the telephone or in person. Sometimes a simple and straightforward explanation of why the president supports the bill will suffice. At other times, the president will argue that the party, or he himself, will suffer grievously unless the legislation is enacted in an acceptable form. Mr. Johnson is known to have made emotional appeals to members whom he wanted to influence, sometimes even reducing them to tears with his plaintive descriptions of the burdens of office. But the more usual approach of administration lobbyists is to appeal to the enlightened self-interest of the member with a judicious blend of threats and promises, presented in a subtle if unmistakable

[15] Other aspects of White House lobbying are discussed in Chapter 4.

form. The promises predominate because even a president can do comparatively little to punish uncooperative congressmen. He can, however, do much to help by providing things of value to the congressmen in his constituency. The gifts that a president can bestow are important enough that the mere possibility that he may withhold them constitutes a threat of some magnitude.

One of the most important things that a president can either grant or withhold is patronage jobs. The use of the appointing power for political gain has a long tradition in the United States. During much of the nineteenth century, it was taken for granted that "to the victor belong the spoils," and government offices were filled with an end no more exalted than the development of an army of campaign workers. To a great extent, the spoils systems is now a thing of the past for the development of the civil service principle in the federal government has brought an increasingly large number of jobs within the purview of the merit system. Yet, although the patronage available to a president today is only a shadow of what could be dispensed in the period after the Civil War, a substantial number of appointments, numbering in the tens of thousands, are still open for the president to fill.

The most coveted patronage controlled by the president consists of federal judgeships. Yet, it is not within the exclusive power of the president to appoint judges because the advice and consent of the senate are required by the Constitution.[16] In practice, the president's power to appoint judges is shared with individual senators. Often, in fact, it is actually delegated to them with the president merely placing his stamp of approval on the selections made by senators. Apart from judges, a wide variety of desirable offices are usually filled on the basis of patronage. United States attorneys, federal marshals, and customs collectors are all patronage appointees. Seats on the independent regulatory agencies are also available as patronage although the president is foreclosed by statute from appointing more than a bare majority of the members on such an agency from his own party. In addition, cabinet members and the heads of independent agencies such as the Veterans Administration have a number of policymaking positions not subject to civil service, which can be used for patronage purposes.

If patronage is no longer the device it once was for bringing congressmen around to the president's point of view, other rewards are available to compensate for it. The enormous growth of government

[16] Article II, Section 2.

contracting, most of it in defense but a great deal in other fields as well, means that the administration can give a fillip to the economy of a state or congressional district by favoring its industries with lucrative and job-creating contracts or with new military installations. The administration also has something to say about where harbor improvements will be made or flood control projects inaugurated, and congressmen know it.

The devices for applying presidential and interest group pressure are by no means used on an everyday basis in the committee rooms of Congress. Usually, in fact, drama is entirely lacking. Unless a high priority administration bill or a bill of great consequence to powerful groups is under consideration, hearings will be perfunctory, often with no one at all appearing in opposition. In this manner, many bills that are of no importance to the nation as a whole but of great significance to the constituency-oriented congressmen go through the stage of committee consideration.

To the Floor When a bill has been approved in committee, a report is prepared explaining why the committee recommends its enactment into law. On the other hand, the committee is under no obligation to persuade other congressmen that it has acted reasonably when its decision is adverse to a bill. The mere failure to report out legislation almost always seals its doom. Not only is there hardly a chance that the bill will ever become law; there is also almost as little likelihood that it will ever even get to the floor to be debated and voted on.

Both the Senate and House, however, do provide techniques through which a determined majority can pry a bill out of committee if its supporters can overcome the traditional reluctance of Congress to invoke extraordinary procedures. One such means enables a majority of the total membership to discharge a committee of responsibility for a bill, thus bringing the legislation to the floor. But, although the means exist, in practice the device is rarely attempted and even more rarely is it successful.

Apart from the discharge procedure, the Senate and House have other devices for circumventing an obstructionist committee. Senate practice allows the substance of a bill that is immured in committee to be brought to the floor in the form of an amendment to legislation that has already been called up for debate. Since the Senate, unlike the House, has no rule of germaneness, the rider may concern a completely different subject than the measure to which it is offered as an amendment. There are still other ways for the Senate to deal with the problem of committee pigeonholing. A bill that has already passed the House can be kept from an unfriendly committee by putting it directly on the calendar. Or the Senate can refer the bill to committee with instructions that it must be reported out at a given date.

The House, too, has an alternative to the discharge procedure: suspension of the rules. The suspension procedure, which requires that a bill brought to a vote under the rule receive a two-thirds majority, assumes great importance when a congressional session is drawing to an end. For, although suspension may ordinarily be moved only twice a month, this limitation can be waived during the frenzy at the end of the session when the drive for adjournment coincides with the realization that vital legislation has not yet been acted upon.

None of the methods for getting around committees in either the House or Senate is used successfully except at rare intervals. Tremendous pressure is generally required, either from the public or from the president or from both, to overcome Congress' traditional reluctance to bypass a standing committee. Under normal circumstances, a bill that has been buried by a committee stays buried. Thus a committee's decision on whether to report out a bill and, if so, on what provisions it should contain, is one of the most important factors in the legislative process.

Scheduling The power of standing committees to obstruct legislation they dislike is greater than their power to advance legislation they support. A bill that has been favorably reported by a committee may still not even get to the floor for discussion and decision by the entire membership. For procedures have been established in each house to examine committee-approved bills and determine which of them should be scheduled for chamber action. The need for such procedures is evident: since the legislative committees in every Congress report out many more bills than there is time to debate, someone must decide which ones deserve to be cleared for floor action and the order in which these should be taken up.

With respect to this function, the elected party leadership, headed by the Speaker, in the House, and the majority leader, in the Senate, plays an important role. Members of the majority party in the respective chambers elect those who will occupy these positions, as well as other leadership posts such as the majority leader in the House. The minority also selects its leadership.

Both the Speaker and the Senate majority leader exercise considerable powers. But recent history indicates that these positions of leadership depend more for their success, or lack of it, on the personality of the man and his inclination to use informal but effective methods of persuasion. Take, for example, the contrast between the incumbent Speaker, John McCormack, and his predecessor, Sam Rayburn of Texas. Rayburn was a master at inducing people to cooperate, largely through the board of education sessions held in his office where the use of distilled spirits helped to lubricate proceedings. McCormack, on the other hand, has showed little taste for taking on the competing barons holding committee chairmanships. Much the same contrast can be made between Mike Mansfield, the present majority leader, and his predecessor, Lyndon Johnson.

The nature of the leadership also has a substantial impact on the image a party projects outside of Congress as well as being a reflection of the factionalism inherent in the parties in Congress. Leadership struggles usually occur when dissident elements of the party gather sufficient force to insist on a place in the power structure. As more and more liberal Republicans from Northern urban areas came to Congress in the late fifties and early sixties, restlessness with the old leadership grew. First in 1959, Representative Joe Martin, Republican leader in the House for almost twenty years, was unseated in favor of Charles Halleck of Indiana. Six years later, Halleck was forced to step down in favor of Gerald Ford of Michigan.

In the Senate, both parties experienced leadership struggles at the opening of the Ninety-first Congress in January, 1969. A challenge to the Southern-dominated Democratic leadership succeeded when Edward Kennedy, by a 31–26 margin, defeated Russell Long of Louisiana, the incumbent assistant majority leader or whip. On the Republican side, there was a contest over the same post, occasioned by a retirement. Hugh Scott of Pennsylvania defeated Roman Hruska of Nebraska, the candidate with conservative leanings, who had been strongly backed by Minority Leader Everett Dirksen. Later in the year, after

Dirksen's death, Scott succeeded to the top leadership post by defeating Dirksen's son-in-law, Howard Baker of Tennessee.

On the House side, the Ninety-first Congress opened with an unusual but dramatic challenge to an incumbent Speaker. Many younger and more liberal Democrats, unhappy with the 77-year-old McCormack, lined up behind Morris Udall of Arizona. Although McCormack won easily, 178–58, the young Turks gained promises that the party apparatus in the House would become more responsive to their needs.

House Rules Committee Although the leadership has other functions, scheduling legislation for floor action is one of its principal tasks. In the House, however, decisions on when or if a particular bill should be brought to the floor are not within the sole discretion of the Speaker and his lieutenants. They must share this power with the House Rules Committee.

If a bill is not otherwise privileged, one dealing with appropriations, for example—and many important bills are not privileged—it may never reach the floor unless it receives a favorable recommendation from the Committee on Rules. Such a recommendation comes to the House in the form of a resolution that is reported out by the rules Committee and offered for the approval of the House. The resolution (which is more commonly referred to as a rule) specifies, among other things, how much time will be allowed for debate and whether floor amendments will be in order. If the committee is so inclined, it can compel legislative committees to make substantial changes in bills they are framing as the price for obtaining a rule. A committee with this kind of power is a force to be reckoned with in the House.

For almost a century, the House Rules Committee has enjoyed the right to report privileged resolutions making it possible for bills to be scheduled for debate without waiting their regular turn. During most of this period, the committee operated as an instrument of the majority party in performing this scheduling function. Since it seemed reasonable that the party which had captured control of the House should be master of the legislative program, the majority party was always given the right to name two thirds of the members of the House Rules Committee regardless of how slender its majority might be in the chamber as a whole.

An entirely new factor was introduced, however, during the mid-1930s. In revolt against the New Deal, Southern Democrats on the committee began to vote with their Republican colleagues. The alliance thus forged made the committee a graveyard for liberal legislation in the years that followed. When the Republicans had a majority in the House, conservative domination of the committee was assured and liberal measures on both economic issues and civil rights could not even reach the stage of floor consideration. The situation was not significantly different when a resurgence of liberalism in the country gave the majority in the House to the Democrats. For the conservative Republicans still had exactly the number of Southern Democratic allies they needed to prevent the committee from clearing liberal legislation. In the last decade, the House Rules Committee has had its ups and downs. When heavy Democratic majorities have been elected to the House, this has usually meant more members of the party from the North and West and trouble for the committee. In 1961, the membership of the committee was expanded by adding two Democrats and one Republican, the idea being to give the liberals a one-vote margin. But this technique proved unreliable and the "reformed" committee was responsible for some of the most important defeats suffered by the administration.

After Johnson's large margin of victory in 1964 swept numbers of new Democrats into the House, another device was employed to reduce the committee's tendency to obstruct: the House approved a 21-day rule, which made it possible for the Speaker to bring a bill to the floor after it had been blocked by the House Rules Committee for three weeks. During 1965 and 1966, the 21-day rule was resorted to eight times and eight times it freed legislation from the committee. Not only that, but also, on four other occasions, the mere filing of the necessary resolution prompted the House Rules Committee to recommend that the legislation in question be brought to the floor.

But the joy of the liberals was short-lived. After the midterm congressional election of 1966 in which the Republicans gained a net total of forty-seven seats, a quite different situation was created, and one of the first actions of the new Congress in 1967 was to repeal the 21-day rule.[17] Thus the House Rules Committee once again occupies a highly strategic position in the legislative process.

---

[17] History was repeating itself when the House adopted and promptly repealed the 21-day rule. In 1949, a somewhat similar curb on the committee's powers had been adopted, only to be set aside two years later.

The committee has come in for heavy criticism, usually from those with a liberal bent, in and out of Congress, because of its conservative cast. But many members of Congress, in candid conversation often express their pleasure at the existence of a committee with the power to keep legislation from the floor on which they have no desire to stand up and be counted. Members of the House are quick to insist that the committee serves another, and presumably more noble, purpose. Some bills, they explain, are clearly against the public interest but have so much support from selfish or uninformed groups that a negative vote on the floor might prove fatal to an individual member. In such circumstances, say the congressmen, recourse to the House Rules Committee enables a member to accomplish what his conscience demands without subjecting himself to punishment at the polls at the same time. Yet, those who criticize the committee may be ignoring an exceedingly important point. The most significant issue about the committee is not whether it possesses too much power but instead whether or not a body with this much power should not be directly responsible to the elected leadership of the House. The case for giving *some body* the power is unassailable because priorities must be assigned in a legislature where thousands of bills and resolutions are introduced in every session. The basic question, therefore, is why this power should rest in the hands of a committee which is not accountable to the majority party.

It is not that the leadership is totally powerless to bring a bill to the floor against the opposition of the House Rules Committee. In addition to informal pressures, several procedural devices are available although none is simple, and they are used infrequently.[18]

In the Senate, the scheduling of legislation is handled in a completely different way. The nominal counterpart of the House Rules Committee, the Senate Committee on Rules and Administration, exercises no jurisdiction whatever over the scheduling of bills. Instead, the basic decisions are made by the policy committee of the majority party. A bill reported out by a legislative committee is placed on a calendar but the Senate turns to the "call of the calendar" only under one set of conditions: when it wants to obtain swift approval of innocuous legislation. Controversial bills do not come before it unless

[18] Among these devices are the Calendar Wednesday rule, which is supposed to make it possible for the chairman of a legislative committee to bring a reported bill directly to the floor without going through the House Rules Committee; the same discharge procedure that can be used to free bills from legislative committees; and suspension of the rules.

they are taken from the calendar and brought to the floor. Although any senator may call up a bill, it is ordinarily left to the majority leader to perform this function. He may ask for unanimous consent that the bill be considered or he may accomplish the same purpose by means of a motion. In any case, scheduling is normally done in consultation with the minority leader.

On the Floor

In either the House or the Senate, a bill that has been cleared for floor debate has moved a long way toward enactment. For minor or noncontroversial bills, formal passage is assured: in the House, by the call of the consent calendar; and in the Senate, by just as cursory a procedure. Such routine procedure, however, is possible only when the bill is noncontroversial and there has been informal agreement in advance that it should be passed. For those bills that stir up determined opposition, the procedures are not at all routine.

Each house has its own way of handling bills on the floor. The most important difference between the two houses that emerges at the stage of floor consideration of legislation is that senators enjoy the privilege of unlimited debate whereas House debate is conducted under rigid time restrictions. The House agreed many years ago that full and free debate is less important than expeditious decision. As a consequence, obstructionist tactics on the House floor can only succeed in delaying action for a comparatively brief time.

On most bills before the House, the first issue is supposedly not substantive but procedural: whether to agree to the terms recommended by the House Rules Committee for consideration of the bill. The remarks that members of the committee deliver at this juncture are heard by more representatives than one generally finds on the floor of the House at other times. The reason is that this phase of the debate takes place before the House itself—not before the Committee of the Whole, into which the House will soon resolve itself. The importance of this distinction is that a more exacting quorum requirement is in effect when the House meets *as the House* than when it functions as the *Committee of the Whole*. For the House itself to be in session, at least 218 representatives—a majority of the total membership—must be present. In the Committee of the Whole, on the other hand, the attendance of only 100 members is sufficient.

Amendments, Debate, and Voting

The most informative stage in House debate occurs at the time amendments are considered. After disposing of any committee amendments that might have been reported, the House next turns its attention to those offered from the floor if the House Rules Committee has not foreclosed such a procedure in the rule it has reported out.[19] Many amendments are often submitted by representatives who know there is little chance of passage but who are trying to convince constituents or pressure groups that their interests are being represented.

Voting during Committee of the Whole on amendments is carried on under procedures that assure members of virtual anonymity as they cast their votes. If the members were meeting *as the House,* one fifth of those present could insist on a roll-call vote, in accordance with the constitutional provision;[20] when they meet *as a Committee of the Whole,* however, a record vote is not in order. A considerable amount of time is saved because roll-call votes may not be demanded. To call the roll takes more than thirty minutes because after the names of all 435 Representatives have been read, the names of those who did not respond must be read once again. Conserving time, however, is not the only reason why many congressmen appreciate the absence of roll-call votes. A far more basic consideration is involved.

Without roll-call votes, a member can conceal the actual part he is playing from his constituents. Although a bill may have strong backing in his district, he can safely support an amendment to cripple it because no official tabulation of that vote will be made. Then, when the Committee of the Whole has finished its work and the House itself takes a publicized roll-call vote on the entire bill, he can vote in favor of final passage and thus indicate to his constituents, on the basis of that publicized vote, that he has acted in accordance with their wishes.

Although it is true that some time is saved in the Committee of the Whole by avoiding roll-call votes, this point is strictly secondary. If time were really important the House would have long ago installed a system of electrical voting as a number of state legislatures have

---

[19] If the House Rules Committee has reported out a closed rule, there is still a chance to alter the bill on the floor by offering a motion to recommit it with instructions that a particular change be made by the committee. In addition, the minority on the committee that reported out the bill may offer a single substitute for the committee bill.

[20] Article I, Section 5.

done. Through the use of such a device, its members could complete a recorded vote in no more than a few seconds. Electrical voting would take even less time than the system presently employed in the Committee of the Whole. Not infrequently, three separate votes must be taken today on a single amendment before a decision is considered final. First, the chairman of the Committee of the Whole puts the question to a voice vote, in which the outcome often seems to depend more on lung power than on numbers. A single member may then force a division, or standing vote, in which a fairly accurate tabulation may be made. But even that does not always end the matter. On the demand of a mere twenty members—one fifth of the 100-man quorum in the Committee of the Whole—the chairman must order a teller vote. This is a lengthy procedure in which, first, all those supporting a bill and then later all those opposing it march between two members, usually one from each party, who are designated as tellers. The teller method provides an accurate count without revealing the position taken by each individual member.

It is not unusual for the result of a teller vote to be reversed in subsequent proceedings. This can happen if the parliamentary situation permits a roll-call vote on the same question when the House itself meets to pass on the recommendation of the Committee of the Whole. One reason why such switches occur is that, typically, many members participate in a roll call who did not bother to attend for the teller vote, which, perhaps, drew only a bare quorum. The extra votes may have made the difference. But there is another and more important reason. The anonymous vote cast in the Committee of the Whole may have reflected the personal thinking of House members whereas the vote on a publicized roll call reflects more their perceptions of what constituents want them to do.

Unrecorded votes in the Committee of the Whole also account for the fact that final passage of a bill by the full House is often by a lopsided majority. In part this may mean that enough amendments have been adopted to win over some former opponents of the bill. But it is also indicative of the desire of many congressmen to show their constituents that they are on the winning side and support what is considered good legislation. Roll-call votes, therefore, often do not register the intensity with which members may have fought to cripple or defeat a bill through their unrecorded votes in Committee of the Whole. This discrepancy in behavior not only deceives constituents, but also makes roll-call votes an unreliable guide to a congressman's true voting behavior.[21]

The Senate operates under a rule of unlimited debate. Senators take pride in this rule. They say it is the principal reason why the Senate deserves to be considered the greatest deliberative body in the world. Debate should not be cut off, they argue, as long as a single member has something that he wants to say. Senators should be courteous enough to hear out patiently any colleague who wishes to speak. Whatever sacrifice in time may be involved is more than outweighed by the benefits that result from preserving full and free debate in at least one chamber of the national legislature.

The Filibuster

In the terms in which it is presented, this argument may well be unanswerable. It is, however, almost totally irrelevant to the only serious criticism made of the unlimited debate rule: that it enables a Senate minority to kill a bill by refusing to stop talking. The case against unlimited debate thus does not rest on any skepticism about the benefits to be derived from exhaustive discussion. It is predicated instead on the belief that a Senate minority should not be permitted to prevent the majority from enacting legislation it favors. The ostensible aim of a filibuster is to educate and influence public opinion. But the real purpose is to hold the floor indefinitely to prevent a vote from being taken on a bill which its opponents know will pass. Lengthy speeches are designed to convey the simple thought that, until the objectionable bill is laid aside or modified to suit the minority, the Senate will not be able to transact any business of consequence.

The filibuster need not be discussed in purely abstract or philosophical terms, however, for in practice it is not a protection that is available on a continuing basis to every minority whose interests are threatened by a tyrannical majority. Rather, the one minority that has chiefly benefited from use of the filibuster has been the South, in resisting civil rights legislation. Until 1957, any attempt to enact such

[21] The "procedure of Congress is so complex that it is easy for [a congressman] to obfuscate where he stands on any issue and what he has done about it." Raymond A. Bauer et al., *American Business and Public Policy: The Politics of Foreign Trade* (New York: Atherton Press, 1964), p. 424.

legislation was foredoomed to failure, the threat of filibuster serving as an adequate deterrent. Although civil rights bills were passed in 1957 and 1960, they had been stripped of provisions which Southern members really opposed to avoid a filibuster. In both 1964 and 1965, considerably stronger civil rights bills were enacted, and this time the Senate succeeded in breaking Southern filibusters. But the climate of the racial problem had by this time become considerably more heated. When the Republican leader, Senator Dirksen, decided to support the move to end debate, the hopes of the Southern senators were dashed.[22]

Another chapter in the use of the filibuster occurred in 1968 when it was used by a combination of Southern Democrats and Republicans to block the nomination of then Associate Justice Abe Fortas to become chief justice. The filibuster, however, has not been the exclusive province of Southern Senators. In 1962, liberal Democratic senators sought unsuccessfully to prevent consideration of a bill creating a mixed private-public corporation to develop a communications satellite system.

As the rule stands today, a filibuster can be ended only by two-thirds of those present and voting. This procedure is referred to as cloture. For the last twenty years, determined (albeit unsuccessful) efforts have been made to change the rule. Some have proposed that rather than two-thirds, the number needed to invoke cloture be reduced to three-fifths of those voting. It may well be that the Senate will move in this incremental way toward abolition of the filibuster. But the essence of the controversy will not be resolved until a simple majority of senators is allowed to work its will after reasonable opportunity for debate. The irony of the filibuster is that even a proposal to change the rule which makes the obstructive device possible may be prevented from coming to a vote by a filibuster!

When senators are not abusing the rule of unlimited debate to prevent legislation from coming to a vote, they are generally willing to enter into agreements in advance on a cutoff point when discussion will end and voting begin. Such agreements, adopted by unanimous consent, are commonplace. Their use means that the Senate often functions under the same sort of tight limitation on debate as the House. What is more, the time available for debate under a unanimous consent request is normally divided between proponents and opponents of the measure just as it is in the House.

[22] On passage of the 1960 and 1964 acts, see Daniel M. Berman, *A Bill Becomes a Law*, 2d ed. (New York: Macmillan, 1966).

POLICYMAKING: FOCUS ON CONGRESS

The fact that much business is conducted under such agreements throws a cloud on the claim, often made (usually by senators themselves), that the Senate is the world's greatest deliberative body. Debate, in a genuine sense, has practically ceased to exist in the Senate. One reason is the absence of a rule of germaneness. Senators, when they have the floor, may talk about anything; it has been estimated by the Legislative Reference Service that 40 percent of Senate debate is not germane to pending business.[23] Frequently, the only senators present are those who agree with the speaker's point of view and thus serve as mere foils. With senators busy with committee work and with constituents, sparse attendance is the rule.

Debate in both houses, because of the conditions under which it takes place, has only little influence on the way members vote. In the House in the Committee of the Whole, highly technical amendments may be offered in such profusion that even the most conscientious congressman might be left in the dark. Particularly among representatives who are not members of the committee reporting the bill, detailed knowledge of the legislation is bound to be scant. There is insufficient time in the day for any congressman to read the stacks of all the hearings and all the committee reports that gush forth without letup. To make matters still worse, some subjects may be so technical that only a specialist can hope to master them.

Logrolling

Since members of the House cannot think through for themselves all the complex questions put to them during the hectic consideration of a bill on the floor, they tend to be influenced in their voting by colleagues they know and respect. A member may take his cues from one of several sources: the leadership of his party, a committee member whose judgment he trusts, or someone else in his state delegation.

Since so much House business is transacted in the virtual anonymity of the Committee of the Whole,[24] irresistible opportunities for logroll-

---

[23] "Proposed Amendments to the Standing Rules of the Senate," *Hearings* before the Subcommittee on the Standing Rules of the Senate of the Committee on Rules and Administration, 87th Congress, 1st Session, 16 June 1961, p. 18.

[24] No comparable situation exists in the Senate. Since there is no provision for a committee of the whole, roll-call votes are far more common than in the House. Even when voting is by division, Senators are far more readily identifiable to reporters when they stand than House members are.

ing are created with the members agreeing to vote a certain way in return for a colleague's promise of support on another issue. Especially if the matter is of no consequence to the member's own district, he is free to vote as he pleases, perhaps paying back a favor done for him in the past, or possibly establishing a credit that can be used at some later time.

Particularly if the member has been attending faithfully to his errand-boy functions, he need not worry too much about the feeling in his constituency on the question at hand. Even when his constituency has an interest in the problem, the congressman does not necessarily feel obligated to do its bidding. Although that, indeed, may be the safest course of action open to him, there may be no great risk in following an independent line. In such an event, the congressman can always claim that he felt compelled to place the national interest above the interest of his constituency. Alternatively, he could insist that he voted out of his deepest personal convictions, and that he was conscientiously incapable of acting otherwise. Either way, there is likely to be some support in his constituency for the stand he took.

Presidential Pressure   Administration pressure may be especially intense at the time when amendments are being considered on the floor of the House or Senate. Whether the minions of the president are trying to preserve a bill intact that has been reported out of committee or whether they are trying to repair damage done in committee, they will make their presence felt not only by telephone but also in person in the cloakrooms and lobbies immediately outside the House and Senate chambers. Sometimes they will draft amendments on the spot and give them to cooperative congressmen to introduce.

Administration pressure is far more effective in influencing votes than the pressure of congressional party leadership. That leadership, in fact, is most often successful when it takes care to mesh its efforts with those of the administration. For the president's party, the efforts to coordinate strategy have been institutionalized through the Tuesday morning breakfasts at the White House for the congressional leadership. Such meetings provide an opportunity for the president and the party leadership to discuss the status of major administration bills and their prospects in the two houses.

When the president sees, however, that lobbying by his assistants and pressure on the leadership may still be insufficient to move legislation of great importance to him, resort to the people is his ultimate weapon. As with interest groups, a campaign to stir up grass-roots support may succeed when other means have failed. Franklin Roosevelt used his fireside chats on the radio to excellent advantage in surmounting opposition to some major New Deal proposals.

But the instrument most frequently used has been the presidential press conference.[25] Franklin Roosevelt's use of the press and the mass media showed clearly how a president could put these instruments of communication to good political use. Under FDR the press conference became an informal and at times riotous affair, with both Roosevelt and reporters enjoying the give-and-take. The most dramatic innovation in the press conference was the use by President Kennedy of live television. Although it gave him unique exposure to the American people and undoubtedly contributed to his considerable personal popularity as reflected in the polls, it was not a particularly successful weapon in convincing Congress to do his bidding. Just as abruptly as the life of the young president was taken, so was the live television press conference dropped. Because he apparently believed that he might suffer by comparison, Lyndon Johnson developed his own, often erratic, style in dealing with the press.

In his days as Senate majority leader, Johnson literally had the press eating out of his hand. As the active leader of a restless Democratic majority in the Senate, at a time when the presidency often seemed listless, Johnson and what he did was news. But once he became president, Johnson no longer enjoyed the same relationship with the press. The fundamental tensions which must inevitably exist between a news maker like a president and those trying to get news from him seemed to bother Johnson. Regularly scheduled conferences became a thing of the past. Unscheduled, frenetic walks around the White House lawn became the news item rather than what was said by the president. The press frequently complained that the president was trying to use them. Although this is a thoroughly natural attitude for newsmen, the frequency with which it was voiced and the high stature of some of the complainers lent considerable weight to the charge of a credibility gap, which became common by 1966.

---

[25] The development of the press conference is extensively treated in Elmer E. Cornwell, Jr., *Presidential Leadership of Public Opinion* (Bloomington: Indiana University Press, 1965).

Although President Nixon, during his earlier career as a representative, senator, and vice-president, was often a favorite whipping boy of the press, a remarkable turnabout occurred when he became president. In large part this was because of his deft handling of the newsmen and his particularly effective demeanor in the press conference. Without benefit of notes or the protection of a lectern, Nixon faced his first press conference with a confidence and competence which thoroughly impressed the media. In his first 100 days in office, he held five nationally televised press conferences.[26]

Like the Kennedy-Nixon debates of 1960, the presidential press conference is a peculiarly fragile institution. Each president inevitably develops his own style of reaching the people, and he will do this in his own way as he perceives the circumstances and the degree of need for presidential persuasion. But that any president must, in some way, resort to going over the heads of Congress to speak to the people and ask for their support seems a certainty. As with all presidential trump cards, there is a danger of playing them too frequently and diminishing their effect. A president, with the help of his advisers, must make the choice as to when he will unleash his biggest weapons of persuasiveness.

Conference Committees When debate has been concluded and the votes have been taken in both houses of Congress, the legislative process is still not at an end, and the bill that has survived so many obstacles must surmount one more hurdle before it can go to the president. For, before that can happen, the bill must be approved in identical form by both the Senate and the House. On major legislation this rarely occurs. Except where minor changes are involved, a conference, composed of members from each chamber, will be requested by the house that wrote the original bill to compromise the differences.

Almost always, the chairman of the committee which reported the bill will be named to the conference, as well as the ranking majority and minority members of the committee. The function of a conference committee is to seek out middle ground on which both houses can

---

[26] Don Oberdorfer, "Nixon's First 100 Days," *Washington Post*, 27 April 1969, p. A-1.

stand, not to explore entirely new territory. But there are circumstances when a conference committee, in fact, does introduce new provisions. Since conference committee reports are impossible to amend on the floor, such bodies exercise enormous power.

Conference committees also operate in secret. At no other point in the congressional process can so little be learned about why actions are taken and by whom they are promoted. The committees do not even keep minutes or other formal records. This situation is made to order for a lobbyist, either from an executive agency or a private organization. He has only a small number of congressmen on whom to work; he knows that what they decide cannot be effectively challenged; and he has an atmosphere of secrecy in which to campaign. Because of the absence of publicity, conferees need not fear being held accountable for what they do.

To the White House After a bill has been approved in the same form by both houses, it is sent to the White House. The Bureau of the Budget collects the views of interested agencies and also makes its own independent recommendation to the president as to whether he should sign or veto the bill.[27] Advice from his White House assistants will also help the president make up his mind.

Early chief executives used the veto power sparingly and operated under the theory that it should be exercised to prevent unconstitutional bills from becoming law. Andrew Jackson, however, saw the veto power otherwise, and since that time presidents have justified their votes of no on grounds of policy. The most extensive use of the veto power came during the administration of Franklin Roosevelt, who turned down 631 bills, and who was the first president ever to veto a tax bill. Since FDR, the number of vetoes has drastically declined. Truman vetoed 250 bills whereas Eisenhower turned down 181. During his brief tenure, Kennedy disapproved 25 measures; in his five years in office, Johnson vetoed only 27 bills. The decline reflects, at least in part, a greater will-

[27] The president may simply not sign a bill within the ten days stipulated in the Constitution, in which case it becomes law. In this way, he can indicate his disapproval without actually vetoing the measure.

ingness on the part of Congress to heed expressions of probable presidential disapproval in advance.[28]

When the president vetoes a bill, the Constitution requires him to return it to the house where it originated together with a statement of his objections.[29] If two-thirds of those present do not vote to override the veto, the bill is dead. Only during a period of the most acute tension between the president and Congress is a large number of vetoes overridden. More than one-fourth of the instances in which Congress overcame presidential vetoes took place during the feud between Congress and President Andrew Johnson in the Reconstruction era.

The president also possesses what is popularly known as a pocket veto. Any bills passed by Congress during the last ten days of a session do not become law unless the president makes an affirmative decision to sign them; without his signature, they die. The pocket veto is essentially an absolute veto since no congressional majority, however mighty, can overcome it. Ironically, an extraordinarily large number of major bills are subject to the pocket veto; because Congress always lets its work pile up, it must invariably approve dozens of bills in the closing days of a session.

The veto and the threat of the veto are so efficacious that Congress can seldom succeed in enacting legislation to which the president really objects. Thus presidential frustrations do not ordinarily stem from the necessity of accepting obnoxious legislation but rather from the inability to obtain passage of desired legislation.

Appropriations After a bill has been passed, the policy struggle continues. For even though it has survived all the trials and tribulations of the congressional process, the bill may still remain for all time a complete nullity, its purposes frustrated and its provisions mocked. This lamentable condition will exist unless Congress bestirs itself a second time and appropriates money to finance the program it has approved. The bill that has been enacted into law is only an *authorization*. It signifies approval of a pro-

---

[28] The decline in the number of private bills considered by Congress is undoubtedly a factor because a substantial percentage of such measures have historically met with executive disapproval.
[29] Article I, Section 7.

gram but by itself provides no funds for putting that program into effect. What must come next is an *appropriation*.

Countless bills never get the appropriation that would be required to give them the meaning their sponsors originally hoped them to have. As a general proposition, it is far easier to obtain approval for programs or constituency projects from legislative committees and from Congress as a whole than to convince the appropriations committees to recommend that the necessary funds should be provided. Starving an already authorized program is, in fact, one of the major ways in which Congress makes public policy, taking advantage of the fact that the appropriations process affords those who opposed the authorizing legislation another opportunity to assert their disapproval.

It has become a commonplace to say that Congress' control over the federal purse is the most important source of its power. Although policy initiative belongs almost exclusively to the president, he can never act to translate an idea into an activity unless Congress provides the necessary funds. Without bills that supply funds no wheel of government can turn. This is so because of the existence of a short and simple constitutional provision: "No Money shall be drawn from the Treasury, but in Consequence of Appropriations made by Law." [30]

To a considerable extent, Congress has delegated the power of the purse to its appropriations committees. Few committee assignments are more coveted than an appointment to one of them. In a very real way, those who supervise the appropriations process sit as a committee of review over all the other committees of Congress. Legislative committees in both houses may have recommended the enactment of a bill and the two chambers may have approved it but, before the program that has thus been authorized can go into effect, it must undergo the scrutiny of the committees on appropriations.

The House Appropriations Committee has the strongly developed tradition that its proper function in the legislative process is to stand at the door of the federal treasury to guard public funds against raids by legislative committees and executive agencies. This attitude is exemplified by the distinctive vocabulary used by committee members. When describing what they do to the budget bills submitted by the administration, they use verbs such as cut, curb, slice, prune, whittle, squeeze, wring, chop, and slash. The tools of the trade are likewise referred to

[30] Article I, Section 9.

as knife, blade, meat-ax, scalpel, meat-cleaver, hatchet, shears, wringer, and fine-tooth comb.[31]

Appropriations committee members are a perpetual study in righteous indignation. The indignation stems principally from a feeling of frustration because the hard fact is that it is simply impossible to cut some of the most expensive items in the president's budget. In the untouchable category are such items as veterans' benefits, interest on the national debt, and programs of such long standing that to curtail them would be political suicide; these programs constitute a kind of permanent obligation that is perpetually honored. In addition, neither Congress in general nor the appropriations committees in particular have shown any inclination to reduce expenditures in the field of defense, which is by far the largest single budgetary item. Instead, congressmen who pride themselves on being economizers in other fields have often tried to compel the president to spend even more than he wants on military hardware.

Thus it is primarily on newer program areas—controversial at their inception and still lacking firm political support—that the House Appropriations Committee concentrates. In this category have been most of the major social programs of the Roosevelt, Truman, Kennedy, and Johnson administrations, most recently the war on poverty.

The House Appropriations Committee goes about its budgetary work in a way much different than do the president and the executive agencies. To begin with, there is no mechanism for coordinating or even comparing expenditures with income because these two aspects of the budgetary process are dealt with as though they had nothing whatever to do with each other. Income is within the province of the Ways and Means Committee in the House and of the Finance Committee in the Senate whereas expenditures are the responsibility of entirely separate appropriations committees. Moreover, the budget is broken up into bits and pieces and farmed out to the dozen or more appropriations subcommittees, never to be put together again. Although subcommittee actions are all technically subject to reversal by the full committee, in actual fact a gentleman's agreement operates to assure that the principle of reciprocity will be respected and that the recommendations made by the various subcommittees will almost automatically be converted into decisions. As a consequence, Congress, as

[31] Richard F. Fenno, Jr., *The Power of the Purse: Appropriations Politics in Congress* (Boston: Little, Brown, 1966), p. 105.

a whole, never looks at the financial state of the nation in any systematic and unified way.

Nor do House appropriations subcommittees have to be concerned with public scrutiny of the manner in which they conduct their hearings. For almost all appropriations hearings take place in executive session with neither reporters nor members of the general public admitted. It is felt that the executive officials who testify are generally more candid when the press is excluded. In addition, open hearings, covered on a day-to-day basis by the press, might generate irresistible pressures on committee members to abandon their role as guardians of the public purse. That congressmen prefer arrangements under which they are free from pressure is, of course, understandable. From the viewpoint of individual voters in a representative democracy, however, to insulate congressmen from pressure is to deprive citizens of the right to make their views known to their representatives in an effective manner.

Although House appropriations hearings are closed (in the Senate they are often open), transcripts of their hearings are eventually made available, and a clear picture emerges from these of what generally takes place. The only witnesses before the subcommittees are agency officials whose requests for funds are under consideration. The hearings, which are generally dominated by the subcommittee chairman, are trying experiences for the head of an agency. Although the appropriation that the White House requested for his work may be smaller than the amount he favored, the subject for discussion at the hearings is almost invariably not whether the budgetary figure should be increased but by how much it should be decreased. The figure that the president has accepted is treated by the subcommittee as the point of departure for further cuts.

In the course of the hearings, the subcommittee, typically, does not confine itself to the examination of budgetary requests for the future operations of the agency. Instead, it devotes considerable time and effort to a review of the agency's performance in the past. In this manner, the subcommittee performs what has become increasingly the major preoccupation of Congress: the supervision of administration in the executive branch. This function of oversight affords subcommittees ample opportunity to have an impact on agency policy. Critical comments made by subcommittee members about the ways an agency has been performing are disregarded only at extreme peril. Retaliation in the form of budgetary cuts the next time around provides a sanction of great effectiveness. On occasion, specific policy directives are contained in the subcommittee report which accompanies the appropriations bill to the floor. The appropriations process thus serves a dual policymaking role. It establishes the level of funding for an agency and also provides the agency with specific policy guidelines.

The Pork Barrel   Few members of Congress go out of their way to offend the sensibilities of appropriations committee members. It is a fact of congressional life that it does not pay to antagonize the committee to which one will some day have to appeal for funds to support a cherished local project. Such projects are commonly referred to as pork. The word is not inappropriate because vital programs that pour money into a constituency and give contracts to its businessmen and jobs to its people are indeed juicy political morsels for the congressman whose state or district will benefit.

So important a part of the congressional process is this kind of legislation that almost all members of the appropriations committees want seats on subcommittees dealing with pork projects for which their constituencies might be eligible. Probably the most important of these subcommittees are the ones that supervise the Department of Defense, Interior, and Agriculture, the scientific and space programs, and the civil functions of the army. Each of these subcommittees handles spending programs that have an immediate economic impact on particular geographical areas. The programs that the army is in charge of, for example, include rivers, harbors, and flood control projects, which always have an exhilarating economic effect on the areas in which they are built. Water projects constructed by the Bureau of Reclamation of the Department of the Interior have a similar effect where they are established.

Every such project represents the use of tax money, obtained from the country at large, to benefit a particular locality and, even more directly, private concerns situated there. Why does a congressman vote to spend his constituents' money on projects that will be of value only to constituents of other members? The answer, of course, is that he is likely to do so only in exchange for a similar courtesy that will redound to the benefit of his own district or state. That is why logrolling—or what congressmen like to call mutual accommodation—is so prevalent in Congress. It is practiced when the original legislation for authorization is being formulated; it is practiced among members of the appropriations committees; and it is practiced when the appropriations bill comes to the floor. There was more truth than poetry in the statement by former Senator Paul Douglas (D., Ill.) that public works appropriation bills are the product of "a whole system of mutual accommodation in which the favors are widely distributed, with the implicit promise that no one will kick over the applecart; that if Senators do not object to the bill as a whole, they will 'get theirs.' "[32]

The policymaking process in Congress is exceedingly complex and cumbersome. If not by design, then by history, the process has all the earmarks of being calculated to prevent action rather than to promote it. The committee and subcommittee structure, the seniority system, the filibuster in the Senate, and the conference committee system—all raise serious questions about the representativeness of Congress, its capacity to act decisively and intelligently, and its accountability to the nation as a whole. In part because of the deficiencies in congressional structure and process and also partly because of the nature of many of the issues with which Congress deals, much public policy is made elsewhere.

---

[32] Quoted in Donald R. Matthews, *U.S. Senators and Their World* (Chapel Hill: University of North Carolina Press, 1960), p. 100.

Chapter 11 Policymaking: Presidency and Bureaucracy

The mere enactment of a federal statute is only a part of the dynamic process of policymaking. Before the policy that Congress has enunciated can become a reality, it must be determined how the statute is to be applied in particular circumstances. For legislation, by its very nature, is general. This is true whether it is a criminal statute, making certain conduct punishable or whether, at the other extreme, it is a social welfare measure, making benefits available to specific classes of persons under certain circumstances. In the first instance, someone must decide whether the conduct of a particular individual falls within the category proscribed by Congress. In the latter instance, someone must decide whether specific persons are eligible to receive the benefits that Congress has made available. This is just one function performed by the administrative machinery of the federal government.

The bureaucracy, however, does far more than merely administer the statutes enacted by Congress. It is the major source of policy ideas

POLICYMAKING: PRESIDENCY AND BUREAUCRACY

many of which eventually become incorporated as part of the president's program. Even those ideas that do not gain a place on the official agenda may nevertheless result in public policy. This is so because the bureaucracy has a policymaking role quite apart from the authority granted in any specific statute. Programs often evolve into their contemporary form not because Congress delegates new powers but because agency rule-making authority is "simply assumed in practice through custom and usage."[1]

The Constitution put the president squarely in charge of administering the acts passed by Congress. The president, it said, "shall take Care that the Laws be faithfully executed. . . ."[2] It is possible that at least some of the framers conceived of this responsibility more as a burden than as a power, considering that there would be little discretion for the president to exercise. Things, however, have not worked out that way in practice, and presidents, especially in modern times, have played anything but a perfunctory and automatic role in their capacity as chief administrator.

This is so largely because the problems with which government is involved are far more complex and the areas in which it must act are far more numerous than could have been anticipated. This development was probably inevitable, given the fact that the industrial and technological revolutions transformed the United States almost in the twinkling of an eye from a small agricultural nation on the shores of the Atlantic into a continental colossus with the most advanced industrial plant in the world. Whatever the cause, Congress found itself inundated with more problems than it could handle and at a time when the philosophy of the welfare state encouraged individuals to expect more of government than they had in the past.

As early as 1887, Congress took cognizance of its own technical incapacity to deal with complex problems. Desirous of regulating the railroads and controlling their rates, it despaired of its own ability to make the necessary decisions on the basis of highly specialized data. As a consequence it created the first independent regulatory agency, the Interstate Commerce Commission, to do the job on its behalf. When new social and economic problems came to the fore in the years that followed, the same kind of solution was resorted to again and again. Just as often, however, it gave authority to one of the regular cabinet-

[1] Charles E. Jacob, *Policy and Bureaucracy* (Princeton: D. Van Nostrand, 1966), p. 45.
[2] Article II, Section 3.

level departments, such as the Department of Agriculture or the Department of the Interior, to regulate or promote some aspect of the national economy.

In vesting responsibility for important economic decisions in agencies of either type, Congress was relieving itself of more than just the burden of struggling with intricate technical problems. It was also ridding itself of the uncomfortable political pressures that were sure to be directed against whatever instrumentality of government that made decisions of such great economic importance. For it was no mere technical task that Congress was sloughing off on the agencies. Decision-making in the economic field must of necessity be a highly political operation involving a ceaseless tug-of-war between competing interest groups.

Administration and Policy Accordingly, administrators are very far from being economic eunuchs making decisions in accordance with the will of Congress. In most instances, Congress lays down the standards that are to guide the economic regulators in the most general terms. The Federal Communications Commission, for instance, was told that it should allocate radio frequencies and television channels on the basis of "the public interest, convenience, and necessity." Similarly, the National Highway Safety Bureau, in the Department of Transportation, charged with the administration of the Automobile Safety Act of 1966, was directed to impose only those safety standards which are "practicable." Often, the administrators are told little more than that they should perform the regulatory function in a just or a reasonable manner. Moreover, even when the statutory standards are somewhat more precise, administrative agencies must still make countless policy decisions, some of which are of great significance.

On at least some occasions, decisions made in the course of administering a statute may be even more important than the statute itself. The antitrust activity of the federal government provides an example. Congress has enacted two fundamental statutes on the subject: the Sherman Act of 1890 and the Clayton Act of 1914. Although economic conditions in the nation have changed radically since these two statutes were placed on the books, the decisions on whether and when to institute remedial action against monopolization have all been made outside Congress by the Department of Justice, acting through its antitrust division, and by an independent regulatory agency, the Federal Trade

Commission. The Supreme Court, too, has been left free to render momentous interpretations of the congressional statutes. Thus it can be seen that, for more than half a century now, antitrust policy has been largely a compound of administrative policy and judicial policy with little congressional involvement.

Just as Congress cannot be considered the only formulator of national policy, neither is it, realistically speaking, the sole and exclusive fount of national legislation. For although, in theory, only Congress has the constitutional power to legislate, the practice is quite different with the rule-making power exercised by administrators almost indistinguishable from the legislative power of which Congress professes to be so jealous. Sometimes, in fact, Congress itself bestows such quasi-legislative power on officials in the executive branch, insisting all the while that the entirely metaphysical distinction between rule-making and law-making is a real one. Content with this purely verbal formulation, it delegates vast power over the lives of individuals to the president and to the heads of a variety of organizational entities in the executive branch.[3]

Like laws passed by Congress, rules and regulations issued by the president, or by executive agencies of one type or another, prescribe a course of conduct which government officials or ordinary citizens must follow. Most people who become involved, either voluntarily or involuntarily, in dealing with the government find that the relevant law is not an act of Congress but the rules or regulations of an administrative agency instead. Often a sanction is attached to the failure to obey. This may take the form of a criminal penalty (a term of imprisonment or a fine), a civil penalty (a fine), or the withholding of benefits or privileges that would otherwise be available.

The president's rule-making power is expressed through the issuance of executive orders. These orders may range from relatively minor matters, such as the procedures of executive agencies, to matters of great consequence, such as the 1952 order by President Truman seizing the strike-bound steel mills, and the 1958 order by President Eisen-

[3] The most important of these organizational entities as far as policymaking is concerned fall into four broad categories: (1) the department, encompassing a multitude of bureaus, agencies, offices, and services, and almost always headed by a secretary, who is ex officio a member of the president's cabinet; (2) independent executive agencies, such as the Selective Service System, the Veterans Administration, and the National Aeronautics and Space Administration, each headed by a director or administrator; (3) the independent regulatory agencies, such as the Interstate Commerce Commission, the Federal Communications Commission, and the Federal Power Commission, each headed by a board of commissioners; (4) government corporations, such as the Tennessee Valley Authority and the Federal Deposit Insurance Corporation, each organized along the lines of a private business corporation.

hower putting the Arkansas National Guard under federal control during the racial integration crisis at Little Rock. It was also by executive order that far-reaching loyalty-security programs for federal employees were established by Presidents Truman and Eisenhower. At all times, the president must be able to show that there is a legal basis for any executive order, either in a statute passed by Congress or in the Constitution itself.[4]

Only the president is authorized to issue executive orders. But the heads of executive departments and agencies may issue rules and regulations, which possess the same quasi-legislative character. Daily, these pronouncements pour forth in great profusion from government agencies large and small, actually exceeding in volume the statutes enacted by Congress. Thus, on the shelves of any law library, the **Code of Federal Regulations**, in which such rules, as well as presidential executive orders, are collected according to subject matter, will occupy four or five times as much space as the United States Code, which is a similar compilation of existing federal statutes. Like executive orders, the rules and regulations issued by agencies must have a legal basis, either in a presidential delegation of power or in a congressional authorization.

Although the rules and regulations that issue forth from the executive agencies are almost always supposed to do no more than implement congressional legislation, they are often more important than the laws themselves, for they may embody highly significant policy decisions. Federal tax law provides one illustration. To taxpayers, the interpretations of the Internal Revenue Service, an executive agency that is part of the Treasury Department, may be more important than the sometimes vague provisions of the tax law itself. What are, for example, necessary and reasonable business expenses? Where, for tax purposes, is an individual's home—the place where he lives or the place where he works? If Congress does not like the interpretations rendered by the Internal Revenue Service, it is, of course, free to reverse them through legislation. It did just that in 1962, when it upset a long-standing ruling by IRS that money spent by a business concern for the purpose of lobbying is not deductible from taxable income as a business expense. But for forty-three years, the IRS policy had prevailed.

Even though a rule may be issued in the name of a department head,

---

[4] Almost any reference to the vague executive power in the Constitution will suffice. Occasionally, as with Truman's seizure of the steel mills, the courts may see it otherwise [Youngstown Sheet and Tube Co. v. Sawyer, 343 U.S. 579 (1952)], but the peculiar circumstances of that situation and case by no means make it a certainty that the courts can be counted on to slap the president's wrist.

or even of the president, chances are that the idea behind it originated in one of the lower echelons of the bureaucracy. For it is the highly specialized subunits of an executive agency that are most closely in touch with problems that have arisen in a particular field. It is these subunits which hear the complaints and demands of the interest groups, the subcommittee chairmen, and the individual congressmen who are most directly concerned.

Since the tendency in any bureaucracy is for those in higher positions to approve the recommendations of their subordinates, the likelihood is that the department head, or even the president, who signs his name to the proclamation of a new policy, may not be signifying anything more important than that he sees no harm in a recommendation that was made at a much lower level than the one he inhabits. The sheer number of decisions that must be made each day by executive officials makes it humanly impossible for the president to know more than a minute fraction of what goes on. Department heads are in a somewhat better position to keep track of developments in their individual bailiwick, though they, too, will seldom have any but the most controversial problems brought to their attention.

Policy Subsystems

If administrative policy is not made too often at the top of the executive hierarchy, neither is it often made exclusively within the executive establishment. Administrative policymaking is far more frequently the product of interactions that involve executive agencies, interest groups, and congressional committees and subcommittees. In the field of education, for example, the major participants in the development of policy have been the United States Office of Education (a part of the Department of Health, Education, and Welfare), the National Education Association (a private interest group), and the subcommittees in the House and Senate that deal with education bills. These groups constitute a kind of subsystem in the field of education.[5] A multitude of subsystems abound in the political process and play a major role in administrative policymaking as they do in all phases of the policymaking process. The elements within a particular subsystem need not neces-

---

[5] See J. Leiper Freeman, *The Political Process: Executive Bureau-Legislative Committee Relations,* rev. ed. (New York: Random House, 1965) for an analysis of the subsystem concept as applied to Indian affairs.

sarily be allies in the same cause. At times, two of them may be ranged against a third, or the interest groups may be at odds with each other and look to either the agency or the subcommittee for protection. There is simply no uniform pattern of relationships. What is uniform is the existence of the relationship.

Since important actors in these subsystems include administrators there can be little doubt about the basically political nature of rulemaking in the executive branch. Thus, to characterize the work of executive agencies as the routine execution of legislative policy obscures the essential reality that the administering of policy is just as much political as the initial formulation and enactment of policy. While ostensibly doing nothing more than administering legislative policy, executive agencies are often modifying that policy or even negating it. Almost always, moreover, they are laying the foundation for the development of new policy.

The fact that congressional subcommittees and executive agencies often enjoy such a high degree of autonomy makes it an easy matter for them to relate freely to each other and to the interest groups within their orbit. A number of subcommittees have considerable independence as a result of the dispersion of power in Congress, and the fact that they are so strongly interest-oriented makes them ready partners for interest groups and executive agencies that share responsibility for similar functions. Specialized agencies in the bureaucracy, too, have considerable autonomy from departmental and presidential control, not only because of the vast size of the executive establishment, but also because the career civil servants who often run them have usually had the time to develop so much expertise that superiors find it difficult to frustrate their designs.

It is thus a common occurrence for firm alliances to be welded between executive bureaus and legislative subcommittees. Though no president views this situation with satisfaction, there is little that can be done about it because the congressmen may take the agency head under their wing, making it clear to the president that he would be well advised to make peace with reality. That explains why more than one president, who may have concluded that J. Edgar Hoover richly deserves to be retired from government service, has, upon reflection, decided that he would be stepping into a hornet's nest in Congress if he so much as hinted that he was considering a replacement for the first and only head of the Federal Bureau of Investigation. Although not all administrators have been as successful as Mr. Hoover in making friends and influencing people on Capitol Hill, this seldom stems from any lack of effort on their part. For the canny executive official knows that he must be more politician than administrator if both he and his programs are to survive.[6] It is for this reason that administrators do not consider it a waste of time to help congressmen (especially those on the legislative and appropriations subcommittees having jurisdiction over their agencies) with the handling of constituents' requests of all kinds. The administrator, in fact, will be just as eager to serve "his" congressmen as the congressmen are to serve their constituents.

Although administrators do not have to run for reelection, they may well think of themselves as serving a distinct constituency. Congressmen are members of this constituency, but there are others as well—principally, the segment of the public with whose affairs they deal. Believing as they do that they serve administrative publics[7] just as congressmen serve electoral publics, they are intent upon convincing those whom they serve and those whom they regulate of their open-mindedness and goodwill.

For this reason, and also because of certain legal requirements,[8] their agencies perform the task of decision-making in much the same way that congressional committees do in their own spheres. An agency that is considering the issuance of rules and regulations to implement a statutory policy is likely to invite a degree of public participation in its work, just as legislative committees make use of public hearings to allow those who will be affected by a policy to state their views. Public participation in the administrative process may be accomplished by nothing more elaborate than informal conferences. Sometimes it takes the form of the creation of an advisory committee on which interest group representatives are invited to serve. Or there may be formal public hearings, either because these are required by law or because the agency feels that it would be politically unwise to proceed without developing support both in the general public and among interest groups.[9]

Administrative policymaking is beset with some of the same difficulties as policymaking in Congress. Any new idea will almost certainly encounter some opposition from interest groups, within the agency

---

[6] Morton Grodzins, *The American System: A New View of Government in the United States*, ed. by Daniel J. Elazar (Chicago: Rand McNally, 1966), p. 270.

[7] The term is from Robert S. Friedman, Bernard W. Klein, and John H. Romani, "Administrative Agencies and the Publics They Serve," *Public Administration Review* 26 (December 1966): 192.

[8] Principally, the Administrative Procedures Act of 1946.

[9] On the variety of agency practices, see William W. Boyer, *Bureaucracy On Trial* (Indianapolis: Bobbs-Merrill, 1964), pp. 17–38.

itself, and in Congress. Such conflict is especially characteristic of the large, cabinet-level departments where, typically, many disparate agencies have been haphazardly collected under one fragile roof. In such departments fierce interagency battles break out each year when the time comes to draw up the budget. Responsibility for refereeing these battles is the unhappy lot of the secretary of the department.

The nature of administrative policymaking indicates that conflict in the governmental process is not confined to the relations between president and Congress. What appears to be a struggle between the legislative and executive branches is often a contest between parts of one institution and parts of the other, or between two coalitions, each consisting of members from both branches. On occasion, of course, the president does find himself in a direct confrontation with Congress. But even in such instances, his antagonists may not be Congress as a whole but, rather, an important committee or its chairman.

Controlling the Subsystems The existence of coalitions and subsystems that cut across institutional lines means that no president, however resourceful, is ever truly the master of his own house. The centrifugal pressures within the bureaucracy mean that the president often finds himself chief executive and chief administrator in name only. But the president is not without tools to impose at least a semblance of unity on the warring factions that comprise the branch he is supposed to head. The same executive office which assists him in the crucial process of policy initiation also helps shoulder the burden of controlling and directing the administration. The staff members of one of its components, the White House Office, work long and hard to establish lines of communication for the president with all levels of the bureaucracy. The president must depend on the people of the White House Office to spot trouble, to overcome foot dragging and inertia, and, generally, to put his own stamp on his administration. It is they, too, who try to mediate the recurrent conflict among executive agencies and between them and the committees of Congress. In helping to overcome the conflicts that are built into the administrative process, the efforts of the Bureau of the Budget are also of paramount importance. Through the function of budgetary coordination that it performs, and also through its legislative clearance work, the bureau tries to prevent the executive departments and agencies from working at cross-purposes with the president.

The impact that these two staff arms of the president—the White House Office and the Bureau of the Budget—have on the bureaucracy is directly related to the fact that these agencies, unlike the components of the executive branch that they help to coordinate, feel a sense of undivided loyalty to the president. Both the staff assistants who comprise the White House Office and the director of the Bureau of the Budget are the president's men in every sense of the term, with their appointments not even subject to senatorial confirmation. At other levels of the buraucracy, too, the president can use his power of appointment with telling effect. An incoming president can, and usually does, replace all the heads of executive departments with people of his own choosing. He can exercise the same power with respect to under secretaries and assistant secretaries as well as some bureau and agency heads. These, in turn, pick many of their immediate assistants. In this fashion, at least the upper layer of the bureaucracy takes on the president's own political coloration.

Presidential Appointments Although it is the prerogative of the president to nominate his subordinate officials in the executive branch, the individuals whom he selects must, in general, receive majority approval in the Senate before they can begin exercising the powers of their office. There are some exceptions to this general rule. Not wishing to be bothered with a host of nominations to comparatively minor offices, Congress has by law given the president, or in some cases the head of a department or agency, complete discretion in choosing those who are to serve under him. Occasionally, Congress chooses to give the president a free hand with respect to offices which are not minor.

It is not necessary, for example, for the president to seek the advice and consent of the Senate when he names the director of the Federal Bureau of Investigation. The present FBI Director, J. Edgar Hoover, has held office for more than four decades without ever having to undergo screening by the Senate. Similarly, the director of the Bureau of the Budget and the president's special assistants at the White House do not require senatorial confirmation. The theory is that the president is entitled to select whatever men he wants for positions that will involve the closest and most intimate relationships with him in the discharge of his most characteristic duties. Moreover, any vacancy at all that arises in the executive branch after the end of a congressional session may be filled through unilateral presidential action although the appointee must be confirmed during the next congressional session if he is to remain in office.

Many a president has learned to his sorrow that it is prudent to clear prospective nominations with key members of Congress rather than merely send a name to the Senate and hope for the best. Otherwise, even the nominee to a cabinet-level position may be unceremoniously denied confirmation by the Senate. That was precisely what happened in 1959, when President Eisenhower nominated the Chairman of the Atomic Energy Commission, Lewis L. Strauss, to be secretary of commerce. Strauss had managed to alienate many senators long before he was nominated to the cabinet, and, when he proved uncooperative and even evasive in responding to questions at his confirmation hearing, the stage was set for his undoing. By a margin of three votes the Senate declined to confirm his nomination, and Strauss was retired from public life. But such a rebuff of a president with respect to his choice of a cabinet member is extremely rare. Altogether, only eight cabinet appointments had been rejected by the Senate prior to the Strauss case; there has not been a rejection since. The Senate seems to give the president the benefit of the doubt whenever any question is raised about a man he wants in his cabinet. Just as the Senate tends to approve any presidential nominee at the cabinet level almost automatically, ambassadorial nominations also seldom encounter any serious obstacles in the Senate. Not too many senators seem prepared to challenge the prevailing theory that no restrictions should be placed on the right of the president to choose the men who will represent the nation abroad.

The president is also almost universally conceded the right to remove his appointees if he grows dissatisfied with their performance. The only exceptions, in addition to judges, are the members of the independent regulatory agencies such as the Interstate Commerce Commission, the Federal Power Commission, and the Securities and Exchange Commission. Although the president selects these officials of the executive branch, the Supreme Court has held that he may not remove them because they exercise what is often referred to as quasi-judicial powers and should thus be left free from political pressures.[10] Quasi-judicial power is the term sometimes given to the adjudicatory function of the regulatory agencies. The invention of such a term followed the realization that a number of executive agencies were, in fact, engaged in much the same kind of adjudication as courts. Emotional attachment to the doctrine of separation of powers necessitated adding the Latin word *quasi,* meaning as if or in a manner, to assure purists that the judicial power reserved to the courts was not really being used by administrative agencies.

The Court's decisions have created an anomalous situation. The security of tenure which is given to members of the independent regulatory agencies on the ground that they perform quasi-judicial functions is denied to other governmental officials such as the secretary of agriculture or the postmaster general, though these officials, too, discharge, at least occasionally, a similar task. The secretary of labor, for example, adjudicates disputes arising out of the statutes governing wages and hours. Also overlooked is the fact that commissioners of the independent regulatory agencies exercise extensive policymaking powers in addition to their adjudicatory functions. When the Federal Trade Commission moved against the cigarette industry, for instance, it was operating as a rule-making body.

Although the Supreme Court has helped make the regulatory agencies independent of presidential control, no one yet has succeeded in conferring on the agencies the same degree of independence from private pressure groups as they have from the White House. More than one agency has been captured by the interest it is supposed to be regulating, the Interstate Commerce Commission, for instance, by the railroad industry, though the very reason why the ICC was called into existence in 1887 was to keep the railroads in line and to prevent them from preying on the public. Similarly, the Federal Aviation Agency and the Civil Aeronautics Board often act more like spokesmen for the airlines than like policemen of their operations; nor are the regulatory agencies independent of congressional influence. Quite the contrary, congressional committees and subcommittees, as well as their chairmen, have not hesitated to put pressure on the agencies while at the same time insisting that the president keep his proper distance. There are, in fact, many in Congress who believe

[10] Humphrey's Executor v. United States, 295 U.S. 602 (1935), and Wiener v. United States, 357 U.S. 349 (1958).

firmly that the commissions should function as arms of the legislative branch. The term *independent* is evidently supposed to mean independent of the president and nothing else.

Legislative Oversight The power of appointment and removal, although seemingly potent weapons in the hands of a president, hardly assure him that in fact he will be chief executive. Apart from the sheer size of the bureaucracy and the centrifugal force its specialized nature generates, the president must compete with Congress in efforts to control policymaking by executive agencies. The passage of an act by Congress by no means represents the final act of interest in a particular policy on the part of the law-makers. Those who were in favor of the proposal will want to be assured that their expectations are being adequately fulfilled by sympathetic and efficient administration. Those who were in opposition, on the other hand, may be concerned that overly sympathetic administration may be giving more than Congress intended. Members of Congress and the committees of Congress, therefore, have an intense interest in following through on the administration of policy and the performance of executive agencies, so much so that supervision of administration or legislative oversight is probably the most important single role Congress plays today.

The place of legislative committees in the supervision of administration was explicitly recognized by the Legislative Reorganization Act of 1946. But congressional supervision of the executive branch is not exercised in a unified or even in a coherent fashion. Typically, an agency must expect its activities to be scrutinized by the legislative committees and subcommittees that authorize its programs, by the appropriations subcommittees on which it depends for funds, and by the government operations committees, which are licensed to roam about in the entire executive branch. In some instances, Congress even provides that prospective executive actions be subject to a committee's approval.[11] Presidents have been deeply resentful of such congressional interference in administration. In several instances, they have vetoed legislation making

---

[11] The first such provision dates from 1944, when the secretary of the navy was required to come into agreement with the House and Senate Naval Affairs Committees before spending money to acquire land for naval purposes. Joseph P. Harris, "Congressional Committee Veto of Executive Decisions," paper presented at the 1959 annual meeting of the American Political Science Association.

committee approval a prerequisite for certain executive actions. At other times, however, they have been obliged to concur in such arrangements or resign themselves to the defeat of legislation they favored.

The usual provision for a committee veto requires the department to submit a detailed report in advance of certain actions it plans to take. The committee is given a specific period of time in which it may disapprove the step. In practice, a committee sometimes chooses to delegate this veto power. The delegation may be to the committee chairman or to a subcommittee. On occasion it has even gone to professional staff members.[12] The two committees on government operations have often in effect subcontracted their veto to individual congressmen—whether committee members or not—whose constituencies would be directly affected by certain types of executive actions. An agency plan to dispose of surplus property, for example, is usually referred to the representatives and senators from the area where the property is located. If the proposed action does not meet with their approval, one of the government operations committees can usually be counted on to exercise its veto.[13]

Congress seems particularly concerned to give its committees a veto power over administrative action threatening the effectiveness of pork barrel legislation. Thus it has required committee clearance for military construction contracts, military real estate transactions, and the acquisition of public buildings.[14] In addition, it has used committee clearance when it is dissatisfied with the way in which established governmental programs are administered or when it is concerned about how new and untried programs will work out.[15]

Control by Appropriations The strategic position that the appropriations committees occupy in the legislative process enables them to play a highly important role in congressional supervision of the administration. If the committees were content to make lump sum appropriations to large departments and

[12] Walter E. Rhode, *Committee Clearance of Administrative Decisions* (East Lansing: Michigan State University Bureau of Social and Political Research, 1959), p. 51.
[13] Ibid., p. 59.
[14] George B. Galloway, *History of the House of Representatives* (New York: Thomas Y. Crowell, 1962), p. 188.
[15] Rhode, *Committee Clearance of Administrative Decisions*, pp. 48–49

then leave it up to the administrators to determine how to spend the funds, their supervisory power would be only minimal. Although they could threaten to cut a budget total, they would be unable to express themselves effectively on a particular program being carried out by a bureau tucked away in one of the corners of a vast department. To avoid being equipped only with an ax when a scalpel might be needed, the appropriations committees often follow the practice of writing reports that describe in minute detail how funds are to be apportioned to the subordinate units of a department.

Such detailed specification has been called "the most positive and flexible single method of legislative control of administration." [16] Its effectiveness stems from the fact that no administrator can afford to forget that anything he does may be examined by the appropriations committees. He knows that if his actions displease the committees, he may be punished by a budget cut when the next appropriations bill for his agency is drawn up. He pays careful heed, therefore, when he receives unsolicited advice as to how his office should be administered. He may even try to fill vacancies in his agency only with personnel satisfactory to the appropriations subcommittees with which he must deal. Sometimes the appropriators go so far as to recommend individuals for jobs with the agency. They also often issue what amounts to instructions as to how the work of the agency should be carried out as well as requiring periodic reports to assure that their directions are not being ignored.[17]

On occasion, Congress has provided in so many words that certain executive actions were not to be undertaken without advance approval from the appropriations committees. Regardless of party, presidents have been up in arms over such provisions. There have even been threats that legislative vetoes would be ignored. But in the final analysis, the executive branch has bowed to Congress, sometimes covering up its retreat by means of a face-saving formula.

Such was the case, for example, in 1955 when Congress attached a rider to the big defense appropriations bill. The rider gave the appropriations committee the right to prevent the secretary of defense from closing certain local installations and activities of the military establishment. President Eisenhower, although violently opposed to the provision, had no real alternative but to sign it into law because a veto

---

[16] James M. Burns, *Congress on Trial: The Legislative Process and the Administrative State* (New York: Harper & Bros., 1949), p. 104.
[17] Ibid., pp. 105–06.

of the entire bill was out of the question, and it is generally accepted that the Constitution does not sanction the veto of only part of a bill. According to the rider, the Defense Department would have to justify to the appropriations committees any plan to close a facility that had been in existence for at least three years. If within ninety days either one of the committees disapproved the shutdown, the plan would have to be dropped. Although executive officials at first let it be known that they would ignore the rider as unconstitutional,[18] they did nothing of the sort. Defense Secretary Charles E. Wilson kept the committees fully apprised of all closing plans, and, when a committee expressed its disapproval—as was the case in nine instances—there was no defiance. In all nine cases, the department contented itself with insisting, after it had capitulated, that its decision to cancel the closing plan had been arrived at independently of the committees' action.[19]

The use of such a congressional veto has been subjected to serious criticism. Perhaps the most interesting argument, and certainly the most ironic, is that the practice actually impairs the ability of Congress to supervise administration effectively. For when an executive official clears an administrative decision with Congress, he is no longer fully responsible for that decision and cannot be held accountable if it turns out to have been unwise.[20] Another criticism of the committee veto and of congressional interference with administration generally is that only an administrator is close enough to programs to make intelligent decisions as new problems arise. Unless he is given sufficient flexibility, he will be unable to act in response to a continuously changing situation. But the appropriations subcommittees are not deterred by arguments resting on principles of effective administrative management.

The Power to Investigate In the performance of their legislative and supervisory functions, congressional committees are aided immensely by their investigatory power. Such power, in fact, constitutes one of the principal devices enabling Congress to supervise the executive branch and compete with it for

---

[18] Edith T. Carper, "The Defense Appropriations Rider," in Edwin A. Bock and Alan K. Campbell, eds., *Case Studies in American Government* (Englewood Cliffs, N.J.: Prentice-Hall, 1962), pp. 47–48.

[19] Ibid., pp. 67–81.

[20] Harris, "Congressional Committee Veto of Executive Decisions."

public attention. The upsurge of congressional investigations in recent decades has accurately been termed "one of the unanticipated consequences of the Presidency's enlargement." [21] The congressional power to investigate, though nowhere mentioned in the Constitution, was already taken for granted when Congress was only in the third year of its existence. The first investigation was conducted in 1792, after a band of American soldiers, under the command of Major General Arthur St. Clair, experienced a disastrous defeat at the hands of the Indians. Six hundred American lives were lost. The House of Representatives proceeded to empower a select committee to investigate the debacle. It gave the committee authority to compel witnesses to appear, testify, and turn over relevant papers.[22]

In this very first inquiry, Congress came up against a problem that was to recur frequently: how to compel the president to produce documents needed in an investigation. When Washington was asked for certain papers relating to the St. Clair campaign, he enunciated the principle that the president "ought to communicate only such papers as the public good would permit, and ought to refuse those the disclosure of which would hurt the public." Jefferson, Monroe, and Jackson chose to follow this precedent, and executive privilege became a firmly established constitutional principle. It is generally conceded to mean that the president cannot be ordered to appear before a congressional committee. In addition, both the substance of conversations in which he has participated and the content of White House files are beyond the reach of Congress.[23]

Not all congressional investigations, of course, are directed toward supervision of executive activities although that was most frequently their subject during the first century of the nation's history. Toward the end of the nineteenth century and in the first three decades of the twentieth century Congress turned increasingly to quite another matter: economic and social problems that might call for legislative solutions. The muckraking atmosphere that characterized the period of Theodore Roosevelt's administration prompted investigations into such important sectors of American society as the stock market, the rail-

---

[21] Andrew Hacker, "Voice of Ninety Million Americans," *New York Times Magazine*, 4 March 1962, p. 80.
[22] Telford Taylor, *Grand Inquest* (New York: Simon and Schuster, 1954), pp. 19, 22.
[23] Joseph P. Harris, *The Advice and Consent of the Senate* (Berkeley: University of California Press, 1953), p. 103. But the scope of executive privilege is by no means clearly delineated. It is in dispute, for example, whether the privilege extends beyond the office of the president himself and encompasses the departments and agencies

roads, and the giant financial combines. Investigations of the same type were important to the administration of Franklin Roosevelt, too. Senators, for example, conducted a sensational investigation in 1935 into the high-handed methods employed by power companies to defeat a bill providing for the regulation of public utility holding companies. This investigation was carried on under the chairmanship of Senator Hugo Black of Alabama. The facts it turned up helped convince Black that proper investigations were an invaluable adjunct of the legislative process. On many occasions, he said, they had resulted in the enactment of salutary legislation, the saving of public funds, and the focusing of "the rays of pitiless publicity" on special interest groups, "who can defy every other power." [24] These words indicated that Congress had come to accept a broad view of its investigative authority during the 150 years following the inquest into General St. Clair's defeat.

The Legislative Reorganization Act bestowed on the committees of the Senate the power to subpoena both witnesses and documents needed to investigate "any matter within its jurisdiction." This was something of a revolutionary development, for previously no congressional committee had ever been granted the subpoena power on a permanent basis. Whenever either house had felt that a matter warranted investigation by a committee, it had been obliged to pass a special resolution particularly describing the subject to be studied. Under the 1946 law, however, every Senate committee was given blanket authorization to issue subpoenas. The break with the past was especially sharp because the use of subpoenas would no longer have to be confined to a specific subject certified by the Senate as ripe for investigation; subpoenas could now be used throughout the length and breadth of the spacious area over which each committee was given jurisdiction. In the House, the situation is different. There, only three committees have permanent authority to issue subpoenas: Appropriations, Government Operation, and Un-American Activities (the name of this last committee was changed in 1969 to the House Internal Security Committee).

The importance of the subpoena power, of course, is that it enables a committee to compel the presence of an unwilling witness and to insist, under threat of punishment, that he answer its questions and produce records it wants. A recalcitrant witness runs the risk that he will be held in contempt. In the present century, Congress has wholly abandoned the practice of punishing contempt on its own as it once

[24] Hugo L. Black, "Inside a Senate Investigation," *Harper's Magazine*, February 1936, p. 275. Black was appointed to the Supreme Court by Roosevelt in 1937.

did. It now prefers to rely on the Justice Department to prosecute balky witnesses and on the federal courts to punish them after citing them for contempt. In the last two decades no other committee of Congress resorted to the contempt power with as much frequency as did the formerly named House Un-American Activities Committee. Part of the reason for the change of the committee's name to the Internal Security Committee was to remove the negative image which had developed because of HUAC's abuses of the contempt power. To some extent, it was HUAC's practices which served to discredit Congress as a whole and weaken its investigatory power.[25]

General Accounting Office The overwhelming number of congressional investigations are quite different in nature and method from those made notorious by HUAC. In fulfilling their investigatory function, committees rely heavily on their professional staffs, as they do when conducting hearings on proposed legislation. Also available to Congress in exercising its function of legislative oversight are the services of the General Accounting Office. When Congress endorsed the executive budget concept in the Budget and Accounting Act of 1921 it also saw the need for having some means of supervising expenditures. It thus created the GAO, placing it under congressional control,[26] with the broad mandate to review expenditures of the executive agencies to be certain that they had been made in compliance with the laws under which they had been authorized.

The principal function of GAO is to audit the accounts of the executive departments and agencies. As part of this task, the office evaluates the management of agencies in terms of the economy and efficiency of their operation. Thus it does far more than merely audit vouchers to determine whether or not documentation is sufficient and whether or not expenditures were authorized and made in accordance with law. Its comprehensive review encompasses studies of the overall management of an agency and the detailed administration of a program or function. This is what differentiates its activities from those of public

---

[25] Such an observation was made almost twenty years ago. Robert K. Carr, *The House Committee on Un-American Activities, 1945–1950* (Ithaca, N.Y.: Cornell University Press, 1952), p. 458.

[26] Its head, the comptroller general, although appointed by the president and confirmed by the Senate, can be removed only by Congress. He also has a term of fifteen years and cannot be reappointed.

accounting firms, which never question the policy decisions of management. The purview of GAO is wider than government agencies, because colossal sums of federal money are spent under contracts with private enterprise.

The work of the agency is seldom publicized widely except when sensational revelations are involved. There was an abundance of publicity in 1962 when GAO discovered that both a brothel and a nudist colony were flourishing in national forests which were controlled by the Department of Agriculture. The brothel (in the Tonto National Forest in Arizona) and the nudist colony (in the Boise National Forest in Idaho) were being conducted under the guise of mining claims.[27] In a different vein, it was the GAO which found evidence of extensive corruption in the handling of American military and economic aid to South Vietnam as well as in the supplies intended for the American forces.

While the General Accounting Office has a well-deserved reputation for its efficient and exacting operations, there is some doubt whether Congress has fully exploited the potential of the agency. Its many reports are forwarded to the appropriations committees and to other committees as well. If Congress could gear itself to more long-range policy development and control in the appropriations process, the work of the GAO might be a useful tool. Often, however, the reports of wrongdoing or administrative errors in judgment are simply used by individual congressmen to gain publicity.

The elaborate array of mechanisms available to Congress in supervising the activities of the bureaucracy has important implications for the political system. For if Congress is vigilant and exercises a close watch over the agencies, it is unlikely that the federal bureaucracy will ever pose a serious threat to American freedoms. The danger is always present because the bureaucracy is such an imposing center of political power. But there is at least one factor that can be counted on to keep it in check: its pluralistic nature. The very diversity of the functions and interests represented by the bureaucracy constitutes a built-in counterweight to the possibility that it will ever become monolithic and hence dangerous. Individual agencies may well pursue policies adverse to civil liberties, but chances are that other agencies, representing other

[27] *Washington Post,* 2 June 1962, p. A-4. It was not the immorality that distressed GAO, but rather the fact that a mining claimant "has no right to use any part of the surface of his unpatented location for other than mining purposes. . . ." "Review of Administration of Mining Claims Located on National Forest Lands Reserved from the Public Domain," Report by the Comptroller General of the United States, May 1962.

interests, will find it expedient to mount a counteroffensive. Moreover, the processes used by the Civil Service Commission to recruit new employees into the executive branch tend to make the bureaucracy democratic in terms of such factors as the income level and associations of those who man it. It has even been argued that the bureaucracy as a whole is more representative of the American people than Congress itself.[28]

In any event, it seems that even the most uncompromising critics of bureaucracy must reconcile themselves to the fact that the system is here to stay. For it is inconceivable that the bureaucracy can be dismantled without dismantling at the same time the vast and complex edifice that is American society today. Nostalgia for the good old days can lead to nothing but frustration. Far more important is the development of mechanisms which, although presuming the continuation of a vast federal bureaucracy, will assure the public accountability of the bureacratic policymakers. The challenge of the future is to make the bureaucracy responsible without at the same time hampering its ability to advance the public interest.

The Foreign Policy Dilemma   The pluralistic nature and relative openness of policymaking indicate that such a goal is at least within reach on domestic issues and problems. But no such optimism can be justified when it comes to questions of the nation's relations with other countries. Here, the preeminence of the president's role and powers and the cloak of secrecy which hangs so heavily over decision-making pose a perhaps insoluble dilemma: how to square norms of self-government with the demands of foreign policymaking.

Presidential domination of the nation's foreign affairs might not be readily recognized upon a mere reading of the Constitution. All that is accorded the president is the power to make treaties (provided two-thirds of the Senate concur) and the power (again with the advice and consent of the Senate) to appoint ambassadors, other public ministers and consuls, as well as the power to receive ambassadors of other

---

[28] Norton Long, "Bureaucracy and Constitutionalism," Chapter V in *The Polity* (Chicago: Rand McNally, 1962), p. 70. This would not be true of the top rung of politically appointed executive officials who generally bear the same socioeconomic characteristics as congressmen.

countries.[29] In exercising two of these three powers, the president is required to share with the Senate decision-making authority. There are other areas, also, where the Constitution confers power on Congress in fields touching on our relations with other nations. It has, for example, power to regulate commerce with foreign nations; it can define and punish piracies as well as offenses against the law of nations; it has the power to declare war and to raise and support an army and navy. And, of course, Congress has the all-important appropriations power. Nowhere, however, to either Congress or the president, is a specific power given to conduct foreign relations.

The constitutional assignment of functions might well have resulted in a much closer partnership between president and Congress, and especially the Senate, in the field of foreign relations. But the expediency of events has dictated otherwise. The lines of historical development were early foreshadowed when John Marshall, while still in the House of Representatives, asserted: "The President is the sole organ of the nation in its external relations, and its sole representative with foreign nations."[30] Although Marshall's remark was made in the context of partisan dispute between Federalists and Republicans over foreign policy, it has been reiterated time and again by the Supreme Court.

Throughout much of American history, our relations with foreign nations have not been a major preoccupation of presidents. The twentieth century, and especially the last half of it, however, has seen a dramatic reversal of the United States' physical as well as diplomatic isolation from the rest of the world. On those sporadic occasions when the United States became involved in world affairs, it was the secretary of state, acting for the president, who was the principal figure. Wilson's personal effort on behalf of the Treaty of Versailles, however, ushered in a new style of foreign-policy making. Since FDR, the president has become a personal diplomat. What is done is not only done in his name—as it always has been—but often is done by him personally.

Crisis Policy Nonetheless, day-to-day conduct of the United States' affairs with more than 130 nations is carried on by the personnel of the Department of State

---

[29] Article II, Sections 2 and 3.
[30] Quoted in Edwin S. Corwin, *The President: Office and Powers,* 4th ed. (New York: New York University Press, 1957), p. 177.

and its affiliated agencies, such as the United States Information Agency and the Agency for International Development. If the Department of State has exercised a monopoly over such affairs in the past, it now must share responsibilities with a host of other agencies. The Department of Defense has become an intimate partner in the pattern of our foreign relations, as also have the Departments of Agriculture, Commerce, and Treasury. And perhaps, foremost of all of these, in terms of its impact on United States policy and action, is the Central Intelligence Agency. The representatives of all such agencies assigned to a foreign country are nominally under the control of the United States ambassador, the man the president has chosen to be his personal emissary to that nation. Whether the country ambassador can, in fact, control the often divergent and conflicting tendencies of all of the people under him is a question often posed by events.

It is not day-to-day operations, however, which occupy the mind and attention of the president. The detail is too great and the facts are too many. A president must be content that he has the right men as secretaries of state and defense and their principal assistants and then hope that they can infuse their departments with the appropriate values and spirit. Most presidents have found, however, that the bureaucracies in the Departments of State and Defense are almost impermeable.

It is, rather, in situations of crisis—which occur with such frequency that they appear to be normal—that the president becomes the major force in the making of American foreign policy decisions. Though he is practically never the originator of such policies, it is his act of choosing what United States policy will be which makes the president the chief architect of that policy. In modern times, the president has been given a great deal of organized machinery to help him discharge this function. Chief of these devices is the National Security Council. Yet the style of presidential operations in the field of foreign policy merely serves to emphasize the intensely personal nature of such decision-making. More than the apparatus of the Departments of Defense and State and the NSC, it has been the president's own man in the White House—his national security adviser—who has counted.

Whether done by the president personally, or in his name, most of the actions undertaken by the United States with other nations stem from the basic power of the president to send diplomatic representatives to other countries and to receive similar personages. It is the president—at least nominally—who must make the decision with which of the world's nations the United States will do diplomatic business. It was Franklin Roosevelt who made the decision in 1933 to recognize the U.S.S.R. as a nation—sixteen years after the Russian Revolution. And it has been Presidents Truman, Eisenhower, Kennedy, Johnson, and Nixon who thus far—twenty years later—have refused to extend recognition to the People's Republic of China. In this, all five presidents have been strongly encouraged and supported by Congress. Any chief executive, in fact, who undertook the step of recognition would do so at great peril unless public opinion were carefully cultivated in advance.

Treaties and Executive Agreements

The power to recognize—or withhold recognition—establishes the basis for relations between nations. To undertake particular policies in conjunction with another power, however, usually requires some form of agreement. Traditionally, the treaty has been the means of establishing some special relationship between or among nations. For most of American history, the treaty, in its constitutional form, requiring concurrence of two-thirds of the Senate, was the means whereby the United States agreed with other nations on mutual undertakings. Wilson's monumental defeat at the hands of the Senate over the Treaty of Versailles and United States adherence to the League of Nations, however, brought a shift away from the treaty. In its place, Wilson's successors have increasingly resorted to the device of executive agreements, which are unlike treaties in that they do not require the concurrence of the Senate. As a consequence, the treaty is now used only in situations of great importance (NATO, Test-Ban Treaty, Consular Treaty), especially when presidents find it politically expedient to secure the support of the Senate.

The term executive agreement does not appear in the Constitution. The authority of the president to negotiate such pacts is inferred from his constitutional powers as commander-in-chief of United States armed forces and from his position as sole organ of foreign relations. It was on this basis that President Roosevelt traded American destroyers for British bases in World War II and President Truman committed American troops to the postwar occupation of Germany. Agreements have been used in a wide variety of cases when treaties would have been in order. The precise difference between an executive agreement and a treaty is somewhat obscure. One possible distinction is that some question exists as to whether an executive agreement binds the successors of the president who signed it; no such question can arise concerning the more solemn treaty obligation. Another observable difference is that in practice executive agreements have generally been used only for bilateral compacts; agreements that involve a joint enterprise of a group of nations have usually taken the form of treaties.[31]

Unlimited use of executive agreements is open to serious question. The American people can be kept completely in the dark about the contents of an executive agreement; a secret treaty, however, is almost inconceivable under the system requiring senatorial ratification. At a time when foreign policy decisions may determine the fate of the species, a curious paradox exists: The nation which once was unwilling to accept taxation without representation does not rebel today against the possibility that it may be consigned to extinction without representation. Still there will doubtless continue to be a temptation to resort to executive agreements because they avoid the requirement of ratification by two-thirds of the Senate. The ironical fact is that the two-thirds rule, instead of operating to preserve the power of the Senate, has actually resulted in an erosion of that power.

The House once approved a constitutional amendment providing for ratification of treaties by a simple majority in each of the two houses of Congress, but the resolution, as might be expected, was buried by the Senate Judiciary Committee.

The War Power

The power to make executive agreements and to accord recognition to other nations is indeed a formidable weapon in forging foreign policy decisions. But if this were all the president had to rely on, his power would be nowhere as awesome as it is in practice. Since Lincoln, however—who first claimed it—presidents have exercised a vaguely defined but vast war power. No such power is anywhere mentioned in the Constitution, particularly with reference to the president. And only Congress, of course, has the power to declare war. The absence of any

---

[31] Yet the United States joined specialized organizations of the United Nations (such as the Food and Agriculture Organization and the International Bank for Reconstruction and Development) not through treaty but by means of joint resolutions of Congress.

such specific power was no embarrassment to Lincoln. Having decisively determined to preserve the Union, he just as decisively decided to take the actions he thought necessary toward that end regardless of their constitutional sanction. Although his military actions might have had some constitutional or statutory warrant, the suspension of habeas corpus raised a serious constitutional question.[32]

Nonetheless Lincoln did not have the slightest doubt that his actions were thoroughly appropriate; and, to rationalize his exertion of authority, he developed the notion of the war power, asserting that it naturally arose out of his power as commander-in-chief of the army and navy, together with the injunction in the Constitution that "he [the President] shall take Care that the Laws be faithfully executed . . ."[33] With reference to the suspension of habeas corpus, Lincoln sought to justify his action to Congress by asking a disarmingly simple rhetorical question: "Are all the laws *but one* to go unexecuted, and the Government itself go to pieces lest that one be violated?"[34] In his unprecedented interpretation of the Constitution, Lincoln simply assumed not only military power but political power as well, law-making or policy-making power in its baldest sense. He continued to exercise such power throughout the war, the Emancipation Proclamation of January 1, 1863, being the outstanding example. History justified Lincoln's actions but no amount of favorable gloss can obscure the fact that the Constitution is indeed a fragile thing in the hands of a determined chief executive.

Although Lincoln developed the theory of war power in response to a domestic situation of rebellion, subsequent presidents have found it just as useful to wage foreign wars. In both world wars, even before formal entry, Wilson and Roosevelt, on their own as well as with congressional sanction, fully used the war powers of the president. Increasingly, moreover, the president's power as commander-in-chief, together with his authority in foreign relations, has been able to commit the nation to war. The great difference between World Wars I and

---

[32] In Article I, Section 9, it is provided that "The Privilege of the Writ of Habeas Corpus shall not be suspended, unless when in Cases of Rebellion or Invasion the public Safety may require it." Since this appears in Article I, dealing largely with the legislature, it was argued at the time that only Congress could suspend the writ. The writ of habeas corpus is a basic guarantee of civil liberty because it requires that an arrested person be brought before a magistrate or judge and the confining officer required to show cause why the prisoner should not be discharged. It thus prevents arbitrary imprisonment without specification of some wrongdoing in violation of law.
[33] Article II, Sections 2 and 3.
[34] Message to Congress, July 4, 1861, James D. Richardson, *Messages and Papers of the Presidents*, Vol. VI (Washington: Government Printing Office, 1896–99), p. 25.

II and Korea and Vietnam is that in the large-scale conflicts the nation, through Congress, formally declared a state of war. In Korea, and more so in Vietnam, unrestrained presidential war power has effectively abrogated the power of Congress to determine when the nation should be at war. Hardboiled realists may attribute this to the nature of modern conditions and the struggle against communism. But, whatever the reasons, the plain fact is that a nation of over 200 million people can be sent down the path of destruction by a single man. And, as the nation discovered, the Senate, not to mention the House, provides very little check either before involvement or after the commitment has become irrevocable.

In policymaking in the fields of foreign relations and military affairs, the courts are even less significant a factor. Historically, in fact, the courts have been content to mind their own business and only occasionally have summoned enough courage to interfere with executive conduct in these fields. Such was the case with Lincoln and the Supreme Court. It was only after the war had been won by the North that the Court ventured to declare that the trial by military commission in Indiana of a suspected rebel agitator was unconstitutional.[35] A similar pattern prevailed during World War II when the Court showed no inclination to interfere with the presidentially endorsed military program of relocating Japanese-American citizens in detention camps on the West Coast. Only when the presumed threat of a Japanese invasion had waned toward the end of the war did the Court begin to question this cruel deprivation of constitutional liberties of American citizens.[36] And in a case reminiscent of *Milligan* the Court decided that the trial of a civilian in Hawaii by a military tribunal, after the imposition of martial law, was unconstitutional. Even though the issue had been presented to the Court as early as February, 1945, at least six months before the war ended, the Court did not hand down its decision until a year later.[37] The courts have not shown any inclination toward questioning the president's conduct of the war in Vietnam, whether the issue was raised in a case involving the draft or one concerning freedom of expression under the First Amendment.

---

[35] Ex parte Milligan, 4 Wall. 2 (1866).
[36] Ex parte Endo, 323 U.S. 283 (1944).
[37] Duncan v. Kahanamoku, 327 U.S. 304 (1946).

Suppressing Domestic Violence

Keeping peace or waging war abroad is not the only preoccupation of American presidents. On occasion they have felt the necessity to exert their power to quiet domestic violence. The ink on the Constitution had hardly dried when Washington was confronted with an insurrection of sorts in western Pennsylvania. Objection to an excise tax levied on distilled spirits so aroused some of the inhabitants of the Appalachians that there were threats to secede from the state and the Union. A statute passed by Congress in 1792 had authorized the president to call up the militia of the state involved or other states to put down opposition to the execution of the laws of the United States. Washington issued the required proclamation in August, 1794, called out 15,000 militiamen from four states, and led the force himself over the mountains. This show of strength put to flight most of the rebels and their resistance was broken.[38]

Congress in 1795 broadened the president's authority in putting down trouble at home. It extended his power to situations involving domestic violence as well as insurrections and made him the sole judge of when the authority could be invoked. Previously, a federal judge had to notify him of the disturbance before he could act.[39] The 1795 statute has proven useful several times. It was invoked by President Eisenhower when, in 1957, he ordered paratroopers to Little Rock, Arkansas, to maintain order after the state's governor had shown no disposition to control the mobs seeking to prevent integration of Central High School.[40] President Kennedy also relied on this authority in 1962, when troops were sent to Oxford, Mississippi, to quell rioting at the University of Mississippi over the admission of James H. Meredith ordered by a federal court. A year later, a Kennedy order "federalizing" the Alabama National Guard induced Governor George Wallace to unlock the schoolhouse door, in this case the University of Alabama, to two Negroes. The same power was the basis for the dispatch of the guard as well as regular troops to quell racial disturbances in the cities.

Such presidential assertions of power are, of course, far from the ordinary way in which the laws of the United States are executed day

[38] Samuel Eliot Morison, *History of the American People* (New York: Oxford University Press, 1965), pp. 340–41.
[39] Corwin, *The President*, p. 131.
[40] Under other statutory authority of long standing, the president took the Arkansas National Guard out from under the governor's control by "federalizing" it.

in and day out. Incidents involving clashes between national and state authority, although dramatic, are hardly typical of the normal relationships between these two levels of government. What is significant, however, is that in such situations the president—and not Congress—makes the decisions and exercises on his own account awesome power.

Chapter 12 Policymaking by Courts

Like Congress, the president, and the bureaucracy, the courts are major participants in the policymaking process. This is true because the end result of the activities of courts is the promulgation of rules of behavior, just as is the case with Congress, the president, and the executive agencies. Yet the policymaking role of judges is often lost sight of, largely because the special traditions and procedures of the courts appear to be entirely nonpolitical.

Indeed, the foremost function of courts is not to make policy but rather to settle disputes among individuals. In form, at least, most judicial decisions do nothing more than determine the respective rights and obligations of the particular litigants who are the parties to a dispute. Over the long term, however, such decisions often come to be used as precedents for adjudicating similar cases that may arise. It is for that reason that a series of court decisions in a particular field may be looked upon as the expression of general policies to which individuals are expected to conform.

Dispute settlement was perhaps the first of all government functions to develop. In primitive societies, even those lacking formal institutions of government, some mechanism for reconciling conflicts existed. Paradoxically, the violence that characterized "primitive societies occurs because the rules to which everyone subscribes in principle are broken in particular cases."[1] In enforcing the broken rules, the aggrieved parties often resorted to violent means to redress the wrong. Force is still a factor—even in modern civilized societies—in settling disputes, although it lurks in the background. Administration of the death penalty is an example of a societal-sanctioned application of force in the taking of a human life. But even the mildest of sanctions imposed in the enforcement of rules has behind it the power of organized government.

Enforcement of law or public policy is made a great deal easier because members of society learn to obey the rules. An important part of the process of political socialization is especially aimed at inculcating those values of respect for law and order without which organized society would be virtually impossible. Although most citizens accept the decisions of society, as embodied in public policy, disputes still arise. In modern, complex societies, the sheer quantity of rules and regulations touching so many daily activities inevitably makes dispute settlement a major governmental task.

Judicial Policymaking

Many of the same characteristics of legislative policymaking which give rise to the necessity of administrative policymaking also require that courts make policy in the course of dispute settlement.

When an executive agency applies the provisions of a general statute to particular cases, questions inevitably arise. Did the agency misinterpret the intent of Congress in the action it took? Were the procedures employed by the agency in accordance with applicable constitutional standards? Was the statute itself free from any constitutional infirmity? The responsibility for answering questions such as these falls to judges and injects them into the policymaking process. The political nature of the judicial process is a basic fact of life in the American governmental system.

Since the policymaking process is so often a struggle among different

---

[1] Lucy Mair, *Primitive Government* (Baltimore: Penguin Books, 1962), p. 35.

interest groups, it is not surprising to discover that in an impressively large number of instances group conflict lurks in the background of what appears on the surface to be a legal controversy between two individual litigants. For, although the formal parties to a lawsuit involving public policy may be individuals, or perhaps corporations, such parties often only stand in for large and powerful groups whose interests may be vitally affected by the outcome of the litigation. The judicial process, in fact, is often resorted to by those who have failed to gain their objectives in the legislative or administrative arenas. Viewed in this light, the courts are just another forum in which competing interest groups continue, renew, or initiate their struggles over public policy.

The two most important public policy decisions made by the courts in the last two decades—those on legislative apportionment and school segregation—illustrate the group nature of the judicial process.

In 1959, a Chattanooga voter named Charles W. Baker filed a legal suit against Joe C. Carr, the Tennessee Secretary of State. He claimed that the state legislature had violated the federal constitution by its failure to reapportion itself in more than a half-century. In order to have standing in court, one must prove that one has more than a bystander's interest in the outcome of the litigation. Accordingly, Baker made the point that the state legislature's inaction had diluted his vote. His argument was that the urban areas, including the one where he lived, were entitled to select more members of the state legislature than an ancient law, enacted when Tennessee was overwhelmingly rural, provided.

But, although Baker was the moving party in the litigation, all other city dwellers in Tennessee—and the state's rural population, as well—had just as much at stake as he did in the suit that he instituted. So, also, for that matter, were millions of other voters throughout the country affected since Tennessee was by no means the only state where legislative apportionment did not reflect the actual distribution of population. It was understood from the beginning that a favorable decision for Baker would open the federal courts to citizens in any state who felt that judicial action was the only feasible way to overcome the constitutional evil of malapportioned state legislatures. Such a decision was, indeed, forthcoming,[2] and, as expected, the result was an avalanche of legal actions to compel legislative reapportionment.

The school segregation cases were no different. Although the case that

[2] Baker v. Carr, 369 U.S. 186 (1962). For a study of the reapportionment controversy, see Royce Hanson, *The Political Thicket* (Englewood Cliffs, N.J.: Prentice-Hall, 1966).

was decided by the Supreme Court in 1954 ostensibly did no more than pit the parents of thirteen Negro school children against the Board of Education of Topeka, Kansas, its outcome would obviously determine the fate of segregated public schools wherever they existed. The suit, in fact, was brought as a class action so that the decision would apply directly not only to those personally involved in the litigation but also to all others similarly situated.[3] And when the Supreme Court decided the case in favor of the Negro litigants, no one could doubt that it had enunciated public policy not only for Topeka but also for the rest of the United States.[4]

In the school segregation cases, the role played by an organized interest group, the National Association for the Advancement of Colored People, was not difficult to discern. The cases were actually financed by the NAACP, and the organization's chief counsel, Thurgood Marshall,[5] was the lawyer who argued them. Sometimes the participation of an interest group is less direct. Interest groups, for example, make extensive use of *amicus curiae,* or friend of the court, briefs. Through the filing of such briefs, a group that is not a party to a suit in which it feels it has a vital interest can present its argument to the court. During a recent term of the Supreme Court, in some 250 decisions, no fewer than 54 *amicus curiae* briefs were filed by groups as diverse as the National Association of Broadcasters, the National District Attorneys Association, the American Humanist Association, and the Planned Parenthood Federation of America. Private groups, moreover, are not the only ones to take advantage of the *amicus curiae* procedure. In 1963, when the Supreme Court held that states must provide counsel to defendants who are too poor to hire their own,[6] the justices had before them an *amicus* brief filed by twenty-three of the states, urging them to make exactly the decision that they did.[7] And in 1954, when the Supreme Court placed the stamp of unconstitutionality on public school segregation, its path was made easier by the fact that the United States government, acting through the solicitor general, had filed a supporting brief and participated in the oral arguments as well.

Whether interest groups are involved directly or only indirectly,

[3] See Daniel M. Berman, *It Is So Ordered: The Supreme Court Rules on School Segregation* (New York: W. W. Norton, 1966), p. 30.
[4] Brown v. Board of Education, 347 U.S. 483 (1954). Also decided by the Brown case were three suits from other states and one involving segregation in the District of Columbia.
[5] Now a justice of the Supreme Court.
[6] Gideon v. Wainwright, 372 U.S. 335 (1963).
[7] See Anthony Lewis, *Gideon's Trumpet* (New York: Vintage Books, 1966), pp. 147–48.

judicial decisions with an impact on public policy are an everyday occurrence. A court may be called on to draw the line between television commercials that merely embroider the truth and those that amount to simple deception, or it may be asked to decide whether the Federal Power Commission took into account the public interest in scenic beauty when it granted a license for the building of hydroelectric power facilities on the Hudson River. Although the issues vary, the cases have one thing in common: they all represent the participation of judges in the formulation of public policy.

Judicial Review The involvement of courts in the policymaking process is a phenomenon that is by no means confined to the United States. But in this country the courts play a distinctly more important role than elsewhere, primarily because judges have the power to interpret the Constitution to which all governmental actions, both state and federal, must conform. Not that the idea of judicial review, as the power of courts to declare legislative enactments unconstitutional is called, originated in the United States. Well before the United States Constitution was written, an English judge, Sir Edward Coke, had planted the seeds of such a theory by asserting that statutes of Parliament which violated common right and reason should be invalidated as violations of the common law.[8] But the theory advanced by Coke was never accepted in England, and to this day no British court would dare assert the power to nullify what Parliament has decreed to be public policy. The assumption in England is that it is the solemn obligation of Parliament not to infringe the right of individuals, and that Parliament must be relied on to discharge this obligation faithfully.

But the theory of legislative supremacy, so firmly entrenched in England, was not to survive in the United States. A written Constitution and a cultural inclination to cast political issues in legal terms have almost from the first given American courts extraordinary powers. The idea of putting into written form the basic scheme of government reached its flower among the generation which wrote the American Constitution. The milestones of English constitutional evolution reaching back even before the Magna Carta of 1215 had been recorded in a variety of written documents. When the colonies declared their inde-

[8] Dr. Bonham's case (1610).

pendence from England in 1776, it seemed a perfectly natural act to write down the form the new state governments would take. The pervading notion was "that the basis of governmental power is a contract between governor and governed."[9] Although other nations have had, and presently do have, written constitutions, in no other country is a constitution regarded with such a degree of reverence as is characteristic of American attitudes toward this basic document.

Political Law Constitutions of government were regarded by Americans of the eighteenth century as law, often in the equivalent sense as scripture was regarded as law. As Tom Paine expressed it, politically and prophetically:

> But where, say some, is the King of America? Yet that we may not appear to be defective even in earthly honors, let a day be solemnly set apart for proclaiming the charter; let it be brought forth placed in the divine law, the word of God; let a crown be placed thereon by which the world may know that so far as we approve of monarchy, that in America the law is King.[10]

All that remained was to supply constitutions with authoritative interpreters. In time, the judges became the high priests of the law of American constitutions. But the law of which they would become the guardians after the American Revolution and the adoption of the Constitution in 1789 was law of a different kind. American judges, both national and state, were to become the authoritative interpreters of political law—constitutions of government—as well as of torts and contracts and crimes, subjects of the common law, largely made by judges in the beginning. The basic organization of powers and rights in a political system is an entirely different matter, however. Yet judges responded to this task of guardianship with much the same outlook as they pursued their functions in interpreting the common law. And in the middle and last part of the eighteenth century, this function was conceived of as an almost automatic, transhuman endeavor.

[9] Arthur E. Sutherland, *Constitutionalism in America* (Waltham, Mass.: Blaisdell, 1965), p. 6.
[10] Quoted in Edward S. Corwin, *The "Higher Law" Background of American Constitutional Law* (Ithaca, N.Y.: Great Seal Books, Cornell University Press, 1955), pp. 1–2.

The eighteenth century's leading legal commentator, William Blackstone, had described judges as

> the depositaries of the law; the living oracles, who must decide in all cases of doubt, and who are bound by an oath to decide according to the law of the land.[11]

But how did a judge know what the law of the land was? Presumably he could find it by an informed reading of the mass of previously decided cases which had something to do with the problem. Implicit in such a process is the notion of a preexisting body of law. To a generation seeking to overcome the pernicious effects of arbitrary government, there was great comfort and security in the belief in the rule of known and standing laws.

When it came to the field of political law, however, the judge was in a much better position because he could look to the Constitution itself. The answer could be found in the text of the document. "The idea of reducing to writing such a compact is part of the concept of government of laws and not of men . . . [giving] the fundamental writing . . . a mystique greater than its words can explain by themselves." [12] Statutes, of course, are also written. But it has been to political constitutions, and especially the one of 1787, that Americans have accorded a quality of higher law.[13]

Much of the infirmity of the Blackstonian view of the law, however, carries over to the interpretation of a written constitution. Although a written text may provide a more explicit basis for interpretation, there are still instances when words are ambiguous or situations arise which were unforeseen by its drafters. No writing, no matter how detailed, can possibly cover all conceivable human situations, nor can words and combinations of them ever be totally free of all ambiguity. Language is simply not a precise tool of expression as is mathematics. The inherent ambiguity of constitutions together with the higher quality accorded such documents as opposed to ordinary law produces the ingredients for political law made by judges.

---

[11] William Blackstone, *Commentaries on the Laws of England* (Philadelphia: Geo. T. Bisel, 1922), p. 58. Blackstone was widely read in America, and his book served as the text for the training of many American lawyers of the period and for some time thereafter.
[12] Sutherland, *Constitutionalism in America,* p. 6.
[13] Corwin, *The "Higher Law."*

Myth and Reality

Judicial review as it has come to be practiced in the United States was almost unknown at the time of the adoption of the Constitution. The tradition of legislative supremacy had been assumed in the political consciousness of Americans of the day, most of whom were but two or three generations removed from the revolution of their forebears in 1689. Legislative supremacy, moreover, was much more in line with the attitudes of the day toward popular government. Judges during the colonial period were most often the appointees of the governors, who stood little better than the king in the eyes of the colonists. Less than ten instances, in fact, are cited where courts in the states asserted a power of judicial review—of declaring acts of the state or lesser governmental bodies contrary to the state's constitution and therefore void—before 1787. Several of these are of extremely dubious value as precedents.[14]

Nevertheless, it has become traditional American history to assert firmly that the framers of the Constitution of 1787 intended to grant to the Supreme Court of the United States (and other federal courts as they might be created) the power of judicial review. Evidence, in addition to the cases where it is claimed courts exerted the power, usually is drawn from the remarks made at the Constitutional Convention. Most of these, however, when closely examined reveal that the subject being discussed was how to keep the states from flouting the Constitution and laws of the national government by passing their own inconsistent laws. Some tribunal would be needed, it was argued, to declare when the states had transgressed the bounds of their own power and interfered with national authority.[15] But this is a decidedly different matter from conferring on the Supreme Court the power to declare laws of Congress void because they are contrary to the Constitution. Although such a power seems quite natural to Americans of today, long-continued acceptance of a practice ought not to be confused with belief in the deliberate creation of such a practice.

The controversy is largely an academic one, however, because American courts have exercised the power of judicial review since early in the nineteenth century. And federal courts have held not only acts of the states, but laws of Congress as well, unconstitutional. Judi-

---

[14] The cases are extensively discussed and criticized in W. W. Crosskey, *Politics and the Constitution in the History of the United States*, 2 vols. (Chicago: University of Chicago Press, 1953), vol. II, chap. XXVII.

[15] The subject is more fully discussed in the context of federalism in the next chapter.

cial review has come to be an accepted feature of the American political system because it has satisfied the public policy demands of enough groups of citizens enough of the time to escape permanent destructive attack. Or, to put it another way, the practice has not dissatisfied enough groups so consistently as to sustain a successful attack on it. Ultimately, the Supreme Court, as the principal political organ exercising the power of judicial review, has been adept and astute enough to adjust its constitutional doctrine to a safely acceptable level of public disapproval.

The historical truth seems to be that the political decisions of the Supreme Court, although offending many, have also pleased others. There are usually two sides to a lawsuit, even those involving great constitutional questions. One side wins and the other side loses. The triumph of either side means that the interest of many others is likely to be affected. This was as true in 1824 when the Supreme Court invalidated the monopoly of the steamboat trade on the Hudson River conferred on Ogden by the state of New York [16] as it was in 1954 when the Court held in favor of Linda Carol Brown and against the Board of Education of Topeka, Kansas.

The ability of courts to make political decisions palatable is, in large part, because of the tendency of Americans to regard such decisions in precisely the opposite light. Courts and judges in American political culture are regarded as impartial arbiters of the law. The Constitution is viewed as a particularly important and binding law. When the Supreme Court makes a decision based on the Constitution, therefore, the tendency is to accept it. As at a baseball game, a few decisions now and then will provoke heated and passionate denunciations, particularly from among the most zealous of fans. But, in the end, the umpire is accepted as part of the scene. Neither the players nor the fans would know how to play the game otherwise. So, too, for better or for worse, has the American political culture accepted the supposedly impartial role of the Supreme Court. That the picture of impartiality and aloofness from politics may not have always accorded with reality makes little difference. It is the myth which counts far more.

Much of the myth can be traced to the two men who made the doctrine of judicial review respectable. Although the theory was first extensively developed by Chief Justice John Marshall in 1803 in *Marbury v. Madison,* it was Marshall's mentor, Alexander Hamilton, who had provided much of the rationale. Marshall's opinion in *Marbury*

[16] Gibbons v. Ogden, 9 Wheaton 1 (1824).

was, in fact, almost a carbon copy of Hamilton's argument in *Federalist* paper No. 78, written fifteen years before. In 1788, Hamilton was a zealous partisan on behalf of the adoption of the Constitution, offering explanations of how the new system would work. His arguments were largely directed at swaying the New York ratifying convention and to some extent the Virginia convention. In 1803, Marshall was an equally zealous partisan on behalf of those principles which he thought pure and consistent with the Constitution, specifically the ideas of the Federalist party. It was, after all, Marshall, as Chief Justice of the United States, who was the only remaining visible symbol of the party which had breathed life into the new nation.

The Hamilton-Marshall argument was seemingly irrefutable. What would be the purpose of a written constitution if its terms could be violated at will by the legislative power? A written constitution containing limitations on governmental power would be meaningless if there were no way to enforce those limitations. Some agency must, therefore, declare when those limitations have been passed. Who else but the judges of the Supreme Court, who have sworn to uphold the Constitution, should serve in this capacity? To those that asserted that this gave to the Supreme Court a political power supreme over that of Congress, Hamilton had a deceptively simple answer:

> Nor does this conclusion by any means suppose a superiority of the judicial to the legislative power. It only supposes that the power of the people is superior to both, . . .[17]

Thus is the mythical power of the people vindicated, not by their elected representatives, but by the appointed judges of the Supreme Court. Arguments that legislators also take an oath to uphold the Constitution and that they, equally with judges, are competent to determine the constitutionality of legislation have fallen on an unreceptive public. Assertions by no less dominant figures than Thomas Jefferson and Andrew Jackson that the president is also empowered to make his own constitutional determinations have met a similar fate.

Whatever the abstract merits of the argument might be, the Hamilton-Marshall notion took root. Rather early in the development of the American political character, the Frenchman, Tocqueville, could comment that

---

[17] *Federalist* No. 78, in Clinton Rossiter, *The Federalist Papers* (New York: The New American Library, 1961), pp. 467–68.

> Scarcely any political question arises in the United States that is not resolved sooner or later into a judicial question. Hence all parties are obliged to borrow, in their daily controversies, the ideas, and even the language, peculiar to judicial proceedings.[18]

If this were true in 1830, it became even more so as the commerce and industry of the nation developed. It has meant that all courts in the United States—national and state—have been involved in the judicial process of answering political questions as well as economic and social ones.

What Kinds of Cases? The role of courts in the policymaking process is not confined to those cases in which constitutional questions are raised. The Supreme Court of the United States, moreover, is not the only federal court which makes political or policy decisions. The structure of the federal court system, as well as the kinds of cases that can be heard, determines the role of the courts in the policymaking process.

There are several types of cases in which a federal court may become involved. One of these has little consequence as far as public policy is concerned. These are the cases heard in a federal court because the parties are citizens of different states. There were those at the Constitutional Convention who feared that the courts of New Hampshire, for example, would give short shrift to a citizen of New Jersey suing a resident of New Hampshire. It was argued that national tribunals, with no state attachments to prejudice them, would provide a mutual forum for such suits. Accordingly, federal courts were given jurisdiction to hear these kinds of cases—involving diversity of citizenship.[19]

Diversity of citizenship cases involve the same areas of the law—contracts, torts, wills, and so on—which ordinarily would be fought out in state courts. Until 1938, however, the fact that these issues could be heard in federal courts resulted in the development of legal rules which a federal court sitting in a state might follow while the courts of that same state might apply different principles. Often, the mere fact of diversity of citizenship could result in different decisions in the same state on similar problems. In 1938, however, the Supreme Court of the

---
[18] Alexis de Tocqueville, *Democracy in America*, 2 vols. (New York: Vintage Books, 1960), vol. I, p. 290.
[19] Congress has required that any such suit must involve a claim for at least $10,000.

United States decided that federal courts in a state should adhere to the law as accepted by the state's courts. The federal court should reach the same result as if the case had been brought in the state court.[20] The possibilities of federal courts making public policy in such areas of the law, although not entirely eliminated, were sharply reduced.

Diversity of citizenship cases form a part of the civil jurisdiction exercised by federal courts. Civil cases concern disputes between members of society embracing a wide variety of relationships, normally the rights of persons as against other persons. By contrast, criminal cases involve the wrongs done by individuals against society at large, even though the specific wrong is done against a particular person. In the one case—the civil—an individual is seeking to redress a wrong alleged to have been done to him by another person. In the criminal case, on the other hand, society is seeking to punish an individual for antisocial behavior committed against another person. If Jones hits Smith in the mouth, Smith may bring a civil action against Jones seeking damages for the assault and battery. But the local prosecutor may also bring criminal charges against Jones for assault and battery or breach of the peace. Thus Jones may have to pay Smith fifty dollars in damages and at the same time pay a fine (which would go into the local public treasury) and/or spend a few days in jail.

Most courts exercise both civil and criminal jurisdiction, state courts more so than federal courts because their jurisdiction is generally much broader. Federal courts, moreover, are usually confined (except in diversity of citizenship cases) to civil cases where jurisdiction has been conferred specifically by act of Congress. Nonetheless, the jurisdiction of these courts is wide, extending to cases arising under the Constitution, laws or treaties of the United States, and in other cases authorized by statute. The general language is broad enough to encompass almost any attack on public policy which can be phrased in legal terms.

Federal courts also exercise extensive criminal jurisdiction. Unlike the states, Congress has no general power to specify and punish crimes. Federal criminal statutes depend for their authority on the power of Congress to protect its other powers from interference. Thus, under its power to regulate commerce, Congress has made it a crime to transport a stolen automobile in interstate commerce. Only the states may punish car theft as such (except where the car involved

[20] Erie R.R. v. Tompkins, 304 U.S. 64 (1938).

belongs to a federal agency) but Congress has seen fit to aid in the apprehension of car thieves by discouraging flight across state lines. Making the transportation of the auto in interstate commerce a crime also enables the FBI to assist in the apprehension of the offender. If the federal aspect were not involved, the FBI would not have any authority in a case of simple auto theft.

Interpreting Statutes   Whether a federal court is involved with a civil or criminal case, it is usually concerned with an act of Congress or regulations of an administrative agency. It is in the interpretation and application of these rules to the case before it that policymaking can and often does occur. Statutory interpretation is thus the principal task of the federal courts and the one which requires them constantly to make decisions having policy implications. Only rarely is the wording of a congressional act so clear and precise that reasonable men cannot differ as to its meaning. Ambiguity and imprecision are necessary by-products of the use of language, even when draftsmanship of the statute is done with painstaking care. But the reasons why a variety of possible interpretations of a law may exist are also closely related to the dispersion of power in Congress and the lack of party leadership and discipline in the development of a legislative program.

Political realities in Congress are such that support for a measure tends to melt away with every effort to spell out exactly what is intended. In order to enhance the possibility that a bill will receive majority support, its sponsors are frequently led to sacrifice clarity for votes. In the words of one student of Congressional behavior, "ambiguity and verbal compromise may be the very heart of a successful political formula, especially where the necessity for compromise is recognized but [where compromise] is difficult to achieve in explicit terms." [21] There may, that is, be majority support for some sort of bill to discourage secondary boycotts, but no agreement on what the bill should contain. The result in all probability will be a statute which is phrased in terms of calculated ambiguity. The allies in the uneasy coalition approving the bill agree tacitly to let the courts choose between

[21] David B. Truman, *The Governmental Process* (New York: Alfred A. Knopf, 1951), p. 393.

the two or more interpretations that can validly be made of the legislative formula agreed on.

Even when Congress has thus almost commanded the courts to formulate policy, judges are unwilling to admit that they must perforce make a decision based in part on subjective factors. They accept the view that the courts can continue to play an important part in the American system of government only if they do not appear to be framing policy decisions.

This may help explain why judges, when engaged in the task of statutory interpretation, work so long and hard at what seems to be a completely objective aspect of their task: ascertaining the legislative intent. They pore through materials such as committee reports and statements made on the floor with such a consuming interest that they have been accused, only half in jest, of consulting the statute itself only when its legislative history is doubtful.[22]

Leaving to one side the nagging question of whether it is defensible to treat the heavily edited *Congressional Record* as if it were a verbatim account of floor proceedings, a larger problem suggests itself. That problem goes to the heart of the legislative process, for it is concerned fundamentally with the underlying assumption that such a thing as legislative intent exists at all. It is difficult enough to ascertain the intent of an action or statement by a single individual; when one goes a step further and seeks to learn the intent of a group, he may be in quest of a logical absurdity. And the absurdity is compounded if Congress is the group with which one is dealing.

Congress is so heterogeneous, its procedural machinery is so ill-adapted for rational decision-making, and the motives of its members are so unrelated to their verbal professions that it may be completely unreasonably to inquire after its intent. On what premise, for example, is it assumed that the chairman of a House committee speaks for his chamber as a whole, not to mention the Senate? What can one really infer about the will of the Senate from the fact that a certain provision was dropped from a bill to avert a filibuster? Can a compromise reached secretly in conference and presented to each chamber on an all-or-nothing basis really be said to reflect the will of a majority in each house? And in addition to such questions, there is also the problem of whether presidential statements should be considered as part of the relevant record. The president, after all, may have had a completely

[22] Howard N. Mantel, "The Congressional Record: Fact or Fiction of the Legislative Process," *Western Political Quarterly* 12 (December 1959): 989.

different motive in signing the bill than any member of Congress did in voting for it.[23]

Even if the courts would like to escape the often unenviable task of doing that which Congress either refused to do or could not do, they have little choice in the matter. There are some situations in which it is possible to reject a case because the matter is declared not to be within the jurisdiction of the court. Over the years, in self-defense, certain kinds of issues have been deemed by the courts too politically charged to be handled. Such was the attitude toward cases challenging malapportioned state legislatures until *Baker* v. *Carr* declared otherwise. Suits against the president will not be entertained by the courts, and even indirect challenges to his power in the fields of military and foreign relations policy are difficult to mount. Federal courts refused to hear, for example, suits brought by draftees against the secretary of defense to prevent him from sending them to Vietnam.

Interpretation as Policy The great bulk of the task of statutory interpretation arises because the law of Congress has already received one interpretation and this is being challenged. In acting under the authority of a statute, some federal agency has undoubtedly issued rules and regulations making the public policy operative. Some individuals or interest groups, believing that the administrative interpretation is disadvantageous to them, may bring suit. Such an action may allege either that the administrator exceeded his authority under the statute, or that he gave to the law an erroneous interpretation. The court is thus faced with two alternative interpretations: that of the administrator and that of the challenging party. The nature of the Anglo-American adversary process, which casts the courts in a largely passive role, means that one of these two interpretations normally will be adopted. It is possible, and it occasionally occurs, that a court may reject both of the interpretations urged on it and produce its own. More than likely, however, and because one or the other of the parties must win the suit, the court will support the position of one of the adversaries.

[23] Supreme Court Justice Robert H. Jackson remarked: "It is not to be supposed that, in signing a bill, the President endorses the whole *Congressional Record*." He also attacked what he considered the common judicial policy of selecting "casual statements from floor debates, not always distinguished for candor or accuracy." Mantel, "The Congressional Record," p. 990.

The Fair Labor Standards Act passed by Congress in 1938 resulted in several controversies about its scope and meaning. This law established minimum wages and maximum hours for employees engaged in production for interstate commerce, and it also attempted to discourage the use of child labor by denying the use of the channels of interstate commerce to companies who employed those under sixteen.[24] The FLSA was a complicated and bitterly contested statute, bringing into the open for the first time the antagonisms of conservative Southern Democrats toward the social welfare policies of the New Deal. After passage of the act, the head of the Children's Bureau, then in the Department of Labor, ruled that the scope of the law included the messenger boy employees of the Western Union Telegraph Company. The company disagreed. Under the act, the procedure for enforcement was to obtain an injunction against the offending company which is what the head of the Children's Bureau sought in a suit brought in a United States district court. The injunction was issued and a court of appeals affirmed the lower court's decision.

Ultimately the dispute came before the Supreme Court. As the Court readily confessed, the situation before it had not been foreseen at all by Congress. Although disclaiming any purpose on its part to legislate where Congress had failed to, this is precisely what the Court proceeded to do. It resorted to interpreting the words Congress used, finding that messenger boys were not engaged in the production of goods for shipment in interstate commerce because telegrams are sent rather than shipped.[25] In reality, the Court was not willing to accept the obvious language of the statute because in this particular case the consequences would be too onerous for the country to bear: that is, to be deprived of the services of Western Union. And so it took upon itself the task of deciding what Congress would have done if the problem had been considered by it.

Application of the FLSA to elevator operators in an office building provides another illustration of the policy choices which the courts are constantly asked to make. One office building in New York was owned by a national company which occupied slightly more than half of the premises as its corporate headquarters. Another building had no such dominant tenant, but almost half of its occupants were in businesses in interstate commerce. Nonetheless, the Supreme Court decided that

---

[24] Interpretation of the commerce power of Congress is discussed more fully in the next chapter.
[25] Western Union Tel. Co. v. Lenroot, 323 U.S. 490 (1945). Four justices dissented.

the employees of the first building were covered under the FLSA whereas those of the second building were not.[26] To the employees concerned, this was a policy decision of the first magnitude because it would make a substantial difference in their respective paychecks. Yet it was a policy decision made by the courts and not by Congress.

In these controversies arising under the FLSA, the courts were engaged in policymaking through statutory interpretation. The fact that the Supreme Court of the United States made the final decision in these cases, and otherwise receives great publicity, on occasion, should not obscure the fact that there are other courts in the federal judiciary. Although the Supreme Court sits at the apex of the federal court system, it hears only a fraction of the total number of controversies fought out in the courts.

The Federal Court System The workhorses of the federal judiciary are the United States district courts, of which there is at least one in every state, one in the District of Columbia, one in Puerto Rico, and as many as four in some of the states. There are also district courts in the territories (Guam, the Virgin Islands, and the Canal Zone) of slightly different status. Some district courts may also have many sitting judges. Thus, the District Court of the Southern District of New York (one of four in that state) has twenty-four judges. District courts are courts of orginal jurisdiction, that is, courts in which suits are commenced and trials held. All of the jurisdiction conferred by the Constitution and by statute may be exercised by the district courts except for a few types of cases which must be brought in other courts.

The Constitution, for example, confers original jurisdiction in suits between two states on the Supreme Court. By statute, some cases involving claims against the government must be brought in the Court of Claims, one of the special courts of the United States. Another special court is the Customs Court, exercising jurisdiction over matters conferred on it by statute. The federal courts of appeals exercise jurisdiction over appeals from most of the regulatory commissions. Apart from these and other exceptions, the district courts hear the overwhelming number of cases brought in the federal system.

[26] Borden Co. v. Borella, 325 U.S. 679 (1945); 10 E. 40th St. Bldg. v. Callus, 325 U.S. 578 (1945).

It is at this level that a regular trial is held, with a single district judge presiding, with or without a jury, depending on the type of case. Testimony is given by witnesses, who are cross-examined by the counsel for the opposing party (one of whom is frequently the United States in the form of one of its many agencies) under the rules of evidence. In short, these are the courts (with comparable ones in each of the states as part of their own court systems) in which most people are likely to encounter the workings of the judicial process. The district courts of the United States hear more than 100,000 cases a year, not including bankruptcy proceedings. Of these, about two-thirds are civil cases, whereas the remainder are criminal cases. In about 95 percent of these cases, the controversy will end at the district court level. Many suits are settled by compromise agreements before the trial is concluded or even before it begins. Most criminal cases are disposed of on guilty pleas. For those who lose, the expenses of appealing a civil case are simply too burdensome and the matter is dropped. In criminal cases, although counsel for indigent defendants is usually provided, appeals are few.

There are ample opportunities at the district court level for a judge either to make policy or at least to initiate a round in the policymaking process. Many district court judges in the South were noticeably reluctant to push local school boards too hard in the direction of desegregation. Though such judges were much less hostile toward federal desegregation policy then were state court judges, they still reflected to a degree their cultural affinity with the region which had influenced their values. In other instances a federal court judge can force the Supreme Court into a policy area from which it might otherwise prefer to remain aloof. In the spring of 1969, for example, a district court judge in Boston ruled that profound moral beliefs, not necessarily connected with any established religion and upon which repugnance to the war in Vietnam was rested, was a legitimate basis for a claim of conscientious objector status with regard to the draft. By excluding such a basis, said the judge, Congress had infringed the First Amendment by giving preference to opposition to war based on religious belief. In declaring the applicable portion of the selective service law unconstitutional, the judge indicated that the government could appeal directly to the Supreme Court, thus bypassing the normal process of review by a United States court of appeals.

Appellate Court Policymaking

In the overwhelming number of cases, however, it is one of the eleven United States courts of appeals which will hear appeals from the decision of a district court. There are ten such courts covering geographical circuits into which the country has been divided, and one which sits in the District of Columbia. Unlike the district courts, a trial is not held in a court of appeals; rather, an appellate hearing is conducted. Such a hearing is intended to serve as a review of the lower court decision to ascertain its legal correctness. The facts as found by a district court (by judge or by jury) are therefore not usually reviewed. A court of appeals is primarily concerned with the appropriateness of the legal rules applied by the district judge in disposing of the case as well as with his conduct of the trial in order to determine that no prejudicial errors occurred. Thus, what may have been a relatively routine matter at the district court level is often transformed into a case where significant policy issues are raised for the first time in the appellate court.[27]

Review of a district court decision takes the form of an oral argument after written briefs have been submitted by opposing counsel. A court of appeals normally sits in panels of three judges when it hears cases. Some of the courts of appeals have as many as nine judges, one has twelve, and one as few as three. On occasion, when there appears to be disagreement among all the members of a court of appeals over the decision of one of its panels, the full court may sit *en banc*.

There exist many opportunities for policymaking by the courts of appeals for it is these tribunals which must give approval to the meaning of a statute as determined by the district judge, or reject his interpretation and substitute their own.

What makes the appellate function of the courts of appeals even more significant is that very few cases they decide are ever heard by the Supreme Court. Out of the more than 100,000 or so cases originally begun in the district courts, only about 5 percent are even appealed to a court of appeals. In addition to the 5,000 or more appeals from district court decisions, the courts of appeals also hear about 1,200 appeals from decisions of administrative agencies. But of the approximately 6,500 decisions handed down by the courts of appeals, the parties in only about one in six even bother to file a request that their particular case be heard by the Supreme Court.

---

[27] Richard J. Richardson and Kenneth N. Vines, "Review, Dissent, and the Appellate Process: A Political Interpretation," *Journal of Politics* 29 (August 1967): 600–601.

Whether the Supreme Court will choose to hear a case appealed from a court of appeals is a matter entirely within the discretion of the highest Court. It expresses its decision to hear or not to hear a case by granting or denying a petition for a writ of *certiorari*. The power to control its docket through the use of the *certiorari* procedure was given to the Supreme Court by Congress in 1925. It was felt necessary at that time to save the Court from an overburden of appeals which it had to accept. The courts of appeals, created only in 1891, were intended to relieve the Supreme Court of much of its appellate burden, which had grown tremendously in the post-Civil War period. But not until the number of mandatory appeal cases was reduced could the full benefit of the courts of appeals be felt.

Congress accomplished this in 1925 when it made *certiorari* practically the only way of getting a decision of a federal court of appeals before the Supreme Court. For all practical purposes, therefore, at least as far as the federal court system is concerned, the courts of appeals are the courts of last resort. The finality of decision of these courts is illustrated by the low percentage of its decisions the Supreme Court hears on the merits.[28] Of the 1,000 or so requests for *certiorari* filed by one of the parties in a case decided by a court of appeals, less than 10 percent is granted. Thus, of the more than 100,000 cases originally begun in the federal court system, the Supreme Court hears a minute fraction. It hears an even smaller percentage of all the cases begun in the state courts, a figure which probably approaches one million cases a year, perhaps hearing only 150 or so.

The policymaking role of the courts of appeals is also enhanced by the relationship of these courts to administrative policymaking. Although the number of such cases heard is not great (about 1,200 a year), many of them involve significant public policy disputes. Generally, both the courts of appeals and the Supreme Court give considerable support to the government side in administrative policy disputes. This is reflected in the number of times the courts affirm agency decisions and thus reject attacks on agency policy launched by disaffected interests. In some areas, the courts, and especially the Supreme Court, have been more zealous in pursuit of the public interest than the regu-

---

[28] In considering a *certiorari* petition, the Supreme Court is in a sense reviewing the decision of the lower court, even though such review may be perfunctory. When the Court grants *certiorari*, however, and agrees to hear the case on its merits, much more extensive briefs are then filed by the parties, and, in most cases, their counsels will argue the case orally before the nine justices.

latory agency concerned. Public power advocates have frequently found more support in the courts than in the Federal Power Commission, which has often sided with industry advocates of private power.

The normal case in the federal judiciary follows the path of district court trial and court of appeals review, if there is an appeal at all. Others go from an administrative agency to a court of appeals. Decisions of the Interstate Commerce Commission constitute a major exception to the usual pattern which administrative agency cases follow. Because the ICC was created before the courts of appeals were, review of the decisions of this agency takes place in a district court, with appeal then lying directly to the Supreme Court. The courts of appeals are also bypassed in another category of important cases. Whenever a party seeks an injunction against the enforcement of a federal or state law because of its alleged unconstitutionality, such a case must be heard by a special three-judge district court. Such a court normally consists of two district judges and one court of appeals (or circuit) judge. Appeal from the decisions of such a court go directly to the Supreme Court for review. In any case where there is not an intermediate appellate review by a court of appeals, the Supreme Court has little option in the matter of hearing the case on its merits.

The three-judge district court was of particular importance in the segregated schools and reapportionment controversies. Three of the four cases attacking the system of segregated schools in the states were heard by three-judge courts, appeal going directly to the Supreme Court. Many of the cases attacking malapportioned state legislatures were also heard by three-judge district courts. In both areas, the statutory requirement of such courts guaranteed that the Supreme Court would have to become involved in these significant policy disputes.

Cases heard by one of the special courts of the United States also bypass the courts of appeals. Decisions of the Court of Claims are reviewable, but only by *certiorari* in the Supreme Court. Few such decisions are ever heard by the highest court. On occasion, however, a case of great national import may find its way there from the Court of Claims. After cancellation in 1955 of the Dixon-Yates contract to build steam-power facilities in the TVA area, the private power combine sued the United States for damages. The Court of Claims decided in favor of the company, but this decision was reversed by the Supreme Court.

THE POLICYMAKING PROCESS

Policy at the Top The structure of the federal judicial system is such that the court at the apex hears very few cases. Most of the cases, however, have rather important implications for national public policy. But even those cases which present controversial issues of public policy may not involve an interpretation of the Constitution. Heavy newspaper coverage of cases involving segregation, school prayers, reapportionment, or the rights of defendants would seem to indicate that the Supreme Court does nothing but decide cases involving provisions of the Constitution. Such cases, in fact, account for only about a third of the decisions reached on the merits. The major part of the Court's work, as is true of the lower courts, is devoted to interpreting the laws of Congress or to determining the validity of administrative policy actions taken under such laws.

The Supreme Court is also the final judicial authority for cases involving a federal question, which arise in state courts. The First Congress conferred on the Supreme Court the power to review decisions of the highest courts of the state in the Judiciary Act of 1789. It did so as a means of insuring that laws of the states contrary to the United States Constitution or laws of Congress could be rendered inoperative. Giving this kind of power to the Supreme Court was seen as the principal way to keep the national government intact. Without such authority resting in the national government there would be little to stop the states from going their own way, as had been the case under the Articles of Confederation. As to this kind of use of the power of judicial review, there was considerable discussion and agreement in the Constitutional convention that such would be necessary. The Judiciary Act of 1789 provided the specific means for making judicial review over the state courts effective.

The basic outlines of review established in 1789 are still operative today. The Supreme Court may review a decision of the highest court of a state [29] when such a court holds an act of Congress invalid. Review is also possible when a party in a state court attacks a state statute on the grounds that it is inconsistent with a federal law or the United States Constitution and the state court upholds the validity of the state statute. A third possibility for review exists when a party in a state court claims

---

[29] In some situations, a state supreme court may not hear all cases which may raise a federal question. The Act of 1789 provided, however, for review from the highest court of a state in which a decision could be had. This provision, in effect even today, means that decisions of lower courts in a state may sometimes be reviewed by the Supreme Court if that is the highest court which, by the laws of the state, can hear the particular case.

a right or privilege under the Constitution or federal law. Cases in the first two categories are said to be reviewable by the Supreme Court by *appeal*—supposedly as a matter of right—as opposed to *certiorari*, which is the method applicable to the third category, as well as to cases from the federal courts of appeals. In practice, however, the Supreme Court accepts an appeal case only if a substantial federal question is presented. And it is the Court, of course, which decides whether the question is substantial. It does so in the same manner it follows when deciding whether to grant *certiorari*. Only if four of the justices vote to grant *certiorari* or vote to hear an appeal case will either kind be heard on the merits.

Altogether, about 2,500 requests for review are filed each year with the Supreme Court by disappointed litigants in the federal court system and from the state court systems. Only about 10 percent of these requests are granted by the Court so that full consideration will be given to the dispute. Even when the Supreme Court decides to hear a case, it may still dispose of the matter either with no opinion or a very short one.[30] In slightly more than 100 cases, the Court will devote a full discussion to the legal or policy questions raised in the form of a written opinion.

Although the Supreme Court's other functions in the policymaking process are often unjustifiably neglected, there is no gainsaying the overriding importance of its task of interpretation of the Constitution. So much has the shape and character of the American political system been a product of the Supreme Court's collective hand that it has, as Woodrow Wilson once commented, served as a "continuous Constitutional Convention." And as Charles Evans Hughes, before he was appointed to the Court, said: "We are under a Constitution, but the Constitution is what the judges say it is. . . ."[31]

The Supreme Court has almost never been hesitant about stamping on the public consciousness its view of the constitutional and political world. As Chief Justice, Federalist John Marshall managed to fight a fairly successful rearguard action against the Jeffersonian interpretation of the Constitution. The nationalist overtones which had been predominant in 1787–89 might well have been erased entirely were it not for the efforts of Marshall and his brethren. By the time Federalist

---

[30] The Supreme Court usually decides more than half of its cases by *per curiam* opinions, that is, an unsigned opinion for the court.
[31] Speech before the Elmira, New York, Chamber of Commerce, May 3, 1907, quoted in Sutherland, *Constitutionalism in America*, p. 203, n. 118.

influence on the Court had waned, Federalist constitutional doctrine had been sufficiently absorbed by the political culture to withstand Southern disaffection and even secession.

Marshall was succeeded as Chief Justice by no less a fighter for the causes he thought just, Roger B. Taney of Maryland. Taney and his Southern-dominated court even thought that the magic of constitutional interpretation might provide an effective political solution to the problem of slavery and its extension. This was a miscalculation, however, as the *Dred Scott* decision did little more than inflame the passions of the North. Both Marshall and Taney, no matter how their views on the political form of the Constitution might differ, agreed on the proposition that the Constitution and the Supreme Court were the appointed guardians of property rights. Although Taney was much more sympathetic toward giving the states greater discretion in such matters, like Marshall, he was suspicious of legislative attempts to violate the rights of creditors.

In less than a half-century after its ill-fated *Dred Scott* decision, the Supreme Court had once again ascended to the heights of political power. Reflecting the corporate background of most of its members, the Court served as the official vehicle for the propagation of the *laissez-faire* economic faith. At the turn of the century, many of the states, as well as Congress, had perceived that the industrial revolution was not without tragic economic and social consequences. But attempts to ameliorate some of the more exploitive conditions were often turned back by a Supreme Court which, in the dissenting words of Justice Oliver Wendell Holmes, had engrafted onto the Fourteenth Amendment "Mr. Herbert Spencer's Social Statics." Holmes' reference was to the English sociologist who developed a Darwinian concept of human economic activity emphasizing the survival of the fittest.

For another thirty-five years, the economic philosophy of the Supreme Court served as a sort of brake on social and economic change. But when the New Deal sought to accelerate the rate of progress, it ran smack into a Court unwilling to step aside and let the electorate have its way. Finally, in 1937, under the threat of packing the Court by President Roosevelt, the Court backed away and resigned itself to the inevitable. A rapid change in personnel followed in the next few years so that, by 1941, by its own choice the Court took itself out of the realm of economic policymaking, except to give free reign to Congress and the state legislatures.

Contemporary Role: Civil Rights and Liberties

Never content to be without a major policy role, however, the Court since the late 1930s has been the chief architect of public policy regarding civil rights and liberties. The Supreme Court bore the burden of undoing the system of segregation which had previously gained the sanction of an earlier Supreme Court. In 1896 the Supreme Court membership had one view of the sociology of race relations.[32] The doctrine of separate but equal was read into the Fourteenth Amendment, not to be read out until almost fifty years later, when a different Court expressed a contrasting view of race relations.[33] From that decision in 1954 have flowed consequences the end of which is not yet in sight.

In the field of criminal procedure, the Supreme Court has also wrought revolutionary change. The Bill of Rights to the Constitution was early held to be applicable only to the national government. As a consequence, the protections of the Fourth, Fifth, and Sixth Amendments were not considered binding on the states. Among these constitutional protections are some of the most important safeguards of a fair criminal trial. The Fourth Amendment protects against unreasonable searches and seizures. The Fifth guarantees the privilege of not being forced to testify against oneself in a criminal case. The Sixth guarantees the assistance of counsel. After the Civil War, the adoption of the Fourteenth Amendment was thought by many to have made the guarantees of the Bill of Rights applicable to the states. Such a theory has been repeatedly urged on the Court, but in a series of decisions extending even to recent times, it has consistently rejected such a proposition.

Nonetheless, by interpretation of the due process clause of the Fourteenth Amendment, the Supreme Court, in recent years, has succeeded in making most of the guarantees of the Bill of Rights applicable to the states. The states must respect the provisions against unreasonable search and seizure and are forbidden to use such illegally obtained evidence in a criminal trial.[34] So, too, must the states respect the privilege against self-incrimination.[35] And they are also bound to provide

---

[32] Plessy v. Ferguson, 163 U.S. 537. Justice John Marshall Harlan, grandfather of the present Justice Harlan, was the one exception. He dissented.

[33] Brown v. Board of Education, 347 U.S. 483 (1954).

[34] Mapp v. Ohio, 367 U.S. 643 (1961).

[35] Malloy v. Hogan, 378 U.S. 1 (1964). In 1969, the Court held that the states must also respect the privilege against double jeopardy.

counsel to those too poor to pay for it, and in other ways make the assistance of counsel meaningful.[36]

The political role of the Supreme Court is paralleled by the political considerations which contribute to its composition. From the first, presidents have viewed their appointing power of Supreme Court justices as a prime way of implanting their own ideas of public policy on the nation. Although Presidents frequently cross party lines in making such appointments, nominal party membership is often a poor guide to how a justice will react to the policy choices thrust upon him. More often than not, Supreme Court justices have been appointed not because they are great legal technicians, but because they are men who have distinguished themselves in political capacities. Neither has extensive judicial experience often been considered a necessary prerequisite to service on the Supreme Court. Presidential and congressional unwillingness to adopt such criteria for appointment is a realistic recognition of the essentially political role which the Court fulfills.

Other considerations also intrude on the appointing process. For years, there has been an effort to balance the Court geographically so that most sections of the nation have representation in the Court. In recent decades, ethnic considerations have grown in importance. Although not begun with an explicit intention to create a so-called Catholic seat or a Jewish seat, the expectation has developed and the practice has conformed to it. It was not surprising, therefore, as many had predicted during the late fifties and sixties, that the expectation of a Negro seat was fulfilled with the appointment by President Johnson of Thurgood Marshall, former counsel of the NAACP. In Marshall's case, however, intervening positions as a court of appeals judge and then as Solicitor General of the United States would be enough to satisfy the demands of prior judicial experience.

President Nixon's first two appointments to the Court both confirmed and departed from these expectations. To replace retiring Chief Justice Warren, Nixon named Warren E. Burger, who had sat for more than ten years as a judge on the important United States Court of Appeals for the District of Columbia Circuit. Before that, Burger was Assistant Attorney General in charge of the Civil Division of the Department of Justice. During his tenure on the court of appeals, Burger had often been critical of decisions which he felt leaned too far in the direction of protecting the rights of criminal defendants. Burger's appointment as

---

[36] Gideon v. Wainwright, 372 U.S. 335 (1963); Escobedo v. Illinois, 378 U.S. 478 (1964).

Chief Justice was therefore interpreted as a partial fulfillment of one of Nixon's campaign themes of at least stemming the tide against overly liberal decisions in this area.

For his second appointment, to replace Justice Abe Fortas, who resigned under pressure after disclosures which cast some doubt on the propriety of his relations with a wealthy financier, President Nixon chose Clement F. Haynsworth. A fifth-generation South Carolina lawyer, Haynsworth had served on the United States Court of Appeals for the Fourth Circuit since 1957 (covering South and North Carolina, Virginia, Maryland, and West Virginia). He had not earned a reputation for eagerness in supporting school desegregation nor for a tender regard for the interests of organized labor. As a consequence, civil rights groups and the AFL-CIO opposed his confirmation. What proved to be more of an obstacle to gaining his seat on the Supreme Court, however, was the suggestion that his ethical behavior was not beyond reproach, the very thing that had led Fortas to resign. Haynsworth's nomination also showed Nixon's disinclination to abide by the expectation of a "Jewish" seat, as Truman had done before him by not appointing a Catholic when Justice Frank Murphy died.

Power Within Limits Although the Supreme Court is a potent policymaker in the American political system, it is not without limitations. In addition to those self-imposed canons of restraint which the Court has historically found expedient in the interest of its own self-preservation, the nature of the judicial process helps to confine judicial policymaking. Courts cannot reach out and initiate policy changes. Before courts can become involved in policymaking they must be presented with a controversy in the form of a legal suit. Early in its development, the Supreme Court declined to give advisory opinions but, in a political culture as litigious as is America, courts are quite readily thrust into the midst of political, economic, and social controversy. Nonetheless, the shape of such disputes is largely determined by the parties to the case, and not by the courts.

The way disputes are settled in the judicial process also differs from comparable conflicts in Congress or the bureaucracy. The mystique and reverence accorded the law and courts and judges has meant that an atmosphere of decorum and detachment pervades judicial proceedings to a degree quite lacking in other decision-making processes. The fact that members of the Supreme Court and lower courts are judges evokes in them a psychological urge to live up to the expectations associated with such a role. To an extent which varies widely from judge to judge, this is a factor which restrains somewhat the expression of their own values and sentiments and notions about public policy. Personal predilections, of course, are prime influences shaping the way a judge decides; to suppose otherwise is to confer on judges qualities which all other men lack. Yet, to the extent that personal preferences must be adjusted to the conventions of the legal process, they are tempered.

There are other constraints in the policymaking powers of the Supreme Court. The Court does not operate in a vacuum; it is part of a complex of political institutions, all with constituencies, all serving a representative function, and all making policy.

A prime political institution with which the Court must interact is the Department of Justice, especially the solicitor general of the United States. The solicitor general is the government's chief legal counsel in the sense that it is he who has historically argued the government's side before the Supreme Court in cases in which it is a party. The solicitor general also plays an influential policy role in deciding which cases the government will bring before the highest court. One solicitor general, for instance, declined to sign the government's brief in a case involving allegations regarding the security clearance of a State Department official. The task of arguing the case fell to Warren Burger, at that time an Assistant Attorney General.

The composition of the Supreme Court and hence its policies can be drastically altered by the appointing power of the president. The vagaries of fate, of course, determine when a president will be able to exercise this power. Since the justices (as do most all federal judges) enjoy tenure during good behavior—tantamount to life tenure—only death or the decision to retire opens vacancies on the Court as long as Congress chooses to keep the number at nine.

If the appointing power of the president is not a consistently useful weapon to shape the course of Supreme Court policy, the chief executive's general political position is. Few Supreme Courts have been willing to force a showdown with a president. John Marshall's unwillingness to do battle with Jefferson was, in fact, the reason he contrived a way out by using judicial review in *Marbury* v. *Madison*. If the Court were to have issued the mandamus (order) to Madison to give Marbury his commission as a justice of the peace in the District of Columbia, few thought that Madison or Jefferson would comply. To avoid the disgrace of having his writ ignored, Marshall held that Marbury was in the right legally but in the wrong court because the act under which he sought relief had unconstitutionally conferred jurisdiction on the Supreme Court in the matter. In this way, the astute Chief Justice could make his point that Federalist Marbury had been wronged by the Jeffersonians, and at the same time avoid a direct confrontation.

The Supreme Court has also been reluctant to interfere with presidents, particularly in their conduct of foreign relations or in the exercise of their war powers. On occasion, however, the Court does stand up to the president successfully. It has done so in restricting his right to remove the members of regulatory commissions because they are said to exercise quasi-judicial powers. The most recent major instance when the Supreme Court found itself in a direct clash with the president occurred in 1952. To head off an impending steel strike which could have caused serious problems for the American forces then fighting in Korea, Truman ordered his secretary of commerce to seize the steel mills and place them under government operation.

The steel companies immediately went to court seeking an injunction to restrain the secretary of commerce. A district court decided for the companies and the United States appealed to the Supreme Court, even asking that the court of appeals be bypassed. With unusual alacrity, the Supreme Court heard and decided the case, affirming the decisions of the lower court. Six of the nine justices agreed that the seizure was unconstitutional but for somewhat different reasons, represented by six separate opinions. Three justices joined in one opinion and dissented.[37] The fact that President Truman refused to invoke the strike settlement procedures under the Taft-Hartley Act distressed some whereas others were concerned that his act threatened the separation of powers. When viewed in the context of Truman's unpopularity, the fact that he had announced he would not run again for the presidency, and the great outcry in Congress and the press over the seizure, the Court seemed on safe ground in defying the president. Given a different set of circumstances—a much more popular president and a more imminent threat to the national security—it is not at all unlikely that the limitations on presidential power imposed in 1952 would be ignored by a subsequent Supreme Court.

[37] Youngstown Sheet & Tube Co. v. Sawyer, 343 U.S. 579 (1952).

Congress and the Supreme Court

The relations between the Supreme Court and Congress are a different matter. Simply by virtue of the function of judicial review of challenged acts of the legislature, the Court is much more likely to find itself embroiled in conflict with Congress. Congress quite naturally views with disdain decisions invalidating a law that it or some previous Congress has enacted. But more than hurt pride is involved. Since the Supreme Court has often aided disadvantaged minorities in its decisions, Congress is the logical place for majorities to express their disapproval vociferously.

In more recent times, decisions of the Supreme Court in the areas of freedom of political expression and criminal procedure have aroused heated denunciations. Such decisions have been characterized as aiding Communists and coddling criminals and, if put to a vote of the people, would undoubtedly be overturned. But such is the fate of a political institution which insists on standing for principle against the tyranny of the majority. The reapportionment decisions and those in the field of racial discrimination have also aroused the hostility of many groups. Perhaps no other decisions in recent years have provoked as much public wrath as those that held that both prayer and Bible reading in the public schools were unconstitutional.[38]

When Congress is offended by a Supreme Court decision based on an interpretation of the Constitution, it can do nothing by itself to prevent the justices from having the last word. Only by initiating a constitutional amendment can it even attempt to overcome the decision. But when the Court rests its decision on statutory construction rather than constitutional interpretation, a quite different situation is presented. If the Court has found a meaning in legislation that members of Congress think unwarranted, an attempt may be made to reverse the effect of the judicial action by promoting passage of a new law. For instance, a Supreme Court decision that Congress had not meant to prevent the Department of Justice from obtaining access to copies of confidential census reports was overturned by an act of Congress prohibiting such access.[39] In cases when Congress does not pass legislation to repudiate the judicial interpretation of a statute, the Supreme Court assumes that its interpretation has been accepted. Considering how

---

[38] Engel v. Vitale, 370 U.S. 421 (1962); School District of Abington v. Schempp and Murray v. Curlett, 374 U.S. 203 (1963).
[39] St. Regis Paper Company v. United States, 368 U.S. 208 (1961), overturned by 76 Stat. 922.

much inertia and irrationality are built into the federal legislative process, the Court, in refusing to desert an interpretation of the congressional will that Congress has failed to disown, may be inferring far too much from the failure of Congress to act.

If Congress gets angry enough with the Supreme Court, several courses of action are available to it. One of these is the removal, by means of impeachment, of an offending justice. Not a single member of the Supreme Court, however, has been removed in this manner, and only one—Samuel Chase, in 1805—even had to undergo a trial in the Senate. Short of impeachment, Congress has no weapon it can use against individual members of the Court. The framers of the Constitution saw to that when they provided that all members of the federal judiciary should serve for life and be paid salaries that Congress could not diminish.[40]

Even if the independence of the Supreme Court is constitutionally safeguarded, Congress is not entirely powerless to translate into action its displeasure with what the Court has done. For one thing, it can increase the size of the Court and thus enable the president to appoint members who will neutralize the incumbents.[41] President Franklin Roosevelt tried to persuade Congress to pack the Supreme Court in 1937, after the justices who had been popularly labeled "The Nine Old Men" had invalidated some of the most significant New Deal measures. Congress declined to expand the size of the Court to conform with the president's wishes, but Roosevelt won his main point when the justice, whose vote had been crucial in giving the conservatives a majority [42] suddenly began to throw his support to the other side.

If Congress is averse to packing the Court, it can try to curtail the appellate jurisdiction of the Supreme Court, thus preventing the justices from handling cases in certain categories. Although this extreme action has not been taken since 1867,[43] it has been promoted vigorously in recent years as a way to prevent the Supreme Court from supposedly interfering with governmental activities directed against political dissenters.

---

[40] Article III, Section 1.

[41] This method, of course, is usable only if Congress does not find the political philosophy of the president as obnoxious as that of the Court. At times Congress has been in such violent disagreement with the president that it has wanted to prevent him from making any Supreme Court appointments at all. On such occasions it has sometimes provided that any vacancies arising on the bench were not to be filled until the number of justices fell to a given level.

[42] Owen J. Roberts.

[43] In Ex parte McCardle, 7 Wall. 506 (1869), the Court acquiesced.

Even when the Supreme Court does not encounter opposition to its policies from Congress or the president, it may well face an overtly hostile or at least uncooperative lower court system. In many ways lower court judges (both federal and state) can twist, distort, or simply ignore the mandates or legal norms laid down by the highest Court.[44] Supreme Court decisions may also suffer the fate of being ignored by segments of the public. Almost a decade after the decisions invalidating Bible reading in the public schools, noncompliance with this constitutional policy was reported to be rather common in some areas of the country. Where local traditions were strongly in favor of such rituals, and where there was no one willing to challenge the practice, it continued despite the ruling of the Supreme Court. Although the appearance may be that the Court has the last word, the reality is often otherwise. The still slow pace of school desegregation in the South more than fifteen years after the decision is ample testimony of that truism.

Dispute Settlement: By Commissions

Although settlement of disputes is the principal function of the courts, other governmental institutions carry a share of this burden. Under statutes passed by Congress, a number of executive agencies and regulatory commissions discharge adjudicatory responsibilities.[45] The areas of policy over which these agencies exercise jurisdiction, although not so inclusive as those of the federal courts, nevertheless often involve substantial economic stakes. Decisions of the Interstate Commerce Commission, for example, are vital to the economic health of the railroads, the trucking industry, and other forms of transportation. An award of a television channel by the Federal Communications Commission can mean millions of dollars in profits to the successful company. The cost of power to the consumer and the rate of profit of natural gas producers and power companies are direct concerns of the Federal Power Commission. Almost the entire climate of labor-management relations is set by the decisions of the National Labor Relations Board as it handles thousands of labor disputes each

---

[44] See, for example, Walter F. Murphy, "Lower Court Checks on Supreme Court Power," *American Political Science Review* 53 (December 1959): 1018–1031.

[45] Other aspects of the policymaking role of such agencies were discussed in Chapter 11.

year. Policy regarding trade practices, honesty in advertising, and threats to competition from corporate mergers results from decisions of the Federal Trade Commission.

Since the stakes are high in those disputes settled by regulatory commissions, there is understandable interest in their proceedings on the part of other agencies, congressmen, and interest groups. Yet, there is considerable effort made to hide these direct public policy controversies behind a façade which closely resembles all of the judicial trappings of regular courts. In effect, the regulatory process has been judicialized. When, for example, the Federal Communications Commission must decide among several competing applicants for a single radio or television broadcasting license, it holds a hearing that bears more than a superficial resemblance to a trial. The parties to the controversy are permitted to introduce evidence. The hearing examiner who presides is often addressed as "Your Honor" by legal counsel. Oral testimony is taken, with witnesses subject to cross-examination. Attorneys raise objections on familiar grounds such as incompetency or irrelevancy, and the hearing examiner must rule on these.

The resemblance to a legal trial does not end when the hearing officer comes to a conclusion about how the case should be decided. Since his decision cannot very well be pleasing to all parties to the dispute, it will almost always be appealed to the five commissioners who sit at the apex of the FCC. With the record of the hearing, as well as the recommendation of the examiner, before them, the commissioners will often take additional testimony and then decide, just as does a court, whether to affirm, modify, or set aside the initial decision. In everything but name, a judicial proceeding has taken place.

The immediate impact of the decision in such a case falls, of course, on the parties directly involved. But broadcasting interests from far and wide know that it is out of a series of such decisions that a general policy, affecting all of them, will evolve. As a consequence, they understand fully that they have a stake in what appears to be merely a private proceeding on the allocation of a wave length, just as a host of other companies will have their eyes focused on the Federal Power Commission when a decision is being made about the licensing of a hydroelectric power plant.

Like Congress itself, the regulatory agencies do their work in a kind of goldfish bowl, in full view of a large and extremely interested group of spectators. Members of the general public, however, are effectively excluded from access to the proceedings. The press, on which the public must depend for news of government, devotes far less attention to the administrative agencies than to Congress or the president. Usually the only reporters who cover the agencies intensively are those who write for trade association papers or for other communications media of the interest groups concerned. Those who are already involved, therefore, have access to thorough coverage, whereas members of the general public can hardly even be aware that a fight is in progress. And the president, though his sources of information are quite adequate, may be entirely helpless to influence a decision that may be of vital importance to the program of his administration.

Whether settlement of disputes is by courts or commissions, public policy is frequently the outcome—either immediately or in the long run. On many issues a decision by a court or commission may be the end of the policy road. But for many others it is only a way station in the continuous round of policymaking. For the decision may simply set in motion efforts aimed at initiating still another policy change, perhaps through legislation by Congress or by agency rule-making.

Part Four

Constitutional Theory and Political Reality

Chapter 13 Dispersing the Powers of Government

Were a student of American government of today able to take a trip into the future, what he would observe in the year, say, 2151, would likely be totally unrecognizable. So, too, would a citizen of the United States in the year 1789 have been amazed if he could have projected himself 181 years into the future and have seen the American political system in the year 1970. Historians generally credit the Founding Fathers with considerable foresight. But no group of human beings, no matter how gifted, could have foreseen the changes wrought by almost two centuries.

American folklore would seem to suggest that the framers of the Constitution deliberately created a system of government that could grow with the times and changing conditions. Yet it is unlikely that even the most egotistical of individuals could or would lay a very strong claim that the Constitution he helped to fashion bears much resemblance to the way American government operates in 1970. The

Constitution, even as amended, remains fairly intact. The institutions which it created are still in existence. But the American political system —as it is constituted today, or, to put it another way, its contemporary constitution [1]—differs radically from its original Constitution.

The growth of the American president into perhaps the most powerful political leader in the world would no doubt have distressed some of the framers. The time consumed by congressmen or their staffs in pacifying their constituents might well be regarded as sheer tomfoolery. That Congress spends more time poring over the details of administrative action rather than fully participating in the development of policies for the nation would no doubt be of great disappointment to the men of 1787. Such disappointment would be compounded were one of the framers to spend a day in the often almost vacant chamber of the Senate, listening to the desultory monotone that passes for debate. The shock might even be greater were the visitor to take in a session of the raucous, restless, and unruly House.

Rude awakenings occasioned by current legislative behavior would be dwarfed, however, by the continual exposure to a variety of strange and bewildering political institutions and decision-making processes. The men of 1787 would no doubt be left speechless by the spectacle of a national party presidential nominating convention. It would not be surprising to find them quite suspicious of the existence of political parties and their uses of communications media to influence the electorate. Their amazement at the great number of executive departments, agencies, commissions, and boards would be more than matched by their incomprehension of the vast number of subcommittees in Congress. The power of committee chairmen, the relative weakness of the elected party leadership, and the extraordinary powers of conference committees would all be matters of great curiosity.

Even more unfamiliar, with hardly a hint to go by in the Constitution, would be the regulatory commissions, gathering under one roof the powers of rule-making, rule-application, and dispute settlement. This innovation in the policymaking process might not be the only one noticed by the men of 1787. The close relationship between interest groups, executive agencies, and congressional subcommittees might occasion considerable surprise as to the way public policy is made by these autonomous subsystems supposedly in the national interest. The

---

[1] The small "c" is used deliberately to distinguish the currently operative set of political institutions and processes from the Constitution of 1787.

pervasive influence of such an organization as the Central Intelligence Agency on American foreign policy might also cause some misgivings.

And, a framer of the Constitution might justifiably ask, why are all of these vast changes not recorded in the amendments to the Constitution? The theory of a written constitution, so strongly held in the eighteenth century, was that it laid down the will of the people as to the basic form and institutions of government and could only be changed by further similar acts of the people. But the formal provisions for amending the Constitution have produced far less in the way of fundamental change in the institutions and processes of government than have the informal means. By a simple doing of things—constitutional warrant or not—presidents, Congresses, Supreme Courts, and the political activities of people have wrought far more change than have the people through the amending process.

The Bill of Rights, adopted so soon after the Constitution itself was ratified, and insisted upon by many of the states as a condition of ratification, can be considered part of the basic framework. Even these ten amendments would have accomplished little, were it not for the process of judicial interpretation which has filled them with meaning. How different are the conceptions of freedom of speech and religious liberty now, as compared with 181 years ago! Apart from the Bill of Rights, only the Fourteenth and Sixteenth Amendments have had a really profound and lasting impact on the American political system. The Fourteenth, as it has been interpreted by the courts, has worked a fundamental rearrangement of the relations between nation and states in the sense of making the central government a more effective protector of the civil rights and liberties of the American people. Through the powers of raising revenue that the Sixteenth granted to Congress, the United States, as a nation, has been able to promote a much broader and higher level of social and economic justice than would have otherwise been possible.

Yet, in some very fundamental aspects, the American political system bears a great resemblance to some of the conceptions held by many of the framers. In one grand respect, a commonly held idea of the time has triumphed notably. This is the notion that dispersing governmental powers was the surest way to restrain arbitrary political power. The generation that wrote the Constitution of 1787 had a perception of the world of politics much different from that commonly held by Americans of today. Most men of the time endorsed the principle of popular government, or, as Madison expressed it in *Federalist*, No. 39, "a government which derives all its powers directly or indirectly from the great body of the people" and "not from an inconsiderable proportion or a favored class of" society.[2] Popular government, however, might take two forms. In the one form, democracy, citizens assemble and administer the government; in the other form, a republic, the citizens exercise their political authority through chosen representatives. At the time, a republic was vastly to be preferred.[3]

Fear of the Majority A republic was thought to be a superior form of popular government because, to many of the founding generation, democracies as then known and understood

> have ever been spectacles of turbulence and contention, have ever been found incompatible with personal security or the rights of property; and have in general been as short in their lives as they have been violent in their deaths.[4]

Nor was the history the only guide in forming such an opinion. Since the middle of the eighteenth century, France had become the center of democratic political thought, most comprehensively expressed in the *Social Contract* of Jean Jacques Rousseau, published in 1762. To its opponents, democracy meant that the property and privileges of the few would be at the mercy of the many. To the advocates of republicanism, the negative liberty of being free from governmental restraint was far more important than the freedom of full participation in making governmental decisions, which became the essence of the democratic faith.

A republic as a form of government was therefore viewed as a necessary way to restrain the passions and the power of the people. Republicanism was hostile to the aspirations of democratic theory and resisted the ideas which today have become intimately associated with the idea of democracy. Such fundamental notions as "universal suffrage of men

---

[2] References are to the edition of the *Federalist Papers* edited by Clinton M. Rossiter (New York: The New American Library, 1961), p. 241.
[3] Martin Diamond, "Democracy and The Federalist: A Reconsideration of the Framers' Intent," *American Political Science Review* 53 (March 1959): 54.
[4] Madison, in *Federalist*, No. 10, p. 81.

and women, the equal participation of all classes, especially the labor class, in political life, and the elimination of racial and religious discrimination. . . ."[5] gained ground only slowly in the nineteenth century. Not even today, in the United States or other advanced democracies, have all the goals of democracy been adequately realized.

How to make government as harmless as possible was, therefore, the major preoccupation of those who had any substantial stake in society and thus an interest in protecting what they had acquired. To many Americans of the day, government as an oppressive force was feared, whether the crushing power of it came from the arbitrary acts of a single man or from the equally arbitrary acts of a rampant majority. Experiences of both kinds were visible enough, either as recent history or as present fact. Americans of 1787 were only a century removed from the turbulent events of 1689, when the constitutional struggles of England during the seventeenth century finally resulted in the triumph of legislative supremacy over the arbitrary power of the English monarch.

Since early in the seventeenth century, the Stuart kings had increasingly sought to rule arbitrarily. Not even the events of 1648 and the ensuing Cromwell protectorate deterred a renewal of arbitrary pretensions on the part of Charles II and then James II, following the Restoration. The events which precipitated the bloodless revolution of 1689 were similar to those which had created turmoil throughout the century: the king, in this case James II, making decisions without gaining the consent of Parliament, or at times even against the expressed will of Parliament. Arbitrary political power is therefore, not surprisingly, the major problem treated in John Locke's *Second Treatise on Civil Government*.

Locke became the principal expositor of a theory of government which gained ascendancy in 1689. Rather than a new theory, however, it was, in fact, merely a return to the policymaking process which had been slowly developing in England over the preceding five centuries. As Locke expressed it:

> This slowness and aversion in the people to quit their old constitutions has in the many revolutions which have been seen in this kingdom, in this and former ages, still kept us to, or after some interval of fruitless

---

[5] Carl J. Friedrich, *Constitutional Government and Democracy*, rev. ed. (Boston: Ginn, 1950), p. 31.

attempts still brought us back again to, our old legislative of king, lords, and commons . . .[6]

England had become a constitutional government, not because it possessed a written constitution, but because it had developed a system of decision-making in which there was expected and regularized participation of the king and the two houses of Parliament. The aberrant departures from this process by the Stuart kings were terminated in 1689, and the old system essentially reaffirmed.[7]

But to the colonists of the 1760s and 1770s, all of the familiar attributes of arbitrary government seemed to reappear in the way decisions were being made in England regarding the lives and fortunes of Americans. The most visible form of such oppression, of course, was King George III. Although many of his ministers were more to blame, it was much easier to focus one's wrath on the singular figure of the monarch. Once again, highly arbitrary power could be seen as the prime evil. The governors of the colonies were also almost always viewed as the direct representatives of the king and the intolerable policies of the mother country. There was ample evidence to convince most Americans that the major problem of government was curbing arbitrary power.

Once independence had been secured and the new states had time to begin to function as political entities, fresh evidence of the dangers of arbitrary power appeared. This time, however, the source of the danger was not one-man arbitrariness, but the collective efforts of legislative bodies. During the 1780s, as an aftermath of the burden of fighting the Revolutionary War, debtors and taxpayers were caught in a financial squeeze. They "faced the problem of paying in hard money when none was to be had; and when they demanded paper money, the creditors rose in violent opposition." [8] The advocates of paper money proved politically more potent, primarily because they were more numerous. By 1786, seven states had adopted paper money schemes.[9] The lesson was not lost on creditors and other men of property. The

---

[6] John Locke, *The Second Treatise of Government*, ed. by Thomas P. Reardon (New York: The Liberal Arts Press, 1952), sec. 223, p. 125.

[7] The political settlement of 1689 did, however, change the basic power structure in England. Although the division of power between king, lords, and commons was retained, the real foundation of it became "the electorate behind the Commons, rather than the ecclesiastical authorities and feudal landowners behind the Lords." Friedrich, *Constitutional Government*, p. 28.

[8] Merrill Jensen, *The New Nation* (New York: Vintage Books, 1965), p. 303.

[9] Ibid., p. 313.

successful vehicle of the paper money advocates was the legislative majority, unrestrained by specific limitations on its power. It is not surprising that in later extolling the virtues of the new form of government under the Constitution, Madison could argue that it would make the "rage for paper money . . . or for any other improper or wicked project . . . less apt to pervade the whole body of the Union. . . ."[10]

One of the principal preoccupations, therefore, of many of the delegates who assembled at Philadelphia in May, 1787, was how to guard against arbitrary power, whether from a too strong executive or from an unrestrained majority. Added to these general considerations was a matter of great practical consequence. The thirteen states prior to 1787 did not really constitute a single government. For some purposes, the Articles of Confederation adopted in 1781 did provide for organs of a central government, and to that central or general government was accorded a limited amount of power. But, by any modern standards, the general government created by the Articles could hardly be called a government.[11] It provided for only one organ of central power—Congress. It did not make provision for any effective executive authority. The Articles did mention a committee of the states, and contemplated creation of other committees "as may be necessary for managing the general affairs of the United States . . ." and authorized the committee of the states to execute the powers of Congress when that body was in recess.[12] But committees are notably inadequate in exercising executive authority. The committee of the states, not appointed until 1784, might have, in time, developed into a cabinet, comparable to the British model, and been able to centralize executive power. The junking of the Articles in 1787, however, precluded such development.

The Articles, moreover, failed to provide for a national judicial system. A few narrow areas of jurisdiction were conferred on the general government, but the procedure for establishing courts was unwieldy and unworkable. Congress itself, in a complicated procedure, could also adjudicate disputes between states over conflicting land claims. Even the legislative power was sharply circumscribed, and, in two important areas—regulation of commerce and taxation—it was largely impotent. Such decisions that it could take, moreover, were made difficult

[10] *Federalist Papers*, No. 10, p. 84.
[11] "Strictly speaking, neither the friends nor the enemies of the Confederation regarded the Articles as having created any kind of *government* at all, weak or otherwise." Martin Diamond, "What the Framers Meant by Federalism," in Robert A. Goldwin, *A Nation of States* (Chicago: Rand McNally, 1961), p. 28 (italics in original).
[12] Articles of Confederation, IX and X.

by the requirement of the assent of nine of the thirteen states. The government created under the Articles, therefore, did not possess the requisite functions of an effective political system. Although it possessed a rule-making power, this was woefully inadequate. The functions of applying rules and settling disputes were practically nonexistent.

Another major defect characterized the government under the Articles of Confederation. It lacked what is in essence the most fundamental of all governmental attributes: it did not exert its authority directly on people. Although Congress did carry on some of its assigned functions directly, for the most part its decisions depended for their effectiveness on the states as intermediary agents. In the vital matter of raising revenue for the support of the general government, the states simply failed to perform as Congress expected, "to such an extent that they put the Confederation government into chronic bankruptcy." [13]

The government created under the Articles was, in fact, not intended to be a general government with effective power. This was made clear when it was proclaimed that "Each state retains its sovereignty, freedom, and independence. . . ." [14] The prospect of a central or general government with any real power was odious to large numbers of people who had had enough of the centralized and arbitrary authority exercised by England. A war had been fought to escape from this kind of domination. Thus, there were many who were perfectly satisfied with the political and economic conditions in the 1780s under the Articles of Confederation. Any move to upset the status quo was bound to meet with determined opposition, the rallying cry being the specter of centralized authority.

Toward Government

Nonetheless, there were powerful forces which were greatly interested in change. The chaotic economic conditions resulting from the control by each state of its own commerce was viewed as a most serious problem. The inability of Congress to raise money and adequate forces to repel the very real possibilities of foreign intervention—from England or Spain—in the north, west, and south dismayed many. Military in-

---

[13] Alfred H. Kelly and Winfred A. Harbison, *The American Constitution, Its Origins and Development,* 3rd ed. (New York: W. W. Norton, 1963), p. 106.
[14] Articles of Confederation, II.

capacity also made it more difficult to protect settlers as they pushed the Indians from frontier areas. The rage for paper money in some of the states and the lack of impartial national courts to settle disputes between citizens of different states was viewed as a threat to property rights. And the fact that individual states could, with impunity, flout the policies of Congress and so easily abort the new nation impressed many with the seriousness of the problem of an effective national government.

It was men with such views who took the initiative in trying to bring about change. The purpose of the call for a convention in 1787 was to examine ways in which the Articles might be revised. To those uninterested in change, it appeared that there was little such a convention could do to effect major alterations in the scheme of things because the Articles required that each and every state agree to any amendments. Because the opponents of centralized government felt comfortable in the assurance that drastic change was highly unlikely, they showed little interest in the convention called for May, 1787. As a result, the membership of that convention was strongly stacked in favor of drastic revision of the Articles. It did not take long for them to perceive that simply amending the Articles would not be enough. An entirely new system of government was needed.

The proposal put before the convention in its early stages and adopted as the basis for discussion was indeed a radical departure from the existing state of things. It was offered by the leader of the Virginia delegation, Governor Edmund Randolph, and is most often referred to as the Virginia Plan. But the Virginia Plan was largely the work of James Madison, a series of proposals he had been shaping for some time and which he had sent off during the spring to Jefferson, Washington, and Randolph.[15] As originally presented by Randolph, the plan went to the heart of the difficulties under the Articles of Confederation. It proposed the creation of a government which would possess legislative, executive, and judicial authority.

More importantly, the Virginia Plan recognized that it was not only the lack of governmental functions from which the articles suffered, but also the failure of the government to operate directly on the people. This was overcome in the form of a proposal substituted for the first of the original points that made up the Virginia Plan. The revised version went as follows: "That a National Government ought to

---

[15] James MacGregor Burns, *The Deadlock of Democracy* (Englewood Cliffs, N.J.: Prentice-Hall, 1963), pp. 8–15.

be established consisting of a supreme Legislative, Executive and Judiciary."[16] The key word is national, for it had a particular meaning well understood at the time. "National," explained George Mason of the Virginia delegation, meant a government which would "directly operate on individuals and possess compulsive power on the people of the United States."[17]

The scheme of government thus proposed sought to overcome the basic structural and power difficulties of the Articles. But it went much further than even this. It struck directly at the principle of the equality of the states so carefully recognized and preserved in the Articles. The Virginia Plan provided that in choosing the national legislature, either population or wealth should be used as the basis for determining how many voting representatives each state should have. Not surprisingly, such a proposal came from the most populous of the states; Virginia, with a population of about 740,000, had almost 275,000 more people than the next most populous state, Massachusetts. Together, the three leaders in population (the third being Pennsylvania), had nearly as many people as the nine least populous states.[18] Without much doubt, the Virginia Plan would have made the three or four most populated states (North Carolina was the fourth) easily dominant in the national legislature.

The heavy weight the most populous states would carry, moreover, would be compounded by the arrangement for electing the second of the houses of the national legislature. The members of the second branch, as it was called, were to be chosen by those of the first branch. Thus, the domination of the heavily populated states would be felt in the entire legislative body. As if this were not enough, the Virginia Plan also provided that the national executive was to be chosen by the national legislature! Little wonder that some of the smaller states balked at the scheme of representation offered by Virginia. Controversy over this proved to be the most formidable obstacle to agreement during the convention.

The basic conflict was over representation. It was not, as often depicted, between the advocates of a national or central government and those who favored continuation of the system of the Articles. It was not between those who were nationalists and states'-righters, because the

[16] Quoted in Charles Warren, *The Making of the Constitution* (Boston: Little, Brown, 1928), p. 146.
[17] Quoted in ibid., p. 147.
[18] Based on figures in Arthur E. Sutherland, *Constitutionalism in America* (Waltham, Mass.: Blaisdell, 1965), p. 173, n. 60, which are derived from the census of 1790.

dominant sentiment at the convention supported the idea of national government.[19] The problem facing the delegations from small states was one of trying to achieve a fairer share in policymaking than the Virginia Plan contemplated. How difficult a task it would have been for the delegates from the small states to return after the convention and try to win support from their people for a scheme of government in which they would carry so little weight.

For some weeks, the work of the convention was held up by this conflict over representation between large states and small states.[20] The possibilities of compromise were readily at hand, however. The existing system provided for the equal representation of the states in the Congress under the Articles. Almost as soon as the Virginia Plan had been introduced, there had been suggestions that two methods of representation be employed: population and the states as equals.[21] When the advocates of domination by the large states saw that there could be no constitution at all without the smaller states, they capitulated to the demand for equal representation in one of the houses of the legislature. The national character of the new scheme of government thus remained intact while the states had retained in part their political autonomy through their representation as equals.

Federalism—The Republican Remedy

In retrospect, American historians have acclaimed this arrangement as *federalism*. Ironically, James Madison is frequently credited with conceiving this scheme although he bitterly opposed the compromise which destroyed the purity of the national government he sought.[22] What Madison did do, during the convention, was to argue effectively against a purely federal plan and thus insure that at the least the defective government of the Articles would be replaced.[23] At the time of the convention, the terms national and federal

---

[19] John P. Roche, "The Founding Fathers: A Reform Caucus in Action," *American Political Science Review* 55 (December 1961): 802–08.

[20] It was not that the opposition to the Virginia Plan came only from small states. Chief among those states against it were New York and Maryland (the fifth and sixth largest in population); Georgia, one of the least populous (82,000), often sided with the large states. Sutherland, *Constitutionalism in America*, p. 173.

[21] Max Farrand, *The Framing of the Constitution* (New Haven: Yale University Press, 1963), p. 107 (first published in 1913).

[22] Roche, "The Founding Fathers," p. 810.

[23] Martin Diamond, "What the Framers Meant," pp. 32–40.

had quite definite and distinctly different meanings. Today they are used almost interchangeably to describe the government in Washington. But in 1787, national was a term used to describe a government having power over its people. Federal, on the other hand, quite clearly conveyed the idea to the men of the time of a league or compact among sovereign states for limited purposes, usually mutual defense.[24] Federalism in 1787 accurately described the Articles of Confederation; the third article emphatically stated that the "states hereby severally enter into a firm league of friendship with each other. . . ."

It was only after the Constitution became a matter of public record that the lines of a nationalist versus states'-rights struggle emerged. During the convention, the newly developing scheme of government was among comparatively friendly forces. Once the battle for ratification began, however, those attached to the status quo perceived the effectiveness of arguing against the Constitution because it did such violence to federalism as then understood. The Constitution, it was argued by its opponents, represented the greatest threat to republicanism imaginable because it centralized authority by consolidating the states into one national government.

This is the argument which Madison strove to refute in the *Federalist*. It is a measure of Madison's ability as a politician and propagandist that, within a few months after so stoutly opposing the compromise which gave the states equal representation, he could turn around and make such a brilliant argument in support of the idea. The result has been to credit him with the idea of federalism, understood in the modern sense, whereas in reality he merely concocted a persuasive rationalization for it. Madison was effective because he managed to turn the argument of his opponents upside down.

The proponents of federalism in 1787–88 believed that republicanism could thrive only in small states. To swallow up the states in a national government would be to create arbitrary power with nothing but bad consequences for the rights of the people. Madison, however, proceeded to demonstrate that the system the Constitution embodied was, in fact, a mixed system, partly national and partly federal. Moreover, its large size, rather than being a threat to the rights of the people, was the surest guarantee of their rights. In *Federalist,* No. 10, for instance, where Madison was concerned with the evils of faction, he argued that by extending the sphere of territory, a greater variety of

[24] Ibid., pp. 27–29.

parties and interests could be included. This made "it less probable that a majority of the whole will have a common motive to invade the rights of other citizens. . . ." His conclusion was that "in the extent and proper structure of the Union, therefore, we behold a republican remedy for the diseases most incident to republican government." [25]

Madison returned to this theme in *Federalist,* No. 51. In this paper, the dispersion of power between the national government, on the one hand, and the state governments, on the other, was linked to the notion of separation of powers. Each of these devices, as Madison saw them, aided in securing the rights of the people. In combination, they provided "a double security":

> In the compound republic of America, the power surrendered by the people is first divided between two distinct governments, and then the portion allotted to each subdivided among distinct and separate departments. . . . The different governments will control each other, at the same time that each will be controlled by itself.[26]

By this argument, Madison was able to turn the tables against the opponents of the Constitution. He demonstrated that the proposed scheme, rather than being a threat to republicanism, would, in fact, assure precisely those values which the friends of republicanism sought. Federalism was rationalized as one of the major means of dispersing power and thus preventing arbitrary government.

Madison, of course, was not extolling the virtues of the new Constitution in a vacuum. The *Federalist* papers were written primarily to rally support for the new plan of government in the state of New York. Except for New York City, the state was firmly in control of the anti-Federalists, under the leadership of Governor George Clinton. Madison, along with John Jay and Alexander Hamilton, both New Yorkers, began writing their series of articles defending the Constitution soon after the convention adjourned. Their arguments appeared in the form of letters to the public in the pro-Constitution press of New York City, over the signature of Publius, but "they were smothered by the deluge of anti-Federalist propaganda and were of virtually no influence in deciding votes except in the immediate vicinity of the City." [27]

---

[25] *Federalist Papers,* pp. 83–84.
[26] *Federalist Papers,* p. 323.
[27] Forrest McDonald, *We The People, The Economic Origins of the Constitution* (Chicago: University of Chicago Press, 1963), p. 284. When the election of delegates to the convention in the state ratifying the Constitution was finally held in April of 1788, the Federalists were badly defeated. Ibid., p. 286.

In an environment largely hostile to the Constitution, Jay, Hamilton, and Madison were attempting to soften some of the national aspects of the new form of government so as to make it more palatable to the anti-Federalists of New York. It is in this context that Madison's exposition of federalism was designed to make such a strong appeal to believers in republicanism, guarding at the same time both the position of the states in the new government and the rights of property. New York eventually ratified the Constitution, but not because of the *Federalist* papers. The threat of secession of both the city and county of New York was apparently a more potent influence in the decision to ratify than the arguments of Jay, Hamilton, and Madison.[28]

The whole tenor of the *Federalist* papers is exemplified in the name the authors chose. If, to the men of 1787–88, the term federal denoted decentralized, confederated government, how was it that the advocates of national government were able to style themselves as Federalists? The proponents of change in the political system of the Articles of Confederation simply appropriated the term which carried the most favorable connotation. And by designating the opponents of the new Constitution as "Antifederalists," they managed to attach to them "the reverse of their true beliefs" and also to cast them as obstructionists.[29]

Taken out of its contemporary context, however, the *Federalist* has come to be regarded as the one true exposition of the meaning of the new Constitution, as well as the most original American contribution to political theory.[30] Whether such accolades are fully justified or not, the fact remains that the system of divided power which Madison described has turned into the single most important characteristic of the American political system. The concept of federalism pervades all thinking about politics and government in the United States. Federalism has had a major impact on the development of the system of political parties. It has nurtured the attachment to local government, which is a strong attitude in American political thought. More importantly, however, the concept of federalism and all that has been associated with it has not only shaped the way public policies are made in the United States, but also the kinds of policies that are produced by the political system.

---

[28] Ibid., pp. 287–88.
[29] Jackson T. Main, *The Anti-Federalists* (Chapel Hill: University of North Carolina Press, 1961), pp. xi–xii.
[30] *Federalist Papers,* pp. vii–xvi.

Who Has the Power? For much of American history, federalism was viewed primarily as a legalistic concept. Supposedly, federalism meant that the national government had certain powers, but that the states were free to exercise all those powers not given to the central government. The Constitution was even looked to as an authoritative source for defining what kinds of powers properly belonged to each level of government. Or, if the Constitution failed to provide an explicit guide to the distribution of power, the Supreme Court could be depended on to decide in cases of conflict based on its interpretation of what the fundamental law demanded. From the very first, those who opposed the new Constitution, even after its ratification, saw the possibilities of disputing national public policy on the grounds that federalism precluded the central government from doing certain things. The ease with which such policy disputes could be cast into legal and constitutional terms, and the readiness of the Supreme Court to cast itself in the role of arbiter, early guaranteed that there would be an endless series of such disputes.

Conflict has therefore been a major byproduct of federalism. The struggles over interpretation of the national government's power to regulate commerce are as illustrative as any in demonstrating the way such conflicts were cast into legal disputes and ultimately settled by the Supreme Court. The commerce clause received its first extended exposition in the steamboat monopoly case, *Gibbons* v. *Ogden*, decided in 1824. New York had sought to confer a monopoly to operate steamboats from that state across the Hudson to New Jersey. Gibbons challenged this exclusive franchise on the basis of a license granted under an act of Congress. In upholding the monopoly, the courts of New York claimed that, under the Constitution, the states had a concurrent power, together with Congress, to regulate commerce among the states.

The Supreme Court decided in favor of Gibbons and against the state-conferred monopoly. Chief Justice Marshall gave a broad definition to the word commerce and said that Congress could exercise its power to the fullest. But he also acknowledged that commerce completely within one state was subject to local regulation, and he hedged on the question whether or not the states could exercise a concurrent power even over commerce that was concededly within the power of Congress to control. The decision in *Gibbons* v. *Ogden* received general approval. The blow against monopolies struck a responsive chord, and the concessions made to the states satisfied all but a few of the most ardent advocates of extreme localism.[31]

The ambiguity of the decision, however, merely compounded the ambiguity of the commerce clause. In subsequent years, a mighty battle ensued between those who advocated that the power of Congress was exclusive, leaving no room for state regulation, and those who were devoted to the concurrent theory. State power over regulation of commerce, in fact, became the principal rallying point for the advocates of states' rights, an additional reason being that it was linked to state control of slavery. An uneasy and not much less ambiguous compromise was reached by the Supreme Court in 1851.[32] Those matters of commerce which were national in character, declared the Court, were exclusively within the power of Congress to regulate. Other matters, peculiarly local in character, might demand diverse solutions, and the states were free to regulate such aspects of commerce among the states as long as Congress had not exercised its power.

The industrial revolution drastically changed the American economic system. From essentially an agricultural and local economy, the system became an industrial and national one. Toward the end of the nineteenth century, Congress for the first time began to see the possibilities of its commerce power. Not always, however, was the Supreme Court willing to endorse the public policies of Congress. Federalism and the commerce power increasingly provided the materials of conflict.

Congress, for instance, discovered that by prohibiting the movement of goods in commerce among the states certain supposedly obnoxious practices could be suppressed. In this way, Congress lent its weight against lotteries in the states by prohibiting the shipment of lottery tickets across state boundaries. It struck a blow against the white slave trade when it forbade, in the Mann Act, the transportation of women from state to state for immoral purposes. Elimination of fraudulent practices in the food and drug trade was the aim of Congress when it passed the Pure Food and Drug Act of 1906.

In each of these instances, the Supreme Court sustained these exercises of the commerce power, although it was widely recognized that prohibition of particular practices deemed evil by Congress was the real aim of the statutes. In each of these cases, the major challenge was based on the theory that Congress was in reality invading the reserved powers of the states. But the Court, although often divided, turned a

---

[31] Kelly and Harbison, *The American Constitution,* p. 296.
[32] Cooley v. Board of Wardens, 12 Howard 299.

deaf ear to such pleas, and at times it endorsed far-reaching excursions of national power into matters considered strictly local. Such was the case, for example, when the authority of the Interstate Commerce Commission to disapprove the rates of a railroad for trips wholly within a state was upheld by the Supreme Court. The theory was that if such state-approved rates were injurious or would have an adverse effect on the rates between states, the supremacy of the national power was justified.

The Commerce Power Undone

The record of the Supreme Court, however, was not entirely consistent. In 1890, Congress passed the Sherman Anti-trust Act. The first major test of the act resulted in crushing defeat for the government. Through contracts, one company had gained control of more than 90 percent of the manufacture of sugar in the United States. But the Supreme Court chose to apply an antiquated and wholly unrealistic conception of commerce, one that even in the year 1895 was hopelessly out of date. Because the monopoly was in the manufacturing of the sugar, said the Court, it could not be reached under the act, since "commerce succeeds to manufacture, and is not a part of it." [33] This disposed of the problem, since the Court had already proclaimed its view of federalism: "That which belongs to commerce is within the jurisdiction of the United States, but that which does not belong to commerce is within the jurisdiction of the police power of the State." [34]

In time, subsequent Supreme Courts overcame this initial hostility to antitrust policy.[35] But the decision in the sugar trust case showed how a mechanical and legalistic view of federalism could be used to oppose unwanted national economic policies. This was dramatically illustrated in 1918, when the Supreme Court struck down an attempt by Congress to stamp out the widespread evils of child labor. Since the Court had approved of the use of the commerce power to aid in the elimination of lotteries, prostitution, and impure foods and adulterated drugs, Congress undoubtedly felt on sure ground in using the same technique with regard to child labor. Congress, as in the other

---

[33] United States v. E. C. Knight Co., 156 U.S. 1 (1895), p. 12.
[34] Ibid.
[35] In dissenting in the sugar trust case, Justice Harlan had said: "While the opinion of the court in this case does not declare the act of 1890 to be unconstitutional, it defeats the main object for which it was passed."

situations, could not directly outlaw the use of child labor. All that it tried to do was discourage the practice by forbidding products made by children from using the channels of commerce from state to state.

A bare majority of the Supreme Court, however, condemned the statute in the name of federalism. Congress, said the Court, was really trying to control production in the states. But production was not commerce and therefore the national government had no authority to invade this reserved power of the state. The Court, moreover, could see a difference in using the commerce power to discourage child labor, on the one hand, and lotteries and prostitution, on the other hand. In the child labor case, the specific products made had been furniture. Although lottery tickets and immoral women were harmful commodities in themselves, furniture, argued the Court, was not.

By way of invoking the Constitution as authority, the five-member majority relied on the Tenth Amendment. This, it was said, carefully reserved to the states power over local matters.

> In interpreting the Constitution it must never be forgotten that the Nation is made up of states to which are entrusted the powers of local government. And to them and to the people the powers not expressly delegated to the National Government are reserved.[36]

Mr. Justice Day, who wrote the opinion, thus permitted the Tenth Amendment to override the power delegated to Congress to regulate commerce among the states. Moreover, in paraphrasing the amendment, he managed to distort its meaning by including the word "expressly."[37] When the proposal which resulted eventually in the Tenth Amendment was before the First Congress, three separate attempts were made to insert the word expressly as a modifier of the powers not delegated to the national government. On each occasion, twice in the House and once in the Senate, the attempts failed.[38]

Neither the wording nor the intent of the Tenth Amendment was properly invoked by Justice Day. All that the amendment did was to confirm that which had already been accomplished by adoption of the Constitution. In ratifying the Constitution, the people of the states had merely authorized a different distribution of powers between them-

---

[36] Hammer v. Dagenhart, 247 U.S. 251 (1918), p. 275.

[37] The amendment reads as follows: "The powers not delegated to the United States by the Constitution, nor prohibited by it to the States, are reserved to the States respectively, or to the people."

[38] W. W. Crosskey, *Politics and the Constitution in the History of the United States,* 2 vols. (Chicago: University of Chicago Press, 1953), vol. I, pp. 680–81.

selves, their states, and the new central government. Instead of the very limited number of powers exercised by Congress under the Articles of Confederation, Congress under the Constitution was delegated a rather lengthy series of powers, most of them enumerated in Article I, section 8. Those powers not transferred to the national government were to remain exactly where they had been: either in the hands of the states or prohibited to the states or Congress.

It is for this reason that the powers of Congress have been referred to as *delegated* or *enumerated* powers, whereas those powers exercised by the states are termed *reserved* powers. But trying to fix labels to something as dynamic as governmental power is illusory. In recognition of this, Congress was given, in Article I, section 8, a final, very general, and vaguely defined power "to make all Laws which shall be necessary and proper for carrying into Execution the Foregoing Powers. . . ." It is this clause which became the battleground between Jefferson and Hamilton over the establishment of the Bank of the United States. Jefferson read over the powers of Congress and nowhere did he see a power to create a bank. He acknowledged that Congress had power to lay and collect taxes, pay the debts of the United States, as well as other fiscal powers which might suggest that a bank would be useful in exercising them. But, he argued, a strict reading of the "necessary and proper" clause would show that a bank was not absolutely indispensable.

Hamilton, on the other hand, argued that "necessary and proper" should be interpreted loosely or broadly; and that if merely expedient or convenient, a bank would be constitutional. Marshall, as he had done in *Marbury* v. *Madison*, embraced Hamilton's argument when the dispute finally came to the Supreme Court some twenty-eight years later. The case involved an attempt by Maryland to impose a tax on the branch of the Bank of the United States in Baltimore. Such was unconstitutional, argued the Court, because it would interfere with the operations of the bank, the constitutionality of which was sustained. The case gave constitutional sanction to the doctrine of implied powers.[39]

It is the combination of a more specific power and the implied power conferred by the "necessary and proper" clause which lies at the basis of much of what Congress does. The National Defense Education Act, passed in 1958, under which college students can get national government loans, is an example. This is the meaning of "Defense" in its

---

[39] McCulloch v. Maryland, 4 Wheaton 316 (1819).

title. It is an exercise of the power of Congress to "provide for the Common Defense" and to do that which in its judgment is "necessary and proper" toward that end.

As always, however, the exercise by Congress of its powers was subject to the veto of the Supreme Court. In the child labor case of 1918 the Court chose to exercise that veto largely because it felt that this extension of national power was unwarranted. In a matter where there was a difference of opinion, five justices had decided public policy. The inappropriateness of the use of the Tenth Amendment as the rationale becomes clear when it is remembered that the amendment, by its own terms, refers to those power *not delegated*. The commerce power, however, *is* a delegated power. But the Court chose to ignore this straightforward interpretation.[40]

The Commerce Power Restored

A narrow view of the powers of Congress, especially the commerce power, as exemplified in the sugar trust and child labor cases, was used by the Supreme Court as the major weapon of attack on much of the major legislation of the New Deal. It was not until the Court's reversal of policy in the spring of 1937 and subsequent changes in personnel that the Court adapted itself to the realities of the twentieth-century American economic system. In 1941, the child labor case was overruled.[41] A year later the Court sanctioned a far-reaching use of the power of Congress to regulate commerce under the Agricultural Adjustment Act of 1938. It held that regulations on the amount of grain a farmer could grow for consumption on his own farm were constitutionally valid. To permit one farmer to grow as much as he wanted would be to permit all farmers to do the same. The result would be to defeat the congressional policy of reducing surpluses which had seriously depressed farm prices. The farmer would rely on his own sources, rather than going out and purchasing from the market. Even though the farmer's excess production in this case was local and

[40] Walter Berns, "The Meaning of the Tenth Amendment," in Goldwin, *A Nation of States*, pp. 126–48.

[41] United States v. Darby, 312 U.S. 100. In the course of that decision, Justice Stone put the Tenth Amendment in proper perspective: "The amendment states but a truism that all is retained which has not been surrendered."

would never become commerce among the states, national power could properly regulate it if there was a substantial effect on such commerce.[42]

The Supreme Court also recognized what had been the situation all along. The commerce power and the Supreme Court had been the battleground for competing economic interests in the name of federalism. No longer would this be the case, announced the Court. Since 1942, Congress has been free to exercise its power over commerce without much fear of Court intervention. Whether Congress should regulate some phase of economic activity no longer became a constitutional question. If the necessary political support could be mustered in Congress to form majorities in support of regulation, the matter would be ended.

It came as little surprise, therefore, when Congress used the commerce power as the major basis for the Civil Rights Act of 1964. As earlier Congresses had done regarding the evils of lotteries and prostitution, the commerce power was now to be used to strike at the evils of discrimination. Thus were places of accommodation along routes of travel between states prohibited from refusing service to travelers because of their race or color. So, too, were places of eating which depended on the channels of commerce among the states for their supplies forbidden to discriminate. The Supreme Court readily acquiesced in this use of the commerce power. The decision to use the commerce power, wrote former Justice Tom C. Clark,

> is a matter of policy that rests entirely with Congress, not with the courts. How obstructions in commerce may be removed—what means are to be employed—is within the sound and exclusive discretion of the Congress.[43]

That the latest exposition of the powers of Congress under the commerce clause concerned racial discrimination is testimony to the historical importance of this problem in the tug-of-war between nation and states. The slavery controversy, which erupted into an armed struggle over the relations between nation and states, and recent disputes arising from attempts of the national government to solve the problem of racial discrimination are examples of the almost continuing instances of conflict in the context of federalism. When such con-

---

[42] Wickard v. Filburn, 317 U.S. 111 (1942).
[43] Heart of Atlanta Motel, Inc. v. United States, 379 U.S. 241 (1964), pp. 261–62; also, Katzenbach v. McClung, 379 U.S. 294 (1964).

troversies have not been in the forefront, economic interests have often used the rhetoric of federalism in an attempt to avoid regulation imposed on them through Congress.

Conflict and Cooperation   Conflict, however, has been only one of the major characteristics of the system of policymaking in the context of federalism. Although conflict amply fulfills the prescription for divided power which Madison described, cooperation in the system of federalism has been of equal historical importance. Cooperative efforts between national, state, and local governments, however, have not lent themselves to dramatic presentation in the textbooks. Not until recently, in fact, has the full dimension of such cooperation been known. The prevalence of conflict throughout the nineteenth century seemed to imply that the national government and the states acted in their own respective spheres of power, and it was when either attempted to intrude on the other that conflict resulted.

The facts of history indicate otherwise. The pattern of American federalism has been one of partnership, and constantly so since the very beginning. Careful research has revealed that "virtually all the activities of government in the nineteenth-century United States were co-operative endeavors, shared by Federal and state agencies in much the same manner as government programs are shared in the twentieth century." [44] All that has changed in this picture of more or less constant cooperation has been the means whereby the different levels of government cooperate. In an early period, the joint stock company for long-term cooperative projects was used. As the United States expanded westward and great amounts of public land came under control of the national government, the land grant became the predominant form of cooperative venture. Finally, as land became scarce, the cash grant moved to the forefront as the principal vehicle for intergovernmental cooperation.[45]

Under the first means, a great number of the internal improvements, particularly in water transportation, so important to the development of commerce in the nation, were made. Education became the major

---

[44] Daniel J. Elazar, *The American Partnership, Intergovernmental Co-operation in the Nineteenth-Century United States* (Chicago: University of Chicago Press, 1962), p. 1.
[45] Ibid., p. 34.

cooperative venture benefiting from the land grant policy, although internal improvements and welfare programs also owed their existence to this system. Today, education, highways (a modern form of internal improvements), and a variety of social and welfare services are provided through the cash grant-in-aid. Most of the programs of cooperation to provide services to the public in the nineteenth century "originated as a result of what is usually termed 'grass-roots' pressure (of educators, veterans, or conservationists)."[46] What was true then is equally true today and accounts for the great proliferation of cooperative programs.

The Marble Cake

When placed alongside the rhetoric of conflict which the principle of federalism normally evokes, the evidence of cooperation indicates that, quite pragmatically, "the American people have by and large endeavored to use both federal and state governments as means to achieve specific ends. . . ."[47] In truth, "the history of American governments is a history of shared functions."[48] The result has been aptly described by use of a symbolic marble cake. In contrast to the traditional picture of the system of federalism as a neat layer cake consisting of three levels of government, the marble cake shows a blending and sharing of functions and powers that follows a variety of patterns, making "government in the United States . . . chaotic."[49]

Such chaos is simply the modern-day application of the notion of divided and dispersed power which Madison said the system of federalism embodied. To the extent that it makes it difficult to reach decisions, it is faithful to the desires of those of the late eighteenth century to guard against majorities and the possibility of arbitrary decisions. Complicating the modern picture even more is the presence of the cities as a major factor in the political equation of federalism. The traditional view has taken the nation and the states as the given forms of the federal system. In this century, however, the cities have exercised their own political potency to become an important consideration in the policymaking process. Rural domination of the state legislatures, even at a time earlier in this century when a major population shift to

[46] Ibid., p. 263.
[47] Ibid., p. 297.
[48] Morton Grodzins, "Centralization and Decentralization in the American Federal System," in Goldwin, *A Nation of States*, p. 6.
[49] Ibid., p. 1.

the cities had occurred, meant that the problems of the cities often went neglected.

The cities went directly to Congress. Since the early thirties, many programs of intergovernmental cooperation have been forged on a nation-city basis. Public housing, urban renewal, mass transportation, and airport construction are among major grant-in-aid programs where the relations are between nation and city, with little or no state involvement. One of the major controversies that pervades the politics of federalism today is not whether the national government should undertake aid at all, but how are the states and cities to share in the cooperative venture. The politics of contemporary federalism, as well as of its history, indicate that traditional views of federalism as a legal or constitutional device of separation have missed the point. Federalism is in reality simply a way in which the policymaking process in the United States has been and is structured. It is a question of at which levels of government and in what manner will there be cooperative endeavors in a great variety of fields of public policy.

Recent debate about federalism exemplifies this. Strong sentiment exists for the replacement of the traditional specific grant-in-aid, at least in part, by open-ended grants to the states to be used as they determine. To those in favor of such a plan, as well as to those opposed to it, the basic argument revolves around by whom and at what level should decisions about national, state, and local cooperation be made. Part of the support for revenue sharing comes from the dissatisfaction with the multiplicity of grant-in-aid programs and the bureaucratic maze which is so often difficult to penetrate in obtaining federal funds. Here again, the importance of who exercises authority, and at what level, is a basic point of conflict. Whatever forms federalism takes in the last third of the twentieth century, the twin themes of conflict and cooperation are likely to persist.

To those wary of the increasing scope of governmental authority, the traditional view of federalism as separated sovereignties will continue to provide a rhetorical rallying point. But the reality of the twentieth century is that government at all levels continues to grow. It is often simply a case of which government is going to intervene. When economic or segregationist interests, for example, have felt that it would be easier to influence and control state policy, opposition to national policy is most effectively premised on preserving federalism and the Constitution. When they do so, they are modern-day counterparts of the Madison of the *Federalist* papers.

The age-old issue of decentralization within the political system has taken on a new twist in recent years. One of the principal issues thrust up by the Black revolution is that of community control—of schools and police and other public services. The struggle in New York City in the fall of 1968 brought the problem into public view in a dramatic way. The controversy centered over the degree of control the governing board of a local school district in the Ocean Hill-Brownsville area in Brooklyn was to have over the hiring and firing of teachers.[50] A common reaction across the country was that the insistence on local control, not only of the hiring and firing of teachers, but also of curriculum, was no different from white Southerners exercising community control for the purpose of running segregated schools.

Yet, this reaction overlooked a factor fundamentally differentiating the two situations. For the Blacks, it is not a matter of subjugating a white minority to the decisions of a majority. It is, rather, a case of Blacks being able to control the education of their own children in what already are *de facto* segregated schools. And in such a situation, it is essential to the goals of establishing Black identity and community that Black children not be subject to a curriculum and to instruction which is a product of a white society. For it is this society which, in the past, has essentially failed to serve adequately the educational needs of the Black.[51]

The issue is no less emotionally charged when it comes to the problem of community control of the police. In most major cities, the proportion of Blacks on the police force is far less than the ratio of Blacks to whites in the population. A good many white policemen, moreover, tragically display attitudes of prejudice toward Negroes, and Blacks have developed a counterreaction of hatred toward white cops. Under such circumstances, the issue of community control becomes basic. Resolution of the problem will be one of the most vexing of all political issues in the decade of the seventies. Once again, the rush of events has served to put a constant problem of American politics into a different—and perhaps paradoxical—context.

---

[50] The teachers' union struck over this issue, and for most of the fall the schools were closed.

[51] See, for example, the indictment in Jonathan Kozol, *Death at an Early Age* (New York: Bantam Books, 1968), subtitled "The Destruction of the Hearts and Minds of Negro Children in the Boston Public Schools."

Separating Powers The dispersion of power embodied in a policymaking process where federalism is such a pervasive factor is only half of the double security Madison found in the new Constitution he was defending. After dividing power "between two distinct governments . . . the portion allotted to each [is] subdivided among distinct and separate departments." [52] Like federalism, the separation of powers was to make it more difficult for majorities to form and impose their will on minorities. As commonly understood in contemporary America, the principle of separation of powers means that each of the three branches of government —legislative, executive, and judicial—are separate and coequal in the political process. Just as frequently, it is also asserted that each branch has a distinctive function not to be usurped by the others. Consider the words of Justice Black in the steel seizure case:

> In the framework of our Constitution, the President's power to see that the laws are faithfully executed refutes the idea that he is to be a lawmaker. The Constitution limits his functions in the law-making process to the recommending of laws he thinks wise and the vetoing of laws he thinks bad. And the Constitution is neither silent nor equivocal about who shall make laws which the President is to execute. The first section of the first article says that "all legislative Powers herein granted shall be vested in a Congress of the United States." [53]

Practice is often widely at variance with the constitutional theories sometimes expressed by justices of the Supreme Court. But in the case of the doctrine of separation of powers, the modern version of the theory is also at odds with its supposed eighteenth-century origins. The notion of a separation of powers has a long history in the development of political theory. Two principal sources for its American offshoot are usually cited. There are the writings of John Locke and the Frenchman, Charles Montesquieu.

Locke's formulation of the idea of the separation of powers is a prominent aspect of his *Second Treatise*. His discussion of it comes in the context of his analysis of the powers of government and their appropriate arrangement. He talks of the legislative power and the need for persons other than the lawmakers to have the power of

---

[52] *Federalist Papers*, No. 51, p. 323.
[53] Youngstown Sheet & Tube Co. v. Sawyer, 343 U.S. 579 (1952). Justice Black, of course, was speaking for himself, inasmuch as there were six separate opinions, one for each of the six-man majority which held against the president. But Justices Frankfurter, Burton, and Douglas also relied to some extent on the doctrine of separation of powers

DISPERSING THE POWERS OF GOVERNMENT

executing the laws. Otherwise, the lawmakers might be tempted to exempt themselves from the application of the law. In this regard, Locke is assigning a moral reason for the separation of powers.

Another reason, however, is also assigned as the rationale for a separation of the legislative and executive power. The business of legislating in seventeenth-century England was decidedly a part-time occupation, as it still is in many of the states today. Thus, Locke argued, the legislators would be around but a short time, whereas there was a need for "a power always in being which should see to the execution of the laws that are made and remain in force. And thus the legislative and executive power come often to be separated." To the moral reason, Locke had added one of convenience and expediency without indicating which was the more important.[54]

Locke, moreover, had a much different conception of what the powers of government consisted of than is commonly taken for granted today. To him they were the legislative power, the executive power, and the federative power, which is what would be called, in modern language, the foreign relations power or function of a government. Nowhere does Locke single out a judicial power for separate treatment, although in earlier parts of the *Second Treatise,* he frequently alluded to application of the known and standing laws by authorized judges.[55] It was common to think of the judicial power as a function of the executive power. But as with so many historical figures of political thought, it is not what they wrote but what people subsequently choose to believe they said that seems to matter.

If Locke failed to develop fully the rationale for the separation of powers, Montesquieu did, more than a half-century later. Montesquieu's model, in fact, was the England Locke had written about, which Montesquieu visited during the years 1730–31, thus having an opportunity to observe how the system Locke had rationalized was functioning. His observations are contained in Book XI of his extensive analysis of government, *The Spirit of the Laws,* first published in 1748.

Montesquieu tied his theory of a separation of powers directly to the goal of trying to prevent the exercise of arbitrary political power. He perceived that it was in the way the process of lawmaking was structured that the surest guarantee against arbitrariness would result. If all legitimate interests had a share in this process, he argued, it was not likely that one of them could arbitrarily impose its will on the others.

[54] Secs. 143 and 144 in *The Second Treatise of Government,* pp. 82–83.
[55] Ibid., sec. 136.

To this Frenchman, living under the absolutist Bourbon monarchs, it came as a natural proposition, as it did to so many in the eighteenth century, that political power is likely to be abused. Thus, said Montesquieu, it is necessary from the very nature of things that power be checked by power. And this could be accomplished by the way a government is constituted.

Unlike Locke, Montesquieu identified the three powers of government as legislative, executive, and judicial. But like Locke, he derived the judicial power from the executive power. Following his identification of the three powers, Montesquieu goes on to make his oft-quoted statement about their separation:

> When the legislative and executive powers are united in the same person or in the same body . . . there can be no liberty. . . . There is no liberty if the judiciary power be not separated from the legislative and executive. . . .
> There would be an end of everything, were the same man or the same body, whether of the nobles or of the people, to exercise those three powers, that of enacting laws, that of executing the public resolution, and of trying the causes of individuals.[56]

In relying on Montesquieu as an authority for the doctrine of separation of powers, most commentators stop quoting him at this point. But when his discussion of the judicial power is examined, it becomes clear that Montesquieu was talking about something quite different from the power of judicial review American courts exercise. Montesquieu, as befit a student of government in the eighteenth century, had in mind the function of judge and jury when he discussed the judicial power. In his time, the judge was viewed as a living oracle of the law with the simple function of pronouncing what the law was. The jury, on the other hand, representing the peers of the accused in criminal cases or the parties to a civil case, had the important responsibility of deciding what the facts in a dispute were. Through judge and jury, justice was dispensed.

Both of the venerable institutions of judge and jury had come under attack during the arbitrary pretensions of the Stuart kings during the turmoil in England in the seventeenth century. The kings had used judges as tools in their persecution of political opponents and had likewise tried to interfere with the functioning of juries. Both of these practices had been put to an end by the parliamentary triumph of

[56] Montesquieu, *The Spirit of the Laws* (New York: Hafner, 1949), p. 152.

DISPERSING THE POWERS OF GOVERNMENT

1689. And in 1701, the English made it a constitutional principle [57] that judges should serve during good behavior, rather than at the pleasure of the king, thus establishing their independence.

Montesquieu saw the virtues of a nonpolitical judiciary, and it is for this reason that he extolled the necessity of its separation from both the legislative and executive power. But by this he meant its independence from these powers in the sense that the judge would not be subject to their whim for continuance in office. Having described judicial power in this manner, Montesquieu concluded that it would thus "come next to nothing." It would become "invisible." This kind of judicial power bears no resemblance to the fundamentally political power of vetoing legislative acts which American courts later claimed to possess.

From this point on, Montesquieu's discussion of the separation of powers nowhere includes a mention of the judicial power. Later, he summarizes his findings and makes the major point of his analysis:

> Here, then, is the fundamental constitution of the government [English] we are treating of. The legislative body being composed of two parts, they check one another by their mutual privilege of rejecting. They are both restrained by the executive power, as the executive is by the legislative.[58]

Montesquieu had in mind, of course, the bicameralism of Parliament, developed, not because the English thought two houses were better than one, but because each came to represent over historical time the major social and economic interests of the nation. The House of Lords, derived from the council of great barons, represented the landed aristocracy and their agricultural interests. As commerce developed in England in its urban centers, a newer class of bankers and merchants finally gained representation—when, at their insistence, the House of Commons was formed.

A State of Repose Thus far Montesquieu has described a system for dispersing power to prevent arbitrary decisions, seemingly without any way to get the three powers to act. In his own words, he said that these three powers "should

---
[57] In the Act of Settlement.
[58] Montesquieu, *The Spirit of the Laws*, p. 160.

naturally form a state of repose or inaction. But as there is necessity for movement in the course of human affairs, they are forced to move, but still in concert."[59] Here was the magic of balancing powers: action in governmental affairs, but only at the price of agreement from the principal interests, represented in the two houses of the legislature and in the person of the king. In a century not far removed from utter absolutism, it was a sound prescription for nonarbitrary government.

Montesquieu is said to have had a wide audience in the thirteen states, men of learning having been acquainted with his theory of the separation of powers. But Americans were also acquainted with the notion of separation of governmental power by their own experience, for, as a practical matter, this is how the political situation had developed in the colonies. Governors and their councils were ranged against the lower, popularly based, assemblies, with judges on the side of those to whom were owed their positions. As might be expected, the doctrine became part of most state constitutions, in some of them in such a rigid form as to be unworkable in practice. As a matter of fact, however, in disregard of the idea of separated and balanced powers, legislative supremacy was the general fashion.[60]

The doctrine of the separation of powers was more rhetorical than real, but its value as a symbol against arbitrary government compelled Madison to elaborate on the notion in the *Federalist* papers. Ironically, as with federalism, Madison had started out, in the Virginia Plan, with a scheme of government as far removed from the separation of powers as possible. The executive was to be chosen by the national legislature, which was also to choose the members of the national judiciary. All power was to issue from the legislative head.

It was as a result of the discussions in the Constitutional convention about the method of selecting the president that the notion of an independent and hence separate executive emerged. So, too, is there little evidence that few of the delegates began their deliberations in May with a conscious awareness of the necessity of separating legislative, executive, and judicial power. The most compelling inducement recommending an independent executive was the spectacle of some of the legislatures of the states and the utter weakness of the governors in such states. The separateness of the judges, by the same token, arose from the conviction that they should also be independent in the sense of enjoying tenure during good behavior. What discussion there was

[59] Ibid.
[60] Kelly and Harbison, *The American Constitution*, p. 97.

about the power of the courts to annul legislation came in the context of the problem of state legislation at odds with the national constitution or the laws of Congress.

It is sometimes argued that proof of the framers' intention about the separation of powers is evidenced by the fact that each of the powers is covered in a separate article. This argument, however, hardly stands analysis when it is recalled that a most important power of the president—the veto power—comes not in Article II but in Article I, where it is described as part of the process whereby a bill becomes a law.[61] Not all of Congress' legislative powers, moreover, are enumerated in section 8 of Article I. In Article III, otherwise concerned with the judiciary, Congress is given the power to alter the appellate jurisdiction of the Supreme Court, as well as the power to declare the punishment of treason. Yet, the appointment of judges is not covered in Article III, as might be expected, but is included in Article II, as part of the president's appointing power. Other powers of Congress not mentioned in Article I are described in Article IV, where Congress is given authority, for example, to make rules respecting the territories of the United States. As a guide to the separation of powers, the fact that the institutions of government are described in three separate articles has little meaning.

Yet Madison felt compelled to answer those who charged that the Constitution departed too much from the separation of powers, a central canon of the republicanism of the day. In defending the Constitution in this regard, Madison chose the model of Montesquieu. And, in his reinterpretation of it, he was remarkably faithful to the ideas of the Frenchman. For, in his extended discussion, Madison also identified the three powers as consisting of a two-house legislature and an executive. He does mention the judiciary and makes it clear that their independence needs to be guaranteed. But when he writes about the necessity of giving each department "an equal power of self-defense," his remedy is "to divide the legislature into different branches." By basing them on different modes of election,[62] he asserted, they would be "little connected" with each other.

This might not be adequate, however, because in "republican government the legislative authority necessarily predominates." Further precautions are necessary, therefore, and this requires that the "weakness of the executive . . . be fortified" by arming it with at least a

[61] Section 7 of Article I.
[62] The House, by the "people"; the Senate, by the state legislatures.

qualified veto.[63] And thus, in Madison's elaborate discussion of the separation of powers, there is no mention of the judiciary serving as one of the elements in this system of "separated" powers.[64] In a system where the legislative power necessarily predominates, it would be inconsistent to assert that the judiciary, the Supreme Court, would actually be supreme because of a power to annul acts of Congress.

The contemporary American version of the separation of powers owes little to Madison. It was not until Hamilton asserted the power of judicial review, in *Federalist,* No. 78, that the judiciary was moved into the scheme of things. The popular reverence accorded at that time to the doctrine of separation of powers, together with the willingness of the judiciary to step into the role of predominant policymaker, simply transformed the Montesquieu-Madison model into something distinctively American. Thus, it is not always the case that revered tradition and basic principles of American government necessarily owe their authority to the Constitution or to its framers or to James Madison. Practice and the accumulation of tradition have a logic all their own.

Mutual Relations In many respects, the contemporary realities of separation of powers bear a remarkable resemblance to the Madisonian conception and little likeness to the formalistic and rigid notion of it which subsequently developed. The key to the problem lies in the word separate. For, although each of the branches owes its existence to a different mode of selection, neither Montesquieu nor Madison meant them to be separate in a functional sense. For both Montesquieu and Madison, the central idea was not to separate power but to diffuse it, that is, to make the effective exercise of power depend on mutuality of agreement and at the same time prevent each center of power from subverting the other. Madison's own words reveal this, when he wrote that the way to insure, in practice, the partition of power laid down in the Constitution was to so contrive

> the interior structure of the government as that its several constituent parts may, *by their mutual relations,* be the means of keeping each other in their proper places.[65]

[63] One, that is, that can be overridden.
[64] Madison discusses the separation of powers in *Federalist Papers,* Nos. 47–51. The remarks quoted above are from No. 51.
[65] *Federalist Papers,* No. 51, p. 320. Italics added.

DISPERSING THE POWERS OF GOVERNMENT

It is doubtful if Madison could have perceived the modern form such mutual relations would take. But it is precisely the development of the president's role as chief legislator, along with his supporting staff, which has established the mutual relations of Congress and the executive in the legislative process. By the same token, it is the development of the role of supervision of administration which has brought Congress into intimate mutual relations with the president and the bureaucracy. And it is the basic character of legislation which has inevitably required administrators and judges to be rule-makers, along with Congress.

In the realities of the policymaking process, there is little in the way of separation. The emergence of subsystems has served to bridge whatever gap was intended to exist between branches, as interest groups, executive agencies, and congressional subcommittees all operate in a particular policy area serving their specialized constituencies. As Montesquieu noted, the "necessity for movement in the course of human affairs" requires that there be action, but action in concert. The development of the conditions for concert—or consensus, in more modern terminology—assures the interests involved that policy inimical to them will be hard to come by.

The modern significance of the separation of powers, however, extends well beyond the idea of keeping the powers of government apart. In the American political system, the dispersion of power *within* each of the branches is the real triumph of the eighteenth-century thinking, which saw little good in any governmental action. The Madison of *Federalist,* No. 51, no doubt, would have marveled at the creation which the events of history have produced.

Both federalism and the American variant of the separation of powers operate to color strongly the policymaking process. That process is, in fact, one where effective rule is often not in the hands of a majority but in those of minorities. The complexity of the process and the excessive dispersion of power allows strategically placed minorities to exercise a veto over policies which seemingly enjoy wide public support, simply because it is exceedingly difficult in many situations to form a policymaking majority. Because of the lack of discipline party does not provide a ready-made majority. Only *ad hoc* coalitions of minorities actuated by a sufficiently common interest can form a majority. The obstacles, however, strewn in the path of such a transient majority are so formidable throughout the policymaking process that success is more often than not difficult. When success is possible, it is only because the majority coalition has granted enough concessions to those minorities in a position to block the path of the majority. The veto power of minorities built into the policymaking process has converted rule by majority into rule at the sufferance of minorities. And in the real world of American politics, some minorities are infinitely less equal than others in their ability to obstruct.

The consequence has been to weight the policymaking process in favor of the defenders of the status quo. Although insistent majorities may triumph, it usually requires a great deal of time, often measured in decades. It also means that serious and fundamental concessions often have to be made. It is hardly a system of compromise where a minority can make the majority give up much more than the minority is willing to concede.

Dispersion of power in the American political system and all its consequences are in opposition to the principle of majority rule. To protect the rights of the minority is an admirable principle of democratic theory. But does the right of the minority include the proposition that it is entitled to govern in preference to the majority? In spite of the implications which it entails, the principle of dispersion of powers —reflected in federalism and separation of powers—is well ingrained in American political culture. Reality, however unintended, has conformed to expectation. It is only likely to give way to the inexorable demands of a people not content to let obstructions stand in the way of the achievement of specific political, economic, and social goals.

Chapter 14 The Burden of the Future

Judged by almost any quantitative standard, American society easily leads all other nations. The distance between the United States and other countries in economic terms is tremendous—and it keeps growing. Even the advanced industrial nations of Europe find our expanding economic and technological power menacing to their own well-being. For the newer and largely undeveloped countries of the world, the gap between what they can produce for their people and what America produces is staggering.

Moreover most American citizens need not consult economic statistics to learn of their nation's material success. Affluence and abundance are in sight (if not in reach) of nearly everyone. Among those attending college, the vision of a mighty and productive United States is even more visible. For most of those engaged in pursuit of higher education are themselves the children of those who have been economically successful. And for most of those who graduate, their skills will become devoted to increasing the measures of economic success.

Yet, in spite of all the obvious material success in the United States, there was uneasiness for many in the decade of the sixties. For some, and particularly for Black Americans, their concern was a product of an inability to share in the material benefits otherwise so abundant. But, for others who did not lack anything economically, uneasiness resulted from their appreciation that quantitative standards were not the whole of a nation's character. These two groups, each heterogeneous and each a small minority, have become the voices of criticism of American society.

There have always been dissident elements in American society. States'-righters, abolitionists, populists, and progressives among others have at various times aimed the arrows of criticism at traditional American values and institutions. In many respects the dissatisfactions of the last decade bear a striking resemblance to those voiced during earlier periods of turmoil. During the sixties, however, there seem to have been some distinctive characteristics associated with dissent.

Never before had the United States enjoyed the status of the world's undisputed economic and military giant. All of the ailments of American society singled out for criticism need to be viewed in this perspective. The dual characteristics of economic-military power each produced their own consequences. Economically, the sixties produced unprecedented boom. Beginning in the first Kennedy year, the economy has advanced steadily with just a slight softening during only part of 1967. Militarily, the nation has been involved in war for most of the decade. At first, the few hundred advisers in South Vietnam were hardly visible to the American eye. But by the end of 1968, more than a half-million men had been committed to that struggle which many, though perhaps a minority, still questioned as to basic purpose and goals.

War and economic boom—and, yet, it was only during the sixties that the nation began to recognize that unparalleled American prosperity was shared only by four of every five Americans. In a nation where the tendency is to compare ourselves with the Russians or Europeans, it is hard to realize that, for every triumph of economic statistics, there are real men, women, and children—in the United States—for which such superiority is meaningless. It also came as a realization that many—though by no means all—of such economically disadvantaged people also happened to carry the curse imposed by society of being Black. For these people, color and poverty were inextricably woven together in a pattern of rejection and discrimination by an economic and political system created and managed by an overwhelming white majority.

Toward the end of the decade it also became apparent that there was a link between domestic poverty and racial discrimination and the massive commitment of men and money in Vienam. Never before, perhaps, in American society, did a domestic problem seem to be so highly related to a foreign policy. The fact that the social and economic system resulted in a disproportion of Negroes serving in the armed forces and in Vietnam according to their numbers in the population heightened the sensitivity to the link between civil rights and Vietnam.

A final characteristic of the decade of the sixties is the impact the domestic problem of civil rights and the foreign policy of war in Vietnam has had on the younger people of the nation. It was, after all, young men whom the country was asking to go to Vietnam, to make, perhaps, the ultimate sacrifice. But self-interest in avoiding the horrors of war or death was not the only reason for the growing sensitivity of young Americans to the problems of their nation. For one thing, there were far more young people as a proportion of the total population than ever before, a situation which will prevail for some time. Secondly, far more of these young Americans were going to college, to be confronted, often for the first time, with some of the gaps between American ideals and practice. That many of these students were not themselves victims of social or economic injustice did not at all lessen their condemnation of those things they perceived to be wrong.

Qualitatively, the young, as well as other segments of society, were not satisfied with the progress of America. Cities in despair, blight, and chaos, ill-suited to humane living, were seen as perhaps the major social problem. For it was in the cities that the ingredients of race and poverty had combined to create an inhumane environment. Surrounding the cities were white suburbs whose patterns of sameness and boredom were seen as the result of the city's decline as a place to live. The concentration of population in urban centers also sharply raised the problem of recreational opportunities in something other than concrete and asphalt playgrounds. And pervading the entire atmosphere in a very real sense were the choking problems of air and water pollution and transportation strangulation.

Although the more immediate crises of a physical nature occupy attention, there is an even more fundamental problem which Americans must confront in the last third of the twentieth century. The pace of technological growth is such that it is not unlikely that physical labor, as traditionally known, may all but disappear. What many men and women do now, often in tedious repetition, may be done by the computer tomorrow. At some time in the future, the rate at which machines replace men is likely to result in a largely automated economic system. When that point arrives, our entire set of attitudes toward work may need revision. For it is not unlikely that means to keep men, women, and children busy without working will be needed.

The problems of American life bother those who criticize as well as those who do not. There is far more agreement that there are such problems than on the means to solve them. It is at such a juncture that the dialogue assumes a political cast. For the question often becomes, Is this particular problem one which can be solved through political means, that is, through government? And if it can be solved through governmental policy and action, which government or governments? The national government, state governments, or local governments?

The Drag of Tradition It is over such questions that the desire for change, innovation, action, and solution presses against the traditional values of the political system and its policymaking processes. There is much to commend those values and the policymaking process. In combination they have produced a country with great material achievements. The stability of our political institutions is pointed to as remarkable testimony to the wisdom of the Founding Fathers. Has not the American Constitution survived for almost 200 years in a world which has seen, since 1789, a continuous parade of new states and new forms of government, of revolutions and counterrevolutions?

Americans enjoy perhaps a more fully protected set of civil rights and liberties than the people of most, if not all, other nations. The United States is, in short, it is often claimed, the freest country in the world and the model to which the newer nations aspire. To many Americans, fairly well satisfied with the state of economic and social progress, what faults there are often are associated with departures from accepted values and ways of solving problems. Too frequently, they lament, has the nation departed from the ideals and purposes of the Founding Fathers. There undoubtedly are problems but solutions should be sought in conformity with accepted American values and practices.

To many, this means that increasing reliance on government for the solution of problems is misplaced. This is especially so when the national government is sought as the cure for all social and economic problems. If government needs to be involved at all, that government closest to the people—the state or the city or town or county—should be the government given the responsibility. But first, people should not look to government but to their own individual efforts, or their efforts combined with those of other private individuals or companies. Government can be a partner in such ventures, but it should most often be the junior partner, so the argument goes.

To millions of Americans, the world of nostalgia and myth is as much a reality as is the world of the future to others who find needed change constantly floundering against the rocks of tradition. The problem of overcoming resistance to change because of the drag exerted by tradition is, in fact, the most fundamental of all political problems. To carry the burden of criticism and the initiative for change is often onerous. Comfort can perhaps be taken in the words of Senator J. W. Fulbright (D., Ark.):

> To criticize one's country is to do it a service and pay it a compliment. It is a service because it may spur the country to do better than it is doing; it is a compliment because it evidences a belief that the country can do better than it is doing. . . . Criticism, in short, is more than a right; it is an act of patriotism, a higher form of patriotism, I believe, than the familiar rituals of national adulation.[1]

If the course of history is an adequate guide, the problems of American economic and social life will be resolved ultimately through political means. And it is through the same process that our position as a nation, and our relations as people with other people, will find meaning, hopefully in a world with law and without war. The agenda of political problems that confronts the nation is coextensive with the forms and conditions of political participation and the nature of the policymaking process. Throughout the consideration of such an agenda, the basic and pervasive question can be asked: Are eighteenth-century political ideas and practices adequate for, and relevant to, the

---

[1] J. W. Fulbright, *The Arrogance of Power* (New York: Vintage Books, 1967), p. 25.

realities of the twentieth century and of the impending twenty-first century?

It is not simply a case of pitting the old and the new against one another. Much of the practice and some of the ideas of the American political system are, in fact, new and innovative; nor is it simply a case of junking old political institutions in favor of new ones, for the sake of change. It is more a question of freeing that which does exist from the constraints imposed by outmoded ideas born of a different time and formed in response to problems of an earlier day.

A Troubled Agenda Of all political problems, perhaps none is so fundamental as is the role of the citizen-individual in the political system. Is the ideal of eighteenth-century democracy, in reality, an illusory one in a large, complex, industrial nation? Can the citizen participate in a meaningful way in the making of decisions which affect his own life? And if so, how? Or must he be written off as disinterested, uninformed, and apathetic, his participation, if any at all, merely nominal and ritualistic? To some, political apathy is good, for, it is claimed, it contributes to the stability of the political system. But to others, it seems much more important to ask: "Why apathy?" To not ask why is to condemn a substantial number of citizens to the political trash heap. A major problem of American politics is, therefore, how to involve more people in participation in the political system and to involve them in more ways. Simply to increase the rate of voter turnout without raising the level of meaningfulness of the act of voting to the voter himself would be pointless. This most basic of all forms of participation in the political process will acquire meaning when the individual is able to perceive a connection between his action and public policy.

Beyond the individual's lone act of voting, there are those organized forms of participation, principally interest groups and political parties. For some, the interest group serves as a significant conduit through which the connection between action and policy is readily visible. But, for the overwhelming number of citizens, the interest group is either a nonexistent or quite remote means of relating to the political system. Thus, although the interest group is a pervasive and often decisive element in the policymaking process, its potency is out of proportion to the numbers it represents or serves. The great number of members of the political community who are unorganized or cannot be organized are not served at all by the narrow focus of the interest group.

Among the spectrum of interests which are organized, moreover, there is great disparity in resources, access, and influence. The bias of the political system toward economic interest groups places others with broader conceptions of the public interest at a serious disadvantage. Inevitably, some interest groups are more equal than others, and the unorganized or disorganized can find scant comfort in a political process built on the bargaining ability of those who have the wherewithal with which to bargain. Effective regulation of interest groups and lobbying, though badly needed, provides only a partial answer. It does not meet the problem of the nonrepresented.

The means of organized political participation which holds out the most promise is the more inclusive, rather than less exclusive, political party. But, in the current maze of bewilderment which the two American political party systems represent, little can be hoped for. In no other area of the political system has there been such a paucity of creative ideas as that concerning American political parties. At one time the fad was to achieve a greater measure of party responsibility. Yet, how can responsibility be achieved in such a diverse and heterogeneous social grouping as a major American political party? It is not a simple matter to make the parties more homogeneous by bringing about a realignment of the groups composing them.

Neither homogeneity—nor the responsibility which would undoubtedly follow—are conditions brought about by a wave of the hand. Parties of national size and scope are organic, evolutionary growths. That they have grown as badly as they have is just as much because of the accidents of history as that yet unforeseen series of future events which might bring about their transformation. Before there can be structural reforms in party composition or organization, changes in the basic set of political attitudes which have elevated decentralization, independence, and lack of discipline to virtues will be needed. Only when the existing party systems no longer seem suited to the demands for pragmatic political solutions to pressing problems are those attitudes likely to undergo change.

Yet the consequences of the party system gravely infect the policymaking process. Localism and the congressional instinct for self-preservation have combined to make the representatives of the people hardly accountable for the policies they produce. The successful pursuit of services for the constituent frequently is a guarantee of tenure.

Although it may free congressmen of external responsibility, it has made them prisoners of the internal system of rewards and punishments which characterizes the congressional existence. In all of this, party often becomes meaningless, especially to the voter.

It is not only the forms of political participation, however, which need rethinking. The conditions under which participation must take place, if at all, go a long way toward determining its meaningfulness. Effective political participation may well require a somewhat high level of intelligence. But even the person possessed with such intelligence is likely to find the communications messages of politics quite difficult to penetrate. It is, moreover, not merely a matter of lack of intelligence. The techniques of modern communication, in fact, seem more calculated to minimize intellectual qualities.

Few would argue that politics is all intelligence and rationality. If it were, few men would be equipped to participate. By the same token, there is no reason to insist that it is all emotion. Increasingly, however, the techniques of modern communications media stress the emotional appeals to the detriment of reason. Spot television announcements and packaged shows on behalf of candidates are more noted for their entertainment and merchandising value than for their capacity to impart intelligent messages to the electorate. The decided emphasis on imagery also denudes the campaign of the possibility of engendering genuine confrontation.

Arguments over the kind of television programs the American public wants are beside the point. Advertisers may choose to spend millions on television shows that attract large audiences because they are in the business of selling products. Parties and candidates have succumbed to the same technique for selling their products all too easily. The result is for political television to play only one side of the voter's personality and reinforce that side to the exclusion of his ability to comprehend intelligent messages. The use of television as a major factor in all campaigns, and especially the nationwide contest for the presidency, can only increase. But, as one commentator reminds us: "Civil responsibility does not increase in proportion to the quantity of television programming on political subjects; it increases only in proportion to the quality and the pertinence of the presentations." [2]

In a system where campaign commercials are bought in the same manner as are the commercials for detergents and deodorants, it may

[2] Bernard Rubin, *Political Television* (Belmont, Calif.: Wadsworth, 1967), p. 193.

THE BURDEN OF THE FUTURE

be asking too much to look to the networks for responsibility. Public policy of long standing has declared the airwaves to be an aspect of the public domain. Regulation by the Federal Communications Commission confers on the broadcasting industry a status of quasi-monopoly. The ownership of television stations is a business not lacking in substantial financial rewards. To require the networks and stations to dedicate to the public specific segments of prime broadcast time during a presidential campaign is the least the public should expect in return.

Television has been the single most important factor in increasing the costs of political campaigns. The necessity to retain public relations men to package and merchandise a candidate's image has also added to the financial burdens which candidates and parties must shoulder. In the end, only individual citizens can supply the money. But the extent to which the citizen opens his pocketbook for political purposes varies widely. Millions upon millions are never convinced to part with their money to help in campaigns. Comparatively few, therefore, must pick up the enormous expenses of political activity. Even among the few who do, an even smaller group contributes amounts which can only be classed as extraordinary. The gross disparities in the way political costs are distributed among the members of society must inevitably confer an inordinate degree of political power on some. That such power may not always be obvious or measurable hardly detracts from the intuitive understandings of ordinary people that tell them otherwise. The principle of public financing of political campaigns, accompanied by strict and enforceable regulation of such spending, holds out some hope that the influence of money as a major factor conditioning political participation will lessen.

Reforms in the area of money and political campaigns might well be extended to the disclosure of expenditures interest groups make in attempting to influence congressional and administrative policy. The major problem is to overcome the narrow definition of lobbying imposed by the Supreme Court and include within its scope the vast sums spent in developing and manipulating grass-roots opinion. This is where the most insidious impact of interest groups is made and where, in many cases, more money is spent than is on the more apparent forms of direct lobbying. Public relations campaigns, institutional advertising, and a variety of other forms of exerting influence, either for specific legislation or for government contracts, are hidden costs which the consumer pays in the end. He should have an opportunity to know how much it is costing him and who is spending the money.

Beyond the influence which the techniques of modern communication and money have on political participation, there is the ultimate condition of the quality of the environment in which the expression of political ideas takes place. The efficacy of political participation depends, in the final analysis, on the willingness of people to pursue the meaning of all that is relevant to the political, economic, and social world. A self-governing society depends on men assuming responsibility for their political destinies. But the "responsibilities entailed by freedom can be experienced only when one is free to discover them—when, in fact, one *must* accept them to keep one's balance."[3] By and large, the American people have been unwilling to tolerate the kind of atmosphere—one concededly not without risks—where discourse seeking to discover the meaning of political responsibility can flourish. Too quickly are majorities prone to suppress—through the power of government—the expression of the politically unconventional. Dissent from the values of tradition so dearly held by the majority is considered odious. The majority reacts as if such dissidence were a cancer trying to destroy the body politic.

The courts have stood—often alone—in defense of the viability of the principle of free expression. But the defense of this most basic of all freedoms should not be thrust on such vulnerable institutions, possessed neither of the purse nor sword. The reliance of the American people on the courts to guard against their own intolerance of free expression is an abdication of a responsibility which a free people must inevitably shoulder themselves. When an atmosphere of public responsibility is achieved, it will be a mark of the maturity of American society. Until such time, what the courts do on behalf of the freedom of political expression serves as a vital factor in the processes of education which lead to maturity.

Process and Policy   Changes in the quality and conditions of political participation are tied closely to reforms in the policymaking process. Structured as the process is to the maintenance of the status quo, it is here that important breakthroughs must occur before the emergence of a politically mature society can occur. It is with regard to the policymaking process that

---

[3] Henry S. Kariel, *The Promise of Politics* (Englewood Cliffs, N.J.: Prentice-Hall, 1966), p. 62, italics in original.

eighteenth-century political ideas exert the greatest drag. Are the devices of dispersing the powers of government—born of an age of antigovernmental negativism—relevant and adequate to the economic and social exigencies of the last third of the twentieth century?

The nature, powers, and functions of the modern presidency and Congress as major institutions in the policymaking process require continuing evaluation. A persistent attitude of American political culture has been hostility to executive power. Its origin lies, of course, in the visible symbol of George III and the hated policies attributed to him. The first state constitutions reflected the hostility by drastically weakening the office of governors. The Constitutional Convention was not united on the kind of executive the new scheme of government should have. An ambiguous set of decisions left the matter open-ended. From that uncertain beginning a political office possessing a quantum of power greater than that even of dictators has developed simply because presidential power is made legitimate through the process of election.

Throughout American history, fears of executive power—of a too strong president—have been constantly voiced. And as the twentieth century unfolds and modern presidents have become seemingly more powerful, the cries of anguish increase. Yet, paradoxically, the American people have come to depend on the president as the cure for all the host of ailments that afflict the nation—and the world. Out of a beginning of hostility, the American executive now serves as a psychologically comforting father figure.

The impression of vast presidential power, however, can easily obscure the other aspect of the problem of power. Although the modern American president is, indeed, a powerful political figure, he is also a weak one. Although master of the executive branch, and in some sense of the entire political process, he is also a prisoner of those same institutions. As with any executive, the outermost limits of his ability and power are marked by the information he has. The president must rely on others for most of his information. The myriad problems and their technical aspects defy the comprehension of the ordinary mortal, and presidents come from this category.

As much danger lies in the president being too weak as in being too strong. The dispersion of power characteristic of the policymaking process cuts both ways. It divides the strength of informed and critical opposition and thus makes competing institutions more susceptible to domination by the president. At the same time, it enhances the ability of narrow and self-interested opposition to impose its discordant wills on the more nationally oriented instincts of the chief executive. To some extent, the development of the staff apparatus of the Executive Office of the President has provided the leadership and management tools to overcome the centrifugal pressures exerted by the array of competing policy subsystems. But even the best advice given by the closest and most trusted associates can mislead the president into taking actions he later regrets, as in the case of Kennedy and the abortive Bay of Pigs invasion.

It is not likely that the electoral system will produce an American president who will consciously act like a dictator. More often than not, the dictatorial tendencies of the chief executive will become apparent when the nation is in genuine crisis. The men selected for the presidency, however, are unlikely to convert such opportunities into permanent dictatorial rule. Success in the gruelling contest which produces presidents put a premium on conventional personality types committed to essentially the same values as the electorate. Such men are likely to shun the opportunities for prolonging constitutional one-man rule beyond the demands of crisis.

Although it is unlikely, it is decidedly not impossible. A president's awesome powers as commander-in-chief put him in the position of being able to commit the nation to war without its expressing any real choice in the matter. Reliance on public opinion as a deterrent to an overenthusiastic president may be wishful thinking. The president manufactures and manipulates public opinion more so than he is guided by it. In a study of public opinion and the war in Vietnam, the authors suggested in conclusion that there was a circular relation between public opinion and policymaking:

> A leader—be it the President or someone opposed to his policies—adopts a position. He then finds support for that position among the public. . . . He then uses this finding to justify and legitimize his position.[4]

Although such opportunities are open to all political leaders, none can compete on an equal plane with the president.

The president deservedly speaks with a national voice as the country's single elected political leader. He is in a much better position to

---

[4] Sidney Verba et al., "Public Opinion and the War in Vietnam," *American Political Science Review 61* (June 1967): 333.

articulate national concerns, reflecting as he does the diverse elements of the electorate which formed his winning coalition. Yet, there should be no reluctance to demand that the needs of the nation as articulated by the president be subject to critical debate to test the accuracy with which he speaks. There is only one other national political institution that can provide the forum for such debate. Although this may not have been the hope of the framers for Congress, it seems to be the one legitimate role it can now play, given the growth of the president as the major source of policy initiatives.

Americans instinctively regard Congress as a legislative body—one that makes the laws. The fact that people elect their own representatives and senators to Congress reinforces their feeling that this body should make the laws. But, as one observer has reminded us, "Representative assemblies have not always been legislatures. They had their origins in medieval times as courts and as councils. An assembly need not legislate to exist and to be important."[5] It was in the eighteenth century, however, the century of the birth of Congress, that legislatures as lawmaking bodies flowered.

The idea that Congress should continue to write the public policy of the nation persists and dies hard, although in practice it has largely withered away. The alternative to a legislative role as now only weakly played by Congress would be for it to serve as the collective public voice of the nation. Such a role would provide the American political system with something it now quite definitely lacks.

Some would argue that Congress does in fact serve as the vocal representative of the people of the nation. Its bases of representation, its composition, its organization, the dispersion of power, and the autonomy of the committee and subcommittee, however, all seem to belie the belief that this is the case. The difference lies in the distinction between Congress as a public voice and Congress as a series of private congeries of interest representation. It seems that the hundreds of hearings held by congressional subcommittees do little to inform the rest of Congress, much less the nation. High officials of the administration constantly appear—not before Congress—but before one of its subunits. If Congress as an organism is broken up into many diverse, unconnected parts, it is difficult to see how it can function in any uni-

---

[5] Samuel P. Huntington, "Congressional Responses to the Twentieth Century," in David B. Truman ed., *The Congress and America's Future* (Englewood Cliffs, N.J.: Prentice-Hall, 1965), p. 29.

fied way to mirror the many voices of the nation. Although national policy is subject to penetrating scrutiny, it is on a piecemeal basis. The merits of a specific piece of national legislation may be weighed, but usually not in relation to the many other specific proposals which together make up the totality.

What is needed is a more genuine confrontation between Congress as an institution and the presidency as an institution, each with differing perspectives on national policy. What occurs now, however, is confrontation between specialized subunits of Congress and specialized subunits of the bureaucracy. Where the influence of Congress is needed is in the stages of the development of the president's program, not after it has been neatly packaged and the president's imprimatur and prestige has been placed on it. Here is where genuine debate is needed, debate which seldom takes place in Congress at any stage of the legislative process.

To enable Congress to play such a role requires that the deadening grip of the seniority system be broken. It is also essential that Congressmen be turned away from the slavish functions of constituent services. A bureau of constituent services and an Ombudsman system to watch over bureaucratic abuses would be far more effective institutions for the discharge of such functions. Above all, the members of Congress must demonstrate to the American people that congressmen deserve to be trusted. Unwillingness to impose meaningful ethical standards on itself while insisting that others adhere to such standards seriously weakens the ability of Congress to gain the confidence of the nation. The punishment of Adam Clayton Powell and Thomas Dodd during 1967 only shows that on occasion Congress can be moved to disown particularly blatant breaches of ethics. Whether it can adopt enforceable codes which will remove the taint of suspicion that hovers over the rest of its membership is another question.

Procedurally, the devices for obstruction so well built into the legislative system must be broken. If Congress chooses to forsake its largely impotent legislative role, such devices will no longer be functional and can be easily discarded. It is precisely the advantages which the built-in obstacles furnish to wielders of power within the congressional system which make them so highly prized. Congress, however, does not seem even close to recognizing the choice of roles it inevitably must make. When it last had the opportunity, it spoke strongly for the status quo. The Joint Committee on the Organization of Congress, established in 1965, was forbidden to make recommendations for changes in the rules.

There are powerful arguments, made by members of Congress as well as political scientists, that basic reforms in the American political system are not needed. The present policymaking processes are not only consistent with the intention of the framers, but they also have proved successful in keeping the nation abreast of social and economic change and solving its problems. The existing system, moreover, guards against sudden and impulsive decisions brought on by the uninformed demands of the people. The slowness of the processes of policymaking helps to ensure that proposals will be carefully considered and all interests will be consulted. In short, brokerage rule, as it is sometimes called, is democratic because the majority eventually prevails while the rights of the minority are preserved.

The notion that power must be dispersed, of which brokerage rule is a modern variation, in order to guard against arbitrary decisions can work both ways. If it insures against arbitrary decisions by the majority, it also gives the minority power to be arbitrary. It all depends on where the balance is struck between the power of the majority to decide and the power of the minority to obstruct and veto.

It is one thing to carve out certain basic political rights—such as expression—and fundamental personal rights—such as religion and privacy—and guarantee these to all whether in the majority now or later in the minority. It is quite another matter to guarantee to the minority—of whomever it is temporarily composed—the right and power to exercise a veto over the majority. If such is the case, what size must the minority be? If 49 percent have such power, why not 29 percent, or 19 percent, or 9 percent? The essence of a democratic, self-governing society lies not in giving the minority the right to rule, but the right to have their interests fairly and legitimately expressed in the policymaking process.

Weighting the balance in a governmental system of dispersed powers toward the side of minorities places a premium on slow and deliberate adjustments away from the status quo. Innovative change is damned; it is given a negative value. This may have made sense in the world of the eighteenth century when the pace of life and events was of a different character from what it is now. More may be required in the years that lie ahead. In short, a prescription for a mature political order might include the following:

> A competitive party system, decision-making procedures that require alternatives to be weighed and choices to be clearly articulated, institutions that encourage popular participation in politics, [and] associations that invite individuals to test and integrate alternative roles . . .[6]

This may well be called idealism but it is idealism of the future, and of those to whom the future belongs.

Change, moreover, will increasingly be demanded in the coming decade. Younger Americans and Black Americans, though perhaps for different reasons, seem to perceive most acutely the gap between American ideal and practice, or between "capacity and performance."[7] The process of political socialization may have succeeded too well in inculcating the values of democracy and self-government. On the other hand, it may have failed by not convincing the young and the Black that real political life requires not only pragmatic but also often cynical compromises with the ideals. Whatever the reason, it falls to the young, both Black and white, to meet successfully the challenge of American politics, if, indeed, it can be met at all.

---

[6] Kariel, *The Promise of Politics*, p. 86.
[7] Fulbright, *The Arrogance of Power*, p. 27.

Appendix

American Politics: Reading and Research

The amount of written material about American politics is overwhelming. The growth of paperback publishing in the last decade has produced more titles than even the most avid reader can devour. Books, of course, are not the only source of information on the American political system. Newspapers, magazines, scholarly journals, and government publications add to the flood of information. Even a selected bibliography of important contributions in the last twenty years presents students with a difficult problem of making choices.

Perhaps the most sensible place to start is with the footnotes in this book. Each of the books or articles cited provides a great deal more information on the topic under consideration and, in turn, many of these books or articles contain either a bibliography or a discussion of other works of importance relevant to the subject. For the student whose appetite for a particular aspect or issue of American politics has been whetted, further reading will be very much like an adventure where "one thing leads to another."

APPENDIX

It would be of considerable help if there were a single source to which the student could turn for an interpretation of the peculiarities of American character that have shaped and continue to shape the nation's politics. There are, however, as many interpretations as there are writers. Perhaps it is the impossibility of the task: attempting to attribute to an aggregate behavioral characteristics that over time continue to change. Sometimes foreign observers seem to be more successful in this kind of endeavor, although it may be that we credit them with greater insight simply because they are foreign. Be that as it may, Alexis de Tocqueville's *Democracy in America* (1835) and James Bryce's *The American Commonwealth* (1889) remain classics. In more recent times, Dennis W. Brogan's *The American Character* (1944) and *Politics in America* (1954), contain the deftly written insights of an English commentator with a long interest in the mother country's offspring.

Much of the writing about American culture as it bears on politics has been done by sociologists or anthropologists. Among the best studies are *And Keep Your Powder Dry* (1942) by Margaret Mead, who continues to delight students with her fresh ideas; Geoffrey Gorer, *The American People* (1948); Robin M. Williams, Jr., *American Society* (1960);* and Jules Henry, *Culture Against Man* (1963). Historian Henry Steele Commager has perceptively analyzed American thought and character in *The American Mind* (1950). Another historian who has specialized in scholarly as well as readable accounts of American political thinking is Richard Hofstadter, whose most relevant books for the student of politics include *The American Political Tradition* (1948) and *Social Darwinism in American Thought* (1944). Economist John Kenneth Galbraith has influenced recent thinking about the relation of economics and politics in America with *The Affluent Society* (1958) and *The New Industrial State* (1967).

Literature is one of the richest sources of insights into American character and its political implications. A few examples of this neglected field of study for the student interested in politics: Henry Adams, *Democracy* (1879); Jack London, *The Iron Heel* (1905); Edward Bellamy, *Looking Backward* (1887). Henry David Thoreau's *On the Duty of Civil Disobedience* (1848) and *Walden* (1854) suggest some of the bases for current philosophical critiques of American society. It is also

---

* Titles marked with an asterisk are *not* available in paperback. In all cases, the dates of books are the original publication dates.

in fiction and autobiography that one finds the most trenchant examinations of life in the United States from the perspective of Black Americans, for example, Ralph Ellison, *The Invisible Man* (1947); Richard Wright, *Black Boy* (1937) and *Native Son* (1940); and *The Autobiography of Malcolm X* (1964).

For the student who is especially interested in contemporary analyses of his own society and culture, periodical literature is the major source. Such sources may range from *The New York Times Magazine, Harper's, Atlantic Monthly,* and *The National Review,* all of which are weekly or monthly general circulation magazines, to less widely circulated literary and critical journals such as *The American Scholar, The Yale Review, The Antioch Review, Public Interest, Trans-Action,* and many others. In the last several years, *The New York Review of Books,* a biweekly, has emerged as a major source of social analysis and criticism. *The New Yorker,* a weekly, has in recent years also become more devoted to articles dealing with political and social criticism. *The Center Magazine,* published by the Center for the Study of Democratic Institutions, features stimulating and provocative articles, dialogues, and interviews on significant issues touching all aspects of American political, social, and economic life.

Political Participation In the general area of participation in American politics, the late V. O. Key stands as a giant. His work is not only of the highest scholarship but graced with wry understatement. *Politics, Parties and Pressure Groups* (5th ed., 1964) * remains a standard text in its field. *Public Opinion and American Democracy* (1961) * is a searching and perceptive examination of this vital factor in the political process. Published after his death (with the assistance of Milton Cummings, Jr.), Key's *The Responsible Electorate* (1966) is a sympathetic analysis of the voter that suggests that he behaves with more rationality than other analyses have implied.

Although now a decade old, the volume by Angus Campbell, Paul Converse, Warren Miller, and Donald Stokes, *The American Voter* (1960) is the most exhaustive presentation of the socioeconomic characteristics of the electorate. Two books by Robert Lane, *Political Life* (1959) and *Political Ideology* (1962), are useful examinations into why people are politically motivated and the ways in which their attitudes are formed. Herbert Hyman's *Political Socialization* (1959) summarizes much of the work in this field, as Richard E. Dawson and Kenneth Prewitt do in *Political Socialization* (1969). A recent study of changes in political thought is Everett Carll Ladd, Jr., *Ideology in America* (1969).* The broad notion of political participation is thoughtfully analyzed in E. E. Schattschneider's *The Semi-Sovereign People* (1960). Although written two decades ago, David B. Truman's *The Governmental Process* (1951)* can still be read with profit for a perceptive and analytical treatment of the role of interest groups. More recent studies in this area include Harmon Ziegler, *Interest Groups in American Society* (1964)* and Abraham Holtzman, *Interest Groups and Lobbying* (1966).

Many books have been written about American political parties with both an historical as well as contemporary focus. Wilfred E. Binkley's *American Political Parties: Their Natural History* (4th ed., 1962),* is perhaps the most readable historical treatment. In *Political Parties in the American System* (1964), Frank J. Sorauf deals concisely with the party system; his *Party Politics in America* (1968)* is a more extensive analysis. For a comparative perspective on political parties, see Leon D. Epstein, *Political Parties in Western Democracies* (1967).

Karl A. Lamb and Paul A. Smith in *Campaign Decision-Making: The Presidential Election of 1964* (1968) have accomplished a useful analysis of that campaign. Journalist Theodore H. White, with a flair for dramatic but generally accurate reporting and analysis, has established himself as the modern chronicler of the parties' fortunes in the last three presidential elections: *The Making of the President, 1960* (1961), *The Making of the President, 1964* (1965), and *The Making of the President, 1968* (1969).*

In addition to the magazines and journals earlier noted, there are several professional journals devoted to the publication of articles dealing with research findings in the area of political participation. There are, of course, the major journals published primarily by and for political scientists: *The American Political Science Review, The Journal of Politics, Midwest Journal of Politics, The Western Political Science Quarterly, Political Science Quarterly, Polity,* and *The Review of Politics.* Other journals which are more directly concerned with studies in voting behavior, public opinion, and political socialization are *Public Opinion Quarterly, American Behavioral Scientist, American Sociological Review, The American Journal of Sociology,* and *Social Forces.*

The Political Process: Conditioning Factors

Many of the magazines and journals already noted often have articles dealing with the communications media, *Public Opinion Quarterly* perhaps more frequently than others. Books which deal with public opinion normally have sections or chapters devoted to various aspects of communications and its social and political impact. The manipulation of opinion to achieve political objectives is well covered in Stanley Kelley, Jr., *Professional Public Relations and Political Power* (1956). The same author discusses the impact of media on the political process in *Political Campaigning* (1960).* A more specific focus on the role of television is contained in Bernard Rubin, *Political Television* (1967). The role of the press has been explored by Douglass Cater, *The Fourth Branch of Government* (1959), Dan Nimmo, *Newsgathering in Washington* (1962),* and James Reston, *The Artillery of the Press* (1967). The *Columbia Journalism Review* contains timely articles dealing with the problems of the press and politics.

No other book has had such an impact on thinking in the area of communication than Marshal McLuhan's *Understanding Media* (1964). The subject is explored in a variety of ways in Bernard Berelson and Morris Janowitz, eds., *Reader in Public Opinion and Communication* (2d ed., 1966).* Another useful analysis is Richard R. Fagan, *Politics and Communication* (1966).

The publications of the Citizens' Research Foundation in Princeton, New Jersey, continue to provide the most comprehensive collection of data and analysis on spending in political campaigns. Recent presidential election years are covered in Herbert Alexander's *Financing the 1960 Election* (1962), *Financing the 1964 Election* (1966), and *Financing the 1968 Election* (forthcoming). In addition, the Foundation supports the publication of numerous monographs covering specific campaigns or elections at all levels. The broad issue of financing campaigns is covered comprehensively in *The Costs of Democracy* (1960), by Alexander Heard, and in a somewhat more abbreviated form by Jasper Shannon, *Money and Politics* (1959). Philip M. Stern in *The Great Treasury Raid* (1962)* was one of the first to point out some of the glaring inequities in the tax structure, which by the late sixties had become a major political issue.

The problem of freedom of political expression is a subject of historic concern. More than three centuries ago, John Milton gave one of the great formulations of the principle in *Areopagitica* (1644). Two centuries later, another Englishman, John Stuart Mill, again reaffirmed the

APPENDIX

vitality of the concept in his essay *On Liberty* (1859). Zechariah Chafee, Jr. in *Free Speech in the United States* (1941)* carefully analyzes the problem in the period during and after World War I. The stoutest and most articulate defender of the principle in the United States has been Alexander Meiklejohn: *Free Speech* (1948),* later expanded into *Political Freedom* (1960). Martin Shapiro succinctly examines the role of the courts in protecting freedom of expression in *Freedom of Speech: The Supreme Court and Judicial Review* (1966) and Thomas I. Emerson in *Toward a General Theory of the First Amendment* (1967) develops a legal rationale for freedom of expression.

The Policymaking Process Central to the notion of the policymaking process is an understanding of systems theory. Significant contributions toward the development of systems theory for use in political analysis have been made by David Easton in *The Political System* (1953)* and *A Framework for Political Analysis* (1965).* See also Gabriel A. Almond and G. Bingham Powell, Jr., *Comparative Politics: A Developmental Approach* (1966).

An explicit policymaking approach was developed to study local politics in Robert E. Agger, Daniel Goldrich, and Bert E. Swanson, *The Rulers and the Ruled* (1964).* A corollary concept, the policymaking subsystem, is developed by J. Lieper Freeman in *The Political Process: Executive Bureau-Legislative Committee Relations* (rev. ed., 1965).

Applications of the systems and policymaking process approaches can be found in the following representative sampling of works, many of them studies of the making of specific policies: Stephen K. Bailey, *Congress Makes a Law* (1950) [Employment Act of 1946]; Daniel M. Berman, *A Bill Becomes a Law* (2nd ed., 1966) [Civil Rights Acts of 1960 and 1964]; Aaron Wildavsky, *The Politics of the Budgetary Process* (1964); William W. Boyer, *Bureaucracy on Trial* (1964); A. Lee Fritschler, *Smoking and Politics* (1969); Raymond A. Bauer, Ithiel de Sola Pool, and Lewis Anthony Dexter, *American Business and Public Policy: The Politics of Foreign Trade* (1963);* and Daniel M. Berman, *It Is So Ordered: The Supreme Court Rules on School Segregation* (1966). Douglass Cater, a journalist, who later became a White House advisor, has provided a perceptive and highly readable account of the policymaking process in *Power in Washington* (1964).

The role of the president in the policymaking process has been best described in recent years by two White House advisors to President Kennedy, Richard W. Neustadt, *Presidential Power* (1960) and Theodore C. Sorensen, *Decision-Making in the White House* (1963). A monumental historical, legal, and constitutional description of the presidency is Edward S. Corwin's, *The President: Office and Powers* (4th ed., 1957), which contains almost as much footnote material as text. Also historical, but very readable, is Wilfred E. Binkley's *The President and Congress* (1962), an account of the evolving relations between these institutions. The capacity of the president to develop support in the public is analyzed in Elmer E. Cornwell, Jr., *Presidential Leadership of Public Opinion* (1965).* The ambiguous role of the cabinet and its relation to the President, especially since Wilson, is the subject of Richard F. Fenno, Jr., in *The President's Cabinet* (1959).

Congress, both as an institution and as a participant in the policymaking process, has been the subject of voluminous literature. Three quite different viewpoints and approaches are represented in George B. Galloway, *The Legislative Process in Congress* (1953); Daniel M. Berman, *In Congress Assembled* (1964);* and (also including data on state legislatures) Malcolm E. Jewell and Samuel C. Patterson, *The Legislative Process in the United States* (1966).* Other useful analyses of Congress are: Lewis A. Froman, Jr., *The Congressional Process* (1967); James A. Robinson, *Congress and Foreign Policy-Making* (1967); Norman C. Thomas and Karl A. Lamb, *Congress: Politics and Practice* (1964); and Bertram M. Gross, *The Legislative Struggle* (1953). A collection of perceptive essays can be found in David B. Truman, ed., *The Congress and America's Future* (1965). A useful compendium of different facets of the policymaking process in Congress is John Bibby and Roger Davidson, *On Capitol Hill* (1967).

The difficulties inherent in treating Congress as a coherent entity are suggested by the many excellent studies dealing with either one of the houses separately or with a particular committee. Considerable insight into congressional behavior can be gained by a reading of Charles L. Clapp, *The Congressman: His Work As He Sees It* (1964) and Donald R. Matthews, *U.S. Senators and Their World* (1962). A delightful excursion into the conflicts confronting a representative is presented in a collection of letters of the late Clem Miller, in John W. Baker, ed., *Member of the House* (1962). The most systematic and informed study of committees is Richard F. Fenno, Jr., *The Power of the Purse: Appropriations Politics in Congress* (1966).* Also instructive is James A. Robinson, *The House Rules Committee* (1963).

APPENDIX

The need for Congressional reform has been the subject of books by members of Congress; among them are former Senator Joseph S. Clark's, *Congress: The Sapless Branch* (1964) and Representative Richard Bolling's, *House Out of Order* (1965). The same subject is dealt with in Roger Davidson, David M. Kovenock, and Michael K. O'Leary, *Congress in Crisis: Politics and Congressional Reform* (1966).

In recent years, books dealing with the bureaucracy have laid less stress on management theory and practice and placed more emphasis upon the social organization and political behavior of bureaucracy. Representative and readable examples are Peter Woll, *American Bureaucracy* (1963) and Charles E. Jacob, *Policy and Bureaucracy* (1966). Crucial to an understanding of bureaucratic behavior are Peter M. Blau, *Bureaucracy in Modern Society* (1956); also significant is Michael Crozier, *The Bureaucratic Phenomena* (1964). A sophisticated theoretical treatment with an extensive bibliography is Anthony Downs, *Inside Bureaucracy* (1967).

Most of the writing dealing with the role of the courts in the policy-making process has focused on the Supreme Court and on constitutional law. The single most useful treatment of the evolution of constitutional policies and the role of the Supreme Court is Alfred H. Kelly and Winfred A. Harbison, *The American Constitution* (3rd. ed., 1963).* There are any number of case books in constitutional law; one by William B. Lockhart, Yale Kamisar, and Jesse H. Choper, *The American Constitution: Cases and Materials* (2nd. ed., 1967)* deals topically with the subject matter and contains copious notes and comments. Robert G. McCloskey's, *The American Supreme Court* (1960) is a succinct and well-written history of the Court. A persuasive and informed defense of the Court's power of judicial review is developed in Charles L. Black, Jr., *The People and the Court* (1960).

More useful in understanding law as policy and the role of courts in making it are Victor G. Rosenblum, *Law as a Political Instrument* (1955) and Jack W. Peltason, *Federal Courts in the Political Process* (1955); the latter dealing to some extent with lower courts. A brief but useful analysis of the relation of courts to the political process is Henry J. Schmandt, *Courts in the American Political System* (1968). Herbert Jacob also deals broadly with courts and the judicial process in *Justice in America* (1965). Courts as policymakers is the subject of Glendon Schubert, *Judicial Policy-Making* (1965).

Recent treatments of the Supreme Court have stressed its role in civil rights and liberties. A fairly comprehensive collection of cases may be found in M. Glenn Abernathy, *Civil Liberties Under the Constitution* (1968). Other analyses of the Court's role in developing individual rights are George W. Spicer, *The Supreme Court and Fundamental Freedoms* (1967) and Arthur A. North, S. J., *The Supreme Court* (1966). An important book that focuses on other areas of policy in which the Court is involved is Martin Shapiro, *Law and Politics in the Supreme Court* (1964).*

There are few Supreme Court justices about whom biographies have not been written. Two of the more significant works that go beyond more conventional biography are Alpheus T. Mason, *Harlan Fiske Stone* (1956)* and J. Woodford Howard, Jr., *Mr. Justice Murphy* (1968).* Allison Dunham and Philip B. Kurland have edited *Mr. Justice* (1964), a collection of twelve essays dealing with various members of the Court from Marshall to Wiley Rutledge. Although not biography, Walter F. Murphy's *Elements of Judicial Strategy* (1964),* develops a theory of how justices can maximize their policy influence on the Court based on a study of the private papers of several justices, among them Charles Evans Hughes, Harlan F. Stone, and William Howard Taft. David Danielski has written an excellent study of the politics of the appointment of a single justice, Pierce Butler, in *A Supreme Court Justice is Appointed* (1964). A collective portrait of the justices, analyzing their socioeconomic backgrounds, is presented in John R. Schmidhauser, *The Supreme Court: Its Politics, Personalities and Procedures* (1960).

Decisions of the Supreme Court are published by the Government Printing Office as *United States Reports* (abbreviated in case citations to U.S.). Two private companies also publish Supreme Court decisions: *The Lawyers' Edition* (L. Ed., now L. Ed. 2d, denoting second series) and the *Supreme Court Reporter* (S. Ct.). One of these sets of reports is usually found in most college libraries but the same is not generally true of lower court decisions. United States courts of appeals' decisions may be found in the *Federal Reporter* (Fed., now F. 2d, to denote second series) and district court cases in *Federal Supplement* (F. Supp.), both published by the West Publishing Co.

Constitutional Theory and Political Reality

Reading about the origins of the American political system can often be as entertaining as it is confusing. Historians have a tendency constantly to reinterpret American history and fashions in historiography change as do approaches in political science. The historian who did more to arouse interest in the motivation behind the framing of the Constitution than perhaps anyone else was Charles A. Beard. His *An Economic Interpretation of the Constitution of the United States* (1913) remains as controversial as when first published. More recent studies have found much to criticize in Beard, for example, Robert E. Brown, *Charles Beard and the Constitution* (1953). Forrest McDonald has considerably added to the knowledge of the period in two books, *We the People: The Economic Origins of the Constitution* (1958) and *E Pluribus Unum: The Formation of the American Republic 1776–1790* (1965) [in paperback version titled: *The Formation of the American Republic 1776–1790*]. Although Beard may have overstated his case on the basis of less than complete evidence, that there were economic motivations, admittedly complex, seems now well established. Other historians of the Revolution and Constitution period whose writings are helpful include Merrill Jensen, *The New Nation* (1950) and John C. Miller, *The Federalist Era* (1960).

The most frequently relied-on document to support notions of what the framers of the Constitution intended is the collection of essays in its defense written by John Jay, Alexander Hamilton, and James Madison, *The Federalist* (1788). Madison, who wrote most of the papers, is also the prime source of information on what occurred during the Constitutional Convention. His notes are the most extensive, and along with those of others, are collected in Max Farrand, *The Records of the Federal Convention of 1787* (4 vols., 1911). So much has been attributed to the *Federalist* papers as representing the prevailing opinion on what the Constitution meant at the time of the ratification, that it is useful to read Jackson T. Main's *The Anti-Federalists* (1961) for a view of what equally well-meaning men of the time thought.

Federalism, as it always has been, is a subject of interest that continues to fascinate and frustrate students of American politics. An excellent collection of essays appears in Robert A. Goldwin, ed., *A Nation of States* (1961). Daniel J. Elazar has made a substantial contribution toward putting the endless controversies about federalism in a better perspective in two volumes: *The American Partnership* (1962)* and *American Federalism: A View from the States* (1966). A useful essay exploring the theoretical dimensions of the concept of federalism is William H. Riker, *Federalism: Origin, Operation, Significance* (1964). Morton Grodzins did some of the most original thinking in the area of federalism. Many of his essays are collected in Daniel H. Elazar, *The

American System: A New View of Government in the United States (1966).* The Grodzins-Elazar interpretation of the evolution of intergovernmental relations has been disputed by Harry N. Scheiber, *The Condition of American Federalism: An Historian's View* (1966), a study prepared for the Senate Subcommittee on Intergovernmental Relations.

The nature and vitality of the American political system has been the concern of practically all the writers whose books have been mentioned. The prevailing tendency of political scientists has been to find, and approve of, pluralist democracy as the basic characteristic of American politics. Foremost among these writers has been Robert Dahl. His study of local politics, *Who Governs?* (1961) suggested a number of basic propositions about the strength of the American system, which were later elaborated on in *Pluralist Democracy in the United States: Conflict and Consent* (1967).* A growing body of writing disputes some of the normative judgments underlying the conception of pluralist democracy and argues for a strengthening of the participatory bases for democracy. Two brief but persuasive statements are Peter Bachrach, *The Theory of Democratic Elitism: A Critique* (1967) and Henry S. Kariel, *The Promise of Politics* (1966). From quite another point of view the basic character of American politics is criticized in Theodore Lowi, *The End of Liberalism* (1969). Perhaps the most vexing of all American political problems is succinctly and forcefully analyzed in Stokely Carmichael and Charles Hamilton, *Black Power: The Politics of Liberation in America* (1967). A valuable and varied collection of essays is contained in Floyd B. Barbour, ed., *The Black Power Revolt* (1968). The mood of the current generation of young Americans is the subject of Kenneth Kenniston's, *Young Radicals* (1968). Critical views of American politics and society are represented in Priscilla Long, ed., *The New Left: A Collection of Essays* (1969).

American Politics: Research Whether he wants to do a term paper or research project on an historical or contemporary topic, the student of American politics will have little difficulty in securing information. Contemporary problems and political issues generate a host of written material from a variety of sources.

Newspapers are the single most important source of information on the day-to-day development of an issue. Unfortunately, there are too few newspapers that do an adequate job of detailed and interpretative reporting. *The New York Times* is without peer in this regard. Its news reports are not only usually accurate and well-informed, but it frequently prints the text of major speeches, significant court decisions, and other official documents. Its Sunday *Magazine* frequently contains valuable articles on political issues and affairs; and its Sunday section *The Week in Review* is a well-written summary of events stressing interpretation. Use of the *Times* is facilitated by its massive *Index* and many libraries keep back issues on microfilm. *The Washington Post* and *The (Washington) Evening Star,* morning and evening competitors, do a thorough, accurate, and informative job of reporting. Other newspapers highly regarded for their reporting of national news are *The Milwaukee Journal, The St. Louis Post-Dispatch,* and *The Los Angeles Times.* The *Christian Science Monitor* has earned a deserved reputation for intelligent coverage of Washington events and *The Wall Street Journal* frequently contains some of the most original and perceptive pieces of reporting of national political events. A Sunday edition, *The National Observer,* is a useful summary and interpretation of the week's news.

The weekly newsmagazine is a convenient, though less thorough way, of keeping abreast of political developments. *Newsweek,* owned by the same corporation that controls *The Washington Post,* now challenges *Time,* long the dominant publication of this kind. Both stress interpretative reporting and analysis and need to be supplemented by other sources. *U.S. News and World Report,* another newsweekly, emphasizes business and economic issues and publishes original interview material with leading political figures. *Time* and *Newsweek* represent a moderate-to-liberal viewpoint; *U.S. News* has a more conservative bias. Also representing the conservative viewpoint is *The National Review,* more a journal of opinion than a newsweekly, as are *The New Republic,* and *The Nation,* both with a liberal orientation. The *Saturday Review,* also a weekly, emphasizes cultural affairs, but often contains excellent articles on political issues. *Washington Monthly,* a fairly recent entry into the opinion journal field, features lengthy think pieces by some of the nation's best known reporters and commentators. *Science* and *Scientific American,* although appealing primarily to a specialized audience occasionally have pertinent articles on scientific or technological issues that have political implications.

Many of the scholarly journals have been noted previously. Law reviews, publications of the nation's law schools, are a fertile source of information on a variety of political problems and issues. There are more than one hundred law journals being published, and among the more prestigious are *The Harvard Law Review, The Yale Law Journal,* and *The Columbia Law Review,* which frequently contain exhaustive analyses of significant public issues. Much of the writing and commentary on reapportionment, for example, appeared in the law reviews. *Law and Contemporary Problems,* as its name implies, focuses each issue on some public controversy and the *Journal of Public Law* emphasizes public policy discussions. The *Index to Legal Periodicals* provides the same kind of access to the articles published in law reviews, as does the *Readers' Guide to Periodical Literature* for the more general circulation magazines. The professional and scholarly journals in political science, sociology, economics, and other fields are indexed in the *International Index,* and the *Business Periodicals Index* covers the vast number of magazines put out by trade associations and business organizations. Also useful for research purposes is the *Public Affairs Information Service Bulletin.* An indexing service begun only in 1969 that should prove to be a valuable research tool is a publication called *ABC POL SCI.* Issued eight times a year, it is intended to serve as a current guide to periodical literature in political science by reproducing the table of contents of some two hundred and sixty journals and law reviews concurrently or in advance of their publication.

Most of the sources for information that have been discussed are secondary in nature; that is, they report on or analyze some subject of public policy concern. A vast amount of primary materials is available from the world's largest source of information, the United States government and its publisher, the Government Printing Office. Many college and university libraries are designated as depositories for government documents and routinely receive practically every congressional and administrative document, such as the *Congressional Record,* congressional committee hearings and reports, the *Federal Register,* and agency reports ranging from census data to agricultural marketing information. Other libraries usually maintain an adequate collection of important government documents. Perhaps the easiest way to obtain needed information on a specific term project is to write the congressional committee or agency involved for the appropriate hearings, reports, and staff studies. A student's congressman or senator should not be overlooked as a source of information or to facilitate obtaining documents from committees or agencies; such service has become an accepted part of the burden of constituent service provided by congressional offices. The *Congressional Directory*, issued each year by Congress, contains much useful information including short (and laudable) biographies of the members, committee and subcommittee memberships, and considerable statistical information on past elections. Also published annually is the *Government Organization Manual*, a comprehensive guide to the organization of the departments, agencies, and miscellaneous boards and commissions that make up the bureaucracy.

For library work, the office of the Superintendent of Documents, which handles distribution for G.P.O., issues a *Monthly Catalog* to facilitate finding needed publications. The Superintendent also issues free price lists in more than forty subject fields such as "Political Science," "Education," "Foreign Relations of the United States," and "American History." These can be obtained by writing to: The Superintendent of Documents, Government Printing Office, Washington, D.C. 20402.

For more than twenty years, *Congressional Quarterly* has served as a standard reference work for research into governmental and political affairs. The *Congressional Quarterly: Weekly Report* is a thorough review of events focusing mainly on Congress but with adequate attention to the activities of interest groups, the political parties, the presidency and the bureaucracy, and the courts. The *Congressional Quarterly Almanac,* published annually, is a comprehensive review of the year's political events. In 1965, CQ published *Congress and the Nation, 1945–1964,* a massive (2,000 page) compendium of political information. A new publication, *The National Journal,* brought into being by several former editors of CQ, who organized the Center for Political Research, is intended to provide more extensive coverage of the policymaking process in the administrative and regulatory agencies. Information on such activities has always been more difficult to obtain than has been the case with congressional activity, and *The National Journal* should serve as a useful complement to CQ. Congressional Quarterly, Inc. now distributes the series of election statistics compiled under the direction of Richard M. Scammon, Director of the Elections Research Center of the Governmental Affairs Institute. Under the title of *America Votes,* this series provides statistical data on elective offices from president to state governors. The latest volume, *America Votes 8,* covers the 1968 election.

Interest groups are often an overlooked source of information on political issues and policymaking controversies. Such groups are usually more than happy to provide their point of view to the general public in the form of policy statements and studies. The names and addresses of interest groups can be located in the *Encyclopedia of Associations.* A less comprehensive listing may be found under the heading of "Associations" in the Yellow Pages directory for Washington, D.C.

The Constitution of the United States of America

We the People of the United States, in Order to form a more perfect Union, establish Justice, insure domestic Tranquility, provide for the common defence, promote the general Welfare, and secure the Blessings of Liberty to ourselves and our Posterity, do ordain and establish this Constitution for the United States of America.

ARTICLE I.

SECTION 1. All legislative Powers herein granted shall be vested in a Congress of the United States, which shall consist of a Senate and House of Representatives.

[NOTE: Items which have since been amended or superseded, as identified in the footnotes, are bracketed.]

SECTION 2. The House of Representatives shall be composed of Members chosen every second Year by the People of the several States, and the Electors in each State shall have the Qualifications requisite for Electors of the most numerous Branch of the State Legislature.

No Person shall be a Representative who shall not have attained to the Age of twenty-five Years, and been seven Years a Citizen of the United States, and who shall not, when elected, be an Inhabitant of that State in which he shall be chosen.

[Representatives and direct Taxes shall be apportioned among the several States which may be included within this Union, according to their respective Numbers, which shall be determined by adding to the whole Number of free Persons, including those bound to Service for a Term of Years, and excluding Indians not taxed, three fifths of all other Persons.]* The actual Enumeration shall be made within three Years after the first Meeting of the Congress of the United States, and within every subsequent Term of ten Years, in such Manner as they shall by Law direct. The Number of Representatives shall not exceed one for every thirty Thousand,** but each State shall have at Least one Representative; and until such enumeration shall be made, the State of New Hampshire shall be entitled to chuse three, Massachusetts eight, Rhode-Island and Providence Plantations one, Connecticut five, New-York six, New Jersey four, Pennsylvania eight, Delaware one, Maryland six, Virginia ten, North Carolina five, South Carolina five, and Georgia three.

When vacancies happen in the Representation from any State, the Executive Authority thereof shall issue Writs of Election to fill such Vacancies.

The House of Representatives shall chuse their Speaker and other Officers; and shall have the sole Power of Impeachment.

SECTION 3. The Senate of the United States shall be composed of two Senators from each State, [chosen by the Legislature thereof,]*** for six Years; and each Senator shall have one Vote.

Immediately after they shall be assembled in Consequence of the first Election, they shall be divided as equally as may be into three Classes. The Seats of the Senators of the first Class shall be vacated at the Expiration of the second Year, of the second Class at the Expiration of the fourth Year, and of the third Class at the Expiration of the sixth Year, so that one-third may be chosen every second Year; [and if Vacancies happen by Resignation, or otherwise, during the Recess of the Legislature of any State, the Executive thereof may make temporary Appointments until

---

*Changed by section 2 of the fourteenth amendment.
**Ratio in 1965 was one to over 410,000.
***Changed by section 1 of the seventeenth amendment.

the next Meeting of the Legislature, which shall then fill such Vacancies.]*

No Person shall be a Senator who shall not have attained to the Age of thirty Years, and been nine Years a Citizen of the United States, and who shall not, when elected, be an Inhabitant of that State for which he shall be chosen.

The Vice President of the United States shall be President of the Senate, but shall have no Vote, unless they be equally divided.

The Senate shall chuse their other Officers, and also a President pro tempore, in the absence of the Vice President, or when he shall exercise the Office of President of the United States.

The Senate shall have the sole Power to try all Impeachments. When sitting for that Purpose, they shall be on Oath' or Affirmation. When the President of the United States is tried, the Chief Justice shall preside: And no Person shall be convicted without the Concurrence of two thirds of the Members present.

Judgment in Cases of Impeachment shall not extend further than to removal from Office, and disqualification to hold and enjoy any Office of honor, Trust or Profit under the United States: but the Party convicted shall nevertheless be liable and subject to Indictment, Trial, Judgment and Punishment, according to Law.

SECTION 4. The Times, Places and Manner of holding Elections for Senators and Representatives, shall be prescribed in each State by the Legislature thereof; but the Congress may at any time by Law make or alter such Regulations, except as to the Place of Chusing Senators.

The Congress shall assemble at least once in every Year, and such Meeting shall [be on the first Monday in December,]**unless they shall by Law appoint a different Day.

SECTION 5. Each House shall be the Judge of the Elections, Returns and Qualifications of its own Members, and a Majority of each shall constitute a Quorum to do Business; but a smaller number may adjourn from day to day, and may be authorized to compel the Attendance of absent Members, in such Manner, and under such Penalties as each House may provide.

Each House may determine the Rules of its Proceedings, punish its Members for disorderly Behavior, and, with the Concurrence of two thirds, expel a Member.

Each House shall keep a Journal of its Proceedings, and from time to time publish the same, excepting such Parts as may in their Judgment require Secrecy; and the Yeas and Nays of the Members of either House on any question shall, at the Desire of one fifth of those Present, be entered on the Journal.

Neither House, during the Session of Congress, shall, without the Consent of the other, adjourn for more than

---

*Changed by clause 2 of the seventeenth amendment.
**Changed by section 2 of the twentieth amendment.

APPENDIX

three days, nor to any other Place than that in which the two Houses shall be sitting.

SECTION 6. The Senators and Representatives shall receive a Compensation for their Services, to be ascertained by Law, and paid out of the Treasury of the United States. They shall in all Cases, except Treason, Felony and Breach of the Peace, be privileged from Arrest during their Attendance at the Session of their respective Houses, and in going to and returning from the same; and for any Speech or Debate in either House, they shall not be questioned in any other Place.

No Senator or Representative shall, during the Time for which he was elected, be appointed to any civil Office under the Authority of the United States, which shall have been created, or the Emoluments whereof shall have been encreased during such time; and no Person holding any Office under the United States, shall be a Member of either House during his Continuance in Office.

SECTION 7. All Bills for raising Revenue shall originate in the House of Representatives; but the Senate may propose or concur with Amendments as on other Bills.

Every Bill which shall have passed the House of Representatives and the Senate, shall, before it become a Law, be presented to the President of the United States; If he approve he shall sign it, but if not he shall return it, with his Objections to that House in which it shall have originated, who shall enter the Objections at large on their Journal, and proceed to reconsider it. If after such Reconsideration two thirds of that House shall agree to pass the Bill, it shall be sent, together with the Objections, to the other House, by which it shall likewise be reconsidered, and if approved by two thirds of that House, it shall become a Law. But in all such Cases the Votes of both Houses shall be determined by Yeas and Nays, and the Names of the Persons voting for and against the Bill shall be entered on the Journal of each House respectively. If any Bill shall not be returned by the President within ten Days (Sundays excepted) after it shall have been presented to him, the Same shall be a Law, in like Manner as if he had signed it, unless the Congress by their Adjournment prevent its Return, in which Case it shall not be a Law.

Every Order, Resolution, or Vote to which the Concurrence of the Senate and House of Representatives may be necessary (except on a question of Adjournment) shall be presented to the President of the United States; and before the Same shall take Effect, shall be approved by him, or being disapproved by him, shall be repassed by two thirds of the Senate and House of Representatives, according to the Rules and Limitations prescribed in the Case of a Bill.

SECTION 8. The Congress shall have Power To lay and collect Taxes, Duties, Imposts and Excises, to pay the Debts and provide for the common Defence and general Welfare of the United States; but all Duties, Imposts and Excises shall be uniform throughout the United States;

To borrow money on the credit of the United States;

To regulate Commerce with foreign Nations, and among the several States, and with the Indian Tribes;

To establish an uniform Rule of Naturalization, and uniform Laws on the subject of Bankruptcies throughout the United States;

To coin Money, regulate the Value thereof, and of foreign Coin, and fix the Standard of Weights and Measures;

To provide for the Punishment of counterfeiting the Securities and current Coin of the United States;

To establish Post Offices and post Roads;

To promote the Progress of Science and useful Arts, by securing for limited Times to Authors and Inventors the exclusive Right to their respective Writings and Discoveries;

To constitute Tribunals inferior to the supreme Court;

To define and punish Piracies and Felonies committed on the high Seas, and Offenses against the Law of Nations;

To declare War, grant Letters of Marque and Reprisal, and make Rules concerning Captures on Land and Water;

To raise and support Armies, but no Appropriation of Money to that Use shall be for a longer Term than two Years;

To provide and maintain a Navy;

To make Rules for the Government and Regulation of the land and naval Forces;

To provide for calling forth the Militia to execute the Laws of the Union, suppress Insurrections and repel Invasions;

To provide for organizing, arming, and disciplining the Militia, and for governing such Part of them as may be employed in the Service of the United States, reserving to the States respectively, the Appointment of the Officers, and the Authority of training the Militia according to the discipline prescribed by Congress;

To exercise exclusive Legislation in all Cases whatsoever, over such District (not exceeding ten Miles square) as may, by Cession of particular States, and the acceptance of Congress, become the Seat of the Government of the United States, and to exercise like Authority over all Places purchased by the Consent of the Legislature of the State in which the Same shall be, for the Erection of Forts, Magazines, Arsenals, dock-Yards, and other needful Buildings;—And

To make all Laws which shall be necessary and proper for carrying into Execution the foregoing Powers, and all other Powers vested by this Constitution in the Government of the United States, or in any Department or Officer thereof.

SECTION 9. The Migration or Importation of such Persons as any of the States now existing shall think proper to admit, shall not be prohibited by the Congress prior to the Year one thousand eight hundred and eight, but a tax or duty may be imposed on such Importation, not exceeding ten dollars for each Person.

The privilege of the Writ of Habeas Corpus shall not be suspended, unless when in Cases of Rebellion or Invasion the public Safety may require it.

No Bill of Attainder or ex post facto Law shall be passed.

No capitation, or other direct, Tax shall be laid, unless in Proportion to the Census or Enumeration herein before directed to be taken.*

No Tax or Duty shall be laid on Articles exported from any State.

No Preference shall be given by any Regulation of Commerce or Revenue to the Ports of one State over those of another: nor shall Vessels bound to, or from, one State, be obliged to enter, clear, or pay Duties in another.

No Money shall be drawn from the Treasury, but in Consequence of Appropriations made by Law; and a regular Statement and Account of the Receipts and Expenditures of all public Money shall be published from time to time.

No Title of Nobility shall be granted by the United States: And no Person holding any Office of Profit or Trust under them, shall, without the Consent of the Congress, accept of any present, Emolument, Office, or Title, of any kind whatever, from any King, Prince, or foreign State.

SECTION 10. No State shall enter into any Treaty, Alliance, or Confederation; grant Letters of Marque and Reprisal; coin Money; emit Bills of Credit; make any Thing but gold and silver Coin a Tender in Payment of Debts; pass any Bill of Attainder, ex post facto Law, or Law impairing the Obligation of Contracts, or grant any Title of Nobility.

No State shall, without the Consent of the Congress, lay any Imposts or Duties on Imports or Exports, except what may be absolutely necessary for executing its inspection Laws: and the net Produce of all Duties and Imposts, laid by any State on Imports or Exports, shall be for the Use of the Treasury of the United States; and all such Laws shall be subject to the Revision and Controul of the Congress.

No State shall, without the Consent of Congress, lay any duty of Tonnage, keep Troops, or Ships of War in time of Peace, enter into any Agreement or Compact with another State, or with a foreign Power, or engage in War, unless actually invaded, or in such imminent Danger as will not admit of delay.

ARTICLE II.

SECTION 1. The executive Power shall be vested in a President of the United States of America. He shall hold his Office during the Term of four Years, and, together with the Vice-President, chosen for the same Term, be elected, as follows.

Each State shall appoint, in such Manner as the Legislature thereof may direct, a Number of Electors, equal to the whole Number of Senators and Representatives to

---

*But see the sixteenth amendment.

THE CONSTITUTION OF THE UNITED STATES OF AMERICA

which the State may be entitled in the Congress: but no Senator or Representative, or Person holding an Office of Trust or Profit under the United States, shall be appointed an Elector.

[The Electors shall meet in their respective States, and vote by Ballot for two persons, of whom one at least shall not be an Inhabitant of the same State with themselves. And they shall make a List of all the Persons voted for, and of the Number of Votes for each; which List they shall sign and certify, and transmit sealed to the Seat of the Government of the United States, directed to the President of the Senate. The President of the Senate shall, in the Presence of the Senate and House of Representatives, open all the Certificates, and the Votes shall then be counted. The Person having the greatest Number of Votes shall be the President, if such Number be a Majority of the whole Number of Electors appointed; and if there be more than one who have such Majority, and have an equal Number of Votes, then the House of Representatives shall immediately chuse by Ballot one of them for President; and if no Person have a Majority, then from the five highest on the List the said House shall in like Manner chuse the President. But in chusing the President, the Votes shall be taken by States, the Representation from each State having one Vote; a quorum for this Purpose shall consist of a Member or Members from two thirds of the States, and a Majority of all the States shall be necessary to a Choice. In every Case, after the Choice of the President, the Person having the greatest Number of Votes of the Electors shall be the Vice President. But if there should remain two or more who have equal Votes, the Senate shall chuse from them by Ballot the Vice-President.]*

The Congress may determine the Time of chusing the Electors, and the Day on which they shall give their Votes; which Day shall be the same throughout the United States.

No person except a natural born Citizen, or a Citizen of the United States, at the time of the Adoption of this Constitution, shall be eligible to the Office of President; neither shall any Person be eligible to that Office who shall not have attained to the Age of thirty-five Years, and been fourteen Years a Resident within the United States.

**[In Case of the Removal of the President from Office, or of his Death, Resignation, or Inability to discharge the Powers and Duties of the said Office, the same shall devolve on the Vice President, and the Congress may by Law provide for the Case of Removal, Death, Resignation or Inability, both of the President and Vice President, declaring what Officer shall then act as President, and such Officer shall act accordingly, until the Disability be removed, or a President shall be elected.]

---

*Superseded by the twelfth amendment.
**This clause has been affected by the twenty-fifth amendment.

The President shall, at stated Times, receive for his Services, a Compensation, which shall neither be encreased nor diminished during the Period for which he shall have been elected, and he shall not receive within that Period any other Emolument from the United States, or any of them.

Before he enter on the Execution of his Office, he shall take the following Oath or Affirmation:—"I do solemnly swear (or affirm) that I will faithfully execute the Office of President of the United States, and will to the best of my Ability, preserve, protect and defend the Constitution of the United States."

SECTION 2. The President shall be Commander in Chief of the Army and Navy of the United States, and of the Militia of the several States, when called into the actual Service of the United States; he may require the Opinion in writing, of the principal Officer in each of the executive Departments, upon any subject relating to the Duties of their respective Offices, and he shall have Power to Grant Reprieves and Pardons for Offenses against the United States, except in Cases of Impeachment.

He shall have Power, by and with the Advice and Consent of the Senate, to make Treaties, provided two-thirds of the Senators present concur; and he shall nominate, and by and with the Advice and Consent of the Senate, shall appoint Ambassadors, other public Ministers and Consuls, Judges of the supreme Court, and all other Officers of the United States, whose Appointments are not herein otherwise provided for, and which shall be established by Law: but the Congress may by Law vest the Appointment of such inferior Officers, as they think proper, in the President alone, in the Courts of Law, or in the Heads of Departments.

The President shall have Power to fill up all Vacancies that may happen during the Recess of the Senate, by granting Commissions which shall expire at the End of their next Session.

SECTION 3. He shall from time to time give to the Congress Information of the State of the Union, and recommend to their Consideration such Measures as he shall judge necessary and expedient; he may, on extraordinary Occasions, convene both Houses, or either of them, and in Case of Disagreement between them, with Respect to the Time of Adjournment, he may adjourn them to such Time as he shall think proper; he shall receive Ambassadors and other public Ministers; he shall take Care that the Laws be faithfully executed, and shall Commission all the Officers of the United States.

SECTION 4. The President, Vice President and all civil Officers of the United States, shall be removed from Office on Impeachment for, and Conviction of, Treason, Bribery, or other high Crimes and Misdemeanors.

THE CONSTITUTION OF THE UNITED STATES OF AMERICA

ARTICLE III.

SECTION 1. The judicial Power of the United States, shall be vested in one supreme Court, and in such inferior Courts as the Congress may from time to time ordain and establish. The Judges, both of the supreme and inferior Courts, shall hold their Offices during good Behaviour, and shall, at stated Times, receive for their Services, a Compensation, which shall not be diminished during their Continuance in Office.

SECTION 2. The judicial Power shall extend to all Cases, in Law and Equity, arising under this Constitution, the Laws of the United States, and Treaties made, or which shall be made, under their Authority;—to all Cases affecting Ambassadors, other public Ministers and Consuls;—to all Cases of admiralty and maritime Jurisdiction;—to Controversies to which the United States shall be a Party;—to Controversies between two or more States;—between a State and Citizens of another State;—between Citizens of different States;—between Citizens of the same State claiming Lands under Grants of different States, and between a State, or the Citizens thereof, and foreign States, Citizens or Subjects.

In all Cases affecting Ambassadors, other public Ministers and Consuls, and those in which a State shall be Party, the supreme Court shall have original Jurisdiction. In all the other Cases before mentioned, the supreme Court shall have appellate Jurisdiction, both as to Law and Fact, with such Exceptions, and under such Regulations as the Congress shall make.

The trial of all Crimes, except in Cases of Impeachment, shall be by Jury; and such Trial shall be held in the State where the said Crimes shall have been committed; but when not committed within any State, the Trial shall be at such Place or Places as the Congress may by Law have directed.

SECTION 3. Treason against the United States, shall consist only in levying War against them, or in adhering to their Enemies, giving them Aid and Comfort. No Person shall be convicted of Treason unless on the Testimony of two Witnesses to the same overt Act, or on Confession in open Court.

The Congress shall have Power to declare the Punishment of Treason, but no Attainder of Treason shall work Corruption of Blood, or Forfeiture except during the Life of the Person attainted.

ARTICLE IV.

SECTION 1. Full Faith and Credit shall be given in each State to the public Acts, Records, and judicial Proceedings of every other State. And the Congress may by general

Laws prescribe the Manner in which such Acts, Records and Proceedings shall be proved, and the Effect thereof.

SECTION 2. The Citizens of each State shall be entitled to all Privileges and Immunities of Citizens in the several States.

A Person charged in any State with Treason, Felony, or other Crime, who shall flee from Justice, and be found in another State, shall on demand of the executive Authority of the State from which he fled, be delivered up, to be removed to the State having Jurisdiction of the Crime.

[No Person held to Service or Labour in one State, under the Laws thereof, escaping into another, shall, in Consequence of any Law or Regulation therein, be discharged from such Service or Labour, but shall be delivered up on Claim of the Party to whom such Service or Labour may be due.]*

SECTION 3. New States may be admitted by the Congress into this Union; but no new State shall be formed or erected within the Jurisdiction of any other State; nor any State be formed by the Junction of two or more States, or parts of States, without the Consent of the Legislatures of the States concerned as well as of the Congress.

The Congress shall have Power to dispose of and make all needful Rules and Regulations respecting the Territory or other Property belonging to the United States; and nothing in this Constitution shall be so construed as to Prejudice any Claims of the United States, or of any particular State.

SECTION 4. The United States shall guarantee to every State in this Union a Republican Form of Government, and shall protect each of them against Invasion; and on Application of the Legislature, or of the Executive (when the Legislature cannot be convened) against domestic Violence.

ARTICLE V.

The Congress, whenever two-thirds of both Houses shall deem it necessary, shall propose Amendments to this Constitution, or, on the Application of the Legislatures of two-thirds of the several States, shall call a Convention for proposing Amendments, which, in either Case, shall be valid to all Intents and Purposes, as part of this Constitution, when ratified by the Legislatures of three-fourths of the several States, or by Conventions in three-fourths thereof, as the one or the other Mode of Ratification may be proposed by the Congress: Provided that no Amendment which may be made prior to the Year One thousand eight hundred and eight shall in any Manner affect the first and fourth Clauses in the Ninth Section of the first Article; and that no State, without its Consent, shall be deprived of its equal Suffrage in the Senate.

---

*Superseded by the thirteenth amendment.

THE CONSTITUTION OF THE UNITED STATES OF AMERICA

ARTICLE VI.

All Debts contracted and Engagements entered into, before the Adoption of this Constitution, shall be as valid against the United States under this Constitution, as under the Confederation.

This Constitution, and the Laws of the United States which shall be made in Pursuance thereof; and all Treaties made, or which shall be made, under the Authority of the United States, shall be the supreme Law of the Land; and the Judges in every State shall be bound thereby, any Thing in the Constitution or Laws of any State to the Contrary notwithstanding.

The Senators and Representatives before mentioned, and the Members of the several State Legislatures, and all executive and judicial Officers, both of the United States and of the several States, shall be bound by Oath or Affirmation, to support this Constitution; but no religious Test shall ever be required as a Qualification to any Office or public Trust under the United States.

ARTICLE VII.

The Ratification of the Conventions of nine States shall be sufficient for the Establishment of this Constitution between the States so ratifying the Same.

ARTICLES IN ADDITION TO, AND AMENDMENT OF, THE CONSTITUTION OF THE UNITED STATES OF AMERICA, PROPOSED BY CONGRESS, AND RATIFIED BY THE LEGISLATURES OF THE SEVERAL STATES, PURSUANT TO THE FIFTH ARTICLE OF THE ORIGINAL CONSTITUTION.*

AMENDMENT I. (1791)**

Congress shall make no law respecting an establishment of religion, or prohibiting the free exercise thereof; or abridging the freedom of speech, or of the press; or the right of the people peaceably to assemble, and to petition the Government for a redress of grievances.

AMENDMENT II. (1791)

A well regulated Militia, being necessary to the security of a free State, the right of the people to keep and bear Arms, shall not be infringed.

AMENDMENT III. (1791)

No Soldier shall, in time of peace be quartered in any house, without the consent of the Owner, nor in time of war, but in a manner to be prescribed by law.

---

*Amendment XXI was not ratified by state legislatures, but by state conventions summoned by Congress.
**Date of ratification.

APPENDIX

AMENDMENT IV. (1791)

The right of the people to be secure in their persons, houses, papers, and effects, against unreasonable searches and seizures, shall not be violated, and no Warrants shall issue, but upon probable cause, supported by Oath or affirmation, and particularly describing the place to be searched, and the persons or things to be seized.

AMENDMENT V. (1791)

No person shall be held to answer for a capital, or otherwise infamous crime, unless on a presentment or indictment of a Grand Jury, except in cases arising in the land or naval forces, or in the Militia, when in actual service in time of War or public danger; nor shall any person be subject for the same offence to be twice put in jeopardy of life or limb; nor shall be compelled in any criminal case to be a witness against himself, nor be deprived of life, liberty, or property, without due process of law; nor shall private property be taken for public use, without just compensation.

AMENDMENT VI. (1791)

In all criminal prosecutions, the accused shall enjoy the right to a speedy and public trial, by an impartial jury of the State and district wherein the crime shall have been committed, which district shall have been previously ascertained by law, and to be informed of the nature and cause of the accusation; to be confronted with the witnesses against him; to have compulsory process for obtaining witnesses in his favor, and to have the Assistance of Counsel for his defence.

AMENDMENT VII. (1791)

In suits at common law, where the value in controversy shall exceed twenty dollars, the right of trial by jury shall be preserved, and no fact tried by a jury, shall be otherwise reexamined in any Court of the United States, than according to the rules of the common law.

AMENDMENT VIII. (1791)

Excessive bail shall not be required, nor excessive fines imposed, nor cruel and unusual punishments inflicted.

AMENDMENT IX. (1791)

The enumeration in the Constitution, of certain rights, shall not be construed to deny or disparage others retained by the people.

AMENDMENT X. (1791)

The powers not delegated to the United States by the Constitution, nor prohibited by it to the States, are reserved to the States respectively, or to the people.

THE CONSTITUTION OF THE UNITED STATES OF AMERICA

AMENDMENT XI. (1795)

The Judicial power of the United States shall not be construed to extend to any suit in law or equity, commenced or prosecuted against one of the United States by Citizens of another State, or by Citizens or Subjects of any Foreign State.

AMENDMENT XII. (1804)

The Electors shall meet in their respective states and vote by ballot for President and Vice-President, one of whom, at least, shall not be an inhabitant of the same state with themselves; they shall name in their ballots the person voted for as President, and in distinct ballots the person voted for as Vice-President, and they shall make distinct lists of all persons voted for as President, and of all persons voted for as Vice-President, and of the number of votes for each, which lists they shall sign and certify, and transmit sealed to the seat of the government of the United States, directed to the President of the Senate;—The President of the Senate shall, in presence of the Senate and House of Representatives, open all the certificates and the votes shall then be counted;—The person having the greatest number of votes for President, shall be the President, if such number be a majority of the whole number of Electors appointed; and if no person have such majority, then from the persons having the highest numbers not exceeding three on the list of those voted for as President, the House of Representatives shall choose immediately, by ballot, the President. But in choosing the President, the votes shall be taken by states, the representation from each state having one vote; a quorum for this purpose shall consist of a member or members from two-thirds of the states, and a majority of all the states shall be necessary to a choice. [And if the House of Representatives shall not choose a President whenever the right of choice shall devolve upon them, before the fourth day of March next following, then the Vice-President shall act as President, as in the case of the death or other constitutional disability of the President.—]* The person having the greatest number of votes as Vice-President, shall be the Vice-President, if such number be a majority of the whole number of Electors appointed, and if no person have a majority, then from the two highest numbers on the list, the Senate shall choose the Vice-President; a quorum for the purpose shall consist of two-thirds of the whole number of Senators, and a majority of the whole number shall be necessary to a choice. But no person constitutionally ineligible to the office of President shall be eligible to that of Vice-President of the United States.

AMENDMENT XIII. (1865)

SECTION 1. Neither slavery nor involuntary servitude, except as a punishment for crime whereof the party shall have been duly convicted, shall exist within the United

---

*Superseded by section 3 of the twentieth amendment.

APPENDIX

States, or any place subject to their jurisdiction.

SECTION 2. Congress shall have power to enforce this article by appropriate legislation.

AMENDMENT XIV. (1868)

SECTION 1. All persons born or naturalized in the United States, and subject to the jurisdiction thereof, are citizens of the United States and of the State wherein they reside. No State shall make or enforce any law which shall abridge the privileges or immunities of citizens of the United States; nor shall any State deprive any person of life, liberty, or property, without due process of law; nor deny to any person within its jurisdiction the equal protection of the laws.

SECTION 2. Representatives shall be apportioned among the several States according to their respective numbers, counting the whole number of persons in each State, excluding Indians not taxed. But when the right to vote at any election for the choice of electors for President and Vice-President of the United States, Representatives in Congress, the Executive and Judicial officers of a State, or the members of the Legislature thereof, is denied to any of the male inhabitants of such State, being twenty-one years of age, and citizens of the United States, or in any way abridged, except for participation in rebellion, or other crime, the basis of representation therein shall be reduced in the proportion which the number of such male citizens shall bear to the whole number of male citizens twenty-one years of age in such State.

SECTION 3. No person shall be a Senator or Representative in Congress, or elector of President and Vice-President, or hold any office, civil or military, under the United States, or under any State, who, having previously taken an oath, as a member of Congress, or as an officer of the United States, or as a member of any State legislature, or as an executive or judicial officer of any State, to support the Constitution of the United States, shall have engaged in insurrection or rebellion against the same, or given aid or comfort to the enemies thereof. But Congress may by a vote of two-thirds of each House, remove such disability.

SECTION 4. The validity of the public debt of the United States, authorized by law, including debts incurred for payment of pensions and bounties for services in suppressing insurrection or rebellion, shall not be questioned. But neither the United States nor any State shall assume or pay any debt or obligation incurred in aid of insurrection or rebellion against the United States, or any claim for the loss or emancipation of any slave; but all such debts, obligations and claims shall be held illegal and void.

SECTION 5. The Congress shall have power to enforce, by appropriate legislation, the provisions of this article.

AMENDMENT XV. (1870)

SECTION 1. The right of citizens of the United States to vote shall not be denied or abridged by the United States or by any State on account of race, color, or previous condition of servitude—

SECTION 2. The Congress shall have power to enforce this article by appropriate legislation.

AMENDMENT XVI. (1913)

The Congress shall have power to lay and collect taxes on incomes, from whatever source derived, without apportionment among the several States, and without regard to any census or enumeration.

AMENDMENT XVII. (1913)

The Senate of the United States shall be composed of two Senators from each State, elected by the people thereof, for six years; and each Senator shall have one vote. The electors in each State shall have the qualifications requisite for electors of the most numerous branch of the State legislatures.

When vacancies happen in the representation of any State in the Senate, the executive authority of such State shall issue writs of election to fill such vacancies: *Provided*, That the legislature of any State may empower the executive thereof to make temporary appointments until the people fill the vacancies by election as the legislature may direct.

This amendment shall not be so construed as to affect the election or term of any Senator chosen before it becomes valid as part of the Constitution.

AMENDMENT XVIII. (1919)

[SECTION 1. After one year from the ratification of this article the manufacture, sale, or transportation of intoxicating liquors within, the importation thereof into, or the exportation thereof from the United States and all territory subject to the jurisdiction thereof for beverage purposes is hereby prohibited.

[SECTION 2. The Congress and the several States shall have concurrent power to enforce this article by appropriate legislation.

[SECTION 3. This article shall be inoperative unless it shall have been ratified as an amendment to the Constitution by the legislatures of the several States, as provided in the Constitution, within seven years from the date of the submission hereof to the States by the Congress.]*

AMENDMENT XIX. (1920)

The right of citizens of the United States to vote shall not be denied or abridged by the United States or by any State on account of sex.

Congress shall have power to enforce this article by appropriate legislation.

---

*Repealed by section 1 of the twenty-first amendment.

APPENDIX

AMENDMENT XX. (1933)

Section 1. The terms of the President and Vice President shall end at noon on the 20th day of January, and the terms of Senators and Representatives at noon on the 3d day of January, of the years in which such terms would have ended if this article had not been ratified; and the terms of their successors shall then begin.

Section 2. The Congress shall assemble at least once in every year, and such meeting shall begin at noon on the 3d day of January, unless they shall by law appoint a different day.

Section 3. If, at the time fixed for the beginning of the term of the President, the President elect shall have died, the Vice President elect shall become President. If a President shall not have been chosen before the time fixed for the beginning of his term, or if the President elect shall have failed to qualify, then the Vice President elect shall act as President until a President shall have qualified; and the Congress may by law provide for the case wherein neither a President elect nor a Vice President elect shall have qualified, declaring who shall then act as President, or the manner in which one who is to act shall be selected, and such person shall act accordingly until a President or Vice President shall have qualified.

Section 4. The Congress may by law provide for the case of the death of any of the persons from whom the House of Representatives may choose a President whenever the right of choice shall have devolved upon them, and for the case of the death of any of the persons from whom the Senate may choose a Vice President whenever the right of choice shall have devolved upon them.

Section 5. Sections 1 and 2 shall take effect on the 15th day of October following the ratification of this article.

Section 6. This article shall be inoperative unless it shall have been ratified as an amendment to the Constitution by the legislatures of three-fourths of the several States within seven years from the date of its submission.

AMENDMENT XXI. (1933)

Section 1. The eighteenth article of amendment to the Constitution of the United States is hereby repealed.

Section 2. The transportation or importation into any State, Territory, or possession of the United States for delivery or use therein of intoxicating liquors, in violation of the laws thereof, is hereby prohibited.

Section 3. This article shall be inoperative unless it shall have been ratified as an amendment to the Constitution by conventions in the several States, as provided in the Constitution, within seven years from the date of the submission hereof to the States by the Congress.

AMENDMENT XXII. (1951)

Section 1. No person shall be elected to the office of the President more than twice, and no person who has held the office of President, or acted as President, for more than two years of a term to which some other person was elected President shall be elected to the office of the President more than once. But this Article shall not apply to any person holding the office of President when this Article was proposed by the Congress, and shall not prevent any person who may be holding the office of President, or acting as President, during the term within which this Article becomes operative from holding the office of President or acting as President during the remainder of such term.

SECTION 2. This article shall be inoperative unless it shall have been ratified as an amendment to the Constitution by the legislatures of three-fourths of the several States within seven years from the date of its submission to the States by the Congress.

AMENDMENT XXIII. (1961)

SECTION 1. The District constituting the seat of Government of the United States shall appoint in such manner as the Congress may direct:

A number of electors of President and Vice President equal to the whole number of Senators and Representatives in Congress to which the District would be entitled if it were a State, but in no event more than the least populous State; they shall be in addition to those appointed by the States, but they shall be considered, for the purposes of the election of President and Vice President, to be electors appointed by a State; and they shall meet in the District and perform such duties as provided by the twelfth article of amendment.

SECTION 2. The Congress shall have power to enforce this article by appropriate legislation.

AMENDMENT XXIV. (1964)

SECTION 1. The right of citizens of the United States to vote in any primary or other election for President or Vice President, for electors for President or Vice President, or for Senator or Representative in Congress, shall not be denied or abridged by the United States or any State by reason of failure to pay any poll tax or other tax.

SECTION 2. The Congress shall have power to enforce this article by appropriate legislation.

AMENDMENT XXV. (1967)

SECTION 1. In case of the removal of the President from office or of his death or resignation, the Vice President shall become President.

SECTION 2. Whenever there is a vacancy in the office of the Vice President, the President shall nominate a Vice President who shall take office upon confirmation by a majority vote of both Houses of Congress.

SECTION 3. Whenever the President transmits to the President pro tempore of the Senate and the Speaker of the

APPENDIX

House of Representatives his written declaration that he is unable to discharge the powers and duties of his office, and until he transmits to them a written declaration to the contrary, such powers and duties shall be discharged by the Vice President as Acting President.

SECTION 4. Whenever the Vice President and a majority of either the principal officers of the executive departments or of such other body as Congress may by law provide, transmit to the President pro tempore of the Senate and the Speaker of the House of Representatives their written declaration that the President is unable to discharge the powers and duties of his office, the Vice President shall immediately assume the powers and duties of the office as Acting President.

Thereafter, when the President transmits to the President pro tempore of the Senate and the Speaker of the House of Representatives his written declaration that no inability exists, he shall resume the powers and duties of his office unless the Vice President and a majority of either the principal officers of the executive department or of such other body as Congress may by law provide, transmit within four days to the President pro tempore of the Senate and the Speaker of the House of Representatives their written declaration that the President is unable to discharge the powers and duties of his office. Thereupon Congress shall decide the issue, assembling within forty-eight hours for that purpose if not in session. If the Congress, within twenty-one days after receipt of the latter written declaration, or, if Congress is not in session, within twenty-one days after Congress is required to assemble, determines by two-thirds vote of both Houses that the President is unable to discharge the powers and duties of his office, the Vice President shall continue to discharge the same as Acting President; otherwise, the President shall resume the powers and duties of his office.

TEXT OF THE PROPOSAL FOR AMENDMENT XXVI.

SECTION 1. The people of the several States and the District constituting the seat of government of the United States shall elect the President and Vice President. Each elector shall cast a single vote for two persons who shall have consented to the joining of their names as candidates for the offices of President and Vice President. No candidate shall consent to the joinder of his name with that of more than one other person.

SECTION 2. The electors of President and Vice President in each State shall have the qualifications requisite for electors of the most numerous branch of the State legislature, except that for electors of President and Vice President, the legislature of any State may prescribe less restrictive residence qualifications and for electors of President and Vice President the Congress may establish uniform residence qualifications.

SECTION 3. The pair of persons having the greatest number of votes for President and Vice President shall be elected, if such number be at least 40 per centum of the whole number of votes cast for such offices. If no pair of persons has such number, a runoff election shall be held in which the choice of President and Vice President shall be made from the two pairs of persons who received the highest numbers of votes.

SECTION 4. The times, places, and manner of holding such elections and entitlement to inclusion on the ballot shall be prescribed in each State by the legislature thereof; but the Congress may at any time by law make or alter such regulations. The days for such elections shall be determined by Congress and shall be uniform throughout the United States. The Congress shall prescribe by law the time, place, and manner in which the results of such elections shall be ascertained and declared.

SECTION 5. The Congress may by law provide for the case of the death or withdrawal of any candidate for President or Vice President before a President and Vice President have been elected, and for the case of the death of both the President-elect and Vice-President-elect.

SECTION 6. The Congress shall have power to enforce this article by appropriate legislation.

SECTION 7. This article shall take effect one year after the 21st day of January following ratification.

Index

ABM systems, Richard Nixon and, 49, 76
Adams, John, 96, 168–69
Adams, John Quincy, 144, 197 n.
Adams, Sherman, 210
Administrative Procedures Act of 1946, 277 n.
AFL-CIO, 60–61, 66, 160, 325
  Committee on Political Education (COPE), 73, 148
Agency for International Development, 292
Agnew, Spiro, 140
Agriculture, Department of, 292
Alien and Sedition Laws of 1798, 168–70
Alliance for Labor Action, 61
Amendments to the Constitution. *See* Constitution of the United States
American Association of Railroads, 69
American Automobile Association, 72
American Bar Association, 62–63

American beliefs and paradoxes, 4–8
American Civil Liberties Union, 64
American creed, 4 ff.
  under fire, 3–13
American Farm Bureau Federation, 60, 66, 160
American Federation of Government Employees, 61
American Legion, 160
American Medical Association, 62–63, 70–71, 87, 160, 219–20
American Petroleum Institute, 159 n.
American Public Relations Association, 134
American Trucking Association, 72
Amicus curiae briefs, 302
Antiballistic missile systems, 49, 76
Appellate court system, 317–19. *See also* Policymaking process of the United States: Courts, the

421

INDEX

Articles of Confederation, 341–48, 353.
    See also Constitution of the United States
Associated Press, 131
Atomic Energy, Joint Committee on, 233
Atomic Energy Commission, 213, 280
Attainder, bill of, 167, 167 n.
Automobile Safety Act of 1966, 218, 272

Bailey, John W., 114
Baker, Robert G., 158, 162
Bank of the United States, 353
Bernays, Edward L., 135
Bill of attainder, 167, 167 n.
Bill of Rights, 167, 175, 176, 323–24, 337.
    See also Constitution of the United States
Black, Hugo L., 19, 84, 178, 182, 188, 287, 360
Black power, 8, 55–56
Blacks, Black Americans, 31, 38, 55–56, 93 359, 370, 384. See also Negroes
Blackstone, William, 305
Bliss, Ray, 114–15
Brandeis, Louis, 173
Brennan, William J., 24
Buchanan, James, 145
Budget, the, 202–206
    Bureau of, 202, 206, 207–209, 211, 212, 243, 263, 278–79
Budget and Accounting Act of 1921, 201–202, 206, 288
Bundy, McGeorge, 210, 214
Bureau of the Budget, 202, 206, 207–209, 211, 212, 243, 263, 278–79
Bureaucracy, 203–204
    administration and policy, 272–75
    control by appropriations, 283–85
    controlling the subsystems, 278–79
    foreign policy and, 290–91
    General Accounting Office and, 288–90
    government corporations, 273 n.
    independent executive agencies, 273 n.
    independent regulatory agencies, 273 n., 280–81
        interest groups and, 281
        quasi-judicial powers of, 280–81, 327
    legislative oversight, 282–83
    policy subsystems, 275–78
    presidency and, 270–98
    presidential appointments, 279–82
        Senate approval of, 279–80

Burger, Warren E., 324–25
Burr, Aaron, 96

Campaign contributions, 71–73, 143–55
    big contributor, the, 145–47
    Congressional Boosters Club, 146
    Corrupt Practices Act of 1925, 147
    Hatch Act of 1940, 147
    ineffective regulations, 147–50
    need for reform, 151–55
        Honest Election Law, 155
    President's Club, 145–46
    Taft-Hartley Act of 1947, 148
Campaign expenditures, 149–50, 377
    increasing costs at all levels, 155–57
    public subsidization of, 153–54
    spending patterns, 150–51
Case, Francis, 68
Cases, Supreme Court. See Supreme Court
Celler, Emanuel, 20
Central Intelligence Agency, 213, 292
Chamber of Commerce, United States, 60, 66, 67, 159 n.
Chapman, Oscar L., 77
Chase, Samuel, 329
"Christmas tree bill," 81–82, 153
Cigarettes, health warnings about
    Federal Trade Commission and, 212–22, 280
Civil Aeronautics Board, 281
Civil rights, role of Supreme Court in, 323–25
Civil Rights Act of 1964, 355
Civil rights legislation, 17
    political demonstrations and, 55–56
Civil Service Commission, 290
Clayton Anti-trust Act of 1914, 272
Clements, Earl, 78
Cleveland, Grover, 98
Clifford, Clark, 64, 163
College students, federal loans for, 220–21
Commerce, Department of, 292
Commerce clause, 349–51
Commerce power of Congress, 351 ff.
    restored, 354–56
    undone, 351–54
Commission on Civil Rights, 17
Commissions, settlement of disputes by, 330–32
Commissions and task forces, presidential, 214–15

INDEX

Communication and the political process, 123–42, 376–77
Communist Party, war against the, 176–82
Congress, 215–22, 227–69, 270–98, 341–43, 350–55, 358, 360, 365–67, 381–83. See also House of Representatives; Senate, the
  appropriations committees, control by, 283–85
  appropriations to finance approved programs, 264–68
  bills
    committee recommendations, 248–49
    conference committees, operation of, 262–63
    filibuster, the, 257–59
    on the floor, 254
    hearings on, 238–39, 243–44
    logrolling, 259–60, 268–69
    marking-up stage, 244–46
    presidential pressure, 260–62
    scheduling of, for floor action, 249–51
    to the White House, 263–64
    White House lobbying, 246–48
  on campaign contributions, 152–55
  on child labor, 351–52, 354
  commerce power of. See Commerce power of Congress
  committees, 216–17, 235–39 ff.
    chairmen, 238–39
    investigatory power of, 285–88
    professional staff of, 244–45
    seniority system, 239–42
    standing committees, 236, 249
  delegated or enumerated powers of, 353, 354
  dispersion of power in, 242
  implied power of, 353
  interest groups and, 215–16, 245–46, 248
  Joint Committee on Atomic Energy, 233
  Joint Committee on the Organization of Congress, 382–83
  leadership in, 250–51, 253–54
  Legislative Reference Service, 245
  lobbying regulations and, 84–89
  localism of, 229–31, 375
  policymaking in, 215–18, 227–69
  pork barrel legislation, 268–69, 283
  power of, to increase size of Supreme Court, 329
  presidential pressure on, 260–62
  presidential press conference, 261–62
  seniority system, 239–42
  special tax legislation of, 161–63
  subcommittees, 275–76
    chairmen, 241
  subpoena power of, 287–88
  vs. the President, 228–29
  vs. Supreme Court, 328–30, 351–54
Congressional Boosters Club, 146
Congressional and senatorial campaign committees, 116–18
Congressmen
  constituency service of, 231–32
  case work, 232–33
  former, as lobbyists, 78–79
  lobbyists and, 79–80
Constitution of the United States, 8, 402–20
  amendments to, text of, 412–19. See also Bill of Rights
    first, 69, 82, 85, 87, 128, 166–81, 184–87
    fourth, 323
    fifth, 175 n., 179, 181, 323
    sixth, 323
    tenth, 352, 354
    twelfth, 15 n., 96 n., 197 n.
    fourteenth, 23–25, 175, 224, 225, 322, 323, 337
    fifteenth, 16, 17, 19
    sixteenth, 201, 222, 337
    seventeenth, 229
    nineteenth, 21
    twenty-fourth, 18
    twenty-sixth, proposed, 15 n.
  Articles of Confederation, 341–48 353
  Bill of Rights, 167, 175, 176, 323–24, 337
  commerce clause, 349–51
  framing of, 335–37
  fear of the majority, 340–42
Constitutional convention, 341, 343–47, 364, 379
  Virginia Plan, 197, 343–45
Coolidge, Calvin, 101
Corcoran, Tommy, 64
Corrupt Practices Act of 1925, 147
Council of Economic Advisers, 199, 207, 208, 212
Courts, the. See Policymaking process of the United States: Courts, the; Supreme Court
Cronkite, Walter, 125
Cuban missile crisis, 130

423

INDEX

Day, William R., 352
Defense, Department of, 77, 284–85, 292
Democracy, 338
Democratic Advisory Council, 117
Democratic National Committee, 113–14
Democratic Party, 98–102, 104–106, 108, 111–12, 116–18
   campaign contributions for 1960 and 1964, 150–51
   compared to Republican Party, 105–106
   President's Club, 145–46, 163
Demonstrations, political
   public opinion and, 55–56
Depletion allowance for oil producers, 161–62
Dewey, Thomas E., 101
Dirksen, Everett M., 118, 250–51, 258
Dodd, Thomas J., 132, 152, 157–58, 382
Douglas, Paul, 269
Douglas, William O., 25, 184, 188
Draft-card burnings, 183–85
Dred Scott decision, 322

Economic Opportunity, Office of 221
Education, Office of, 220, 275
Eisenhower, Dwight D., 27, 40–41, 43, 44, 50, 75–76, 98, 104, 112, 118, 138–39, 210, 211, 213, 263, 273–74, 280, 284–85, 293, 295, 297
Electoral college, 96 n., 97, 98, 197, 198 n., 380
Emergency Preparedness, Office of, 207, 213
Espionage Act of 1917, 170
Ex post facto law, 167, 167 n.
Executive Office of the President. *See* President, the: Executive Office
Executive power of government, 360–62, 364
Expenditures
   campaign. *See* Campaign expenditures
   officeholders' costs for maintaining offices, 157–58

"Face the Nation," 132
Fair Labor Standards Act of 1938, 314–15
Farley, James, A., 149
Federal Aviation Agency, 281
Federal Bureau of Investigation, 276, 279, 311
Federal Communications Commission, 222, 272, 273 n., 330, 331, 377

Federal Deposit Insurance Corporation, 273 n.
Federal Power Commission, 273 n., 280, 303, 330
Federal Regulation of Lobbying Act of 1946, 85, 159
   Supreme Court interpretation of, 87, 186
Federal Reserve Board, 208, 212–13
Federal Trade Commission, 78, 217, 221–22, 272–73, 281, 331
Federalism, 345–59
   commerce power and, 351–56
   conflict and cooperation, 356–57
   divided and dispersed power, 357–59
   Madison on, 345–47
   marble cake, theory of, 357–58
Federalists, 96, 98, 168–69
Fifteenth amendment to the Constitution, 16, 17, 19
Fifth amendment to the Constitution, 175 n., 179, 181, 323
Filibuster, the, 257–59
Finch, Robert, 62
First amendment to the Constitution, 69, 82, 85, 87, 128, 166–81, 184–87
Fogarty, John, 241–42
Food and Agriculture Organization, 294 n.
Ford, Gerald, 250
Foreign governments, lobbyists for, 77–78
Foreign policy, 290–94
   bureaucracy and, 290–91
   treaties and executive agreements, 293–94
   war power, 294–96
Fortas, Abe, 64, 224, 258, 325
Fourteenth amendment to the Constitution, 23–25, 175, 224, 225, 322, 323, 337
Fourth amendment to the Constitution, 323
Frankfurter, Felix, 23, 25, 46
Freedmen, suffrage of, 16
Freedom of political expression, 166–89. *See also* First amendment to the Constitution
   Alien and Sedition Laws of 1798, 168–70
   clear and present danger concept, 171–75, 177
   Hand, Learned and, 177
   Holmes, Oliver Wendell and, 171–73
   Espionage Act of 1917, 170

Supreme Court decision concerning, 171–72
Hatch Acts, 147, 187–89
public employees and, 187–89
"Red" scare, 173–76
Sedition Act of 1918, 170
Supreme Court decisions concerning, 171–73
Smith Act, 176–77, 178, 179
Vietnam War and, 182–86
antiwar movement, 183–86
Fulbright, J. William, 373

General Accounting Office, 88, 288–90
Gitlow, Benjamin, 174
Goldwater, Barry, 27, 40, 99, 106–108, 118, 139
Grandfather clauses, 16–17
Great Society, 7
Gun control legislation, lobbying and, 82

Habeas corpus, 167, 167 n., 295 n.
Hagerty, James, 210
Halberstam, David, 127
Halleck, Charles A., 118, 250
Hamilton, Alexander, 96, 197, 307–308, 347–48, 353, 366
Harris, Fred, 112
Harrison, William Henry, 98
Hatch Acts, 147, 187–89
Haynsworth, Clement F., 325
Hershey, Lewis B., 184
Holmes, Oliver Wendell, 174, 322
on Sedition Act of 1918, 171–73
Hoover, J. Edgar, 276, 279
Hopkins, Harry, 211
House of Representatives, 228–30, 233–38, 248–49, 286. *See also* Congress
amendments, debate and voting on, 255–57
Committee of the Whole, 238, 254–56, 259
House Appropriations Committee, 234, 265–67
House Committee on Un-American Activities (name changed to House Internal Security Committee), 180–81
investigations of, 180–81, 287–88
House Internal Security Committee (formerly House Committee on Un-American Activities), 287–88
House Rules Committee, 251–54, 255
House Ways and Means Committee, 266
logrolling, 259–60, 268–69
Speaker, the, 250
structure and procedures of, 233–35
21-day rule, 252
Housing and Urban Development, Department of, 204
Hughes, Charles Evans, 321
Humphrey, Hubert H., 27, 108, 111, 112, 139, 141
Huntley and Brinkley, 125

Impeachment, 329
Interest groups, 58–93, 374–75. *See also* Lobbying
campaign contributions of, 71–73
Congress and, 215–16, 245–46, 248
economic, 59–61
agriculture, 60
business, 60
labor, 60–61
government bureaus and, 205, 219–20
independent regulatory agencies and, 281
Internal Revenue Service on tax-exempt status of, 163–65
lavish entertainment expenses of, 74–75
leadership of, 66–67
lobbying of, 68–93
membership in, 65–66
mobilization of grass-roots support, 68–69
mobilization of public opinion, 68
noneconomic, 64–65
professionals, the, 62–64
American Bar Association, 62–63
American Medical Association, 62–63, 70–71, 87, 160, 219–20
public interest groups (PIGS), 63–64
public relations campaign, 69–71
spending of, 158–161
Supreme Court and, 302–303
use of *amicus curiae* briefs, 302
use of public relations techniques, 133–34
Internal Revenue Service, 274
on tax exempt status of interest groups, 163–65
Internal Security Act of 1950, 178–79

INDEX

International Bank for Reconstruction and Development, 294 n.
International Brotherhood of Teamsters, 61
Interstate Commerce Commission, 204, 271, 273 n., 280, 281, 319, 330, 351
"Issues and Answers," 132

Jackson, Andrew, 263, 286
Jackson, Robert, 23 n.
Jay, John, 347–48
Jefferson, Thomas, 95, 96, 169, 286, 343, 353
Johnson, Andrew, 116, 264
Johnson, Lyndon B., 27, 40, 43, 56, 78, 81–82, 91–92, 102, 117, 141, 154–55, 162, 163, 199, 200, 210, 211, 213, 214–15, 218–19, 246, 250, 261, 263, 293, 324
Joint Chiefs of Staff, 213
Joint Committee on Atomic Energy, 233
Judicial policymaking, 300–303
  amicus curiae briefs, 302
Judicial power of government, 360–65
Judicial review, 303–308, 320–21, 366
  myth and reality of, 306–309
Judiciary Act of 1789, 320
Justice, Department of, 272, 326, 328

Kefauver, Estes, 217
Kennedy, Edward, 250
Kennedy, John F., 27, 41, 90, 92, 104, 127, 140–41, 151, 152, 200, 210, 213, 261, 263, 293, 297
Kennedy, Robert, 108, 125
Kerner Commission, 214–15
Kerr, Robert, 162
Kissinger, Henry A., 214
Knowles, John, 62
Korean War, 296
Ku Klux Klan, 16
Kuchel, Thomas, 137

Labor unions, 60–61, 66, 72–74, 160
  campaign expenditures of, 73–74
LaFollette, Robert M., 101
Laird, Melvin, 77
League of Nations, 293
Legislative liaison, 90
Legislative power of government, 360–62, 364–67
Legislative Reorganization Act of 1946, 245, 282, 287

Legislative supremacy, 303, 306
Library of Congress, 245
Lincoln, Abraham, 294–95
Lippmann, Walter, 132
Literacy test, 16–19
Lobbying, 68–93, 377. See also Interest groups; Lobbyists
  campaign contributions, 71–73
  by the executive branch of the government, 89–90
  expenditures of interest groups, 158–61
  for favorable provisions in tax legislation, 161–65
    depletion allowance for oil producers, 161–62
    Sierra Club, 163–64
    United States Savings and Loan League, 162
  Federal Regulation of Lobbying Act, 85, 87, 159, 186
    weaknesses of, 85–87
  first amendment and, 85, 87
  of foreign governments, 77
  gun control legislation and, 82
  interest groups and Congress, 215–16
  interest groups and government bureaus, 205, 219–20
  lavish entertainment expenses, 74–75
  legislative liaison, 90
    coordination of information, 90
  military-industrial complex, 75–78
  patronage, 91, 247
  public relations campaign, 69–71
  regulation of, 84–89
  as supplementary representation, 83–84
  White House lobby, 90–92, 246–48, 261
Lobbyist entrepreneurs, 64
Lobbyists. See also Interest groups; Lobbying
  congressmen and, 79–80
  effectiveness of, 80–82
  former congressmen as, 78–79
Locke, John, 339–40, 360–62
Logrolling, 259–60, 268–69
Long, Russell, 153, 250
Long Amendment, pros and cons of, 153–55
Lucas, Scott, 78

McCarthy, Eugene, 56, 108, 111, 157
McCarthy, Joseph R., 126
McCormack, John, 250–51

INDEX

McCulloch, William, 20
McGovern, George, 111
Madison, James, 58–59, 169, 197, 326–27, 341, 343, 345–48, 356, 357, 360, 364, 365–67
Malapportionment in voting, 22–26
  Baker v. *Carr,* 24–25, 301
  causes of, 22
  Colgrove v. *Green,* 23–24
  population shifts and, 22–23
  Reynolds v. *Sims,* 26
Mann Act, 350
Mansfield, Mike, 250
Marbury v. *Madison,* 307–308, 326–27
Marshall, John, 291, 307–308, 321–22, 326–27, 349, 353
Marshall, Thurgood, 302, 324
Martin, Joe, 250
Meany, George, 61
Medicare, 62, 87, 219–20
"Meet the Press," 132
Mencken, H. L., 23
Meredith, James, 297
Military-industrial complex, 75–78
  retired Army and Navy officers employed by defense contractors, 76
Miller, William, 108
Mills, Wilbur, 219
Milwaukee Journal, 131
Mitchell, John N., 20
Mohr, Charles, 127–28
Mondale, Walter, 218
Money, politics and, 144. *See also* Campaign contributions
  history of, 144–45
Monroney, Mike, 216–17
Montesquieu, Charles, 360–64, 366, 367
Moyers, William, 210
Myrdal, Gunnar, 4

Nader, Ralph, 218
Napolitan, Joe, 137–38
National Aeronautics and Space Council, 207
National Association for the Advancement of Colored People, 66, 225, 302
National Association of Manufacturers, 60, 69, 85, 88, 134, 159 *n.*
National Defense Education Act of 1958, 353
National Education Association, 275
National Farmers Union, 60

National Federation of Federal Employees, 61
National Grange, 60
National Highway Safety Bureau, 272
National Institutes of Health, 241–42
National Labor Relations Board, 330
National Security Council, 207, 213–14, 292
Negroes
  increase in voter registration, 19–20
  National Association for the Advancement of Colored People, 66, 225, 302
  obstacles in right to vote, 15–20
  school segregation, 225, 301–302
  Supreme Court decisions on voting rights of, 17, 19. *See also* Blacks, Black Americans
Neuberger, Richard L., 72
New Frontier, 7
New York Times, 127, 131
New York Times News Service, 132 *n.*
Newspapers, modern, 130–33
  losing individual character by relying on syndicated material, 131–32
Newspapers and the political process, 126–32. *See also* Press, the
  Vietnam War, 127–28
    attempts of administration to suppress news stories about, 127–28
  Washington columnists, 132
Nike-Zeus antimissile system, 75
Nineteenth amendment to the Constitution, 21
Nixon, Richard, 27, 42, 77, 91, 98, 99, 102, 111–12, 139–40, 141–42, 200, 210, 211, 213, 262, 293, 324–25
  ABM systems and, 49, 76
  campaign expenditures, 157
  nomination of, 108
  television debates with John Kennedy, 41, 140–41
Nominating conventions, 106–108, 110, 111–12
  in 1968, 111–12
  control of, 111
Nonvoter, the, 26–31, 34
  reasons for not voting, 29–31
    apathy, 31–33
    registration requirement, 29
    residence requirements, 29, 30

427

INDEX

Nonvoter (*Cont.*)
    suggestions to encourage registration of, 30

O'Brien, Lawrence, 90–91
Office of Economic Opportunity, 221
Office of Education, 220, 275
Office of Emergency Preparedness, 207, 213
Office of Science and Technology, 207
Office of War Information, 134
One man, one vote, 25–26

Packard, David C., 77
Paine, Thomas, 304
Palmer, A. Mitchell, 173
Patronage, 91, 247
Peace marches, effect of, on public opinion, 56
Pearson, Drew, 132
People's Republic of China, 293
Permanent registration, 30
Policymaking process of the United States, 192–332, 378–83
    bureaucracy, 203–204
        presidency and, 270–98
    Congress, 227–269. *See also* House of Representatives; Senate, the
    courts, the, 299–31
        appellate court system, 317–19
        federal court system, 315–16
        judicial review, 303–308, 320–21, 366
        kinds of cases heard, 309–311
        statutory interpretation, 311–13
        Supreme Court, 301–309, 314–19, 320–30. *See also* Supreme Court
    formulating the policy agenda, 195–226
        agencies, 220–21
        Congress, 215–19
        interactions between executive agencies, interest groups, and congressional committees and subcommittees, 275 ff.
        President, the, 196–206
        Supreme Court decisions, 222–26. *See also* Supreme Court
    Supreme Court, functions of, 320–22
Political attitudes, 45–47. *See also* Public opinion
    development of, 45
        family and school in, 46–47
        saluting the flag, 46

Political campaigning and television, 138–42
    debates, 140–41
    suspension of "equal time," 141
Political demonstrations, public opinion and, 55–56
Political expression, freedom of. *See* Freedom of political expression
Political law, 304–305
Political participation, 373–78. *See also* Political parties; Voter, the; Voting
Political parties, 94–119, 375
    choosing presidential candidates, 106–108
    decentralization of, 100–102
    electoral college, 96 n., 97, 98, 197, 198 n., 380
    "King Caucus," 110
    national committees, 113–15
        chairmen of, 114–15
        functions of, 114
    nominating conventions, 106–108, 110, 111–12
        in 1968, 111–12
        control of, 111
    party differences, 105–106
    party membership, 102–104
    permanent party organizations, 115–18
        congressional and senatorial campaign committees, 116–18
    presidential primaries, 111–12
    reason for development of, 95–96
    state and local organizations, 100–104
    statewide party leaders, 103–104
    third parties, 97, 101–102, 154
    two-party system, 96–99
        reasons for, 96–99
    undisciplined parties, 108–110
Politics and money. *See* Campaign contributions; Money
Politics and television, 124–26, 132–33, 376–77
Poll tax, 16, 18
Popular government, forms of, 338
Poverty program, 221
Powell, Adam Clayton, 152, 158, 239–40 n., 383
Powers of government, dispersing the, 335–68. *See also* Federalism
President, the, 196–206, 379–80
    annual economic report, 199
    appointments of, 279–82

428

INDEX

Senate approval of, 279–80
budget message of, 199. See also Budget, the
bureaucracy and, 270–98. See also Bureaucracy
commissions and task forces of, 214–15
decision on how to elect, 197–98, 364
development of powers, 197–99
Executive Office of, 207
   Council of Economic Advisers, 199, 207, 208, 212
   National Aeronautics and Space Council, 207
   National Security Council, 207, 213–14
   Office of Emergency Preparedness, 207, 213
   Office of Science and Technology, 207
   White House Office, 207, 209–214
executive orders, issuance of, 273–74
executive privilege of, 286
foreign policy and, 290–91
patronage, use of, 91, 247
press conferences of, 261–62
pressure on Congress by, 260–62
prime figure in setting policy agenda, 196–99
rule-making power of, 273–74
State of the Union Message, 199
suppressing domestic violence, 296–98
Supreme Court appointing power of, 324–25
treaties and executive agreements of, 293–94
vs. Congress, 228–29
veto power of, 263–64
   pocket veto, 264
war power and, 294–95
White House assistants, 210–11
Presidential candidates
   nominating conventions, 106–108, 110, 111–12
   in 1968, 111–12
   control of, 111
Presidential Commission on Law Enforcement and Administration of Justice, 215
Presidential primaries, 111–12
President's Club, 145–46, 163
President's Council of Economic Advisers, 199, 207, 208, 212

Press, the. See also Newspapers and the political process
   presidential conferences, 261–62
   relationship between government officials and, 128–30
   Cuban missile crisis, 130
Primaries, presidential, 111–12
Proxmire, William, 76–77
Public opinion, 48–53, 380. See also Political attitudes
   ABM program, 49
   characteristics of, 49–50
   communication and, 52–53
   definitions of, 48–49
   formation of, 50–51
   manipulation of, 136–37
   mobilization of, 68
   peace marches and, 56
   political demonstrations, 55–56
   public policy and, 53
   Vietnam War and, 49–50
   voting and, 53
Public relations, 133–42, 377
   campaigns of interest groups, 69–71
   interest groups and, 133–34
   political, 136–42
      television debates, 140–41
      television and political campaigning, 138–40
   rise of, 133–35
   United States Government and, 134–35
Public Relations Society of America, 134
Pure Food and Drug Act of 1906, 350

Quasi-judicial power of independent regulatory agencies, 280–81, 327

Racism, 8, 359
Randolph, Edmund, 343
Rayburn, Sam, 117, 162, 250
Reagan, Ronald, 104, 137
"Red" scare, the, 173–76
Republican Coordinating Committee, 118
Republican National Committee, 113–15
Republican Party, 95, 98–101, 104–108, 111–12, 116, 118
   campaign contributions for 1960 and 1964, 150–51
   compared to Democratic Party, 105–106
Republicanism, 338–39, 346–48

429

INDEX

Reston, James, 132
Reuther, Walter, 61
Ribicoff, Abraham, 218
Rockefeller, Nelson, 107, 137, 156, 157
Romney, George, 111
Roosevelt, Eleanor, 117
Roosevelt, Franklin D., 27, 43, 98, 202, 207, 211, 261, 263, 287, 291, 293, 295, 322, 329
Roosevelt, Theodore, 101, 147, 286
Rostow, Walt W., 214
Rousseau, Jean Jacques, 338
Rowe, James, 64
Rutledge, Wiley, 23

St. Louis Post Dispatch, 131
Salinger, Pierre, 210
Saluting the flag, Supreme Court decisions on, 46
Sanford, Edward T., 174
School segregation, 225, 301–302
Science and Technology, Office of, 207
Scott, Hugh, 250
Securities and Exchange Commission, 280
Sedition Act of 1918, 170
Sedition Law of 1798, 168–70
Selective Service System, 184, 273 *n*.
Senate, the, 229, 230, 233–36, 238, 248–49. *See also* Congress
   approval of presidential appointments, 279–80
   "Christmas tree bill," 81–82, 153
   cloture rule, 258
   Committee on Rules and Administration, 253
   filibuster, the, 257–59
   Finance Committee, 266
   Foreign Relations Committee, 234
   majority leader, the, 250
   Select Committee on Standards and Conduct, 158
   structure and procedures of, 233–35
Separation of powers of government, 360–68
Seventeenth amendment to the Constitution, 229
Sherman Anti-trust Act of 1890, 223, 272, 351
Sierra Club, revocation of tax-exempt status of, 163–64
Sixteenth amendment to the Constitution, 201, 222, 337

Sixth amendment to the Constitution, 323
Smith, Alfred E., 27
Smith Act of 1940, 176–77, 178, 179
Social Security Administration, 204
Sorensen, Theodore, 210
Southern Democrats, 100, 109
Soviet Union, 293
Spencer-Roberts, 137
Spock, Benjamin, 185
State, Department of, 223–24, 291–92
Stevenson, Adlai, 41, 50, 104, 112, 117
Strauss, Lewis L., 280
Subpoena power of Congress, 287–88
Subversive Activities Control Board, 179
Suffragettes, 21
Supreme Court, 273, 301–309, 314–19, 320–30, 349–52, 354–55, 365, 366
   amicus curiae briefs, 302
   antitrust policy and, 351
   appointing power of the President, 324–25
   civil rights and liberties, role in, 323–25
   decisions, 307, 309–310, 328, 349–55, 360
   Abrams v. *United States*, 172–73
   acceptance of, 307
   on Adam Clayton Powell, 239–40 *n*.
   Baker v. *Carr*, 24–25, 301
   on Bank of United States, 353
   Brown v. *Board of Education*, 302, 307
   on child labor, 351–52, 354
   Colegrove v. *Green*, 23–24
   concerning "commerce clause," 349
   concerning House Committee on Un-American Activities, 180–82
   on Congressional lobbying, 87
   on draft resistance and draft-card burnings, 184–85
   on Espionage and Sedition Acts, 171–72
   Gibbons v. *Ogden*, 349–50
   Gitlow v. *New York*, 174–76
   Guinn v. *United States*, 17 *n*.
   on independent regulatory agencies, 280–81
   involving Bill of Rights, 323–24
   involving Fair Labor Standards Act, 314–15
   on labor unions spending money on Congressional election campaigns, 73–74

INDEX

on malapportionment, 23–26, 301
on military affairs and foreign relations, 296
Minersville School District v. Gobitis, 46
on passport laws, 223–24
as policy initiatives, 222–26
on prayer and Bible reading in the schools, 328
on public school segregation, 225, 301–302
Reynolds v. *Sims*, 26
on rights of expression of public employees, 188
on saluting the flag, 46
Schenck v. *United States*, 171
on seizure of steel mills by the government, 327, 360
on Sherman Antitrust Act, 223
Smith v. *Allwright*, 17 n.
South Carolina v. *Katzenbach*, 19
United Public Workers v. *Mitchell*, 188
United States v. *CIO*, 73–74
United States v. *Harriss*, 87, 186
United States v. *O'Brien*, 184
on voting rights, 17, 19
on war against Communist party, 177–79
Watkins v. *United States*, 181
West Virginia State Board of Education v. *Barnette*, 46
Yates v. *United States*, 178
freedom of political expression and, 171 ff.
functions of, 320–22
interest groups and, 302–303
"packing" the, 329
power of Congress to increase size of, 329
power of judicial review, 306, 320–21
power within limits, 325–27
solicitor general and, 326
vs. Congress, 328–30, 351–54
impeachment, 329

Taft, Robert A., 104, 112, 201
Taft, William Howard, 101
Taft-Hartley Act of 1947, 148, 327
Taney, Roger B., 322
Taxes and taxation
lobbying for favorable provision in tax legislation, 161–65

revocation of tax-exempt status of Sierra Club, 163–64
ten percent income tax surcharge, 218–19
Taylor, Zachary, 98
Television and the political process, 124–26, 132–33, 376–77
debates, 140–41
suspension of "equal time," 141
"doctored" documentaries, 125
political campaigning and, 138–40
Tennessee Valley Authority, 273 n.
Tenth amendment to the Constitution, 352, 354
Third party, 97, 101–102, 154
Thurmond, Strom, 101
Time magazine, 127
Times-Post Service, 132 n.
Tobacco Institute, 78
Tocqueville, Alexis de, 48, 62, 308–309
Transportation, Department of, 204, 272
Treasury Department, 161, 208, 274, 292. See also Internal Revenue Service
Treaty of Versailles, 291, 293
Truman, Harry S, 85, 101, 117, 263, 273–74, 293, 325, 327
Twelfth amendment to the Constitution, 15 n., 96 n., 197 n.
Twenty-fourth amendment to the Constitution, 18
Twenty-sixth amendment to the Constitution, proposed, 15 n.

Udall, Morris, 251
Unions, labor, 60–61, 66, 72–74
United Mine Workers, 61
United Nations, 294 n.
United Press International, 131
United States Chamber of Commerce, 60, 66, 67, 159 n.
United States district courts, 315–16. See also Policymaking process of the United States: courts, the
United States Government
agencies of, 203–205. See also Bureaucracy
policy initiatives of, 220–22
budget, the. See Budget, the
bureaucracy. See Bureaucracy
Congress, 227–69. See also Congress; House of Representatives; Senate
Executive agencies. See agency names

431

INDEX

United States Government (Cont.)
Executive agencies (Cont.)
  policymaking process. See Policymaking process of the United States
  President, the. See President, the
  Supreme Court. See Supreme Court
  use of public relations techniques, 134–35
United States Information Agency, 134–35, 292
United States Savings and Loan League, 162

Valenti, Jack, 210
Veterans Administration, 273 n.
Vietnam War, 8, 35–36, 296, 371
  antiwar movement, 182–86
    Benjamin Spock et al., 185
    draft-card burnings, 183–85
  press (the) and, 127–28
  public opinion on, 49–50
Vinson, Fred, 23 n., 177
Virginia Plan, 197, 343–45
Voter, the, 374. See also Voting
  factors affecting voting behavior, 36–42, 47
    candidate personality, 40–42
    partisan preferences, 37–38
    perception of the issues, 42
    socioeconomic factors, 38–40
  independents, the, 42–45
    impact of, in an election, 43
  political activity of, 54–55, 374
  reasons for voting, 35–37
  splitting the ticket, 44
Voter apathy, 31–33
Voter participation in European countries, 27
Voting. See also Voter, the
  Constitution and, 15
  electoral college, 96 n., 97, 98, 197, 198 n.
  fifteenth amendment and, 16, 17, 19
  fourteenth amendment and, 23, 25
  increase in Negro voting, 19–20
  malapportionment and, 22–26. See also Malapportionment in voting
  Negroes and, 15–20
  nineteenth amendment and, 21
  nonvoter, the, 26–31, 34
    reasons for not voting, 29–31
  obstacles in right to vote, 15–21
    grandfather clauses, 16–17
    literacy test, 16–19
    poll tax, 16, 18
    property qualifications, 15–16
    religious and racial, 15
    white primary, 17
  patterns of voting participation, 27–28
  permanent registration, 30
  public opinion and, 53
  Supreme Court decisions, 17, 19
  twenty-fourth amendment and, 18
  voter apathy, 31–33
  Voting Rights Act of 1965, 18, 20
  woman suffrage, 20–21
Voting Rights Act of 1965, 18, 20
  South Carolina suit contesting constitutionality of, 18–19
  dismissal of, 19

Wallace, George, 27, 28, 42, 97, 99, 102, 108, 125, 141, 157, 197 n., 297
Wallace, Henry, 101
Warren, Earl, 19, 26, 87, 180, 181–82, 184, 324
Warren Commission, 214
Washington, George, 95, 286, 297, 343
Whig party, 98
Whitaker and Baxter, 70
White House lobby, 90–92, 246–48, 261
  use of patronage, 91, 247
White House Office, 207, 209–14, 278–79
  presidential assistants, 210–11
Williams, John J., 162–63
Wilson, Charles E., 285
Wilson, Woodrow, 98, 101, 198, 291, 293, 295, 321
Woman suffrage, 20–21
World Wars I and II, 295–96